C E

D1187617

Toward Unification in Psychology

JOSEPH R. ROYCE, editor

Toward Unification in Psychology

THE FIRST BANFF CONFERENCE ON THEORETICAL PSYCHOLOGY

Published by the University of Toronto Press
in co-operation with The Center for Advanced Study in Theoretical Psychology
of the University of Alberta

© University of Toronto Press 1970
   Printed in Canada by
   University of Toronto Press, Toronto and Buffalo
   ISBN 0-8020-1588-3

Contents

I
Prologue

Joseph R. Royce

I
Prologue

Joseph R. Royce

The University of Alberta has established a Center for Advanced Study in Theoretical Psychology, whose inception was first proposed to University officials by Joseph R. Royce in 1962. It was officially approved by the University's Board of Governors in the winter of 1965, functioned in a preliminary way in 1966, and began full-scale operation with its own budget and Director in 1967. The major idea behind the Center is to bring theoretical psychology into clearer focus, to meet an urgent need within the discipline – a need to advance our understanding of behaviour by conceptual analysis and integration, and to train a small, select group of potential theoreticians (at the doctoral and postdoctoral levels) to continue such efforts. It will be claimed by many that a special institute for theory is not needed, and further, that most theorizing is premature anyhow. We would certainly agree that a solid observational base is absolutely essential for the growth and development of a young science. But the mere accumulation of facts does not necessarily lead to unifying theory. Theoretical analysis and integration can only come about as a result of conscious, active effort. And the psychology Zeitgeist of the past three or four decades has been so focused on data that theory has been somewhat neglected. We have, of course, had our theories, but the general level of sophistication in theory construction within the psychology community of scholars has not kept pace with our competence in experimentation and statistical analysis. We think it is time something was done to supplement the pro-data bias with a pro-think bias.

In any event, this conference constitutes the first phase of a long-range commitment which the Center proposes to make to the advancement of theoretical psychology. It was felt that a conference on theoretical psychology would not only be consistent with this general need, but that the proposed Center would gain immeasurably from the advice and guidance of outstanding psychologists who share this concern, and further, that such a conference would serve as a manifestation of the activities of the proposed Center. Invitations to selected potential participants went out in 1963, sounding out interest, and eliciting contributions and suggestions for a conference theme. There was general agreement that the first conference should bring out the full range of our discipline, and that we should pull no punches regarding the evolution of a false sense of unity within the obvious diversity which we call psychology. Hence, while the participants opted for the title, *Toward the Unification of Psychology*, it should be understood that none of us carried to the conference any illusion that unification would, or could, emerge (which is why this book has a slightly modified title). Rather, it was commonly held that the focus should be placed on the word *toward*. Thus, our premise was that we must begin by providing a reasonably complete picture of the 'nature of the beast.' Then, with such full knowledge, we might at least be able to *point* to the ways theoretical integration might follow. The conference planners (primarily the Editor, with the assistance of Professors von Bertalanffy and W. A. S. Smith) met the presupposition of wide coverage by selecting participants representative of the total spectrum. The reader will have to judge for himself how well the participants have pointed us toward unification, keeping in mind that this is merely the beginning of a long, uphill fight with an intractable and elusive foe. Our job was to call attention to this problem in order to elicit continuing and sufficient help so that we may eventually move significantly toward its amelioration. The recent six-volume effort edited by Koch (1959 to 1963) makes it clear that if a ten-year, sixty-man, multi-volume effort cannot provide unification, certainly an eleven-man, long (but hopefully not lost) week-end conference will not. If this be the case, why bother? Our answer is that such integration cannot be achieved by mere data gathering or wishful thinking – it can only be done by active, synthesizing minds. We are suggesting that psychology as a discipline needs to be more *critically active* in its attempts at rational unification, in addition to its methodological concerns and the every-day business of gathering more and more polished data. We are further suggesting that such efforts will always be with us, and that we need to institutionalize these efforts so that they can receive continuing and full support. As the reader gets into the book itself, it will become apparent that in spite of many pages of discussion (not all duplicated here) and in spite of our pre-distribution of the papers, we only scratched the surface of each of the papers prepared for the conference. It will require several years of continued effort to properly explore the several leads toward theoretical analysis and integration which are given here. A centre devoted to theoretical psychology is one way to institutionalize such concern. It is time the implicit inverse "grantsmanship" law was broken. We have formulated this as follows. The more a professor wishes to spend his time thinking, the less he is likely to receive research grant support. A more equitable balance of the present rational-empirical imbalance in psychology will surely move us *toward* greater theoretical unification. Incidentally, we hope it is clear that theoretical unification within our discipline does not necessarily mean greater unity. The point is that theoretical unification is where you find it, and if it results in fragmentation, then so be it, for our primary concern is to understand behaviour rather than perpetuate a historical chapter heading for political or historical reasons.

The Conference convened for four days, April 9–12, 1965 at the University of Alberta's Banff School of Fine Arts, a mountain retreat which handles hundreds of conferences on a year-round basis, plus a large-scale summer school in the arts. All papers, by invitation only, had been prepared and distributed several months before the conference. *No papers were read at the conference itself!* Conference sessions were devoted entirely to in-depth discussion of the pre-digested papers. In short, this was a "working conference" – a manifestation of the kind of activity on which the Center will focus in the years ahead. Discussion was limited to the eleven invited participants: Professors J. R. Royce, Head of Department of Psychology, University of Alberta, Edmonton; W. W. Rozeboom, Department of Psychology, Edmonton; E. H. Galanter, Department of Psychology, University of Washington; S. H. Bartley, Department of Psychology, Michigan State University; L. von Bertalanffy, Departments of Psychology and Zoology, Edmonton; L. K. Frank, Belmont, Massachusetts; R. B. MacLeod, Department of Psychology, Cornell University; H. Tennessen, Department of Philosophy, Edmonton; and O. H. Mowrer, Department of Psychology, University of Illinois. Professors T. Weckowicz, Departments of Psychology and Psychiatry, Edmonton, and David Krech, Department of Psychology, University of California, were present as critics.

The papers appear in the order we originally planned, starting with three general-theoretical papers by Royce, Rozeboom, and Galanter. Royce's paper attempts to summarize the present state of affairs in terms of three underlying epistemologies – rationalism, empiricism, and metaphorism. Rozeboom played the important role of conference meta-theoretician. In Parts I and II of his paper he provides a theoretical taxonomy, and in Part III he exemplifies his approach by way of an analysis of behaviour theory. Galanter shows us how to think deductively, arguing for *a priori* theoretical constructions as crucial for scientific advancement. We then move to the biological end of the behavioural spectrum, particularly in the paper by Bartley. Bartley's paper calls for limiting the term psychology to those aspects of behaviour which can, in principle, be accounted for via biological systems. Although Professor von Bertalanffy's manuscript was originally prepared for this conference, the complete version was not included because of overlap with L. K. Frank's paper. We have, however, included in this book a summary version of Bertalanffy's contribution. Frank maintains that contemporary psychology is hampered by a traditional dependence upon assumptions from a worn-out and outmoded philosophy of science which comes primarily from the physical and other natural sciences. He argues for openness to new modes of thought, particularly of a symbolic and humanistic nature. The next two papers, by MacLeod and the philosopher Tennessen, are consistent with this admonition, even though they do not necessarily agree with the specific suggestions put forward by Frank. MacLeod, for example, asks that we retain openness by involving the naïve attitude of the phenomenologist as a preliminary to subsequent conceptualization. This attitude provides the advantage of seeing the world with the freshness of the child's eye. It also implies a rich immersion in the raw data of behaviour, a reminder of the importance of observation *per se* as a basis for subsequent theoretical integration. If phenomenology demands a greater openness to the introspective, the last paper, by Tennessen, calls for an even greater commitment to the subjective. Tennessen's demand is that we become more aware of existential crisis and the problem of what it means to be a human being. Whereas Mowrer[1] sees the answer to mental illness in terms of developing a stronger social conscience, Tennessen believes the greatest need for the advancement of humanity lies in coming to grips with the absurdities of daily life and the overall meaninglessness of the universe.

In addition to the seminar sessions, each invited participant who gave a paper conducted an "auditors' hour," a question–discussion period between interested auditors and the author of a paper. All seminar discussions and auditor hour ses-

---

1 Mowrer's paper appears in *Morality and Mental Health*, edited by O. H. Mowrer. Chicago: Rand-McNally, 1967.

sions were taped and severely condensed and edited before publication here. Seminar and auditors' hour material appears under the headings "Comments" and "Discussion" respectively. In the case of the seminar discussions each participant was asked to review his remarks on a given paper with an eye on brevity and redundancy, and to submit such remarks for editorial review in the form of a single, condensed comment. In this connection it should be noted that a participant had a right, upon review of his remarks, to offer "no comment" for a given paper. This occurred in several cases; however, the general lack of commentary from S. H. Bartley is due to the fact that he was in attendance at the conference only on the day when he gave his paper. The other invited participants were in attendance at the entire conference. As has been already intimated, one participant, Professor T. Weckowicz, served as a discussant only, and another, Professor David Krech, served as general critic, and was subsequently asked to write the Epilogue. Our concern with the taped material was to mine the available gold in the smallest possible space without destroying the excitement of the conference itself. Incidentally, those who wish to recreate the full discussion can do so by availing themselves of a full set of tapes from the editor.

We mentioned the excitement of the conference. Let us comment on this, for there was true excitement for both participants and auditors. Those of us who had a major responsibility for planning the conference naturally had high hopes that it would be a success. Our hopes were confirmed, and there are many reasons for it. Obviously the major one was the high quality of participation which the invited guests brought to the conference. Several of these participants will be recognized as long-time leaders in psychological and scientific thought in mid-twentieth century. Had you been in attendance you would have had an opportunity to see why. Furthermore, you would have had an opportunity to eavesdrop on professors-in-action. For we followed a format which we believe is unique, and which we believe is a major reason for the 'live' quality of the conference. At the beginning of each session the author gave a fifteen- to twenty-minute summary of his paper. This was followed by an equally brief critique by a pre-arranged discussant. The session was then thrown open to the invited participants seated around the seminar table. The sixty to seventy auditors (and they remained auditors for each of the eight two-hour discussion sessions) were seated in two or three rows around the 'working seminar' so that, from above, the situation appeared as an arena. This seminar-in-the-round technique worked extremely well because everybody felt themselves to be an integral part of the proceedings. Furthermore, informal discussions were possible during meals and between sessions, since we were all housed in the same building, and ate together.

We were able to find a way to involve the auditors, but at the same time preserve the 'working seminar' attitude, and this also contributed to the success of the conference. In our original plans we intended to confine ourselves to the eleven invited participants. Subsequent review of our plans brought forth the idea of the seminar-in-the-round combined with the auditors' hour as a way to involve additional interested persons without having to sacrifice our original notion.

Conferences do not come into existence without human efforts, or financial support. Special mention, therefore, must go to Dr W. A. S. Smith, at that time

Executive Secretary of the Department of Psychology and Assistant Dean of the Faculty of Arts, who served as Conference Manager. He was assisted in the many chores leading to and involved in the conference itself by the Department Secretary, Mrs Rosemary Robertson, who later supervised the typing of 1000 pages of double-spaced typescript from the tape, Mr Paul De Groot, Department Technician, who was responsible for the high-fidelity recording of all the sessions, and Mr D. E. Becker, Assistant Director of the Banff School, who took charge of local arrangements.

We are also grateful to Professors T. Penelhum, Dean of the Faculty of Arts and Science, University of Alberta, Calgary; D. M. Ross, Dean of the Faculty of Science, University of Alberta, Edmonton; A. E. D. Schonfield, Head of Department of Psychology, Calgary; D. E. Smith, Dean of the Faculty of Arts, Edmonton; and K. Yonge, Head of Department of Psychiatry, Edmonton, each of whom sacrificed valuable time and energy to chair at least one seminar discussion.

The lion's share of financial support came from the University of Alberta, without whom the conference simply could not have occurred. We are also indebted to the University for providing a subsidy which has made it possible for the conference proceedings to be published. We are pleased to be able to report that the officials of the University were impressed with the beginning we have made, and they have indicated willingness to support similar conferences in the future as part of the operation of the Center. We are also indebted to the National Research Council of Canada for a small grant in support of the conference. Such support is hopeful to those of us who would like to see a theoretical psychology as viable as theoretical physics. And finally, we are grateful to two local establishments, Lamond, Dewhurst & Associates, industrial psychologists, and Simpsons-Sears, each of whom provided funds which allowed us to establish several stipends to cover living expenses so that worthy University of Alberta graduate students could attend the conference as auditors.

II
The Conference Papers

1
The Present Situation
in Theoretical Psychology*

Joseph R. Royce UNIVERSITY OF ALBERTA

DR ROYCE is Founder-Director of the Center for Advanced Study in Theoretical Psychology. He came to the University of Alberta in 1960 as Professor of Psychology and Department Head. He resigned the latter position in 1967, the year the Center was established.

In 1951 Royce received his PH.D. under Thurstone at the University of Chicago. Beginning with his doctoral dissertation, Royce has been particularly interested in extending factor theory to the domain of comparative-physiological psychology. He prepared for this by minoring in mathematics and biology, and by serving as the first psychology Doctoral Fellow at the Jackson Laboratory, Bar Harbor, Maine, in 1949. During World War II he was a Research Officer in the Aviation Psychology Program of the US Air Force.

Professor Royce's scholarly and research interests cover a wide range, including behaviour genetics, brain damage, autokinesis, and the development of the psycho-epistemological profile. The last-named project is based on his book *The encapsulated man: an interdisciplinary essay on the search for meaning* (Princeton: Van Nostrand, 1964), a wide ranging study which includes many of the theoretical-philosophical issues of contemporary psychology. Other publications include *Psychology and the symbol* (as editor) (New York: Random House, 1965), and around 50 journal articles.

Professor Royce has served on the Associate Committee on Experimental Psychology of the National Research Council of Canada (1962–5), was a Canada Council Senior Research Fellow (1965–6), and was elected to the APA Council of Representatives, 1963–5, and elected President of the Division of Philosophical Psychology for 1969–70. He has lectured widely in Europe and has made brief visits as Distinguished Visiting Scholar to Educational Testing Service, McGill, Hawaii, and Western Michigan, and is presently on the editorial boards for *Multivariate Behavioral Research, Psychological Record,* and *Perspectives.*

PSYCHO-EPISTEMOLOGY AND THE TWENTIETH-CENTURY WORLD-VIEW

I shall begin my presentation with a brief review of the state of affairs in contemporary psychology as a segment of twentieth-century thought as a preliminary to a more detailed analysis of theoretical psychology *per se*.

Several recent publications (Royce, 1959, 1964; Sorokin, 1941) have pointed out that there are three basic ways of knowing: empiricism, rationalism, and metaphorism.[1] While there have been many theories of knowledge expounded in the history of philosophic thought, these three isms have been dubbed basic because of their fairly direct dependence upon varieties of psychological cognition on the one hand, and their epistomological testability on the other hand. This view can be briefly summarized by reference to Table 1.1 below:

TABLE 1.1

THREE BASIC PATHS TO KNOWLEDGE

Cognitive processes	Corresponding epistemologies	Epistemological criteria
Thinking	Rationalism	Logical-illogical
Symbolizing and intuiting	Metaphorism	Universal-idiosyncratic
Sensing	Empiricism	Perception-misperception

The implication here is that each of these isms represents a legitimate approach to reality, but that different criteria for knowing are involved. Rationalism, for example, is primarily dependent upon logical consistency. That is, this approach

* This paper was also presented as a Distinguished Visiting Lecturer Address, Educational Testing Service, September, 1965, and it will be reprinted in B. B. Wolman (editor), *Handbook of Psychology* (in preparation). The last section (i.e. pp. 27–34) was pre-released under the title *Metaphoric Knowledge and Humanistic Psychology*, and appears in J. F. T. Bugental (editor), *The Challenges of Humanistic Psychology*, New York: McGraw-Hill, 1967.

1 Previous publications referred to the third way of knowing as intuitionism and to the underlying psychological process as feeling. In the present text I refer to the third way of knowing as metaphorism and to the underlying psychological processes as symbolic and intuitive. The words metaphoric, symbolic, and intuitive are fraught with semantic confusion. However, it was felt that the present version would focus more adequately on the epistemological criterion of universality on the one hand, and the possible underlying psychological

says that we will accept something as true if it is logically consistent, and we will reject something as false if it is illogical. Empiricism says we know to the extent that we perceive correctly, and metaphorism says that knowledge is dependent upon the degree to which symbolic and intuitive cognitions lead us to universal rather than idiosyncratic insights. While each of these cognitive processes may lead to error, the implication is that each is also capable of leading to truth. The possibilities of intuitive error, for example, are readily apparent. Equally obvious, at least to psychologists, are the errors of perception. The errors of the thinking process are probably more subtle, but I have been led to believe that they have plagued the efforts of the logicians and mathematicians. Furthermore, we recognize that none of these psychological processes operates independently of the others. That is, one does not think independently of sensory inputs and symbolic and intuitive

processes on the other hand. That is, in this context we are concerned with the knowledge-giving qualities which adhere to the word metaphoric – the way in which symbol systems lead to valid awarenesses of reality. The corresponding psychological processes, designated as symbolic and intuitive, imply a more imaginative-creative mode of cognition than is implied for empiricism and rationalism. Greater overtones of affectivity and unconsciousness are also implied.

Additional semantic difficulty is provided by the fact that philosophers (e.g., Montague, 1928 and Cassirer, 1953, 1955, 1957) have defended both intuitionism and symbolism as valid epistemologies, whereas I have shifted these terms to the psychological process side of the ledger. While these words are ambiguous as cognitive process, we can at least argue that this condition is more a function of sheer ignorance than anything else. If the present renewal of interest in cognition continues we can anticipate an eventual operational and empirical clarification of this kind of semantic ambiguity. For example, certain experimental investigations and theoretical analyses of the past decade indicate a possible bridge between the traditional behaviouristic approach to cognition on the one hand, and a revitalized concern for "higher thought processes" on the other hand. Here I am thinking particularly of the introduction of the term "mediators" as exemplified in the writings of Rozeboom (1956), Mowrer (1960b), and Osgood (1957). At a more complex level, we have the emergence of psycholinguistics (e.g. see Miller, 1951 and Carroll, 1953), and the psychology (i.e. beyond the traditional psychoanalytic treatment of the subject) of the symbol *per se* (e.g. see Werner and Kaplan, 1963; Royce, 1965a). In addition, there have been a small number of experimental studies on the nature of the intuitive process as a general psychological phenomenon (e.g., see Westcott, 1961; Westcott and Ranzoni, 1963), as an aspect of creativity (Barron, 1965; Hitt, 1965; Hitt and Stock, 1965 and Taylor, 1964) and as part of the clinician's cognitive repertoire (Meehl, 1954; Sarbin, Taft, and Bailey, 1960; Levy, 1963). Finally, I should state that I decided on the term metaphoric rather than the term symbolic for this third kind of knowledge because it is the lesser of two semantic evils – that is, there is less confusion surrounding the use of the word metaphoric than there is for the word symbolic (e.g. see Langer, 1961; Foss, 1949; Bertalanffy, 1965). In the present context metaphoric is the larger term, a term which implies analogy, simile, and totality. It points to an indivisible unity, a gestalt which is not completely accounted for by its individual symbolic components (e.g. a drama as the metaphoric unit, in contrast to a particular character as a symbolic component).

processes; nor do we perceive independently of intuition and thinking. In short, the correspondences indicated in Table 1 are oversimplified for purposes of analysis and exposition, but they represent all the known ways that man is enabled to come into contact with reality. The major point I wish to make at this juncture is that man needs to invoke all the available ways of knowing for the best possible grasp of his world, but that he tends to be partial to one or the other of these cognitive approaches.

I have developed this theme at some length in a recent book under the title *The Encapsulated Man* (1964), the point being that men of different philosophic commitments (i.e. world-views) reflect limited or encapsulated images of reality as a function of their particular epistemological profiles. This state of affairs is particularly apparent if we look at specialists in contrasting disciplines of knowledge, such as is indicated in Fig. 1.1.

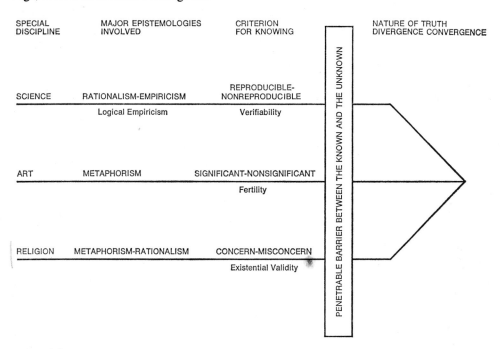

FIGURE 1.1
Representative special disciplines of knowledge (modified version of Royce, 1964, p. 20)

For our purposes I suggest we ignore the right half of this figure and focus on the left hand portion. It is understood that all three epistemologies are involved in each of the three representative disciplines of knowledge, but it is also clear that each discipline gives greater credence to one or more of them. The scientist, for example, "thinks", "intuits", "symbolizes", and "senses" as scientist, but he maximizes the rational and empirical ways of knowing and minimizes metaphoric symbolizing and intuition as final judge. Conversely, the artist, who also invokes his entire cognitive repertoire, maximizes the symbolic and intuitive processes at the expense of the thinking and sensory processes. There are, of course, wide variations in the possible permutations and combinations of epistemological profiles; this brief exposition should be taken as relative and typical rather than as absolute and general.

While my own epistemological hierarchy places rationalism at the apex, I also have strong empirical pressures. Thus, I have initiated a long-range series of investigations on the adequacy of the above mentioned theoretical formulation. Although studies to date represent only a crude beginning, they fortunately tend to confirm my intuitive-rational speculations. I will now briefly summarize these findings.

Our approach was to construct an inventory, the Psycho-Epistemological Profile, as a way to measure a person's epistemological hierarchy. The ultimate goal is to construct a standardized test of fifty to one hundred three-choice items. The choices within each item are designed so as to reflect each of the three[2] approaches to truth. The subject's task is to rank in order the three choices of each item. Response preferences are scored in such a way as to reflect both ipsative and normative data.

It is impossible to specify on *a priori* grounds which items are most likely to be reliable and valid. We have, therefore, included items from several categories in the experimental version of this inventory. This means we have included items which pose hypothetical situations and ask for probable behaviour; items which ask for preferences regarding activities, interests, and people; and items which relate directly or indirectly to epistemological choices. Here is an example of an epistemologically explicit item. In attempting to ascertain the value of a new theory I am most concerned that it be: (*a*) logically consistent; (*b*) validated by direct experimental evidence; (*c*) a new and imaginative idea. An example of the epistemologically implicit item is as follows. Which of the following do you think can ultimately contribute most to our lives: (*a*) mathematics; (*b*) art; (*c*) biology?

The inventory has now been through several revisions, several administrations to selected and unselected samples, and several item analyses and weighting schemes. We believe the present eighty-one item version (Revised Experimental Form III) carries sufficient reliability and validity to be of general research use. A highly compressed summary of specific findings to date is as follows.[3]

2 A fourth approach, purposely not developed in the present context, was labelled believing or authoritarianism. Although it was incorporated in an early version of the inventory as an equal-status way of knowing, we now see it as underlying the other three. That is, empiricism, metaphorism, and rationalism are the basic "truth systems" which are part of the person's total "belief system." Belief systems incorporate a variety of commitments, one of which is cognitive or epistemological in nature. One way to put this is to say we are all "believers" in something, but we make different commitments – some to empiricism, some to rationalism, and some to metaphorism. We anticipate studying the relationships between scores on a specially developed authoritarian scale, and other such measures, and scores on the empirical, rational and metaphoric scales of the PEP.

3 For more details, including additional revision of the inventory, see the publications of my colleague W. A. S. Smith, graduate student associates, and myself (Jones, 1963; Royce, 1962; Smith, Royce, Ayers, and Jones, 1967). We are presently engaged in a long-range theoretical and empirical extension of these preliminary efforts under the rubric of epistemological psychology.

(i) It is possible to assess a person's epistemological hierarchy by way of an inventory known as the Psycho-Epistemological Profile (PEP).

(ii) It is estimated that the test-retest reliability coefficients of the three scales of the present eighty-one item version of the PEP (Experimental Form III) are around 0.90.

(iii) There is preliminary evidence that the inventory is valid in the sense that it can discriminate between contrasting groups. More specifically, the data summarized in Table 1.2 show that empiricism is the dominant characteristic of the

TABLE 1.2

GROUP MEANS ON EMPIRICAL, METAPHORIC, AND RATIONAL SCALES OF THE
PSYCHO-EPISTEMOLOGICAL PROFILE (REVISED EXPERIMENTAL FORM II)

Groups	Empirical scale	Metaphoric scale	Rational scale
Chem-bio N = 48	1.223	1.141	1.337
Mu-drama N = 50	1.102	1.489	1.203
Math-phy N = 44	1.162	1.142	1.452

chemistry-biology group, that metaphorism is the highest in the music-drama sample, and that rationalism is highest for the mathematics-theoretical physics group. This empirical confirmation of theoretical expectations is most encouraging because of the overall consistency of the data. Normative comparisons (i.e. when one compares scale performances *between* groups) turn out as predicted in all cases, and ipsative comparisons (i.e. when one compares scale performances *within* groups) turn out as predicted in all cases except one (i.e. the average scale score for the chemistry-biology group is 1.337 on the rational scale and 1.223 on the empirical scale). All but one (mathematics-physics = 1.142 *versus* chemistry-biology = 1.141 on the metaphoric scale) of the nine possible "t" tests are significant beyond the 5 per cent level.

Now that minimal test construction requirements for reliability and validity have been met, it should be possible to extend the application of the PEP to a wide variety of empirical problems such as cultural (e.g., East *versus* West) and sub-cultural (e.g., "the two cultures") differences, developmental changes, and relationships to other value commitments (such as the six values in the Allport, Vernon, Lindzey Study of Values).

A variety of other theorists have concerned themselves with issues which relate tangentially to what I have called psycho-epistemology. These include Piaget's (e.g. see Flavell, 1963) developmental cognitive studies, Festinger's (1957) theory of cognitive dissonance, Berlyne's (1960) work on epistemic curiosity, the philosopher Wallraff's (1961) analysis of knowing as an interpretation of rather than some kind of correspondence to reality, Jung's (1923) four-fold typology, the Miller, Galanter and Pribram (1960) concept of image as adapted from Boulding (1956), Donald Campbell's (1960) evolutionary epistemology, and Northrop and Livingston's (1964) anthropological epistemology. But the work most directly pertinent to the purposes of this paper is that of the Harvard sociologist, P. A.

Sorokin. He invokes essentially the same three epistemologies in his analysis of the shifts in the dominant values of cultures and epochs of time. He begins with the basic assumption of cultural cohesiveness, as follows.

Any great culture, instead of being a mere dumping place of a multitude of diverse cultural phenomena, existing side by side and unrelated to one another, represents a unity or individuality whose parts are permeated by the same fundamental principle and articulate the same basic value. The dominant part of the fine arts and sciences of such a unified culture, of its philosophy and religion, of its ethics and law, of its main form of social, economic, and political organization, of most of its mores and manners, of its ways of life and mentality, all articulate, each in its own way, this basic principle and value. This value serves as its major premise and foundation (Sorokin, 1941, p. 17).

Then, corresponding to the epistemologies of empiricism, rationalism, and meta-phorism respectively, he analyses culture in terms of the dominant values of sensate, idealistic, and ideational. Thus, the sensate culture is dominated by the truth of the senses, the idealistic culture focuses on the truth of reason, and the ideational culture is symbol-oriented. He characterizes twentieth-century Western society as a weary, sensate culture, a culture which has been dominated by empiricism since the Renaissance, but which has been disintegrating for the last four or five decades – hence, the title of his book *The Crisis of Our Age*. It should be noted that Sorokin's analyses of the rise and fall of civilizations do not follow the organic analogue of Spengler (1932) and Toynbee (1946, 1947), wherein a culture *must* die after living out its natural life span. His position is that the present crisis merely represents a decline in the sensate form of Western society, to be followed by a new integration of the various cultural facets. Let us look at the shifts in European culture since 800 AD as an example of Sorokin's brand of analysis.

He describes the medieval period as an ideational culture, dominated by the truth of religious symbols, a God-centred culture which was supra-sensory and supra-rational. When this theocratic culture declined around 1500, the Renaissance period ushered in the contemporary sensate culture – a culture dominated by the truth of the senses, and secular, present-moment, worldly values. Sorokin also suggests that there was a relatively short transitional period, from around 1200 to 1500, reflecting the domination of reason, an idealistic culture. Thus, while it is oversimplified and the transitional shifts are always less precise than can be diagrammatically represented, I have summarized Sorokin's major value shifts in Fig. 1.2 as follows:

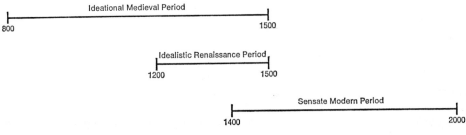

FIGURE 1.2
An analysis of dominant Western cultural values between 800 and 2000 AD

What Sorokin is saying about twentieth-century life is that we are presently shedding our sensory world-view in favour of the other two. The exact direction we shall take is not yet clear, but his guess is that we are moving toward a more "integral" culture, one which reflects a more balanced mixture of all three major values. Sorokin's cultural analyses rarely imply complete cultural disintegration or extinction, but rather, value shifts in terms of the permutations and combinations of the three basic orientations.

The parallels between Sorokin's analysis and my own are obvious. The major world-views are essentially the same, and they form the central plank for subsequent analysis. The difference is that my analysis focuses on the individual and Sorokin's unit of analysis is culture. Because of this my analysis is primarily in terms of psychological processes whereas Sorokin's analysis is primarily in terms of social change. I then turn to philosophy for valid epistemologies – ways of knowing which lead to individual survival. Sorokin then turns to history for valid cognitions – ways of knowing which lead to cultural survival. The two approaches complement one another, providing parallel analyses at the individual and cultural levels, based on the same three cognitive categories of thinking, sensing, and symbolizing-intuiting.

The point of immediate relevance is that twentieth-century Western culture is clearly a sensate culture. Even if we set aside the issue of whether this will necessarily lead to the decline of contemporary civilization, it seems clear from my own analysis at the individual level, combined with Sorokin's analysis at the cultural level, that such a world-view is extremely limited. Furthermore, seen in this context, it comes as no surprise that psychology, being essentially a part of twentieth-century Western culture, is similarly sensate or empirically oriented. There is little doubt, in my mind at least, that contemporary psychology is suffering – stifling might be a more accurate word – from super-empiricism (Royce, 1964, 1965a, and 1965c).

My argument is *not* that psychology should become *less* empirical, but rather, that it should become more *powerfully* rational and more *open* to the knowledge giving qualities of the metaphor. It seems clear that a less encapsulated discipline, one which makes the most of *all* the cognitive processes at our command, will be able to embrace the reality with which it is concerned with greater awareness. I now propose that we take a look at contemporary theoretical efforts within psychology and that we include an analysis of such efforts in terms of the three epistemologies.

AN ANALYSIS OF CONTEMPORARY THEORIES

Theory in a field as immature as psychology cannot be expected to amount to much – and it doesn't. It is my opinion that the major reason psychology cannot point to a great man of the stature of Newton or Einstein is that it simply is not ready for the kind of grand unification which such a man can provide. A great twentieth-century behaviour theorist can only be expected to promote an important point of view which will pervade broad segments of psychology, or develop a theory which covers a rather limited domain such as perception or learning, or perhaps hit the jackpot and accomplish a little of both.

During the first half of the twentieth-century the major contributions to theoretical psychology have been primarily of the first type, namely, the presentation of an all-pervading point of view. The major views of this period are those of the behaviourists, the gestaltists, and the psychoanalysts. Perhaps the outstanding contribution of each of these "isms" to our understanding of behaviour has been to point out an important approach which others had neglected – for example, the psychoanalysts' insistence that we pay attention to irrational and unconscious forces which drive the human oganism. At mid-twentieth century very few psychologists find it necessary to identify themselves with one or another of these camps, as was typical of the twenties. Rather, they take the approach that each of these viewpoints is valid and important, and that they contribute to our understanding of behaviour in a complementary way (see Table 1.3). It is also generally agreed that, in spite of the magnitude of their contributions, none of these viewpoints is adequate as a general theory of behaviour, that they all over-generalized, were based on inadequate data, and were essentially programmatic. In short, they can be characterized more as doctrinal protests than as unifying theories.

While the efforts of neo-behaviourists such as Hull and Skinner started out as reasonably modest statements about very simple learning on the part of very simple animals such as rats and pigeons, it is unfortunately true that these authors have published volumes with such questionable titles as *Principles of Behavior* (Hull, 1943) and *The Behavior of Organisms* (Skinner, 1938). In other words, they have tended to overgeneralize in the same way as did their predecessors, although it must be admitted that the principles which have emerged from these efforts are, in general, more explicit than those of the earlier vintage.

The tendency towards more adequate miniature theorizing which was initiated by the neo-behaviourists is a very healthy development, and it is fortunate that this tendency has continued apace. Thus, we now find perceptual theorists such as Gibson (1950) and Graham (1959) confining themselves to perceptual phenomena, and learning theorists such as Estes (1959) and Spence (1956) staying within the confines of their domain. We need more of this self-conscious concern for developing a theory to account for a relatively limited aspect of the total behaviour of the organism for the simple reason that it is a goal we are more likely to reach in our present state of theoretical anarchy.

On the other hand, there are several very significant general theory efforts currently under way with an orientation radically different from the earlier vintage of general theory. In my opinion, the most promising of these efforts are those which have grown out of the concern for the unification of science and the development of scientific generalists along with the usual scientific specialists – namely, the interdisciplinary efforts of Bertalanffy's general systems theory, and the general behaviour theory which is emerging from the inter-disciplinary team at the University of Michigan Mental Health Research Institute under the leadership of James G. Miller. Efforts such as these are important because they are finding that methodological approaches and concepts developed in one field have relevance for other fields. For example, the methods of factor analysis, developed in psychology, have already had a significant impact on most of the social sciences, and some impact on the biological and physical sciences as well (Royce, 1965b). Similarly, the concept of homeostasis, originally developed in biology, has been shown to

TABLE 1.3

THE COMPLEMENTARY PATTERN OF PSYCHOLOGICAL SCHOOLS (FROM ROSENZWEIG, 1937, P. 97)

Name of school	Structuralism	Gestalt psychology	Functionalism		Geisteswissenschaftliche or verstehende Psychologie
			Behaviourism	Psycho-analysis	
Characteristic problem or field of research	Sensation	Perception	Learning	Motivation	Character
Temporal span of observation in typical methods	●	○	↑	↑	⟶ ∞
Conceptually allied sciences	Physical e.g. Physics		Biological e.g. Physiology		Social e.g. Sociology

have a very deep and significantly unifying impact in more than one area of psychology (Royce, 1957). Thus, it would seem that much of the confusion shared by the various sciences of man is due to the barrage of special in-group terminology, and that considerable headway could be made by the simple-minded routine of translating from one technical language to the other. Furthermore, Bertalanffy has pointed out that there are important generalizations which can be made about all open systems, whether it be the psychobiological unit we call man, or the social system which exists among a species of ants or a nation of men. As long as efforts such as these are seen as they should be seen, namely, as heuristic approaches to the eventual understanding of man, and not as definitive systematic statements, there is real hope that they will eventually move us in the direction of a general theory of behaviour.

Let us now take a closer look at these area and general theories. I'll begin with the area theories or theorettes as they have been dubbed by Krech. I propose that we analyse contemporary theorettes in terms of their underlying epistemological characteristics. Since psychology is primarily committed to the scientific Weltanschauung, the analysis is cast primarily in terms of rationalism and empiricism. However, my statements occasionally carry implications regarding the relevance of symbolic and intuitive cognition, but I will return to metaphorism in the concluding section of this paper.

The essence of what I wish to say about area theories is summarized in Table 1.4 below:

This table shows representative systems by rows and specifies epistemological characteristics by columns. For example, in the area of perception, the Köhler-Wallach theory of figural after-effects (satiation theory) is described as experimental, explanatory, experimental-explanatory, and reflects a "good" empirical-formal fit. The social behaviour theory of Fromm is described as phenomenological, speculative, phenomenological-speculative, and reflects a "minimal" empirical-formal fit. Columns 3 to 6 require brief elaboration. Column 3 refers to the mode of observation which is characteristic of the area in question. While the nature of empirical observations can best be seen as a "degree of control" continuum, ranging from the little or no control of common sense to the relatively complete control of the laboratory (Royce, 1964, pp. 50–1), we have oversimplified the task by utilizing only three terms: phenomenological, correlational, and experimental. Column 4 refers to the degree of formalized rationalization of the area theory in question, ranging from the looseness of "speculation", to the relative tightness of "explanation." The continuum here is in terms of internal consistency, the most stringent, tight system (i.e., "explanatory") being in terms of some form of mathematics or formal logic. The word descriptive is used as intermediary between speculative and explanatory. Column 5 simply refers to the particular combination of terms applied in Columns 3 and 4. It represents what Northrop (1947) refers to as an epistemic correlation. Column 6 represents my guess (and such guesses are loaded with difficulties) as to the adequacy of this epistemic correlation in terms of minimal, fair, and good, the implication being that the adequacy of conceptual-observational fit for *any* extant psychological theory is no better than "good."

TABLE 1.4

REPRESENTATIVE AREA THEORIES IN CONTEMPORARY PSYCHOLOGY

1 Primary area of study	2 Representative contemporary systems	3 Nature of empirical observations	4 Nature of formalization	5 Position on the empirical-formalism spectrum	6 Adequacy of empirical-formal fit
Sensation	Vision, audition	Experimental	Explanatory	Experimental-explanatory	Good
Perception	Helson Köhler-Wallach Gibson	Experimental	Explanatory Explanatory Descriptive	Experimental-explanatory Experimental-explanatory Experimental-descriptive	Good Good Good
Learning	Skinner Mowrer Spence Mathematical models (various)	Experimental	Descriptive Explanatory Explanatory Explanatory	Experimental-descriptive Experimental-explanatory Experimental-explanatory Experimental-explanatory	Good Good Good Fair
Motivation	Variants of psychoanalysis (i.e. Freud, Jung, etc)	Phenomenological	Descriptive	Phenomenological-descriptive	Minimal
Personality	Rogers, Murray Allport, Murphy	Phenomenological Correlational	Descriptive Descriptive	Phenomenological-descriptive Correlational-descriptive	Minimal Minimal
Social behaviour	Fromm Lewin Game theory	Phenomenological Correlational Experimental	Speculative Descriptive Explanatory	Phenomenological-speculative Correlational-descriptive Experimental-explanatory	Minimal Minimal Fair

A similar analysis concerning general theories is summarized in Table 1.5. What conclusions can we draw from inspection of Tables 1.4 and 1.5? I offer the following.

(i) The most adequate efforts (i.e., rated good or fair) in terms of empirical-formal fit are the area theories in sensation, perception, and learning, and general theories covering individual differences and neuropsychology.

(ii) In general, the most successful theories are experimental-explanatory in nature.

(iii) However, both descriptive and correlational approaches have led to convincing theory, as in the cases of Thurstone, Skinner, and Hebb.

(iv) The phenomenological-speculative approach provides provocative leads, but does not eventuate in convincing theory in that form. Note, however, that it plays an important and legitimate role in the scientific enterprise.

Overall, optimal results occur when there is either high *empiricism* (i.e. sticking close to the facts), as in the case of Skinner, or relevant high *formalism* (i.e. high-powered analytic models, such as an *appropriate* mathematics), as in the case of test theory and learning theory, or both, as in the cases of Thurstone and Spence, *and* when the theorist confines himself to a *relatively limited domain* rather than attempting to encompass all of behaviour (i.e., figural after-effects rather than gestalt psychology, conditioning rather than behaviourism, vision rather than all the senses, etc.). This conclusion points up how difficult it is for *any* scientific endeavour to arrive at an advanced state – that is, to develop one all-encompassing theory which adequately accounts for the observed phenomena. Cases where psychological theory manifest relatively high epistemic correlations are either limited to the relatively well-established domains of study (i.e. sensation, perception, learning, individual differences, and neuropsychology), or/and they are confined to a relatively limited segment of behaviour (i.e. even the more successful general theories of individual differences and neuropsychology cover a relatively limited aspect of the totality of behaviour). In other words, one of the conclusions we can draw from this state of affairs is that a high degree of empiricism is pre-requisite to theoretical integration – that is, there must be a large number of observed facts on hand, available for meaningful conceptualization. However, it would appear that the deification of an "experimental only" brand of empiricism reflects a case of well meaning but misguided faith. For the theoretical successes of such correlational approaches as factor analysis and psychometric theory, combined with the promise of a variety of relatively simple probability models, augurs well for a more relaxed attitude toward the apparent lack of precision of psychological data. I say apparent for it is becoming more and more clear that the data of behaviour, even when gathered under the "cleanest" conditions of laboratory control and precision of measurement, do not fall into the patterns of numerical invariance characteristic of the data of mechanics and other strictly nomothetic domains of study. In short, the nature of the behavioural beast is more like the weather than the motions of billiard balls, and we need to adapt our thinking and methodology to this state of affairs. On this point Egon Brunswik has been most incisive and instructive. In one of his last analytic papers, for example, he puts it this way: "So long as the organism does not develop, or fails in a given context to utilize, completely, the powers

TABLE 1.5

REPRESENTATIVE GENERAL THEORIES IN CONTEMPORARY PSYCHOLOGY

1	2	3	4	5	6
Primary area of study	Representative contemporary systems	Nature of empirical observations	Nature of formalization	Position on the empirical-formalism spectrum	Adequacy of empirical-formal fit
Individual differences	Factor analysis (Thurstone)	Correlational	Explanatory	Correlational-explanatory	Good
Neurological (Physiological)	Hebb, Krech Rashevsky McCulloch	Experimental Experimental	Descriptive Explanatory	Experimental-descriptive Experimental-explanatory	Fair Minimal
Information Cybernetics Decision theory	Frick, Attneave Wiener, von Neumann, Luce	Experimental	Explanatory	Experimental-explanatory	Fair
General systems	Bertalanffy J. G. Miller	Various (i.e. all)	Various (i.e. all)	Empirical-theoretical (i.e. all)	Minimal

of a full-fledged physicist observer and analyst, his environment remains for all practical purposes a semi-erratic medium; it is no more than partially controlled and no more than probabilistically predictable. The functional approach in psychology must take cognizance of this basic limitation of the adjustive apparatus; it must link behaviour and environment statistically in bivariate or multivariate correlation rather than with the predominant emphasis on strict law which we have inherited from physics. It is perhaps more accurate to say that the nomothetic ideology was influenced by a somewhat naive and outdated high-school type, thematic cliché of physics which some of us have tacitly carried with us in the process of developing psychology into a science" (Brunswik, 1956, p.158). Thus, his well known insistence that we proceed in terms of a molar-correlational-probabilism.

But even if we broaden our conception of empiricism as suggested, we will not optimally advance our understanding of behaviour by an "empiricism only" approach. That is, radical empiricism can hardly pull its conceptual self up by its own bootstraps – some kind of theoretical lattice work has got to move in on the data. However, the psychologist's traditional trial and error game of importing foreign theoretical models is a mixed blessing. Most of the contemporary models being played with are mathematical in nature, ranging from the well-established relevance of matrix algebra as the basis for factor theory, through the traditional differential and integral calculus and probability theory, to the provocative possibilities of group and set theory. The mathematical models have been attempted primarily in the areas of learning theory (Bush and Mosteller, 1955; Bush and Estes, 1959) and test theory, (Gulliksen, 1950) but they have also been applied to a variety of other domains. Game theory (Luce and Raiffa, 1957; Shubik, 1964) and decision theory (Thrall, Combs, and Davis, 1954; Luce, 1959) appear to be of particular revelance to choice behaviour, social interaction, and value, whereas information theory (Quastler, 1955; Attneave, 1959) and cybernetics (Wiener, 1948) hold most promise as a framework for the data of cognition. Information theory currently shows signs of paying off, for it is already possible to demonstrate many human-like qualities with the use of electronic computers, such as the ability to play chess, translate languages, solve mathematical problems, and perceive. The risk in all this business is that we will forget that a model serves primarily as an analogy, and must not be taken as the thing itself. In other words, it will require a great amount of labour, measuring, experimenting, and thinking before we can ascertain which aspects of the model to retain and which ones must be dropped. For the greatest value of an analogy is heuristic, that is, its tendency to provoke ingenious experimentation and perceptive conceptualization. It is certainly doubtful that a model from one field will be adequate in unmodified form for another field. We must, after much detailed investigation, ascertain what modifications are necessary, or we must be ready to cast aside the analogy completely if we find too few points of empirical contact. For example, early efforts at mathematizing psychology, such as that of Rashevsky (1938), made extensive use of the calculus. Beginning with a differential equation which reflected the rate of change of the neural impulse, Rashevsky introduced a variety of simplifying assumptions, derived a variety of integral equations, and eventually evolved a complete calculus of behaviour which ran the gamut from neurons to war. This superstructure still stands today as a monument to formalization without empirical representation. While it is possible that a tight empirical-formal fit will eventually be found, it certainly seems to be the case that the calculus is a premature (if not actually inappropriate) mathematical model for behaviour. For one thing, differentiation implies the ability to measure very minute rate changes. What aspects of behaviour lend themselves to such precise measurement in mid-twentieth century? Very few – perhaps certain aspects of physiological psychology, such as nerve conduction and the photochemical processes of the retina, and a similarly limited portion of experimental psychology, such as tracking. The point is that the calculus would be relevant only when behavioural data reflect a high degree of veridicality within the framework of a highly quantifiable system – that is, where rate of change can be measured with great precision. In other words, the Rashevsky failure is a case of an inappropriate mathematical model, or what we may refer to as mental dazzle.

Similarly, the electronic brain is probably not an adequate model for its living counterpart. But it seems worth our while at this time to pursue information theory to the limit in order to find out the extent to which this analogy will hold up. I am well aware of the fact that psychology is a pirate science, and its willingness to try on the conceptual raiment of foreign systems of knowledge is well known. In fact, the claim that psychology has been *too willing* to try on the theoretical orientations of other disciplines is somewhat justified (Koch, 1959). It suggests that psychology does not know where it is going. But that is not particularly unusual in academia; it is interesting to note, for example, that the scientific field which knows best where it has been, physics, has been acting in a similar manner lately. The mathematician John von Neuman, at the time of his death, was writing a book (von Neuman, 1958) on the development of computers in terms of the latest developments in neurophysiology and neuropsychology. Here we have an example of the emergence of progress out of pooled ignorance as well as the heuristic value of the analogy in science, for we have the situation of certain men who call themselves psychologists and physiologists looking at computers as a possible model for the functioning of the brain, and another group of men who are computer experts (mathematicians and physicists) looking at men's brains as a possible model for the functioning of the computer.

What prescriptions are indicated? I suggest the following.

(i) That we inductively generate, from *within* the storehouse of existing psychological data, an inventory of basic concepts, functional relationships, and principles of varying degrees of generality. Several years ago I elaborated on the need for such an inventory and gave several examples of what was called for (see Royce, 1957). Recently this kind of effort received a boost in the form of the Berelson and Steiner book, *Human Behavior: An Inventory of Scientific Findings* (1964). Although it omits large domains, such as biological correlates of behaviour, it documents 1045 such empirically based propositions or generalizations. While the adequacy of many of these concepts is questionable, and the degree of generality is limited, this extensive conceptual inventory provides an impressive basis for evolving a large number of functional relationships which are screaming to be brought into sharper focus and subsequent interrelation.

(ii) That we fit our research methodology to the problem at hand, rather than continue the "methodolatrous" forcing of a less appropriate approach to a given domain of study. In the case of psychology this clearly implies a greater utilization of multivariate methods of problem solving in addition to the continued use of the traditional bivariate analyses (i.e., this does *not* imply the elimination of bivariate analysis).

(iii) That we continue to try out a variety of conceptual schemes, both home-grown and foreign, but that we screen these more critically than we have in the past in terms of their relevance to the particular area of psychological study. Let us take model building as a case in point. The history of science shows a trend away from physical analogies to empty, formal, or mathematical models (Schmidt, 1957). But many of the traditional or classical mathematical systems, such as the calculus, seem to have negligible implications for psychology. While a wide variety of mathematical models have been applied to psychology during the past decade (see Luce, Bush and Galanter, 1963a and b) and while it is clearly too soon to assess the pay-off value of these varied efforts, my bias is that the mathematical models most relevant to the study of behaviour are those which will be able to invoke an appropriate combination of (a) statement in terms of probabilities; (b) adequate inclusion of many variables simultaneously, as in matrix algebra; (c) adequate handling of non-mensurational or qualitative data, as in topology, graph theory, and set theory.[4]

(iv) That we focus more on area rather than general theories of behaviour, with subsequent linkages between areas as a basis for moving *toward* the eventual unification of psychology.[5] The hope of moving directly to a general behaviour

---

4 For coverage of the most relevant so-called modern mathematics between the covers of one book see Kemeny, Snell, and Thompson (1957). For a simplified presentation of the most relevant portion of matrix theory, see Horst (1963) or Butler (1962). For varied thumbnail sketches of applications to psychological data see Bush, Abelson, and Hyman (1956). For detailed instruction on the implementation of two probabililistic models to social phenomena see Chapters V and VII of Kemeny and Snell (1962). For detailed instruction on the implementation of two non-metric models to behavioural data see Chapters II and VIII of Kemeny and Snell (1962). For detailed analysis of matrix theory as the underlying mathematics of factor analysis see any of several books, such as Thurstone (1947) and Harman (1963). For a provocative extension of Lewinian-type theorizing, see the monograph on graph theory by Harary and Norman (1953). For an introductory awareness of the relevance of set theory (an approach likely to be of considerable significance for psychology because it provides an analytic method for getting at patterns by way of sets and subsets of organism-environment components which relate to a given response) see Chapter 2 of Bush and Mosteller (1955). And finally, for coverage of multivariate analytic approaches which have gone beyond their traditional non-experimental domains of study see the *Handbook of Multivariate Experimental Psychology* (Cattell, 1966).

5 Mowrer's recent consolidation of learning theory (1960a), and subsequent extension to symbolic processes (1960b), with necessarily (to date) vaguer asides to more complex behaviour such as language, consciousness, socialization, personality, and psychopathology (i.e. primarily in the latter half of Mowrer, 1960b, and in other publications such as

theory without the prior establishment of strong area theories seems to be unrealistic. The fact that no *one* theory has satisfactorily encompassed *any* discipline of study to date, including the various physical sciences, suggests that the notion of a general theory of behaviour can best be thought of as an ideal toward which we should strive, but that it is probably not attainable.

METAPHORIC KNOWLEDGE AND THE EMERGENCE
OF HUMANISTIC PSYCHOLOGY

The question "How do we know?" is an old and difficult one for both philosophers and psychologists. But our intuitions, perceptions, and thoughts regarding symbolic and intuitive knowing are less adequate than our awarenesses of perceptual and rational knowing. Partly because of this, and partly because we are products of a sensate-rational culture, we tend to depreciate, or at least be wary of, the symbol and intuition. On the other hand, we recognize their pervasiveness in all the specialized disciplines of knowledge – the arts, the sciences, and the humanities – particularly when we focus on the insights of "great men" (e.g., see Havens, 1964, and Royce, 1964). The discoveries of Newton and Galileo regarding gravity and the pendulum, the development of new mathematical systems such as the calculus and modern algebra, the works of art created by a Mozart, a Beethoven, or a Shakespeare, reflect a variety of combinations of symbolic and intuitive cognition. In the analysis which follows I take the position that symbolism and intuition are legitimate ways of knowing, in spite of our ignorance about how they work, that they can be brought into play at any phase of the knowing process, and that they have, in fact, manifested themselves to some extent in all domains of psychological study, but that their greatest immediate relevance lies in the present emergence of humanistic psychology. Since humanistic studies are heavily undergirded by the metaphoric epistemology (see Fig. 1.1), it follows that any alliance between psychology and the humanities would, by definition, invoke this approach to reality as primary. However, such alliances imply two-way traffic, so that we can anticipate the welding of the empirical-rational epistemologies with the metaphoric approach in coming to grips with psychological problems of a humanistic nature. This means that the symbolic and intuitive insights typical of humanistic thought would eventually be tempered by efforts to provide appropriate empirical tests. More importantly, however, it also implies an openness on the part of the humanistic psychologist to those metaphoric-rational awarenesses which are *not* immediately testable empirically. In another context (Royce, 1965a) I develop the

Mowrer, 1964) constitutes a provocative example of the possibilities of moving from a hard core area theory toward a more general theory of behaviour. Similar extensions of the well-documented adaptation-level theory have been demonstrated by Helson (1964). My personal bias is that the approach reflected in the examples of Mowrer and Helson is more promising than the earlier "isms" because of the much greater accumulation of empirical evidence available for unification, the integration of earlier (sometimes apparently opposing) theoretical conceptualizations, and the general tightening up of the area theory *before* casting the nomological net abroad to include adjacent behavioural domains.

theme that the key to the difference between scientific and humanistic psychology lies in the distinction between sign and symbol. This point can best be brought out by reproducing the following diagram:

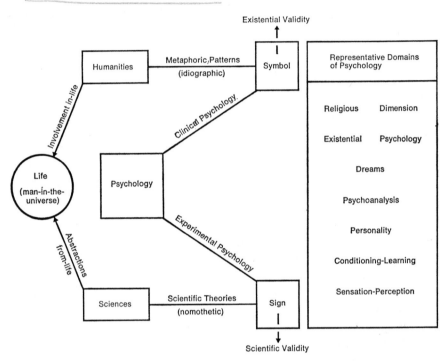

FIGURE 1.3
Psychology at the crossroads (from Royce (1965a), p. 17)

The purpose of this diagram is to bring out the complementary contributions of the sciences and the humanities to the understanding of life, and particularly, to demonstrate how psychology lies peculiarly at the crossroads between the two cultures. Let us concentrate on the upper half of Fig. 1.3. Here we see the humanities as concretely involved-*in*-life as opposed to making abstractions *from* the phenomena of life. And, parallel to the ultimate theoretical goal of science, we see that the humanistic disciplines are also ultimately beamed at making over-arching statements (i.e., metaphoric-rational) regarding man-in-the-universe. However, and this is the main point, the humanities speak through a symbolic rather than a sign language. Hence, the emerging statements take the form of metaphoric patterns or symbol systems rather than scientific theories, and the truth-giving quality of such statements follow the epistemological criteria of symbols rather than signs (e.g., see Fig. 1.1 and note the "fertility" criterion of art and the criterion of existential validity for religion). As used in this context, the essence of the sign-symbol distinction is that the sign reveals a one-to-one correspondence (i.e., A means B, and *not* C. D., and E), whereas the symbol provides a one-to-many relationship (i.e., A may mean B, C, D, or E, or any combination thereof). The multiple meanings of the symbol make the task of empirical analysis extremely difficult, but they open up dimensions of reality which remain unavailable to sign language.[6] Herein lies the challenge for the humanistic psychologist – to tap these symbolic dimensions of reality by invoking the knowledge giving tools of the humanistic trade on the one hand, and by doing all that is possible to provide empirical tests for whatever is so revealed on the other hand. But this must be done without the error of reductionism – that is, by throwing out as invalid those humanistic insights which are *not* amenable, or reducible, to empirical confirmation. If the reductionistic error is committed we simply will not have a humanistic psychology, for we will have reduced it to scientific (or empirical) psychology.

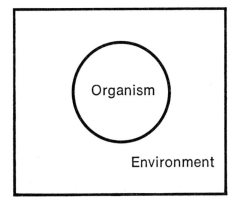

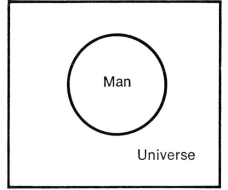

FIGURE 1.4
Basic schematic definition of psychology

FIGURE 1.5
Humanistic schematic definition of psychology

What might a humanistic psychology look like? It is, of course, too early to tell, but I shall point to several possibilities. As a start I suggest we supplement the usual schematic diagram of the organism-in-the-environment (see Fig. 1.4) with a diagram showing man-in-the-universe (see Fig. 1.5).

Such a schematic diagram allows us to cast the more philosophic aspects of man's behaviour within the traditional definition of psychology as involving organism-environment interactions. The only difference is that we are now operating at the more cosmic level of man-in-the-universe. This business of painting man with such a big brush is typical of the humanistic approach, and thereby constitutes a reasonable common ground for mode of study. Also characteristic of the humanities is the effort to unmask the universal by way of the concrete case. Our previous discussion must be kept in mind at this juncture, namely, that such universal-concrete efforts are typically conveyed symbolically rather than via signs. With this as a background we can now take a look at Fig. 1.6.

6 For a more complete exposition of this point see Royce (1965a).

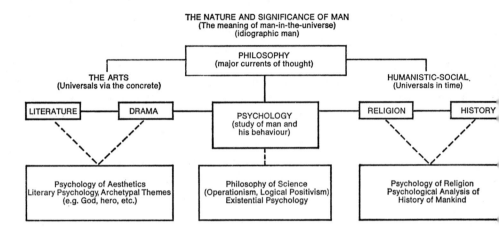

FIGURE 1.6
Psychology and the humanities

This diagram shows psychology as the study of man and his behaviour rather than the science of organisms. The purpose behind this heretical, definitional shift is to legitimize symbolic and intuitive cognition (Royce, 1960 and 1965a). Such a definition, which appears to be a reactionary move, is actually a forward-looking suggestion in the twentieth century because it demands that we re-admit humanistic studies as a way to gain psychological knowledge. Now that we have empiricism as the core epistemology undergirding our discipline there would seem to be little danger that psychology will regress to a pre-Wundtian stage by making such a move. The solid lines indicate alliances with several humanistic disciplines (shown in solid line rectangles), the most relevant lying closest to psychology at the center. The broken lines lead to possible areas of humanistic study which are a result of such alliances. The most obvious examples of humanistic study are those indicated out of the alliance with philosophy[7]: philosophy of science, operationism, logical positivism, and existential psychology (for examples of the latter see Royce, 1962b, and May, 1961). In other words, philosophy of science and existentialism are seen as the most important currents of thought in contemporary philosophical and theoretical psychology (Royce, 1964). Similarly, the psychology of aesthetics and the psychology of religion are seen as examples of studies which have come out of alliances with the indicated humanistic-social and arts disciplines respectively.

The defence for the priority given to drama is that its action-on-a-stage (or on film, TV, or other media) is capable of disclosing a microcosm of man living out

7 Greater recognition for this type of investigation is likely in the near future as the American Psychological Association has recently established a new division devoted to such study – Division 24, Division of Philosophical Psychology.

his life in the everyday world. It is, in a very real sense, the most behavioural of the art forms. It is also one of the more time-compressed forms of artistic expression. These two points, combined with the fact that the dramatic form ordinarily involves a beginning, a middle, and an end, with a build up to a conflict which is resolved, provides the psychologist with material which simulates completed or total "lives". While similar material is also available in literature, it is not as obviously behavioural. Both forms, however, are rich in archetypal characterizations – *the hero*, tragic (e.g., Hamlet, Oedipus), satanic (Mephistopheles in *Faust*, Iago in *Othello*), or God-like (Dion in O'Neill's *Great God Brown*); woman as *great mother* (Cybele in O'Neill's *Great God Brown*) or as *goddess* (the novel *She*); *animus* (*Wuthering Heights*) – and such universal themes as *heaven* and *hell* (*Kubla Khan, Paradise Lost*) and *rebirth* (Job and MacLeish's *J.B.*).

Let me be more concrete about all this by briefly analysing William Golding's *Lord of the Flies* (1954). This is one of those cases where the new corny phrase "big allegory" (i.e. a form of metaphoric knowledge) is completely appropriate, for Golding has focused his attention on the predicament of modern man – possibly man in all time, but particularly twentieth-century man. That is, he makes it clear at the beginning of the story that the kids isolated on the Pacific island had arrived with a cultural tradition, with an awareness of rules and custom. But in due course we observe the disintegration of order and the emergence of evil as the victor. Ralph, the Chief, says to his adviser, Piggy, "What went wrong, why did it all go wrong? We started out all right." This is the big question the story puts, and my interpretation is that the novel is primarily concerned with the forces of good and evil which are inherent in man's predicament. I see "the beast" as an externalization of potentially evil forces, and the pressure from such forces, combined with fear, fear of the unknown, as the key to what went wrong. Jack, the symbolic representative of evil, takes advantage of this fear by promising to provide protection from "the beast", thereby gaining a following. Thus, what went wrong is that fear, a very natural and necessary component for survival in the face of the unknown, dominated the situation at a time when acceptance of ambiguity was necessary. The important consideration, the rational Piggy (symbolizing the egg head) pointed out, was to be "rescued". And surely the important consideration for man, especially in a nuclear age, is for him to be "rescued". There are two clear opportunities for salvation in Golding's novel. The first one occurs when Simon comes to tell them "the truth" about "the beast", and they kill him – a rather obvious Christ symbol. The second chance comes too late at the end of the story when help arrives in the form of the British Navy. This can be taken as symbolic of the Day of Judgment, but it is too late, for all but Ralph have regressed to a savage condition by this time.

It is my view that there is considerable meat in this cosmic type of presentation for psychological analysis. Assuming for the moment that the above is an essentially correct analysis[8] of what Golding's novel is about, it seems clear that the

---

8 Other interpretations are not only possible, but typical of metaphoric knowledge. This does *not* mean that anything goes, that any one interpretation is as good as another. A given

behaviour exhibited in this allegorical treatment of man must be explained.[9] I offered a brief explanation in terms of an outward projection of fear, combined with the always lurking forces of evil and man's inability to tolerate ambiguity. But I have merely pointed to the notion that the psychology of fear and cognition are involved. I have not offered a thorough analysis. Some of Maslow's recent work is directly relevant here, particularly his thinking on what he calls being cognition. In an entirely different context, he says, for example:

Sometimes the safety needs can almost entirely bend the cognitive needs to their own anxiety-allaying purposes. The anxiety-free person [e.g., Simon in *Lord of the Flies*. Brackets by J. R. R.] can be more bold and more courageous ... anxiety kills curiosity and exploration ... especially when anxiety is extreme. ... It seems quite clear that the need to know, if we are to understand it well, must be integrated with fear of knowing, with needs for safety and security. (Maslow, 1962, pp. 62–64)

I see the possibility for a long-range dialogue between the literary picture of man presented by Golding in his provocative novel and the picture of man painted by a traditional scientific psychology. It seems to me that complete psychological analyses of literary products such as *Lord of the Flies*, analysed and empirically investigated à la Maslow and others, could not help but provide valid insights about man and his behaviour patterns, and that the ensuing dialogue between the scientific and humanistic approaches would further provoke an eventual synthesis, thereby leading to greater understanding.

Mythic patterns such as those cited above have recurred throughout recorded history and have transcended geographical and cultural boundaries as well. Continuing failure, in the name of scientific purism, on the part of phychologists to study such a rich storehouse of material borders on the foolhardy. Furthermore, the typical sexual reductionism of Freudian psychoanalysis is simply not up to the requirements of the task, and while Jungian analysis may be more promising,

---

interpretation is constrained by some combination of consistency on the one hand (i.e. external, internal, temporal, theoretical, as amplified, for example, in Royce, 1965a, p. 19), and the extent to which there is universal meaning as opposed to idiosyncrasy on the other hand (at this juncture the reader is reminded of our previous explication of this point, as exemplified particularly in Table 1.1, Fig. 1.1, and Fig. 1.3, and the appropriate portions of the text). Furthermore, additional valid interpretations reflect the one-to-many meanings which are characteristic of the symbol and the metaphor (see p. 28 and, for a more complete exposition, Royce, 1965a).

9 A brief answer to the possible objection that such behaviour does not have to be explained because the characters are fictional is as follows: if the literary product, such as a play or a novel, is valid (i.e., if it reaches for the universal rather than the idiosyncratic), it carries metaphoric reality or truth as a totality. That is, the play or novel says something (metaphorically, or symbolically, rather than in scientific prose) "real" or "true" about the nature of man. Hence, the behaviour exhibited in the literary product should (in principle) also carry metaphoric reality. The extent to which such analyses will converge with scientific analyses can be determined in individual cases.

contemporary psychologists have not yet given serious thought and effort to the possibilities at hand. For example, of the 4500 items listed in Kiell's (1963) recent bibliography on psychology and literature, practically all involve some kind of psychoanalytic interpretation, and further, possibly as many as one third of the drama listings deal with Hamlet. The majority of the references to psychology *per se* are in terms of a very prosaic analysis of audience response to some dramatic production, such as radio, television, or films – i.e., a problem in the measurement of public opinion and/or attitude change. There is very little indication that standard approaches, such as content analysis or projective testing, have been adapted for study in this domain, or that new techniques of analysis, appropriate to the available material, have been developed. There is, in short, a sad lack of imaginative inquiry in what we might refer to as literary psychology.

A similar concern for the symbolic is required for investigation in the psychology of religion, for here we are focusing on the ultimate commitments of man, those commitments around which the meaning of one's existence is built. Penetrating analyses of value, myth, and that which is existentially "real" are all necessary for vital investigation in this area. The typical psychological studies in this area are concerned with such matters as how many people attend church on Sunday and the number of conversions recorded for various denominations as a function of age. Such studies seem to bypass religion almost completely. A humanistic psychology of religion would not lose Tillich's depth dimension; it would not lose the heart of that which is religious in the name of ease of observation and measurement. In short, contrary to the present dominant positivistic Zeitgeist, the humanistic psychological study of religion would deal in whatever way it can with the subjective meaning of life – with that which is existentially valid. Such an approach would begin with ontological anxiety, for example, rather than focusing on the easier neurotic anxiety. It takes more courage "to be" (Tillich, 1952) in the face of ontological as opposed to neurotic anxiety for the simple reason that there is no illusion of "cure" in the case of the former variety. The traditional scientific approach to the psychological study of religion, one of the most important and ubiquitous characteristics of mankind, has not yet penetrated very deeply – it seems to me that the humanistic approach is more likely to probe the "inner man"[10] because of its greater willingness to deal with the fullness of subjective experience via an all-encompassing phenomenology as opposed to a narrow, albeit more rigorous, empiricism.

If we assume, as it seems reasonable to do, that the events of human history are a result of the interdependence between the individual and the culture of his time, then it follows that a more explicit psychological analysis of history is required than has been manifested to date. Due to the overwhelming complexities of life, scholars in all fields oversimplify their domains of study in order to get launched. This approach, however, eventually reveals its simplistic inadequacies. Thus, the study of history has not been of a psycho-cultural order, but rather, it has been

10 For a provocative entree to the implied possibilities see the interdisciplinary roundtable discussion edited by Havens (1968).

dominated by a kind of abstract analysis of political, economic, and military events – "as if" there were no human organisms generating these changes. There are indications that a psycho-historical alliance would lead to a more complete understanding of the evolution of the human psyche on the one hand, and a better understanding of man through time on the other hand. Toynbee, for example, brings psychology to bear in his analyses of the rise and fall of civilizations. A central plank in his approach is the importance of the symbol and the myth as unconscious manifestations of the human spirit. At this juncture his thinking merges with Jung's in their claim that "progress" is crucially dependent upon the validity of symbolic commitments – especially those carrying religious implications. For example, in his concept of "challenge and response" Toynbee indicates that the response to a challenge must eventually become a religious one if the civilization is to survive. Further, Toynbee takes this analysis to the level of the individual personality, particularly the "creative minority" (i.e., the leading artists, scientists, and thinkers of a given epoch), as the source of new values for meeting the challenge of continued existence.

A psychological history is potentially the most empirical of the several humanistic alliances briefly described above, for it can be studied more easily than any of the others within the context of social psychology. However, it does suffer from the fact that behaviour as such cannot be observed directly, only reconstructed from the records and artifacts of the past. Nevertheless, the recent book by Zevedei Barbu (1960) speaks well for the mutual enrichment which should follow the union of the two disciplines.

SUMMARY AND CONCLUSIONS

I have tried to assess the present situation in contemporary theoretical psychology in terms of underlying epistemologies (i.e. empiricism, rationalism, and metaphorism). Because of twentieth century encapsulation within the epistemology of empiricism, contemporary man finds it difficult to be open to symbolic and intuitive cognition. Psychology, as part of the contemporary sensate culture, and psychologists, as part of the contemporary cultural Zeitgeist, can also be characterized as super-empirical, somewhat at the expense of the rational, and almost completely at the expense of the metaphoric, approach to reality.

An analysis of contemporary scientific theories was made in terms of the degree of epistemic correlation between empiricism and rationalism. This analysis revealed that the most adequate theoretical efforts have been made in the domains of sensation, perception, learning, individual differences, and neuropsychology. While the most successful theories are experimental-explanatory in nature, descriptive and correlational approaches have also led to convincing theory. The phenomenological-speculative approach provides provocative leads, but does not eventuate in convincing theory in that form. Overall, optimal results occur when there is either high empiricism, high relevant formalism, or both, *and* when the theorist confines himself to a relatively limited domain.

Prescriptions for action include: (a) That we inductively generate, from within the storehouse of existing psychological data, an inventory of basic concepts, functional relationships, and principles of varying degrees of generality. (b) That we make greater use of multivariate methods of problem-solving in psychology on the grounds that these are, in general, more appropriate than the more traditional bivariate analysis. (c) That we continue to try out a variety of conceptual schemes, both home-grown and foreign, but that we screen these more critically than we have in the past in terms of their relevance to the particular area of psychological study (e.g., appropriateness of certain physical and mathematical models). (d) That we focus more on area rather than general theories of behaviour, with subsequent extensions of well-established area theories and linkages between areas as a basis for moving toward the eventual unification of psychology.

While intuition is involved at all phases of the scientific enterprise it is minimized as final judge in science. However, metaphoric knowledge is crucial in the humanistic disciplines and it would assume a dominant position in a humanistic psychology. The possibilities for the evolution of such a development within an expanded definition of psychology were pointed to but not elaborated in detail. Priority was given to alliances with the humanistic disciplines of philosophy, drama, religion, literature, and history.

References

ATTNEAVE, F., *Applications of information theory to psychology.* New York: Holt-Dryden, 1959

BARBU, ZEVEDEI, *Problems of historical psychology.* New York: Grove Press, 1960

BARRON, F., "The psychology of creativity," in *New directions in psychology II.* New York: Holt, Rinehart & Winston, 1965, pp. 1–120

BERELSON, B. and STEINER, G. A., *Human behavior: an inventory of scientific findings.* New York: Harcourt, Brace & World, 1964

BERLYNE, D. E., *Conflict, arousal, and curiosity.* New York: McGraw-Hill, 1960

VON BERTALANFFY, L., "On the definition of the symbol," in *Psychology and the symbol: an inter-disciplinary symposium,* edited by J. R. Royce. New York: Random House, 1965, pp. 26–72

BOULDING, K. E., *The image.* Ann Arbor: University of Michigan Press, 1956

BRUNSWIK, EGON, "Historical and thematic relations of psychology to other sciences." *Science Monthly,* 83 (1956) 151–61

BUSH, R. R. and MOSTELLER, F., *Stochastic models for learning.* New York: Wiley, 1955

BUSH, R. R., ABELSON, R. P., and HYMAN, R., *Mathematics for psychologists: examples and problems.* New York: Social Sciences Research Council, 1956

BUSH, R. R. and ESTES, W. K. (editors), *Studies in mathematical learning theory.* Stanford: Stanford University Press, 1959

BUTLER, L. E., *Basic matrix theory.* Englewood Cliffs, NJ: Prentice-Hall, 1962

CAMPBELL, D. T., "Blind variation and selective retention as in other knowledge processes." *Psychological Review,* 67 (1960) 380–400

CARROLL, J. B., *The study of language.* Cambridge: Harvard University Press, 1953

CASSIRER, E., *The philosophy of symbolic forms.* New Haven: Yale University Press, vol. 1, 1953; vol. 2, 1955; vol. 3, 1957

CATTELL, R. B. (editor), *Handbook of multivariate experimental psychology.* Chicago: Rand-McNally, 1966

ESTES, W. K., "The statistical approach to learning theory," in *Psychology: a study of a science,* edited by S. Koch. New York: McGraw-Hill, vol. 2, 1959, pp. 380–491

ESTES, W. K., "Component and pattern models with Markovian interpretations," in *Studies in mathematical learning theory*, edited by R. R. Bush and W. K. Estes. Stanford: Stanford University Press, 1959

FESTINGER, L., *A theory of cognitive dissonance*. Evanston, Ill.: Row, Peterson, 1957

FOSS, M., *Symbol and metaphor*. Lincoln: University of Nebraska Press, 1949

GIBSON, J. J., *The perception of the visual world*. Boston: Houghton Mifflin, 1950

GOLDING, W., *Lord of the flies*. London: Faber & Faber, 1954

GRAHAM, C. H., "Color theory," in *Psychology: a study of a science*, edited by S. Koch. New York: McGraw-Hill, vol. 1, 1959, pp. 145–287

GULLIKSEN, H., *Theory of mental tests*. New York: Wiley, 1950

HARARY, F. and NORMAN, R. Z., *Graph theory as a mathematical model in social science*. Ann Arbor: Institute for Social Research, 1953

HARMAN, H. H., *Modern factor analysis*. Chicago: University of Chicago Press, 1960.

HAVENS, J., "Adventurers in experiential knowing." *Main Currents in Modern Thought*, **20** (1964) 83–9

HAVENS, J. (editor), *Psychology and religion: a contemporary dialogue*. Princeton: van Nostrand, 1968

HEBB, D. O., *The organization of behaviour*. New York: Wiley, 1949

HELSON, H., *Adaptation-level theory*. New York: Harper & Row, 1964

HITT, W. D. "Toward a two-factor theory of creativity." *Psychological Record*, **15** (1965) 127–32

HITT, W. D. and STOCK, J. R., "The relation between psychological characteristics and creative behaviour." *Ibid.*, pp. 133–40

HORST, P., *Matrix algebra for social scientists*. New York: Holt, Rinehart & Winston, 1963

HULL, C. L., *The principles of behaviour*. New York: Appleton-Century, 1943

JONES, B., "The psycho-epistemological profile: its scoring, validity and reliability." Unpublished Master's thesis, University of Alberta, 1963

JUNG, C. G., *Psychological types*, translated by H. G. Baynes. London: Routledge & Kegan Paul, 1923

KEMENY, J. G., SNELL, J. L., and THOMPSON, G. L., *Introduction to finite mathematics*. Englewood Cliffs, NJ: Prentice-Hall, 1957

KIELL, N., *Psychoanalysis, psychology, and literature: a bibliography*. Madison: University of Wisconsin Press, 1963

KOCH, S. (editor), "Epilogue," in *Psychology: a study of a science*. New York: McGraw-Hill, vol. 3, 1959, pp. 729–88

KÖHLER, W. and WALLACH, H., "Figural after-effects." *Proceedings of the American Philosophical Society*, **88** (1944) 269–357

LANGER, SUZANNE K., "On a new definition of 'symbol' ", in *Philosophical Sketches*. Toronto: New American Library of Canada, 1964, pp. 53–61

LEVY, L. H., *Psychological interpretation*. New York: Holt, Rinehart & Winston, 1963

LUCE, R. D., BUSH, R. R., and GALANTER, E. (editors), *Handbook of mathematical psychology*. New York: Wiley, vols. 1 and 2, 1963 (a)

LUCE, R. D., BUSH, R. R., and GALANTER, E. (editors), *Readings in mathematical psychology*. New York: Wiley, vols. 1 and 2, 1963 (b)

LUCE, R. D. and RAIFFA, H., *Games and decisions*. New York: Wiley, 1957

MASLOW, A. H., *Toward a psychology of being*. Princeton: van Nostrand, 1962

MAY, R. (editor), *Existential psychology*. New York; Random House, 1961

MEEHL, P., *Clinical versus statistical prediction*. Minneapolis: University of Minnesota Press, 1954

MILLER, G. A., *Language and communication*. New York: McGraw-Hill, 1951

MILLER, G. A., GALANTER, E., and PRIBRAM, K. H., *Plans and the structure of behavior*. New York: Holt, Rinehart & Winston, 1960

MONTAGUE, W. P., *The ways of knowing*. London: Allen, 1928

MOWRER, O. H., *Learning theory and behavior*. New York: Wiley, 1960 (a)

MOWRER, O. H., *Learning theory and symbolic processes*. New York: Wiley, 1960 (b)

VON NEUMANN, J., *The computer and the brain.* New Haven: Yale University Press, 1958

NORTHROP, F. S. C., *The logic of the sciences and the humanities.* New York: Macmillan, 1947

OSGOOD, C. E., SUCI, G. J., and TANNENBAUM, P. H., *The measurement of meaning.* Urbana: University of Illinois Press, 1957

QUASTLER, H. (editor), *Information theory in psychology.* Glencoe, Ill.: The Free Press, 1955

RASHEVSKY, N., *Mathematical biophysics.* Chicago: University of Chicago Press, 1938

ROSENZWEIG, S., "Schools of psychology: a complementary pattern." *Philosophy of Science,* **4** (1937) 96–106

ROYCE, J. R., "Toward the advancement of theoretical psychology." *Psychological Reports,* **3** (1957) 401–10

ROYCE, J. R., "The search for meaning." *American Scientist,* **47** (1959) 515–35

ROYCE, J. R., "Heretical thoughts on the definition of psychology." *Psychological Reports,* **8** (1960) 11–14

ROYCE, J. R., "Studies of value and psycho-epistemological hierarchies," in *Research plans in religion, values, and morality,* edited by S. Cook. New York: Religious Education Association, 1962, pp. 85–8 (*a*)

ROYCE, J. R., "Psychology, existentialism, and religion," *Journal of General Psychology,* **66** (1962) 3–16 (*b*)

ROYCE, J. R., *The encapsulated man: an interdisciplinary essay on the search for meaning.* Princeton: van Nostrand, 1964

ROYCE, J. R. (editor), *Psychology and the symbol: an interdisciplinary symposium.* New York: Random House, 1965 (a)

ROYCE, J. R., "A bibliography of factor analytic studies in fields other than psychology." Unpublished manuscript, University of Alberta, 1965 (b)

ROYCE, J. R., "Pebble picking versus boulder building." *Psychological Reports,* **16** (1965) 447–50 (c)

ROYCE, J. R. and SMITH, W. A. S., "A note on the development of the psycho-epistemological profile (PEP)." *Ibid.,* **14** (1964) 297–8

ROZEBOOM, W. W., "Mediation variables in scientific theory." *Psychological Review,* **63** (1956) 249–64

SARBIN, T. R., TAFT, R., and BAILEY, D. E., *Clinical inference and cognitive theory.* New York: Holt, Rinehart & Winston, 1960

SCHMIDT, P. F., "Models of scientific thought." *American Scientist,* **45** (1957) 137

SHUBIK, M. (editor), *Game theory and related approaches to social behavior.* New York: Wiley, 1964

SKINNER, B. F., *The behavior of organisms.* New York: Appleton-Century, 1938

SMITH, W. A. S., ROYCE, J. R., AYERS, D., and JONES, B., "The development of an inventory to measure ways of knowing." *Psychological Reports,* **21** (1967) 529–35

SOROKIN, P. A., *The crisis of our age.* New York: Dutton, 1941

SPENCE, K. W., *Behavior theory and conditioning.* New Haven: Yale University Press, 1956

SPENGLER, O., *The decline of the west.* London: Allen & Unwin, 1932

TAYLOR, C. W., *Creativity: progress and potential.* New York: McGraw-Hill, 1964

THRALL, R. M., COOMBS, C. H., and DAVID, R. L., *Decision processes.* New York: Wiley, 1954

TILLICH, P. W., *The courage to be.* New Haven: Yale University Press, 1952

TOYNBEE, A. J., *A study of history* (two-volume abridgement). Cambridge: Oxford University Press, 1946, 1957

THURSTONE, L. L., *Multiple factor analysis.* Chicago: University of Chicago Press, 1947

WALLRAFF, C. F., *Philosophical theory and psychological fact.* Tucson: University of Arizona Press, 1961

WERNER, H. and KAPLAN, B., *Symbol formation.* New York: Wiley, 1963

WESTCOTT, M. R., "On the measurement of intuitive leaps." *Psychological Reports,* **9** (1961) 267–74

WESTCOTT, M. R. and RANZONI, J. H., "Correlates of intuitive thinking." *Psychological Reports,* **12** (1963) 595–613

WIENER, N., *Cybernetics.* New York: Wiley, 1948

Comments:
R. B. MacLeod

This paper is so full of substance that it could well provide the basis for a whole week's discussion, but I shall limit myself to a very few points which I feel should be stressed. All my comments are friendly.

(i) The least important of my points has to do with the term "psycho-episte-mology," which I consider to be unnecessary. We can state the essential psycho-logical questions without adding more 'psychos' to our jargon.

(ii) Royce implies that "behaviour" is the agreed-upon subject matter of psy-chology. This might be true, if we had a sufficiently broad definition of the term. He has not given us such a definition. I suggest that psychology has to do with that which is distinctly human about man. This is not a definition, but it raises some good questions.

(iii) Royce would like us to unify psychology. This may or may not be a noble aspiration, depending on what we mean by unification. If the unity we seek is some-thing that is common to all people who call themselves psychologists, then it is a silly quest. The professional label provides at best a spurious semblance of unity. The essential unity of any science, I suggest, is to be found in the questions it asks. What are we really curious about? I happen to be curious about the phenomena of human experience; and to this extent I think I am a psychologist. But I am also curious about the effects of malnutrition on the growth and development of organ-isms. This would seem to make me a physiologist or a biochemist, albeit a very poor one. But this is of no consequence. The important fact is that the sciences unify and diversify as their questions become reformulated. It would not bother me in the least if the questions we now call "psychological" were to be reshuffled and sorted out to a number of other disciplines, provided of course that these other disciplines embodied some meaningful questions. I still think, however, that there are a few persistent questions which might justify the continued existence of a science of psychology.

(iv) Royce has discussed "metaphorism" as one of the modes of knowing. Dis-counting the "ism", which is merely more jargon, I think that he is here emphasiz-ing something of really crucial importance. William James distinguished between the sensationalists and the intellectualists, both of whom were wrong. Between these extremes have been James himself, the gestaltists, and the various humanists, all of whom have insisted that man's apprehension of the world includes the per-ception of tertiary as well as secondary and primary qualities. Metaphor as a medium of communication depends on the apprehension of similarities which do not lend themselves readily to the traditional psychologies of perception. I am not sure that Royce is wise in presenting "metaphorism" as a special mode of knowing. He is, however, calling for a psychology of cognition that takes account of all its data. And this, it seems to me, is precisely what we need if we are to have a unified psychology.

(v) Royce seems to have his doubts about the value of theoretical models, although I suspect that, deep down, he would like to have a model that would unify psychology. Let me speak for myself. Throughout the history of science we have had models. These have served to consolidate existing knowledge and to place curbs on irresponsible speculation. A good scientific model sets the ground-rules for the humdrum digging up of facts upon which science depends. But the really great break-throughs in science have taken place when existing models have been challenged. Newton was at his best when, with an assist from Galileo, he challenged the Aristotelian model. The Newtonian model, which survived him, has paid off in many practical ways, but the really exciting developments in modern physics have come from the challenging, by Einstein and others, of Newton's conception of the physical world.

Psychology's story is similar. We have had an Aristotelian kind of psychology, and also a Newtonian and a Darwinian psychology. Each has produced its fact-finders and its model-builders. In my opinion, however, the psychological model-builders, especially those of the S-R type, have not stimulated enough fact-finding to justify their existence. To put it even more bluntly, the S-R models have seriously restricted the freedom of psychological inquiry. It is a sad commentary on the situation that when courageous rebels, such as Miller, Galanter, and Pribram, break loose from the S-R bonds they are hailed as heroes. They are indeed heroic, for it takes courage to escape from prison. But why did they allow themselves to be captured in the first place?

(vi) My comments seem to have developed into a tirade against theoretical models. I do not wish to damn the model-builders utterly. They are useful as a sort of superego, but they must not be allowed to hamper the progress of science. This permits me to end on a happy note. Royce is pleading for a "humanistic" psychology – a familiar theme in other parts of the world, but slightly heretical in the USA. Royce wants us to deal scientifically with what is distinctively human about man. Aristotle, in his modest way, said the same thing; but it needs to be said again and again, and I think that Royce's restatement should be accepted as a challenge.

L. von Bertalanffy

I wish to comment on some general points:

(i) The feedback model
As is well known, the feedback concept is originally taken from technology. The simplest possible feedback arrangement is given in Fig. 1.7.
Applied to biological and psychological phenomena it is apparent that the feedback model essentially is the s-r scheme with the feedback loop added, thereby making the system self-regulating.

The logical structure of the feedback scheme (and similarly of many other models) is that a model, originally arising in technology, was found to be applicable to phenomena in other fields. This, of course, applies to biology in the explanation of homeostatic regulations, goal-directed movements, and many others. Similarly, the model is applicable to psychological phenomena. The condition for

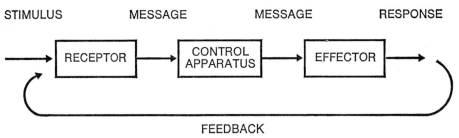

FIGURE 1.7
The basic feedback model

such applications is that the underlying mechanisms can be worked out in the way of a flow or block diagram which will consist of more or less complicated, super-imposed, feedback circuits. The mere word "feedback" (or application of similar general terms) means nothing and is indeed "word magic" to use Krech's expression.

One has, of course, to consider that the feedback model is not a cover-all or nothing-but explanation. Feedback circuits are widely found in physiological and presumably psychological phenomena. As the basic scheme shows, however, it essentially implies one-way (although circular) causality, the existence of a con-trolling center, and so on. Therefore, the feedback scheme is not applicable where it is a matter of interaction between many components and processes, multivariable causality, etc. The German term *Regelmechanismen* correctly emphasizes the essentially mechanistic character of the model.

(ii) Theoretical models in general

Theoretical models, correctly applied to concrete cases, are indispensable. They may be called "metaphors", but the essential thing is that they permit for explana-tion, prediction, and control. This is based on the fact of formal or structural simi-larity between model and phenomena to be explained. For example, the same formal flow diagram may apply to a hydrostatic mechanism, regulation of animal movements, and other phenomena. Of course, there is no material similarity what-ever between, say, hydrostatic mechanism and a nervous system, but the model (if correctly worked out) gives a legitimate explanation. The same is, of course, true in innumerable cases in physics, e.g. the wave model in many physical pheno-mena, the formal homologies between Newton's and Coulomb's law, of Newtonian and wave mechanics. Such homology, far from being trivial, may present important problems for further theoretical development (cf the question of a general field theory).

(iii) "Unification" of psychology

Of course, there is not and probably never will be a "unified" psychology, but only a number of different fields subsumed under this name. But the same also applies to biology; biochemistry, histology, taxonomy, and many others, are fields widely divergent in their methods, problems and theories. Not even physics has a thor-oughly "unified" theory.

Nevertheless, there are *unifying concepts and principles* in science, such as those of atomic theory, molecular biology, evolution, and – hopefully – also in psychology. These certainly do not lead to a "unification" in the grand style, but they do help to bring different phenomena and more special theories into a general framework. I believe working toward such unified concepts is the aim of the present Conference; it is by no means unnecessary or unscientific "word magic," but a development which psychology must follow.

(iv) Theoretical psychology
Of course, "i.e. theories" are preferable to "e.g. theories" (to use Krech's witticism). In other words, mathematically formulated theories permitting quantitative prediction win over loosely constructed, verbal models and theories. However, over-stringent demands will hinder sound development of psychological theory. As a rule, they will either lead to a premature pseudo-exactness or an area theory covering only a very narrow field (or combination of both limitations). It is fantastic to presume that an axiomatic or strict hypothetico-deductive system can be established in psychology if such a system does not exist even in physics (considered as a whole), and hardly a trace of it in biology (excepting genetics). But even verbally formulated theories or explanations "in principle" (Hayek) may be of importance. Such is presently the case in the fields of evolution, meteorology, economics, and others.

Theoretical psychology today is characterized by an over-abundance of methodological sermons and a dearth of original ideas. Hence, discussion is mostly of "classical systems", such as behaviourism and psychoanalysis, the shortcomings of which are apparent. Technological models (e.g. feedback, the electronic calculator as a model of the brain) have been widely adopted but they are applicable only to a limited extent. The call for new, genuinely psychological theory has remained largely unheeded. But science does not grow by prescriptions of "how it should be done" and criticism, but only by novel discoveries and ideas.

(v) Humanistic psychology
I believe the problem of humanistic psychology is essentially simple, although its elaboration will be difficult. It is an elementary fact that the species *homo* is different from rats, pigeons, and monkeys. However, American laboratory psychology was essentially zoomorphic – it wanted to explain human behaviour in terms of rat psychology. That such an enterprise is not legitimate is not a matter of philosophical or theological concern, but is verified by ethology (the naturalistic study of animal behaviour) which reveals important, even inherited differences of behaviour between different species.

Certainly one important facet of human psychology is symbolism and all its implications. It is characteristic of American psychology that not even the term "symbol" is found in the index of leading introductory texts of psychology.

Hence the problem appears to be clearly posed: to elaborate what is specific of human behaviour, and not to try to reduce it to animal psychology or biological factors. This, of course, will imply a different methodology loosely defined by terms such as humanistic and clinical.

W. W. Rozeboom

ROZEBOOM   What does Royce mean by humanistic psychology? Let me cite three alternatives. First, the arts may provide a lore of psychological data which are not available elsewhere, and which humanistic psychology is to analyse in the scientific "cognitive style" (whatever this phrase might mean). Secondly, there may be actual psychological assertions made within the arts from which we as professional psychologists can learn, but that in order to do so we need to recast these propositions in the language of scientific psychology. And thirdly, it is possible that what the arts are saying cannot be grasped within the scientific cognitive style at all, and that humanistic psychology is to be a broadening of our style to include the kind of things the arts are doing and to do it in their terms. Which of these does Royce have in mind?

ROYCE   The third alternative.

ROZEBOOM   In that case humanistic material cannot be discussed within the framework of science at all – instead, we would have to write poems, paint pictures, and compose music.

I am also distressed by the lack of specific meaning for the notions of "feedback" and "symbolic processes" which arose in the discussion as instances of important, humanistically oriented concepts. All behaviour, including Watsonian reflex chains, is feedback-controlled in the generic sense, in so much as each movement leads to a new stimulus input; hence if feedback theory is to give psychology any new ideas, we have to consider feedback mechanisms much more specific than the trivial, abstract case. Similarly, there has been entirely too much talk about "symbolic processes" unaccompanied by any attempt to say how these differ from non-symbolic processes.

L. K. Frank

Royce's paper cites a number of well-recognized categories and assumptions which are derived from earlier concepts and ways of thinking but are no longer valid and, therefore, ought to be replaced. Contemporary science, at least on the frontiers, now emphasizes that the observer is in the picture and that he orders and interprets whatever he observes and records (i.e. his facts, according to his theoretical framework). Moreover, it is being recognized that our observations and experimental manipulations may later determine what we are trying to observe and measure. Finally, the new orientation is toward the dynamics of processes as controlled by the formal laws or static situations and mechanistic sequences. We cannot legislate for psychology and we cannot achieve unification, but we can prepare the way for our successors by reviewing the obsolescent blocks and resistances that must be removed before unification can be attained.

David Krech

I have very grave doubts about the usefulness of any enterprise which sets out to "unify" psychology. Very frequently, attempts to do so fall back on the use of the "empty concept" – generalized metaphors empty of data. The "empty concept" solutions to scientific problems are characterized by the recourse they make to generalized metaphors (such as "feed-back," or "reinforcement," or "life-space") without any serious attempt to show *in detail* how these concepts do *in fact* apply to the wide range of *specific* phenomena which these concepts are supposed to bring together harmoniously under its roof. But we proceed to take these empty concepts and suggest (at first very hesitantly and with becoming – and deserved – modesty) how they *might perhaps be used to help* unify psychology. In our essays entitled *Toward Unification in Psychology* instead of writing a series of specific hypotheses which hopefully might do the job, we content ourselves with setting down a few "suggestive illustrations" of what we have in mind. In other words, instead of using concepts to guide us in the writing of "i.e." statements, we use them to write "e.g." suggestions. A pox on "e.g." theorizing – for we soon forget that we have merely been playing with metaphors and, forsaking our original pose of modesty, we shout ourselves into believing that we have indeed accomplished the job we had set out to do! We become Pseudo-Achievers!

My guess is that he who would seek to unify psychology is doomed to the use of the empty concept. There does not now exist a set of "filled concepts" which can do an "i.e." job of integrating the full range (or any significant portion thereof) of what passes for psychological data. For one thing, there is not, and perhaps cannot be, a "science of psychology." What we have is a mélange of sciences, technologies, professions, arts, epistemologies, philosophies, and humbuggeries – many of them but distantly related to each other – all called "psychology." Indeed, some of these subfields of "psychology" are more closely related to subfields of other disciplines (physiology, anthropology, medicine) than they are to each other. This is as it is, and as it always has been, in matters of knowledge. There are no independently existing bundles of knowledge. Professor Royce knows this as well as the rest of us, but once the call is issued for the *Unification of Psychology* some kind of primeval clan loyalty takes over and we begin to see ourselves as a people apart. Only that can explain Professor Royce's unhappy choice of phraseology when, on page 25 he concedes, apologetically, that psychology is a "pirate science" and is prone to steal concepts from other disciplines. In the name of all that is good in science, what is a "pirate science?" Certainly Professor Royce cannot mean that each science is, and by right ought to be, a sovereign, independent, *self-sufficient disci-pline* with its *own concepts, its own data, its own territory* and perhaps, even its own flag! Every scientist takes his facts and his concepts where he finds them, and, in doing so, he takes not from "another science," but simply from "science." What, then, does it mean when we say that we seek to "unify" *psychology*? Why seek to unify the potpourri of things now called "psychology?" Why not let each element of psychology "unify" itself with whomever and whatever it pleases *at the moment* – this with sociology, this with biochemistry, this with information theory? Are we determined to remain a group set apart from the universe called science?

Rebuttal: J. R. Royce

The comments deal primarily with two points: (i) humanistic psychology, and (ii) the problem of unification. Since both of these points are further amplified in the "Auditors' Hour" material which follows, my reaction here will be very brief.

Let me agree that we need to clarify the meaning of such terms as humanistic, symbolic, and metaphoric. In fact, unless those who identify with the so-called "third force" movement (i.e. humanistic psychology) get on with the job of clarifying meanings, evolving appropriate methodology, and, above all, make the underlying epistemology clear, this movement will just fade away. My concern in the paper is twofold: (*a*) to indicate the fact that there is a humanistic psychology, and that it deserves a hearing, and (*b*) to initiate the inquiry regarding epistemology. With regard to (*b*), my stand is that humanistic psychology *per se* is not science, but, as its name implies, is concerned with the humanistic disciplines. That is, I'm putting metaphorism forward as a third way of knowing, in addition to empiricism and rationalism. If this third mode of knowing is a philosophically valid epistemology (in some sense of truth criterion, but *not* reduced to either empiricism or/and rationalism) then intellectual honesty would seem to demand that we remain open to whatever this approach might reveal concerning man, experience, and behaviour. Logically, however, this implies that (non-reductionistic) humanistic psychology *per se* is essentially a non-scientific (i.e. a humanistic) enterprise.

The logical implication of this position leads to a twentieth-century heresy, namely, that psychology should become the *study* of man and his experience and behaviour, not merely the *science* of behaviour.

My own strong interdisciplinary predilections clearly indicate that I agree with Krech and Bertalanffy when they say that each science must not hoist the flag of independence and claim its self-sufficient autonomy. In this sense psychology should continue to be a "pirate science". And, of course, we will continue to take our facts and concepts wherever we find them.

While I have no objection whatsoever to outside influences, I am challenging psychologists to work more from the inside out. That is, I want us to focus more on the hard core of psychology, and moreover, to go beyond the data to ideas – especially potentially unifying ones – which emerge from within, rather than bringing in concepts from without. If this is done, the conceptual focus of psychology is more likely to relate to the behaviour and experience of real people instead of the motions of billiard balls, hydrodynamic systems, or even the more glamorous-looking simulations of the computer.

Discussion: J. R. Royce

METAPHORISM AND CLINICAL PSYCHOLOGY

AUDITOR 1   How are you using the word "metaphor", and how does it relate to the one-to-many meanings of symbolic language?

ROYCE   I am using it as a bigger term than the word "symbol." If you will, it's the play as a totality which is a metaphor and certain characters and other parts of the totality which are the "symbols." Now we typically get into the business of what the play is all about. We say it's about man's predicament, and we elaborate on what aspects it covers. I believe it's Beckett who says, somewhere, "You're on the earth and there is no cure for it." His play *Endgame* deals with this. He is saying "there is no meaning in life." "It's an absurd universe." He is making statements about the overall predicament of man-in-the-universe. When we analyse this in terms of the symbolic language of the artist there are many meanings involved in this play. The play is there as the product of the artist, and when you ask him what it means he typically says: "There it is. Don't ask me what it means; if I was going to speak in prose I would have done so – whatever it is I have to say I say this way." It's the analyst (and the audience) who looks for meanings at a variety of levels – at the level of interpersonal relationships, the psychological level, the sociological level, and the philosophical level.

AUDITOR 1   It solves things.

ROYCE   This is true in its own meaning of the words "problem solving," but metaphoric is a nasty word when viewed from the scientific framework.

AUDITOR 1   You seem to be talking about something the clinical psychologists have been doing for years, and you're treating the clinician as a play, in a sense.

ROYCE   Yes, partly. The clinician functions, if you will, as an applied scientist, and at that level he is playing the scientific game, using a sign language, multivariate analysis, and so on – all aimed at making a prediction about this person's behaviour, and so on. But at another level he also invokes this other enterprise, which we have labelled metaphoric knowing. And this is one reason why it is said that a good clinician knows literature and art, from which he develops a kind of understanding and awareness about man. Furthermore, any good clinician does this symbolic kind of thing, perhaps most obviously when he interprets Rohrschach and other projective protocols, and dream material. Another parallel to the art form is his focus on the single case.

AUDITOR 1   This is an epistemological syndrome, then, is what you're saying. A syndrome exists, and through empathy or through understanding one can get at it and draw valid conclusions.

ROYCE   All right, and sometimes this syndrome is dealt with empirically and scientifically, and sometimes it is dealt with symbolically. And I would say here that, of course, we should reduce as much of this as possible to a set of scientific statements. But I would argue that there will always be something left over; in short, that scientific reductionism is incapable of dealing with the totality of reality. Incidentally, one reason I got into this epistemological business is that I am convinced that the clinician (or the humanistically oriented psychologist) is not going to get anywhere unless he says something about epistemology, and he'll have to be tough minded about this. That is to say, he's got to come up with a truth criterion which will hold some kind of water, otherwise there really will be the kind of epistemological anarchy which was hinted at earlier in the discussion. It seems highly improbable that we will get valid answers from the artists because they are the last people who seem to be aware of the epistemological issues involved.

AUDITOR 1   If this is a way of knowing, what is it that you know? Is it this co-experience business that Bertalanffy was referring to, that I would get the same emotional experience that you would?

ROYCE   This is part of it, but I would argue that there is a cognitive aspect to metaphoric knowing, that it goes beyond sheer emotionalism. Let us start with a specific example, say Hamlet. When we look at the play Hamlet and the character of Hamlet, what do we know? Obviously we will not have enough time to study this in depth, and in any case I am not qualified to do so, but I can at least *point* us in the right direction. We say that a certain play is "a great play" and that it, therefore, says something about reality. Why? Because it says something about man's "being" on this earth. Because it says something about the predicament of man. It says something about the tragic side of life. It does not say this in the form of a linear equation, or by way of impeccable fact. The great play forces us into greater *awareness*, if you want a single word, awareness about man and his predicament. And it comes to us in a different way from scientific awareness. The crucial place where the difference occurs is in the truth criterion. The scientist has a criterion which he applies for accepting something as true and rejecting something as false, and very briefly, it has to do with a mutuality between the rational structure and the empirical data. And empirical repeatability with a minimum of error is crucial here. That's his game. The artist is not playing that game, I'm arguing; for him intuition (including imagination) is more clearly operative. It is also operative with the scientist but it is not final as judge, it is not the crucial evaluator, whereas in the artistic enterprise it carries much greater weight. The crucial evaluation in the symbolic-intuitive approach of the artist is whether his awarenesses are universal rather than idiosyncratic. To the extent that the artist taps that which is universal about man-in-the-universe as opposed to tapping that which is idiosyncratic, the art form is getting at something "real," something which carries truth value. That's the crucial criterion in metaphoric knowing, *not* the involvement of intuitionism *per se* which is, after all, brought into play by both artists and scientists.

AUDITOR 1   Well, assuming that we have some idea of what it is that we know in this metaphoric way, can you give me any reason why this would be of value to psychology?

ROYCE   I'm struggling with this. I might have a few hints, but that's about all. I felt that I had to deal with this because a tension was created in me when I ran into a valid approach to truth which I was ignoring. I had all the doubts implicit in your line of questioning, but it seemed to me that here was a way to understand man and his behaviour which psychologists were arbitrarily eliminating because of a value commitment to empiricism. With all the scientific structuring which has been going on within psychology for the past 100 years, as a kind of "keeping our feet on the ground," it seems to me that we are pretty safe to go into this humanistic business now. For a variety of reasons having to do with certainty of knowledge, we feel more secure about knowledge which comes through the scientific enterprise. We may be wrong, but we feel more secure about that. What I am saying is that I am willing to accept a less certain knowledge criterion if other approaches, such as metaphorism, can provide us with valid insights concerning man and his behaviour.

AUDITOR 1   Don't you think the artist offers us some kind of fact when he says his product doesn't have to be realistic, for example, a non-realistic play? Don't you think the artist hopes to, somehow in the underlying meaning of this play, reflect reality or some fact?

ROYCE   Reality, yes; but not necessarily fact. The valid artistic product will communicate something about man and his behaviour. Now it may turn out that it will have an epistemic correlation with factual notions from the psychologist, but the factual aspect is the scientific psychologist's business. I don't think the artist is trying to make factual statements.

AUDITOR 1   How aware is the playwright that all his underlying meanings are there, that he is symbolizing? How aware do you think he is? Or is he just writing this?

ROYCE   He may or may not be able to make prose statements about his artistic product.

AUDITOR 2   But such prose statements would not be saying what the play says, so it doesn't mean he had to be consciously aware and construct, as some poets do, all of these complex meanings into a short phrase. He may have done it metaphorically – he brought the mystery into the phrase and you interpreted the mystery in some way and found the truth.

ROYCE   An artistic statement – we have been focused on a play or a literary product – which is "a big symbol," a "big allegory" (and you recognize this phrase as somewhat corny by now), has dimensions of reality which remain to be tapped. How come we can study Hamlet for 400 years and still uncover new awarenesses? This is an important point, it seems to me, about the symbol and the metaphor. There are aspects of reality that keep emerging on analysis and re-analysis.

AUDITOR 1   That may be sheer probability of your unique combination of stimuli.

ROYCE But there are constraints upon what is acceptable as true; it does not follow that anything goes. For example, if the art form is a sheer projection of the artist's personality, then in terms of the idiosyncratic-universal criterion his work is on the idiosyncratic end of the continuum, and we are forced to the conclusion that we are looking at a projective test rather than art. The monkey who threw the stuff on the canvas, you know, did not create art. This was a purely idiosyncratic statement, if you will.

AUDITOR 1   But how do you know it wasn't art? Suppose I didn't know that a monkey threw it on the canvas?

ROYCE   Right. Most people didn't know, and they actually saw meanings there.

AUDITOR 1   I think this is Galanter's argument, though. Galanter says that if you accept this as a criterion of truth, there will be as many different criteria of truth as there are statements about what they are discussing.

ROYCE   We must not fall into the trap of comparing lousy art with good science. Elsewhere I have specified four kinds of constraint for getting at reality through artistic endeavours. They can briefly be summarized as variations of consistency – internal, external, temporal, and theoretical. Not only is it true that there is variability in the interpretation of symbolic material, it is, in fact, *mandatory* that such multiplicity and depth of meanings be characteristic of the art form. But it does *not* follow that this necessarily leads to subjective confusion. Persons who see art and meanings where they do not exist do not bring sufficient insight and sensitivity to the art forms under study, just as persons ignorant of cellular structure and staining techniques fail to interpret the meaningless biological specimens which are so meaningful to the histological expert. The problem of personal ignorance is irrelevant to the issue of epistemological validity.

AUDITOR 1   Are you saying we have to throw out intuitionism then? I mean does the clinician have to explain his intuitive way of knowing in terms of the biological scientist's way of knowing, that is, tie them together?

ROYCE   I'm saying he's got to come up with firm epistemological ground if he wants to step outside the scientific mode, which, in part, he feels he is forced to do.

AUDITOR 1   But you're saying that to go into the intuitive way of knowing is to step out of the scientific mode, but he has to then tie himself back into the scientific mode if he's to be accepted.

ROYCE   No, I didn't. That is Galanter's position, not mine. My position states that he must offer us convincing arguments about the validity of the non-scientific approach.

AUDITOR 1   Well, this proof has to be couched either rationally or empirically.

ROYCE   No. Now you're talking like a scientific reductionist – you begin with the answer.

AUDITOR 1   Well, no. You're saying that the scientist won't take the intuitionist's data unless the intuitionist can give him good proof of it.

ROYCE   No, he's got to offer proof in terms of the underlying epistemology in *his* game, and he's playing a *different* game when he functions in this non-scientific way. No, I'm suggesting he's got to offer us something like "metaphoric knowledge" and "existential validity".

UNIFICATION IN PSYCHOLOGY

AUDITOR 1   I think this issue has important implications for the question of whether one can expect unification within psychology. As long as there are such violent disagreements over epistemological issues it seems to me that this is an argument in favour of fractionation rather than unification.

ROYCE   Well, what would you do about it?

AUDITOR 1   What the University of California did.

ROYCE   I think what you are saying is that you would choose to unify by elimination, which is an acceptable position. You have at least made the problem easier, but it's just a matter of degree in terms of area theories. If you start with a very small theory, such as a theory of colour vision, and work your way outward, you may eventually be able to encompass a fairly large segment of psychology, say all of the experimental-biological area or all of scientific psychology. But now, I would argue, you have sacrificed the whole of clinical and humanistic psychology. And if your question is, "I want to understand the nature of man and his behaviour", it may take you some time before you get to an overall integration with this approach.

AUDITOR 1   Perhaps the approach, then, is to unify via areas, keeping in mind that such efforts do not necessarily imply elimination.

ROYCE   I personally feel this is an important and desirable tactic – to do all we can in a relatively circumscribed sub-domain to evolve watertight theoretical structures, and to use them as a basis for subsequent theoretical extensions and linkages to other area theories. Look at how long we've been trying to get a conclusive theory of colour vision. (If such a theory would hold the field for fifty years I would regard it as worthwhile.) Let us say that we have one. From there we could evolve a theory of perception, which would be a tremendous achievement in terms of our current ignorance. Perhaps we could then see ways to inter-relate our theory of perception with the theory that holds in learning, evolving a theory of perceptual learning. Such an overall strategy would provide a storehouse of area theories and inter-areal linkages as a basis for moving toward a general theory of behaviour. There is some indication that we already have some useful area theories here and there. And I'm convinced by one point, I was *for* the overall, grand theory at one time – I suppose every theory-oriented psychologist must have had that notion at some point in his professional career – but the more one is involved in providing theoretical integration, the more one realizes that the "grand theory approach" is unrealistic, frustrating, and probably impossible.

AUDITOR 1 Isn't reductionism an approach toward unification? For example, if we can reduce metaphorism to purely rational or empirical grounds, haven't we unified the three, in a sense?

ROYCE If you want to be safe but ignorant that's the way to do it. If you want to eliminate a particular way of knowing you can do so in the name of theoretical unification, but at the expense of remaining ignorant in terms of that approach. You may move toward a kind of unification this way and you are privileged to play it this way. We psychologists could say, for example, ye gods! we're in a mess, so let's leave out all this humanistic business, we've got enough trouble! I might buy this if it became overwhemingly apparent that we really were on a trail which led to unification. But as I look around I simply see a variety of interesting approaches to the comprehension of different aspects of the totality of behaviour – I see it as necessary, therefore, to remain open at this time to all valid approaches to the understanding of man and his behaviour.

AUDITOR 1 Perhaps there would be value in the pursuits you suggest, but we might be able to derive the same value by reducing these humanistic concerns to scientific terms.

ROYCE Yes, many take this view, but I think there is adequate argument to show it won't work. Suppose, for example, that we eliminate psychology. After all, is it necessary?

AUDITOR 1 Do you eliminate the people doing the work?

AUDITOR 2 Can physicists handle our problems?

ROYCE Do you think they can?

AUDITOR 1 No, they're not concerned.

ROYCE Let's take you as an example. You're interested in psychology, but you're going to become a physicist now in order to solve psychological problems.

AUDITOR 1 Yes, but if I still define my study as solving a problem in psychology, attacked from the physicist's viewpoint, I am still functioning as a psychologist.

ROYCE Do you think you'll answer the important problems in psychology that way?

AUDITOR 1 No, I don't.

ROYCE   Okay, that's the only point I want to make.

AUDITOR 1   Do you want to unify psychology, or is it rather a question of how to unify it?

ROYCE   We want to do the best we can to make all-encompassing statements about man and his behaviour.

AUDITOR 1   Does this mean that the way Dr Walley (a physiological psychologist in the audience) wants to proceed isn't really psychology in your terms?

ROYCE   My option here would be that I want to deal with the nature of man and his behaviour. That means I've got to be open to all avenues of approach: I want to first look at what it is we are studying, I want to look at the total panorama of what is there, *then* I want to try to unify. Now this is ambitious and probably unattainable. At varying points I may choose to deal with one area theory which is in the scientific realm, and another in the humanistic realm.

AUDITOR 1   Why?

ROYCE   Because I just got interested in it – that's all. And because of a commitment to try to understand the totality of man with all his confusing complexities rather than some oversimplified man.

AUDITOR 1   I don't think the meaning of unification is at all clear, and until we understand what we mean, we cannot clearly lay out the different strategies of unification to see what we are trying to achieve.

ROYCE   If we are concerned with, say, the physical universe, I should think we would mean *a* theory about the physical universe rather than several. When you're in psychology's predicament as in learning theory where we have several theories, it's an indication of the chaotic condition of the field. Whenever you have multiple theories covering the same sub-domain it means you don't know that area well. If you have one theory that really does the trick, that really accounts for the data, then we know something, even if it is eventually replaced by a better theory in the course of time. Incidentally, I hold the view that this idealized goal is impossible in any field, including physics. That is, I maintain that complete unification in any discipline of study, such as physics or psychology, is impossible to attain, although I think it's a goal we should seek.

PHILOSOPHY AND SCIENCE

AUDITOR   There is confusion in my mind as to when an individual speaks as a philosopher and when he speaks as a scientist. I think you have partly answered it, but I wondered if there is any more you could add. Does the scientist have a right to speak as a philosopher?

ROYCE   I would say so, as long as he makes it clear which hat he is wearing. When he says he speaks as a scientist, we demand that he show us his theoretical structure and his data. When he speaks as a philosopher we demand a certain logic, a certain clarity of conceptual analysis. Now, as a human being, or as a good psychologist or a good scientist, if he does not eventually get to these philosophic issues he is not very profound, in my opinion. After all, the Ph.D. is a doctor of philosophy in psychology, or physics, or what have you. Perhaps it is relevant to note in passing that Einstein was a philosopher as well as a scientist.

AUDITOR   Does this mean there is no distinction between the two, they end up being the same thing?

ROYCE   No, but the person in question is one and indivisible, interested in many kinds of questions and curious about a variety of things, and I'm simply saying that the physicist, for example, gets into metaphysics because he is forced to it. There is a quote from Jaspers which reads "The knowledge of science fails in the face of ultimate questions". Well, at that point, we're in the realm of philosophy. Now as far as this conference goes, this kind of confusion is going to remain because of lack of time to fully explain what we mean by this or that utterance. I have come to the conclusion that if you can communicate *anything* which conveys your true meaning this is a time for joy. And we're not doing badly in this department when you think of all the inherent semantic difficulties. It is my firm hope that we will not give in completely to this business of "what you mean" – there just isn't enough time. It would take us at least a year (sitting for a three hour session once a week) merely to clarify terminology and basic concepts. Now I agree that eventually this sort of thing will have to be done. If we establish the proposed Center we can take the long range view which will permit us to take the necessary time to clarify meanings as a basis for more penetrating analysis of important issues.

AUDITOR   Earlier we were talking about the artist and the scientist playing two different games. I was just thinking that if they are playing two different games, but neither of them can grasp reality *per se*, then they are both playing at an illusion about what is there.

ROYCE   I couldn't agree more. But I personally think this is true of all of us, that is, all experts and all specialists. All any of us get is an *image* of reality. We do not get *reality*. We get an *image*, or, if you will, a metaphor. In science we don't use that word, we say "a model". Different experts proceed in different ways; we have axioms and propositions, and so on, but I certainly buy your original position, that it's all illusory. I personally don't think we'll ever get past this. I don't know how we could. One would have to be God to understand reality in any ultimate sense.

AUDITOR   Can we work towards a common goal of some kind by means of the three ways of knowing?

ROYCE   Can you put your question another way?

AUDITOR   Well, if each of these approaches to reality is illusory, and all we can get is an image or metaphor of the real thing, what is it all about?

ROYCE   I think what you're getting at is this – it would be possible for convergences of these different approaches to occur. The philosopher Northrop calls these epistemic correlations. When these convergences occur to the left of what I call the epistemological barrier in Fig. 1.8 we are dealing with "reality images." But when these epistemic convergences occur to the right of the epistemological barrier we are trying to deal with what is labelled ultimate reality. This ultimate reality, I maintain, is unknowable. But if it were possible to know about these convergences to the right of the barrier and all three epistemologies converged, this would point to some kind of monism as the essence of the way things really are. Am I speaking to your question?

AUDITOR   Yes, you are. Doesn't this mean we are speaking about a matter of faith, really?

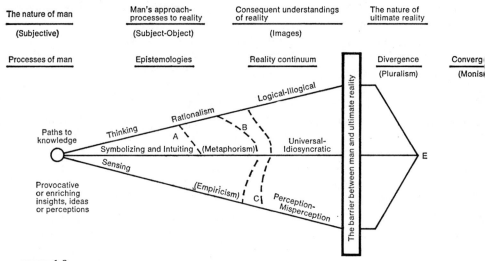

FIGURE 1.8
The basic paths to knowledge (modified version of Royce (1964), p. 12)

ROYCE   If by that you mean all of us have epistemological commitments, you and I, and everybody around this table, if that's what you mean, yes, we all make faith commitments.

AUDITOR   But what about asking the embarrassing question, how do you know there are really three ways of knowing.

ROYCE   I don't. In terms of my analysis that's what I've come up with.

AUDITOR   We may have a pseudo-problem then.

ROYCE   Well, this is possible. I have looked at this problem and have come up with three ways of knowing. However, I would challenge you, you see, to tell me about other ways of knowing, and if you make your case sufficiently convincing I will add them to this scheme.

AUDITOR   I may say, though, why say three, why not one, and I don't even know what that one is.

ROYCE   There is nothing magical about three. In principle, there could be five, one, or ten ways of knowing. My analysis, which carries both epistemological and psychological constraints, led me to three.

AUDITOR   But if there is only one way of knowing, then there really is no problem.

ROYCE   That's right, but I would then just turn this around on you, and ask you to make your case for this one and only way of knowing. And I might then come back to say that there were two more ways of knowing. Do you follow me?

AUDITOR   I follow you, very far behind.

2

The Art of Metascience, or, What Should a Psychological Theory Be?

William W. Rozeboom
UNIVERSITY OF ALBERTA

2
The Art of Metascience, or, What Should a Psychological Theory Be?*

William W. Rozeboom
UNIVERSITY OF ALBERTA

DR ROZEBOOM took both his S.B. (1949) and PH.D. (1956) in bio-psychology from the University of Chicago. He was a National Science Foundation postdoctoral fellow at Minnesota Center for Philosophy of Science and taught at St. Olaf College and Wesleyan University before accepting appointment at the University of Alberta, where he is now Professor in the Department of Psychology and the Center for Advanced Study in Theoretical Psychology. In 1968, he was Visiting Professor in the Department of History and Philosophy of Science at Indiana University. His writings range widely on both sides of the border between psychology and philosophy, with special emphasis on behaviour theory, the logic of science, and occasional digressions into multivariate analysis such as *Foundations of the theory of prediction* (Dorsey Press, 1966).

INTRODUCTION

In order not to lay false claims upon your attention, let me confess at once that the subtitle of this paper is intended more as a stimulus to curiosity than as a serious synopsis of the subject here to be addressed. I shall indeed be concerned at considerable length with the methodological character of psychological theories, but my prescriptions will focus upon process rather than product. Specifically, I shall offer some detailed judgments on how theorizing must be done – or, more precisely, what sorts of metatheorizing must accompany it – if the enterprise is to make a genuine contribution to science; and while on first impression these may seem like no more than the standard broad-spectrum abstractions of one who has nothing specific to say, I assure you that they envision realizable operations which, if practiced, would have a profound effect on our conceptual efficiency as psychologists.

There are at least two formal dimensions along which discussions of psychological theory can vary. One is *level of abstraction,* or *substantivity of concern,* with attention to specific extant theories (e.g. pointing out an inconsistency or clarifying an ambiguity in John Smiths' theory of binocular psychokinesis) at one extreme, and philosophy-of-science type concerns for the nature and functioning of idealized theories in general, detached from any real-life instances, at the other. Distinct from this, though not wholly orthogonal to it, is a second dimension of metatheory which might be called *acuity* or *penetration,* and which concerns the degree to which the discussion makes a serious, intellectually responsible attempt to further our understanding of the matter with which it deals. Here the possibilities range from painstaking attention to technical details, to loose and largely gratuitous generalities built around everyday intuitions, or poorly defined neologisms whose literal relevance to anything in reality is tenuous or nonexistent. Unfor-

---

* Although five years have elapsed since this essay was written, I have not yet been disillusioned of the belief that much of what I say here has considerable significance for the operational thrust of psychological science. Even so, times and conceptions evolve, and in occasional passages which follow I would no longer say exactly the same thing today. None of the changes I envision matter enough to warrant last-minute patchwork revisions, but if here and there the reader takes issue with a particular implication or feels that an important detail has been slighted, it is not impossible that I would agree.

tunately, disciplined thinking *about* science appears to be much more difficult to achieve than disciplined thinking within it, with the result that to date, very little metascience has managed to get far from the casual, dilettante or intuitional end of the acuity scale, especially at the higher levels of abstraction. Since metatheoretical acuity is a major concern of this essay, let me illustrate what I mean by this with three examples of inadequate penetration in abstract metatheory. The first two are narrow aspects of a recently notorious but now moribund metapsychological issue which today can be cited briefly and dispassionately even while a sense of its historical vitality still lingers. The third has contemporary philosophical immediacy, but as yet little if any impact on psychology proper. All three lie on the respectable side of the acuity distribution – at the other end, ideas are muddled about so inchoately that one can scarcely catch hold of anything firm enough to criticize.

(i) Some time ago, when the nature of "intervening variables" was a major bone of metapsychological contention, Feigl (1945) suggested that the conceptual virtue of a single intervening variable V interposed between m independent variables $X_1, ..., X_m$ and n dependent variables $Y_1, ..., Y_n$ might be that the number of laws relating a dependent variable Y_i to an independent variable X_j becomes reduced from the $m \times n$ possibilities $Y_i = \phi_{ij}(X_j)$ $(i = 1, ..., n; j = 1, ..., m)$ to the more parsimonious $m + n$ array $V = g_j(X_j)$, $Y_i = f_i(V)$ $(i = 1, ..., n; j = 1, ..., m)$, wherein each observable relation ϕ_{ij} is analysed as the product $f_i g_j$, i.e. $\phi_{ij}(X_j) \equiv f_i(g_j(X_j))$. This model, often expressed by a visual diagram of form

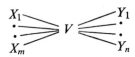

was quickly seized upon as the standard conceptualization of intervening variables, even to the point of serious interpretations of empirical findings in its terms (e.g. Seward 1955; Miller 1959, p. 276f.), with no apparent concern for what could possibly be *meant* by the pairwise relationships ϕ_{ij}, and the visual model showing V at the focus of lines converging from the various independent variables. Dependent variable Y_i (or V) does not have a separate deterministic relation to each of the m independent variables. There is only a single equation $Y_i = \phi_i(X_1, ..., X_m)$ determining Y_i as a joint function of the variables $X_1, ..., X_m$ which affect it. Thus introduction of an intervening variable between the X_j and the Y_i replaces the n equations $Y_1 = \phi_1(X, ..., X_m), ..., Y_n = \phi_n(X_1, ..., X_m)$ with the $n + 1$ equations $V = g(X_1, ..., X_m)$, $Y_1 = f_1(V), ..., Y_n = f_n(V)$ – whence the argument from parsimony must always protest against introduction of the intervening variable. This is not to suggest that no interpretation can be found for the pairwise-relations model – I can think of several, though each has its own methodological complications.[1] The point is that no such interpretation was, in fact, ever provided for it in the literature. A good fifteen years of metatheorizing about the role of constructs

---

1 The best is a Spearman single-factor model in which relation-term ϕ_{ij} is interpreted as the linear correlation between variables Y_i and X_j. However, ϕ_{ij} is then no longer the functional dependence of Y_i upon X_j, but only a measure of how errorlessly linear the relationship is.

in psychological theory allowed a primary sector of its thinking to rest upon a simple fallacy which could have been rehabilitated into fruitful liaison with inferential factor theory by a few moments of critical contemplation.

(ii) Another notion which cropped up repeatedly in the intervening variable literature was that when an intervening variable V is introduced into the relationship $Y = \phi(X)$ between data variables X and Y, V is *the relationship itself*. But this is flagrantly inconsistent with what were cited as paradigm cases, notably, behaviour-theoretical variables such as Hull's Habit-strength, in which the intervening variable V is functionally dependent upon X and in turn determines Y. Regardless of whether V mediates causally between X and Y or is merely a logical construction, it is still a variable which *partakes* of relations to the data variables, in conspicuous logical contradistinction to the fixed function ϕ in $Y = \phi(X)$ which is not *related to* the data variables but is the relationship itself. What is especially ironic about this confusion of variables which intervene with the relationship *within* which they intervene is that at a higher level of logical complexity, data-variable relationships which are themselves variable turn out to be a primary source of inferences to underlying states of the organism which, moreover, are importantly distinct from the internal processes which mediate the relationships from which these states are inferred.[2] Before the logical intricacies of this situation can be effectively navigated, however, it is essential that the concept of "variables" and their relationships be understood with a modicum of technical precision.

(iii) In rebellion against the "covering law" interpretation of scientific explanation, a view has recently arisen in philosophical quarters that the breath of life in an explanatory theory is a distinction between what is "natural" and what is not, namely, that the theory makes first and foremost a commitment to an "ideal of natural order" which is self-explanatory simply because it *is* "natural," and then seeks to account only for apparent departures from this ideal (Toulmin, 1961). The paradigm example for this view is the shift from Aristotelian to Newtonian conceptions of natural motion, the former having expected a moving body to come to rest if left to itself while the latter expects the motion of an unconstrained body to persist without change. There is certainly an intuitive plausability to this thesis, yet a critical search for the role of "naturalness" in the actual conceptual impact of a theory such as Newton's laws of motion has much the same success as looking inside one's television set for the little people who put on the show. The theory simply states what happens (or what *must* happen, if we wish to emphasize the theory's nomic character) under different configurations of values for the relevant variables, and "natural ideals" enter only in the sense that some configurations have simpler consequences than others. Thus Newton's laws tell how a body moves (or what forces direct its motion) for any arrangement of surrounding bodies, and the empty-surround condition is simply one limiting possibility which has no theoretical priority over any other. Neither does the Newtonian theory explain only departures from the "natural ideal" of unconstrained motion. A system's temporal progress from any one initial configuration bears the same logical

---

2 The distinction between state and process variables, and inference to underlying states from mutable parameters in observed process regularities, are discussed at somewhat greater length in Rozeboom (1965).

relation to the theory's postulates as does any other, and the theory "explains" motion in the absence of constraints fully as much and in the very same way that motion in more complex circumstances is explained. I do not wish to imply that the notion of what is "natural" has no significance for metascientific theory. One can feel it hovering impalpably around many practical research tactics such as choice of baselines, reference points, control groups and the like. But whether it has any cognitively *helpful* contribution to make to the development, application, or understanding of science, and if so, what, is still wholly obscure.[3]

In these three examples, as in the overwhelming majority of writings about scientific theory and methodology, one sees through a glass darkly when only a little polishing of the concepts employed would bring their objects into much sharper resolution. Deplorably – and incongruously – the standards of critical evaluation and pressures to clarity which have been such vital forces to progress *within* science have yet to achieve any appreciable impact on research and theory *about* science. I shall not press this complaint just now, for my immediate purpose is only to clarify what I mean by the acuity dimension of metatheory. But when later I argue for the importance of metatheoretical concomitants to substantive psychological theory, it must be understood that I presuppose a much higher level of acuity than is generally found in such work today.

I have begun with this meta-metheoretical statement about dimensions of meta-science in order that I may preview the character of my remarks to follow in its terms. Part I comprises a broad survey of the nature and functioning of scientific theory, followed in part II by some normative prescriptions for practical theorizing. The substantivity of concern in these two sections lies near the extreme of abstract generality, with the result that they have a typical philosophy-of-science flavour with little content that is specifically psychological. In contrast, part III illustrates the precepts of part II by close examination of selected technical components of certain recent and current behaviour theories. Acuity of analysis is a primary objective in part III, and this, unfortunately, likewise contrasts with parts I and II, wherein I shall grudgingly attempt no more than a loose, largely commonsensical coverage. The reason why this discomforts and embarrasses me is that most of the traditional epistemological and semantic concepts employed by contemporary philosophy of science, including what follows below, have outlasted their technical adequacy and need to be hauled back to the shop for reworking.[4] I must slide over these inadequacies if I am to get on with anything having significance for the actual doing

3 Insomuch as it can plausibly be argued that "explaining" an event or phenomenon amounts essentially to making it appear "natural" (cf. Workman, 1964), the notion of naturalness has a legitimate place in the theory of *explanation*. But this is only one more reason for doubting that "explanation" is as such an objective of science. (If the matter were sufficiently germane here, I would argue that explanation is merely one of the pragmatic applications to which the cognitive accomplishments of science can be put.)

4 Two examples of classical black-and-white dichotomies which many philosophers have already come to regard as a continuum of greys are the analytic/synthetic and observable/unobservable oppositions. Faced with the breakdown of traditional philosophic notions, however, far too many philosophers have retreated to the vagaries of ordinary language instead of attempting to hone their technical concepts to a keener edge.

of psychological theory, but the result is that most of what I say in parts I and II is merely a heuristic which should not be mistaken for a technically proficient account of these matters.

I THE CONCEPT OF "THEORY"

Insomuch as our appointed purpose here is to meditate upon the role and reconciliation of theories in psychological science, it is seemly to give thought to where, within the total expanse of human endeavour, our domain of inquiry lies. That is, what is a "theory," anyway?

As is true of any word extensively deployed in ordinary language and quasi-technical discourse, the term "theory" has been and continues to be used in a wide variety of senses, some of which have only tenuous connections with the others. Since what is metatheoretically critical in one such usage need have no special relevance for another, it should be helpful to spread the entire array before us and see what issues emerge from their totality.

The distinctions which, as I sense them, inhabit the manifold uses of "theory" can best be described by a series of contrasts, some of which are "exclusive" in that one pole of the contrast is labelled "theory" to distinguish it from an opposite, while others are "inclusive" in that they express important distinctions within the term's domain of application.

Dimensions of "Theory"
A Inclusive contrasts:
1 Propositional theory *versus* perspectival (programmatic) theory;
2 Interpreted theories *versus* uninterpreted theories (calculi);
3 Warranted (inductively confirmed) theory *versus* speculative theory.
B Exclusive contrasts:
1 Theoretical *versus* observational;
2 Theory (hypothesis) *versus* established fact;
3 Theory (system) *versus* isolated beliefs;
4 Theoretical (idealized) *versus* practical (realistic);
5 Theories (indicative mood) *versus* models (subjunctive mood).

A1 In principle, the phrase "scientific theory" might be applied to any aspect – instrument, method or product – of scientific endeavour according to one's verbal whim of the moment. However, the ultimate goal of any science is to arrive at truthful (veridical) statements about the science's subject matter, and among philosophers of science, at least, it seems to be generally agreed that a scientific "theory" is a specific set of assertions about reality, or at least that the theory is a device for generating such assertions. I, too, shall adopt this position throughout most of what follows. Yet simply to stipulate that by definition, a particular psychological theory *T* corresponds to a specific list of declarative propositions about psychology, appears grotesquely naive when tested against what gets labelled "theory" in psychological practice. What is to be made of such familiar phrases as "behaviour theory," "gestalt theory," "statistical learning theory," "psychoanalytic theory," "S-R theory," "cognitive theory," and the like? Could one conceivably hope to characterize any one of these by a precisely specified set of propositions to which a person who accepts one of these "theories" is committed? We can easily imagine two psychologists who are both recognized behaviour theorists, or gestalt theorists, yet who are unable to agree upon a single substantive principle of psychology – in fact, a psychologist may well be a behaviour theorist or gestalt theorist without having *any* firm convictions about psychological fact. When "theory" is this broadly conceived, it no longer seems quite appropriate to think of the theory as having any specific propositional content which is true or false. (What, for example, would verify or refute statistical learning theory? The very question seems meaningless.) Instead, a "theory" in this sense is primarily a certain *perspective* on psychology, characterized by concern for a particular body of problems and phenomena, by predilection for a distinctive cluster of technical terms even though these may have no fixed usage, by prominence of certain patterns of data organization and interpretation even though what is said through their medium remains flexible, and so on for a host of features which characterize a cognitive style quite apart (or apparently so) from any particular assertive content that might be expressed within this style.

To be sure, it might be protested that use of the singular in "behaviour theory" "gestalt theory," etc., is simply a grammatical error; that the proper wording should be "behaviour theor*ies*," or "gestalt theor*ies*," in order to make clear that each of these is actually a broad category which subsumes a great many specific theories. This is a reasonable stand which helps to drive the concept of theory in the direction of propositional commitment, which is where it most profitably belongs. Even so, the fact remains that in the actual doing of psychology by psychologists, what is *called* a "theory" is more often a configuration of attitudes and special concerns than it is a set of specific beliefs, and that it is frequently very difficult to tease out what if anything a particular theorist actually considers to be true of his subject.

A2 I claimed above that philosophers of science concur that scientific theories are, or at least correspond to, a set of propositions about the way the world is put together, but strictly speaking this is not quite correct. In abstract metatheory, it is not uncommon to find the term "theory" implicitly or even explicitly restricted to just the formal skeleton (schema) of a propositional system, while the flesh of semantic meaning which must be attached to the schema's dry syntactic bones if the theory is to have factual content is known as an "interpretation" of the theory. More specifically, the theory proper (i.e., the uninterpreted theory) according to this usage is a set of patterned concatenations – "postulates" – of abstract elements together with rules for deriving still other element concatenations – "theorems" – from them; while the theory is "interpreted" by adopting a particular co-ordination of the theory's elements and concatenation patterns with meaningful words and syntactical structures, respectively, in such fashion that (i) each postulate and theorem of the theory is thereby co-ordinated with a grammatically well-formed and cognitively meaningful assertion about the science's subject matter while (ii) the rules of derivation correspond to valid principles of logical deduction.[5] As an example, consider the following formal system (abstract calculus) *U*.

---

5 I have stated the notion of "uninterpreted theory" in a form more extreme than any actual usage I have encountered outside of mathematical logic, though Campbell (1920) and

Uninterpreted Theory U

Elements: A symbol s is a *type-1* element of U if and only if s is either (*a*) ∞, ∇, $\diamond$, or $\perp$; or (*b*) s is of form $\tilde{x}$, where x is a type-1 element of U. A symbol s is a *type-2* element of U if and only if s is of form $\dot{x}$, where x is a type-1 element of U.

Postulates: $\dot{\infty}\tilde{\perp}$, $\diamond\tilde{\nabla}$, $\tilde{\diamond}\perp$.

Derivation rules: Symbol concatenation c is a theorem of system U if and only if (*a*) c is a postulate of U; or (*b*) there exist type-1 elements x and y of U such that xy is a theorem of U and c is $\tilde{y}\tilde{x}$; or (*c*) there exist elements x and y, and a type-1 element z, of U such that xz and zy are theorems of U and c is xy; or (*d*) there exists an element x and theorem t of U such that c is the result of replacing $\tilde{\tilde{x}}$ in t with x; or (*e*) there exist elements x and y of U such that $\dot{x}y$ is a theorem of U and c is $\dot{y}x$.

Theorems (*inter alia*): $\nabla\perp$, $\dot{\diamond}\infty$, $\dot{\infty}\tilde{\nabla}$.

While "theory" U entails a number of formally interesting consequences, there is no point in asking what they signify, for at this stage the theory means nothing at all. However, suppose that we construct "interpreted" theory U_1 by augmenting U with the following set of "co-ordinating definitions" ("correspondence rules").

Interpretation of U_1 of U

∞ : "the class of persons troubled by existential anxiety"
∇ : "the class of neurotic persons"
$\diamond$: "the class of well-adjusted persons"
$\perp$: "the class of persons in need of psychotherapy"
xy : "x is included in y"
$\tilde{x}$: "the class of all persons not in x"
$\dot{x}$: "a nonempty subclass of x".

Under this interpretation of U, its postulates hypothesize that

some persons who are troubled with existential anxiety do not need psychotherapy ($\dot{\infty}\,\tilde{\perp}$);
no well-adjusted person is neurotic ($\diamond\,\tilde{\nabla}$);
all maladjusted (i.e., not well-adjusted) persons need psychotherapy ($\tilde{\diamond}\perp$);

its derivation rules are valid (i.e. any interpreted theorem must be true so long as the interpreted postulates are true), and among its theorems are

all neurotics need psychotherapy ($\nabla\perp$);
some well-adjusted persons are troubled by existential anxiety ($\dot{\diamond}\,\infty$);
neurotics aren't the only persons troubled by existential anxiety ($\dot{\infty}\,\tilde{\nabla}$).

Carnap (1956) come close to it. More often, a writer (e.g. Nagel, 1961) will start by defining "theory" as formal calculus plus meaning, but then slip over into talking about the calculus (or the calculus with syntax and logical terms interpreted only) as though it is a theory in its own right. In particular, as soon as one begins to speak of "interpreting" the theory or its terms by introduction of "correspondence rules," "meaning postulates," "co-ordinating definitions" or the like, it is implied that the theory is something to which these make an addition.

However, U_1 is just one of an unlimited number of alternative interpretations for U, e.g.

Interpretation U_2 of U

∞ : "the class of all minerals that dissolve readily in water"
∇ : "the unit class of mineral sodium chloride (salt)"
◇ : "the class of all minerals that ionize poorly in water solution"
⊥ : "the class of all minerals that conduct electricity well in water solution"
xy : "x is included in y"
$\tilde{x}$: "the class of all minerals not included in x"
$\dot{x}$: "a nonempty subclass of x".

Under interpretation U_2, the postulates of U translate into the assertions that

not all minerals that dissolve readily in water conduct electricity well in water solution ($\infty \; \dot{\tilde{\perp}}$);
salt is a good (i.e. not poor) ionizer in water solution ($\diamond \; \tilde{\nabla}$);
all minerals that ionize well (i.e. not poorly) in water solution are good conductors of electricity in water solution ($\tilde{\diamond} \; \perp$);

while the theorems of U_2 corresponding to the ones cited for U_1 become

salt conducts electricity well in water solution ($\nabla \perp$);
some minerals that ionize poorly in water solution readily dissolve in it ($\dot{\diamond} \; \infty$);
salt is not the only mineral that conducts electricity well in water solution ($\dot{\infty} \; \tilde{\nabla}$).

According to the formal-schema sense of the term "theory," then, belief systems U_1 and U_2 both incorporate the same theory, namely U, but interpret it differently through adoption of different sets of coordinating definitions for the theory's ingredients. This meaning of "theory" is a perfectly respectable one in mathematics and formal logic, for a theory's semantic content is quite irrelevant for the structural properties which interest the logician, and realization in depth that a given formal calculus can submit to a multiplicity of interpretations was one of the epochal achievements upon which modern mathematics is grounded. Introduction of this usage into scientific metatheory, however, is much harder to justify. As the term "theory" is actually used in science, it would be intolerable to claim that a certain set of beliefs about existential psychotherapy (U_1) is a manifestation of the *same theory* as certain beliefs about electrochemistry (U_2) merely because they share a common formal structure. Within a science, what is important is not what the theory may be like as an uninterpreted calculus but what it asserts; and its isomorphism, if any, to other structures elsewhere is wholly irrelevant to the theory's factual significance. Except where explicitly indicated, therefore, I shall henceforth use the term "theory" only in the sense of *interpreted* theory, namely, a cognitively meaningful assertion about reality.

In contending that the formal-calculus sense of theory has no value for science, I wish also to express doubts about the utility of views wherein a theory, though defined to include meaning, is thought to be usefully reconstructed for metatheoretical purposes as comprising (i) a syntactic calculus and (ii) a set of correspondence rules or co-ordinating definitions which give the calculus its semantic padding. With one dubious exception to be described in a moment, the calculus/ co-ordinating-definitions partition is entirely otiose. The product of all this fancy formalistic footwork is simply a set of semantically meaningful propositions with cognitive implications, and with very few exceptions, this is the only form in which theory ever originates or gets used in science. I have no desire whatsoever (in fact quite the contrary) to deny that formalization is immensely helpful for explicating the logical interrelations among statements. However, to suggest that a theory's syntax is in some illuminating philosophical sense independent of, or prior to, its semantic meaning, and that in deductions made from the theory the latter is just carried along for the ride, is a dangerously backwards way of looking at the matter (see p. 87 ff.). Metatheoretical partitioning of a theory between formal calculus and co-ordinating definitions clarifies its cognitive status only so far as such a partition brings insight into the cognitive status of *any* set of assertions, whether these compose a "theory" or not. But across-the-board partitioning of this sort is impossible – each co-ordinating definition would itself need to be partitioned between syntactic form and higher-order co-ordinating definitions, thus precipitating an infinite regress – and I see no virtue in submitting theories to this special indignity. While the semantic properties of theories raise some exceedingly challenging, intricate and important questions, the very same questions ultimately apply to semantically meaningful expressions of any sort; and analysis of *what* the meaning or referent of a given expression may be is obfuscated rather than expedited by the sidestep of construing the expression as a syntactic structure and a meaning glued together by correspondence rules.

The one place where a case can be made for metatheoretical reconstruction of theories as formal calculi *cum* co-ordinating definitions is in the thesis that the nature of "theoretical terms" (see B1, below) can be explained through the concept of *partial interpretation*. By a "partial" interpretation of a formal calculus is meant an assignment of semantic significance to some but not all of its elements and structures. For example, let interpretation U^*_1 of U be just like U_1, above, except for omitting the correspondence rule that $\diamond$ is to be translated as "the class of well-adjusted persons." (U^*_1 doesn't substitute any *alternative* translation of this symbol; it simply fails to stipulate any meaning for $\diamond$ at all.) Then U^*_1 is a partial interpretation of calculus U, and the nasty problem which arises is how to characterize U^*_1's cognitive status. It continues to generate the very same theorems as before, but now only some of these are translated into meaningful assertions, namely, only those not containing $\diamond$, even though most of these could not be deduced were the $\diamond$-axioms to be deleted from the theory. Hence U^*_1 cannot, *prima facie*, possibly be *true*, for this would require that each of its postulates be true, contrary to the apparent meaninglessness of $\diamond \; \tilde{\triangledown}$ and $\tilde{\diamond} \perp$. By the same token, neither can U^*_1 be semantically *false*, for this, too, presupposes that all of its postulates are cognitively significant. (We would hesitate, for example, to say that the conjunction, "Grass is red and some blehews farble", is *false*, even though its first component is false.) For this reason, practising scientists of a metatheoretical turn of mind have often averred that theories which cannot be completely stated in observational terms are neither true nor false but only more or less useful. Even before discussing the observation-language issue, however, it may be observed that the concept of "partial interpretation" contributes little if anything to our understanding of a theory's cognitive significance. For if adoption of a "partially interpreted" theory does, in fact, leave its uninterpreted terms meaningless, then the theory may be construed as simply a device for generating those of its theorems for which interpretations are provided, and the theory is then cognitively equivalent to (and is in this sense semantically true or false as a truth-function of) the set of its interpreted theorems. Alternatively, if adoption of such a theory also gives meaning of some sort to its "uninterpreted" terms, the doctrine of partial interpretation does nothing to illuminate what this meaning might be or what factual commitments reside in the theory's "uninterpreted" theorems. In fact, the "partial-interpretation" concept is actively misleading under this latter possibility, insomuch as if assertion of a theory containing terms not supplied with explicit observational meaning does give semantic significance to them, then there remain no semantically meaningless expressions in the theory in virtue of which its interpretation is only "partial."

Before we turn altogether away from the usage in which "theory" is a formal structure with adjustable meanings attached, it should be mentioned that, in practice, theories often have a character which makes their application to various specific cases falsely appear as though the theory were but a calculus which receives different meanings on different occasions from co-ordinating definitions which vary from application to application. This occurs when the main predictive force of the theory resides in postulates or theorems to the effect that if certain observable entities are of kinds (i.e., have properties) $\tau_1, ..., \tau_n$, then these entities will behave in such-and-such a way, but where the theory does not specify a set of antecedently observable conditions which are logically sufficient for something to be of kind τ_i. Then before it can be concluded on a particular occasion that according to the theory, entities $e_1, ..., e_n$ should behave in such-and-such a way, it must first be additionally surmised that $e_1, ..., e_n$ are, in fact, of kinds $\tau_1, ..., \tau_n$; and the auxiliary hypothesis that e_i is an *instance* of τ_i is easily mistaken for the "co-ordinating definition" that in this particular application of the theory, e_i *is* (i.e. is to be identified with) τ_i.[6]

A3 The distinction between *warranted theory* and *speculative theory*, which is seldom properly appreciated either in metascience or science proper, is, of all the issues touched upon in this paper, probably the one with the greatest practical import. However, I defer its introduction until discussion of contrast B2, below, and its elaboration until the end of part II.

B1 Most renowned of all the problems surrounding the epistemological credentials of scientific theories is the one addressed by the sense of "theoretical" which

---

6 The distinction between a theoretical kind τ_i and its empirical (observational) instance e_i is presumably what Koch (1954, p. 28f.; 1959, p. 739f.) is trying to draw by his contrast between "systematic variables" and "experimental (empirical) variables."

contrasts with "observational." What is intended here is primarily a distinction between *terms* (i.e. words or, more precisely, concepts) though derivatively, a sentence is also said to be "theoretical" in this sense if it contains one or more theoretical terms. As the observational/theoretical dichotomy has been traditionally formulated in empiricist metascience, there exist certain entities – objects, attributes, relations and the events they constitute – which we are able to experience directly, or *observe*. (Whether what is so observed are phenomenalistic sense data, ingredients of the more distal commonsense world, or perhaps something still else again, is moot but here irrelevant.) If such an entity has, in fact, been observed by us, then we can add to our vocabulary an "ostensively defined" term which designates (represents, symbolizes, refers to, is about) this entity. (*How* ostensive definition is able to endow terms with meanings that enable them to refer to observed entities is likewise moot and, fortunately, likewise here irrelevant.) Logical terms – i.e., words such as "and," "or," "not," "some" and "all" – and expressions which can be explicitly defined out of logical and previously introduced observational terms are also considered to be "observational." Then any meaningful word in our total vocabulary which is *not* observational in one of the ways just described is by definition a "theoretical" term, and the agonizing epistemological perplexity which then arises is: what do theoretical terms designate and how do they acquire their meanings? *Logical positivism* (which today has virtually disappeared from the philosophical scene) solved this tidily by denying the existence of theoretical terms altogether. In the positivist view, visual or auditory forms which behave syntactically like words but are not observational expressions simply have no cognitive meaning at all; and the sentence-like structures in which they occur (e.g. the postulates of a partially interpreted calculus) are no more than calculation devices which can be used to generate observation-language consequences but semantically assert nothing in themselves. In contrast to this extreme position, *logical empiricism* (which is still very much with us and to which I confess my own allegiance) insists that cognitively meaningful theoretical terms can and do exist, and that they acquire their meanings from the observational connections given them by the theory in which they are imbedded.[7] In particular, according to this view, while the truth or falsity of an observation-language statement (i.e., a statement constructed wholly

7 The thesis that theoretical terms acquire cognitive significance by bumping up against observational terms in an accepted theory has occurred repeatedly in the recent philosophical literature (cf. Feigl, 1956, p. 17f.). *How* this acquisition of meaning takes place, however, has nowhere been spelled out; while what it is that theoretical terms *refer to* has, to my knowledge, been seriously addressed in only two publications, an unnecessarily abstruse monograph by myself (Rozeboom, 1962) and a short article by Carnap (1961; criticized in Rozeboom, 1964). It is sometimes claimed that a theory gives meaning to its nonobservational terms by "implicit" definition (e.g. Nagel, 1961), but the traditional theory of implicit definition proffers only necessary, not sufficient, conditions for the designata of terms so defined – whatever an implicitly defined term refers to must be something which satisfies the definition – and hence fails to say what an implicitly defined term *does* designate.

out of observational terms) is generally verified or refuted by direct observation of
the entities named therein, statements containing theoretical terms can be confirmed or disconfirmed only indirectly by inference from accepted observation
statements and presuppose the truth of the theory by which the theoretical terms
are introduced. To my knowledge, no third alternative to these two theses – positivistic and empiricistic – about how words which allegedly designate unobserved
entities acquire their meanings has ever been proposed, though many philosophers
have apparently felt free to reject both without offering any substitute theory of
meaning.

The simplistic classical conception of the observational/theoretical distinction
as a black-and-white dichotomy has generally fallen into disfavour among contemporary philosophers, partly because the difference between observability and
non-observability can plausibly be regarded only as a matter of degree rather than
of kind (cf. Maxwell, 1962), but more importantly on grounds that there is no
such thing as pure observation. In particular, according to a recently emergent
viewpoint which I shall refer to as the "omnitheoretic" thesis, *all* (non-logical)
concepts used by a science at any given stage of its development are imbued with
meanings given to them by the science's theoretical commitments at that time
(Hanson, 1958; Feyerabend, 1963; Kuhn, 1962) and hence, contrary to empiricist
doctrine, there are no propositions that the science can verify or refute by direct
observation independent of the observer's theoretical beliefs. This view assuredly
has *some* truth in it, for even familiar perceptual concepts in whose application we
feel most secure turn out, under close analysis, to contain implications which go
far beyond anything which can be conclusively verified on the specific occasions of
their attribution.[8] Thus when I see that the basketball on the court before me is a
ball, my perception includes, among other things, a judgment that this object is also
convex on the side turned away from me. A more interesting example with practical
relevance for psychology is the concept of "behaviour." Surely we should be able
to tell by observation whether or not a given organism is behaving, or else what
could justify the behaviouristic thesis that behaviour and environmental events are
the data of objective psychology? Yet suppose that we are watching a play and see
one of the actors suddenly fall to the stage. Is this behaviour or not? Ordinarily we
would say that it is, especially if this event fits the play's dramatic integrity. But
what if we had seen a falling ballast weight strike the actor a crushing blow on the
head just before he collapsed: Would we still think of his floorward movement as
behaviour – i.e. is this something he *did*? Certainly not – but why should information about the blow affect our judgment? A little reflection on this and similar examples reveals that "behaviour" is not *merely* a change in the spatial loci of a living
organism's bodily parts, but also requires that the change have a certain special
kind of underlying cause.[9] Thus to identify an organism's motions as *behaviour* is

8 Contrary to the impression given by recent advocates of this view, empiricists of an earlier
   era were well aware of the "surplus meaning" in ordinary-language concepts (e.g., Ayer,
   1936, chap. 7) and for this reason argued that what we *really* observe directly are sense
   data.

9 Just what sort of underlying cause is envisioned, however, is intriguingly muddy. Com-

to make a judgment far richer in theoretical commitments than anything which could reasonably be called a *pure* observational report.

Realistically, then, it must be admitted that theory-free observation is a limiting ideal which scientific practice never completely attains. Even so, as soon as the omnitheoretic thesis plunges beyond this to allege that no significant difference exists between observation and theory, it becomes a retrograde mystique which has lost intellectual contact with the actual doing of science. As anyone who has ever engaged in serious research is acutely aware, the distinction between facts of which we are most certain – i.e. *data* – and the inferences which we attempt to draw from them is of the utmost methodological importance, and a goodly proportion of the technical aspects of "scientific method" have been developed precisely to keep the perceptual beliefs with which scientific inferences begin as sharply distinguished from the conclusions to which they lead as is humanly possible. Even if none of our observational concepts, scientific or otherwise, are altogether free of theoretical overtones, it does not follow that they prejudge the veridicality of *every* theory to which they are evidence-wise relevant, and it is simply not true, even in ordinary life much less in technical science, that we can never perceive and describe an event without committing ourselves to one or another of rival theoretical interpretations of it. In the example of the collapsing actor, for example, we can perfectly well see that he has fallen to the floor without any commitment (if we make a modicum of effort to abstain from hasty judgment) as to whether or not he was engaging in falling *behaviour*. In actual behaviouristic research, the experimenter usually makes a special point of recording and reporting his data in such fashion that he and his readers can agree about what happened external to his subjects' skins *without* necessarily agreeing about what went on inside. In particular, whether or not the physical motions or environment alterations effected by an organism are instances of *behaviour* makes not the slightest difference for the researcher's protocol record – irrespective of whether, e.g., a rat pushes the lever with grim determination exuding from his clenched jaws and hunched shoulders or just bumps it accidentally with his tail, the response recorder tabulates exactly one pulse from the lever relay. It is precisely *because* behavioural research has become able (albeit still imperfectly) to think about an organism's overt motions and their environmental consequences without *presupposing* any particular underlying cause that behaviour theory has been able to push beyond commonsense mentalism toward a genuine science of psychology. And this is true throughout all of scientific research. Whereas proponents of the omnitheoretic thesis have emphasized the theoretical overtones of slovenly, uncritical concepts drawn from everyday life or the physical theories which underlie interpretation of instrument readings, the former are the very sort of notions that science is most insistent upon replacing with purified technical counterparts, whereas in the latter case most research scientists are not at all reluctant to acknowledge that their theory-dependent instrument interpretations

monsensically, calling a bodily movement "behaviour" implies that it was done on purpose. But this would exclude such actions as heart-beating, pupillary responses and involuntary postural adjustments which are unquestionably – and importantly – included in the technical behaviouristic concept of "behaviour."

are uncertain inferences, and are perfectly able to question the soundness of these inferences without disturbing their perceptual beliefs about what the instrument readings themselves are. I am, admittedly, arguing this point more by loud shouting than by careful analysis of real-life examples, but I submit that anyone who proposes that empirical scientists do not really have an observation language, in which are couched perceptual beliefs that are independent of the theories upon which these data are brought to bear, simply does not appreciate what goes on in actual research. By no means do I wish to imply that this expurgation of theory from data is easily accomplished, or that scientists always maintain high standards in this respect.[10] This is an unceasing challenge to both the science's technical development and the individual investigator's professional skill. But within any empirical science there is an unrelenting *press* toward exhuming and casting out from the science's technical data language any presupposition which, upon critical contemplation, will sustain reasonable doubt – and another way in which "scientific method" leaves everyday habits of thought far behind is in development of professional proficiency at reasonable doubting.

The fact that perceptual judgments, even in scientific data gathering, never attain perfect philosophical incorrigibility, but buy into a broader framework of organized beliefs, complicates analysis of the observational/theoretical distinction but in no way demeans its scientific significance. Whatever is to be made of it philosophically, scientists have *de facto* observation languages within which they formulate what they *take* to be their science's data. However corrigible and theory-saturated (on one level of theory) these professed datum-judgments may be, they are still the bases on which all further inferences in the science are grounded, and the words used to express them are, by definition, the science's observational terms. It is a further undeniable linguistic fact that in most sciences, many of the words which occur in sentences that are seriously (if tentatively) entertained by the science in explanation of certain data or judged for plausibility on the basis of their relation to datum-beliefs are neither observational terms nor are analytically reducible to observational concepts. Words of this sort are then by definition *theoretical* terms in the sense that contrasts with "observational," while any proposition containing a theoretical term is likewise "theoretical" in this sense. Thus the observational/ theoretical distinction remains an obdurate fact of scientific inference with which metascience must reckon, irrespective of how it is to be interpreted epistemologically, and it would be a disaster for scientific practice and metascientific acuity were persuasive proponents of the omnitheoretic thesis allowed to undermine our appreciation of its methodological importance.[11]

10 I have myself called attention to ways in which the orthodox wording of data summaries in behavioral research has prejudged importantly problematic theoretical issues (Rozeboom, 1958; 1960). But rather than contravening my present point, the fact that I *was* able to show this demonstrates that it is not *necessary* to read these inferences into behavioural observations – we can agree about the data even while disputing their interpretation.

11 Most readers who are themselves professional scientists will be puzzled why I have given so much space to arguing this point, which is standard doctrine in the theory and practice of research. Unfortunately, the legitimate dissatisfaction which has burgeoned among phi-

B2 Another way in which the terms "theory" and "theoretical" are commonly used is to stigmatize the propositions to which they are applied as uncertain or hypothetical, in contrast to propositions whose truth-credentials are so strong as to admit of little practical doubt. Thus we say, "That's pretty theoretical," to express our feeling that a certain surmise or speculation has only a tenuous grounding on established facts — not that the facts necessarily *impugn* the proposition in question, but only that they do not strongly support it. Subjunctive considerations incorporating an improbable antecedent are also frequently characterized as "theoretical" in this sense as when, for example, we theorize about what would happen on Earth were the sun's energy output to decrease one per cent, or speculate about how we could most profitably invest our winnings if our ticket in the New Hampshire sweepstakes just happened to hit a big pay-off.

While there is considerable overlap between applications of the term "theoretical" in its non-observational (B1) and hypothetical (B2) senses, the congruence is by no means perfect and it is important that the distinction between these two meanings remain fully appreciated. In the first place, theories in sense B2 need contain no theoretical terms in sense B1. For example, if planetary positions recorded on particular occasions are construed to be astronomical "data," so that astronomy's observation language contains spatio-temporal co-ordinates and the names of planets, the celebrated hypotheses of Copernicus and Kepler are observation-language theories involving no theoretical terms. Again, serious surmise that certain puzzling geological formations were produced by glacial erosion, or that the human species will lose all of its bodily hair within the next million years, is a B2-type theory essentially at the observational level. (I qualify "surmise" with "serious" here because there is a tendency to withhold the title "theory" in sense B2 from hypotheses which are no more than arbitrary guesses.) These theories are "observational" not because they have been or can be conclusively verified by present observation, but because their conceptualization requires us to appeal to no aspects of reality other than what is already perceptually known to us.[12] Similarly, any plausible but inconclusively established generalization about the

losophers and historians of science over traditional reconstructions of scientific methods and concepts is beginning to flow most vigorously into the omnitheoretic stream. To date, the latter is still but a newly started freshet, but it could easily become a torrent precisely *because* it is a bold rejection of past orthodoxies whose occasional shoals and silt accumulations are becoming increasingly intolerable to modern high-powered, deep-draft philosophical navigation. (To belabour the metaphor further, I urge that we put some of these high-powered modern resources to dredging instead of abandoning them and the main empiricist channel for a wilderness portage.)

12 Note that while the hypothesis, e.g., "Marsupials were common in America 50 million years ago," envisions a situation which is no longer itself observable, this proposition is constructed out of concepts that refer only to attributes which we have commonsensically "observed." Thus if we can consider ourselves to have perceptual awareness of brief time intervals, say one-second durations, and of the temporal-precedence relation, we can define the complex attribute *being 50 million years prior to the present* wholly in observational terms.

observable properties of observable things (e.g., extrapolation from an observed sample distribution to a population considerably more inclusive than the one sampled) is a "theory" in sense B2. On the other hand, a term or proposition which is "theoretical" in sense B1 need not be so in sense B2. It is possible for assertions containing theoretical terms to have such strong evidential support that they no longer sustain appreciable doubt. For example, a great deal of chemical theory concerning the atomic constituents of macroscopic substances must surely be regarded by chemists who well understand it to be about as certain as any generalization, observational or theoretical, ever gets, and the same could be said for much of the gene theory of heredity. Similarly, while reflexes and associations are unobserved (i.e., theoretical$_{B1}$) entities postulated by psychologists to explain certain stimulus/ response correlations observed at various times in the lives of certain organisms, the bare existence of reflexes and associations can scarcely be questioned even if many of the more elaborate behavioural theories which have been built upon associationistic concepts well merit continued scepticism. More generally, science and everyday life abound with reference to *dispositional* attributes which are "theoretical" in sense B1 (cf. Rozeboom, 1961, p. 362ff.), yet whose reality – though by no means everything else surmised about them – is so undeniable that there is considerable reluctance to regard them as theoretical at all.

In all these examples of well-established theoretical entities, I have deliberately called backhanded attention to participation of the terms which refer to them in more speculative hypotheses as well as in near-certain beliefs. As discussed more thoroughly in part II, scientific theories are not monolithic wholes which stand or fall in their entirety, but are susceptible to analysis into conjunctive components each of which has its own degree of credibility. Disentangling the components of a theoretical complex which are *warranted* by the evidence at hand from those which are largely unsupported speculation has an importance for practical theory building which cannot be overestimated, and for this reason, if no other, it is essential to be clear that theoretical$_{B2}$ (*uncertain*) does *not* entail theoretical$_{B1}$ (*nonobservational*).

B3 Whereas any aspect of a theory, great or small, may be characterized by the adjective "theoretical," the noun "theory" carries the implication that whatever is so categorized is the whole thing. (Cf.: whereas "my" applies to anything that is mine, "I" refers to all of me as a unit.) Thus while individual words and singular assertions may be "theoretical," we are not likely to call them theories in and of themselves. If we ask what sort of whole is to be dignified by the label "theory," moreover, we feel that whatever else it may be – propositional or perspectival, observational or nonobservational, warranted or speculative – it should have breadth and potency, that it should provide a conceptual framework within which not just one or a few but a great mass of specific facts and possibilities are organized into an intellectually workable pattern. This is why a simple restricted generalization, even if sufficiently uncertain to count as "theoretical" in sense B2 (e.g. hypothesizing on the basis of a sample of size 10 that the linear correlation in a particular strain of dogs between a certain measure of tactile sensitivity and a certain measure of emotionality is about .50) would not generally be considered a *theory* in any meritorious sense, whereas a system of interlocking generalizations of which this is one (e.g. many observed correlations in many different species between various measures of sensory function and motivational arousal) might be subsumable under a few higher-level generalizations which would be admitted to the class of *theory* with much less hesitation. (It is almost impossible to keep theoretical$_{B1}$ concepts from intruding into such higher-level generalizations, but it is not logically essential that they do so in order for the system to qualify as "theory" – e.g., the Corpernican and Keplerian theories of planetary motion cited earlier.) This use of the term "theory" to denote a pattern of organizing ideas is nowhere more apparent than in its application to mathematical systems such as Information Theory, Multiple Regression Theory, and the like. These are neither uninterpreted postulate sets (cf. A2), assertions about unobserved entities (cf. B1), nor indeed hypotheses (cf. B2) of any sort. Instead, they are systems of explicit definitions, and the analytic truths which follow from them, which enable their user to perceive within an otherwise bewildering complexity of raw data an abstract comprehensible empirical structure.

It should be added that while the term "theory" occurs rarely if ever in scientific parlance without connotations of "system" or "conceptual organization," this is by no means true more generally. Historical explanations, in particular, are frequently theories in sense B2 but not in sense B3. Thus when the police chief announces that he has a theory about the mysterious disappearance of Lady Wimbleton's jewellry, or anthropologists entertain theories about the genetic and cultural interactions between Neanderthal and Cro-Magnon man, what is at issue is not organizing principles but specific problematic historical events.

B4 Still another sense of "theory" is the one which contrasts with "practice," as when we compare what "in theory" should happen in some situation with the actual realities of the case. "Theory" as conceived here is not so much a hypothesis whose implications for the situation in question are refuted by the data as it is a *principle*, *rule* or *ideal* to which reality conforms only approximately. In everyday affairs this sense of "theory" subsumes normative as well as natural principles, as in, e.g. "In theory, drivers should come to a complete halt at all stop signs, but in practice the 'rolling stop' is common." In science, theory-as-ideal is what *ceteris paribus* clauses are invoked to protect – i.e., we say that such-and-so is the way things would be were it not for certain secondary disturbances which have not as yet been brought into our systematic account of the matter. Thus we might assert, "In theory (ideally, in principle, as a rule) an adult human has 32 teeth, though decay, accidents and developmental anomalies often cause the actual number to differ from this"; or "In theory, intralist interference in rote verbal learning increases as a function of intralist similarity, but in practice the data are much more complicated than this." In these two examples, the "theory" is not a disconfirmed speculation but an accepted trend which would be expected to hold exactly (or essentially so) were certain other variables, some known, some not, controlled in appropriate ways.

To be sure, the theory in a theory/practice distinction does not have to be inaccurate *merely* in being a simplification – in ordinary language, this contrast not infrequently carries the suggestion that the theory in question is wildly inappropriate to the hard-headed realities of the matter. But it should be emphasized that "theory" in the sense of idealization is perfectly respectable cognitively, and indeed, if buttressed by the proper qualifications, can stand without apology as an aspirant to literal semantic truth. For subjunctive and counterfactual propositions of form "If p were the case, then q would also be so" are not at all impugned by mere failure of p to be the case; and while what does verify or refute subjunctive and counterfactual conditionals is still hotly disputed by philosophers, a theory which tells us how certain variables *would* be precisely related were certain secondary disturbances properly controlled has made a commitment to the way the world *is* put together which may not merely be true but can also have considerable value for practical explanation, prediction and control even when these secondary effects are not eliminated. Similarly, if the imperfect dependence of a variable Y upon variables $X_1, ..., X_n$ under circumstances C is described by, say, the curvilinear regression of Y upon the X_i, the statement "Y is related to $X_1, ..., X_n$ under circumstances C by the function $\hat{Y} = \phi(X_1, ..., X_n)$" can be *exactly* correct *qua* regression (at least within the limits imposed by sampling uncertainty) irrespective of how much residual scatter Y may have around this trend.

B5 One of the most popular catchwords in the behavioural sciences today is the term "model," not least among whose virtues is its union of technical clang with such free-wheeling ambiguities of meaning that an amateur metatheoretician can achieve instant profundity by talking about the role of "models" in science with very little danger that what he has said is wrong in every sense of the word.[13] The variegated meanings of "model" substantially overlap those of "theory"; in fact, theory-as-uninterpreted-calculus (A2), theory-as-simplified-ideal (B4) and to some extent theory-as-system (B3) have all been identified as "models" at one time or another. There is, however, one important usage in which "model" is set in opposition to "theory." Specifically, let T be a set of propositions which entail certain known or suspected empirical phenomena, or at least *ceteris paribus* idealizations of them. Then T is a *model* of these phenomena if we say that it is *as though* T were the case, whereas T is a theory if we hypothesize that T *is*, in fact, so. That is, when "model" and "theory" are contrasted, the difference lies not in propositional content but in the mood of speech, the model being a subjunctive expression of what the theory asserts indicatively.[14] For example, the stimulus-sampling model of probability learning hypothesizes that a molar stimulus S controlled by the experimenter behaves like an ensemble of micro-stimuli, only a randomly fluctuating subset of which confronts the subject on particular presentations of S; but *qua* model, the hypothesis reserves judgment as to whether or not S *in fact* has such a composition.

13 A useful summary of the major meanings of "model" may be found in Kaplan (1964), chap. 7). See also Chapanis (1961) for an excellent discussion of "models" in what I, for one, consider to be the core sense of the term – namely, where "x is a model of y" is to be translated as "x is a system hopefully isomorphic to y in important respects," or more briefly, as Chapanis would put it, "x is analogous to y."

14 Cf. also Boring (1957) and Workman (1964) on the subjunctive/indicative distinction between models and theories.

To attend merely to a model's iffy tone, however, is to overlook the crucial point that it, too, makes indicative commitments about the nature of the phenomena to which it is applied. For we can readily imagine disputing whether or not the phenomena really are as though T were the case. The phenomena must *be* a certain way in order for them to favour one *as-if* assertion over another. That is, to say that something is *as though* T were the case is to allege that some of T's implications *are* true. As a result, proposing hypothesis T as a "model" rather than as a straightforward theory usually has the force of saying, "I think that T is at least partially true, but I would be very surprised if it were correct in all respects and I'd rather not try to say just now which parts are true and which are not." This is a perfectly legitimate attitude to take toward a problematic hypothesis, but it raises some rather basic metatheoretical questions about what a science profits from calling a hypothesis a "model," rather than either (*a*) asserting it indicatively, if tentatively, as a theory, or (*b*) claiming only the known (or suspected) facts about the phenomena in question in virtue of which the model is reasonable *qua* model in the first place. One major benefit from looking at consequences of the model beyond merely those already known to be approximately correct is that this may well promote discovery of previously unsuspected regularities in the data, or suggest rational norms (idealizations) whose empirically determined parameters and/or divergence from the facts in particular instances turn out to define significant data variables; however, this can be accomplished just as well by considering the model indicatively as theory. In part II it will be seen that thinking of hypotheses as "models" in the present sense can be a helpful first step toward what will be argued is the proper way to do theory. But meanwhile, it should also be pointed out that overly facile insistence that a given hypothesis is *merely* a model is a form of methodological irresponsibility. For this attitude encourages one to shrug aside all protests that certain features of the model are theoretically implausible, contrary to known fact, or even logically inconsistent, with the glib rejoinder that a model doesn't claim to be literally true. It is, however, one thing to propose a hypothesis in full expectation that it will not prove tenable in all respects, and quite another to propose it even when it contains specific identifiable components which are strongly believed to be incorrect. A theorist (or modellist) who wishes to pursue the latter course has the burden of responsibility for showing that the use to which he is putting this model is successfully served *even though* it contains these contrary-to-fact ingredients, and to explain why revising the model to eliminate them would not serve this purpose even better.

II   METATHEORY: THE TASK AHEAD

So much for the various senses of "theory." The review has relevance for a conference on psychological theory if only to promote agreement on what we are talking about. But mere facilitation of communication (of which, in my gloomier moments, I sometimes despair altogether) is not my primary purpose in citing them. Each of these themes in the meaning of "theory" has as counterpoint one or more aspects of the technical functioning of psychological theories which are critical for metatheoretical judgments about what theories should be like and how these ideals can most effectively be realized. It is to such judgments that I now turn.

Let me say at the outset that while the prescriptions I shall offer would, if effected, powerfully influence the rapprochement and development of psychological theories, their impact would come to bear in a curiously indirect way. For I want to insist first and foremost that *any psychologist should feel perfectly free, unconstrained by metatheoretical norms, to say anything that he very well wants to say, in observation language or not, precise or vague, guarded or imprudent, earnest or jocular, quantified or qualitative, hesitant or dogmatic, so long as he feels that it contributes something, however obscure, to our understanding of the phenomena under concern.* As I read him, this is essentially the message that Koch (1959) would deliver to us from his official eyrie above the expanse of contemporary psychological thought. Much as I deplore the anti-methodological undertow in Koch's more recent writings, I thoroughly agree with him that it would be foolish for psychological theorists to constrict their thinking only to those conceptual procedures seemingly vouchsafed by positivistic metascience of the '30s and '40s. Unlike Koch, I am sceptical that the doctrines imported into psychology from philosophy of science and other exogenous disciplines during the last few decades have done any appreciable harm – while there was considerable agitation of psychology's verbal surface during this period, I suggest that the only disturbances which penetrated to the level of substantive research were home-grown issues, such as the intervening variable hassle and before that the nature of psychological data, which may have parallelled and eventually made contact with philosophical developments elsewhere, but which arose indigenously out of deeply felt needs to clarify our objectives and methods. These needs (with some reorienting of their cathexes) are as strong as ever, but they will not be met by a childlike appeal to past or present philosophy for advice on how to do psychology. Virtually all philosophers of whose work I am aware stand in awe of the juggernaut of technical science and wouldn't dream of tampering with the machinery. That branch of philosophy currently known as "philosophy of science" is not a school of metascientific engineering for instructing scientists in their profession, but for the most part an approach to epistemological theory which focuses upon the cognitive methods and achievements of science in hope of learning *from* science how human knowledge advances. Thus I repeat: In the proper practice of psychological research and theory, anything goes. The extant body of knowledgeable metascientific opinion comprises mainly tentative generalizations about how science has apparently worked in the past, and apart from the theory of experimental design and some aspects of statistical sampling theory, is still unprepared to say how science *should* be run. A scientist is ever so much more likely to grope, reason, intuit, plunge or blunder his way to novel discoveries and revolutionary insights if he does what comes naturally to his professional instincts than if he is constantly looking back over his shoulder to make sure that he hasn't violated somebody else's rules for the game.

But – this bacchanalia of metatheoretical permissiveness has a cold, grey morning after, and this arrives as soon as the scientist's creative inspiration (which I shall assume is an exemplar of "theory" in some sense of the word) passes over into some form of public document. Once the raw theory is palpably before us, we need to pound, grind and wring it metatheoretically in order to squeeze out just what it actually accomplishes; to make clear the respects in which it is or is not merely a restatement of notions already familiar in previous work on this problem; to recognize what is tenable in it and what is gratuitous; to extract from it what, tenable or not, is conceptually solid and what is too vague or ambiguous to do more than emote – to make, in short, a technically detailed appraisal of what the theory is and does, in as many respects relevant to the cognitive goals of psychology as metatheory has learned to perceive. The operation I am envisioning is something like diamond mining: The first stage, without which all subsequent sophistications come to nothing, is to isolate a mass of ore within which, no matter how messy the matrix may be, there is reason to hope that diamonds are embedded, while this ore is collected in wholesale, indiscriminate, scoops that would rather gulp a ton of waste than lose a gram of gem. But rich or lean, the crude ore still requires a great deal of further processing. Not until the hard stones have been searched out, cleansed of their encumbering dross, cut to exacting shapes and polished to a high brilliance has anything of major value been achieved. Unanalysed psychological theory similarly consists of a sticky gumbo through which uncut gems are occasionally strewn, and it is the task of metatheory to refine this ore.

This analogy breaks down, however, when we come to the methods of refinement. Metatheoretical analysis is most properly conducted in the indicative, not the imperative, mood of speech; and an extant theory can be dissected right down to its last *non-sequitur* and grammatical inconsistency without altering the theory in any way or even recommending that it be revised. One can, for example, point out that a theoretician's verbal definition of a certain technical term is ambiguous or at odds with the use he makes of it, or that an apparently innocuous proposition in the theory actually rests upon concealed presuppositions of controversial nature, or that a certain premise is much stronger than apparently necessary for its role in the theory, without insisting that there is anything *wrong* with ambiguities, concealed presuppositions and unnecessarily strong premises. It could well be that the explanatory power or audience appeal of the theory lies primarily in such subtleties, and the job of metatheoretical analysis is simply to *show* this, not to damn it. Even if it be agreed that certain features of the theory do fall short of optimality, it is still for the theoretician himself (or others who have assumed responsibility for making sense out of the data to which the theory relates) to judge whether these blemishes are serious enough to require attention and, if so, what should be done about them. Metatheoretical analysis of the sort I have in mind should, in fact, lead to considerable enhancement of a theory's keenness and thrust, but only because much of what the analysis discloses will be recognized by the theory-builder himself, out of his own personal sense of cognitive rightness, without coercion from extraneous standards, as features of the theory which he would like to purify or eliminate. Thus it would take a pretty callous theorist to remain entirely unmoved by exposure of a logical contradiction in his basic tenets even if contradictions are not always so disastrous to a conceptual edifice as formal logic would suggest.[15] Similarly, if it were shown that a given theory can be restructured in such fashion

15 Formally, a logical contradiction entails *every* conceivable proposition. But in practice, what has in fact been deduced from postulates containing an inconsistency may or may not depend upon this feature, so that it may be possible to eliminate the inconsistency while leaving the theory's past positive accomplishments essentially unaltered.

that certain suppositions which the theorist himself finds uncomfortable no longer add anything to what the rest of the theory implies for the theory's intended domain of application, it is rather unlikely that the theorist would not wish to make some deletions.

To be sure, normative standards are bound to spin off from metatheoretical investigations in practice. A judgment of form, "Other things equal, the more of quality Q a theory has, the closer it approaches goal G," carries with it the implication that if G *is* a goal the theory is intended to achieve, then development of the theory *should* attempt to maximize quality Q, at least to the extent that this does not impede pursuit of other desired goals; and since metatheorizing will best continue to be done mostly by psychologists themselves, cheek by jowl with their substantive concerns, there will be no shortage of strongly held value judgments to accompany metatheoretical assessments. But I want to stress once again that the metapsychologist's job is first and foremost to work out in technical detail but descriptive neutrality just what the significant properties of a given psychological theory *are* and how they relate to the various possible functions the theory might be expected to perform, and only derivatively, under another hat, to award praise and blame. The distinction I am trying to make is nicely illustrated by the contrast between the two outstanding works of metatheory which have appeared in the psychological literature to date, namely, the brilliantly *con*structive analysis of Tolmanian expectancy theory by MacCorquodale and Meehl (1954) and the brilliantly *de*structive analysis of Hullian theory by Koch (1954). Sympathetically, sensitively and with considerable success, MacCorquodale and Meehl attempted to lay bare the logical structure implicit in Tolman's intuitively appealing but technically obscure behavioural theses. The system which they extracted was no longer pure Tolman, for it is in the nature of explication to become definite or at least to make branching alternatives visible at points which are ambiguous in the original.[16] But the MacCorquodale and Meehl reconstruction allows us to see, ever so much more clearly than before, what is *in* Tolmanian expectancy theory, leaving it for the reader to decide whether or not he *likes* this sort of theory and where it should go from here. In contrast, Koch's essay is an exhaustively detailed listing of ways in which Hull's formulations fell short of certain simplistic ideals which psychological metatheory of the '40s (including Hull's own) borrowed as norms from the prescriptive models of scientific endeavour popular at the time, accompanied by a sustained, thinly muffled shriek of condemnation. Little attention is given to *why*

---

16 It is worth noting here that clarification of an ambiguity does not require commitment to one detailed alternative to the exclusion of others. The explication may amount precisely to making clear what the theory leaves open. For example, a learning theory which speaks of the growth of habit as a function of learning trials without saying *how* habit grows with trials would be clarified by stating that the theory construes this function to be an adjustable parameter, and illuminated even more by spelling out what dimensions of variation the theory envisions for this parameter – e.g. does or does not the theory allow it to assume different values for *inter alia* different habits, different learners, different periods in the life of the same learner? There is no demand that the theory supply numerical details for this parameter or even that it impose restrictions on its manner of variation. One merely wants to know where, and in what way, the theory is *intentionally* indefinite.

a theory should conform to these ideals, or what there might be of methodological interest and substantive importance in Hullian theory despite its manifest imperfections, or how seriously and in what way these blemishes interfere with what the theory could otherwise accomplish, or even whether it would require more than trivial modifications to expunge them. Koch's analysis reveals something of what Hull's theory was *not* – in particular, that it was far from the quintessence of logical rigor which many psychologists had uncritically supposed it to be and that Hull's own metatheoretical characterizations of it were inaccurate – and a number of its technical inconsistencies, but very little on the positive side about what, as a conceptual structure, it *was*, what it *did*, and *how*. (Koch frequently alludes to Hull's status in these latter respects, but either left the actual analysis programmatic in his own thinking or did not consider it of sufficient importance to share with his readers.) In fairness to Koch it must be added that his essay concluded with reservations about the value of these norms in whose light the theory was found wanting, and since then he has come even more sternly to abjure this style of metatheorizing. But it would be most unfortunate if repudiation of *bad* metatheory were overgeneralized into indiscriminate disregard for the deepened understandings and sharpened concepts which emerge when metatheorizing is done incisively but sympathetically.

My emphasis that psychological metatheory must concentrate first and foremost upon norm-free analysis of what psychological theories are in fact like is in no way symptomatic of any reticence or lack of conviction on my part about what is ultimately desirable in a theory. The overriding difficulty is that *metascience simply doesn't know enough as yet to make useful recommendations for the technical elaboration of substantive psychological theory.* "Technical" is the operative word here. If there is anything at all to be learned from the history of science and technology, it is surely that development and application of science in all its phases turn most pivotally upon painstaking exploitation of ever more exacting detail, both in the controlled sensitivity of observations and in the refinement and elaboration of concepts. The greater the demonstrable power achieved by a scientific discipline, the greater the disparity between the articulation and precision of its cognitive machinery and that of everyday life.[17] Inevitably, then, if metatheory is to get at the wellsprings of potency in scientific thought, still muddy though these may be, it will be necessary to study the fine-grained structure of its conceptual mechanisms with a technical precision and subtlety at least as great as that of the science itself. But extant metascience has scarcely begun to achieve any significant technical acuity.[18] About the only developments approaching the degree of pre-

17 I know of no better way to appreciate this than to compare a few issues of *American Scientist* and *Scientific American*. Both are written for an all-purpose audience, but the former presupposes a modicum of scientific literacy while the latter does not, and the difference in conceptual feel is striking. (Both contain much that I, for one, do not understand, but the *way* in which my understanding falters is altogether different in the two cases. One shows me the mountain which I am unprepared to climb; the other leaves me groping for direction in a cloud of feathers.)

18 Throughout this paragraph, I am using "metascience" and "metatheory" in the sense in which "-science" and "-theory" connote some degree of generality and systematization.

cision requisite for metatheoretical assertions to have determinable truth-conditions have occurred in a *few* sectors (e.g., the work of Hempel and Carnap) in which the object-theories studied are highly idealized with no more formal structure than can be comfortably formalized in the propositional calculus with an occasional touch of elementary qualificational logic. In the psychological literature, metatheory has consisted almost entirely of grandiose generalities which hover as word mists far above the concrete realities of theory-building practice, free from any recognizable meaning ties to the metapsychological *data* which should be, but virtually never are, adduced to support them. I have already made reference in my opening remarks to the inadequate acuity of most metatheory, and I hope you will grant at least provisionally the accuracy of this appraisal without demanding that I produce an overwhelming documentation of it at this time.[19] There is nothing particularly surprising or shameful about this condition. It is simply a part of the human predicament, a legacy of brute inarticulateness which mankind is slowly but successfully casting off, and I cite it at this point only to emphasize that the most pressing task for psychological metatheory today is not to teach but to learn – above all, to learn how to discern, to formulate, and to think clearly about the technical refinements which give modern psychological theories whatever cognitive superiority they may possess over commonsense psychological intuitions. To do this, we shall have to trace out in exhaustive detail the conceptual structure found in psychological theorizing as it actually occurs in the systematization of data and evolution of hypotheses at the research level (the difference between working theory in serious research and what is found in secondary sources being something like Mozart *versus* Muzak); and the fact that most of this structure has never been made explicit in the professional literature, but must be dug out of vast, untidy heaps of ellipses, grammatical absurdities, sentence-to-sentence shifts in meaning, and all the other frailties of language in use, only makes the task that much more demanding of determination and skill. This is not a job which can profitably be left for professional philosophers of science. Only a person who has lived the technical concepts and problems in a particular substantive area deeply enough to have acquired a gut-feel for what theories of this material are trying to do has much hope

That is, I do not intend my present remarks to extend to the frequently proficient critiques that appear in the scientific literature on restricted points of specific substantive theories. I am concerned here primarily with metatheory whose level of abstraction is high enough that what is said has relevance (or would have relevance, were it to have sufficient acuity) for more than just a single aspect of one particular theory.

19 It fills me with anguish that, try as I may, I can find no words which can help others to *see*, with the vivid awareness of first-hand experience, the putty-and-wet-sand quality of most of our conceptual tools, not merely in metatheory but in large sectors of substantive psychology as well. (Polemics such as these make evident that I hold this conviction, but do little to demonstrate its truth.) The only way in which this communication can be effected is through an amassing of concrete examples in which flabby concepts in common use are toughened up. This is an enterprise at which I have persisted in most of my previous writings and will continues in part III, below. But what can be accomplished by any one lunge is minute in comparison to the immensity of the task.

of separating what is vital in them from what is not, of empathizing the undercurrents and overtones that turn non-sequiturs into enthymemes, and of working out formalized reconstructions which are faithful more to the spirit than to the letter of the originals. Moreover, the resources of professional philosophy are still not, as they now stand, sufficient for this job. The philosophy of cognition has sought through the centuries to abstract from human reasoning those patterns of thought which still retain normative appeal when stripped to their bare bones of logical form; but whereas the past 100 years has supported a remarkable surge of perspicacity into deductive logic, philosophical command of other belief-governing formal linkages among complex ideas is as yet little more developed than was deductive logic in Aristotle's day.[20] It is all the more important, therefore, that metapsychology now concentrate upon exacting *descriptive* analysis of technical detail in working substantive theories, in full expectation that in order to identify and express what is there we may well have to pioneer new skills and concepts in logic, epistemology and semantics. But this is also a way – and an important one – of developing psychology proper. For as these new or sharpened methodological tools are put to practical use, the architects, builders and renovators of substantive theory (from whose peerage no psychologist should be excluded simply because he practices serious metatheory as well) will be thereby availed of keener awareness of what they are about, in what ways their theoretical products fail to be and to do what their creators intend of them, and how their theory-construction techniques can be honed into a more incisive instrument for these intentions. In short, I conceive of future metapsychology as a technological service adjunct to psychological research, staffed largely by professional psychologists with specially trained skills at conceptual analysis, whose utility for substantive psychological theory is comparable to that of inferential statistics and the theory of experimental design for data collection and of electronics technology for the refinement of research hardware.

To be sure, I have sketched this vision of metapsychology's lusty, trail-blazing future in wispy impalpables such as dreams are made of, and until you are given some operational specifics you have every right to remain sceptical. Let me, therefore, review some of the more urgent metatheoretical problems which protrude from the multiple meanings of "theory" surveyed earlier, and conclude (part III) with a sampler of metatheory in action.

To continue, then, recall that a great deal of what passes for psychological "theory" actually appears to contain little definite propositional content (A1). But this is a remarkable thing. How is it possible – or is it? – for a point of view to have cognitive force and yet not assert anything? In particular, if competing perspectives do not incorporate incompatible beliefs about psychological fact, in what sense can there be conflict among them? To the extent that perspectival theories differ merely in what they are about, as on a grander scale the subject matter of physics differs from that of sociology, or in the murmur and clang of their

---

20 This is not a charge of complacency. There has never been a time when more ferment and probing has vitalized philosophy than in contemporary movements. But no matter how bustling the site, a construction in progress is not the same as an inhabitable edifice.

preferred word-vehicles akin to opting to speak psychology in Russian rather than in English, such disputes are simply non-cognitive quarrels over personal tastes and have no legitimate place in psychological science. But of course there is much more than mere value discrepancies at issue in such oppositions as behaviour theory *versus* phenomenology, trait-theoretical *versus* dynamic approaches to personality, S-R *versus* cognitive interpretations of complex human behaviour, etc., even if it is often hard to make out what the significant points of divergence actually are. Here, then, is a major area for metapsychological research: To analyse various psychological perspectives or "programmatic" theories for how each nuance of expression, pattern of data interpretation, and whatever else may characterize the perspective's style makes a difference for what a person who adopts this perspective believes about psychology, or what it *enables* him to believe, in order that each such detail may be closely examined in naked isolation for its own particular intellectual merits. (Acceptance or rejection of a particular point of view inevitably carries with it adoption of numerous covert beliefs or belief-biasing attitudes to which we would not accede were we to recognize them for what they are, and the more holistic our allegiance or opposition to a given perspective, the more our thinking is corrupted – as judged by our own intellectual standards could we but bring them to bear – by such invisible cognitive demons.) I shall not here attempt to inventory the different *ways* in which a theoretical perspective can have import for what one believes even when the perspective makes no explicit factual commitments – though it is worth passing mention that a great deal of the content in perspectival theory is actually metatheoretical, and that an enormous share of past and present psychological controversy (e.g. the pros and cons of the behaviouristic approach) has been metapsychological conflict rather than disagreement over psychology proper.[21] I would, however, like to give two examples of how acceptance or rejection of a particular manner of speaking (verbal perspective) can carry powerful hidden commitments of which we are seldom aware.

(i) Learning theorists frequently hesitate to use the terms "elicit" and "evoke", to describe the relation between a stimulus S and its empirically correlated response R, on grounds that this implies too severe a reflex-type connection between S and R. The preferred locution for describing the effect of a discriminative stimulus on operant behaviour or (for some verbal learning theorists and virtually any psychologist whose perspective is dominantly "cognitive") the human emission of verbal responses to verbal stimuli is to say that S "sets the occasion for," "selects," or is a "cue" for R. There will probably be little disagreement that saying "S elicits (evokes) R" does, in fact, suggest that the $S \rightarrow R$ relation is akin to a "reflex"; that it has connotations which can be brought out more vividly by speaking of S as jerking, pushing or forcing R out of the organism; and that the physical analogy which comes most readily to mind is that of a doorbell ringing when the button is

21 For example, when one perspective takes another to task for neglect of certain data or possibilities, or contends programmatically that its framework ideas can eventually be worked into a significant and true propositional theory, the thesis concerns the actual or potential achievements of a certain theoretical approach and is hence a metatheoretical proposition.

pushed. Alternatively, to say that S is a cue (selects, sets the occasion) for R is intended to convey merely that presence or absence of S is correlated with the organism's propensity to emit R. But are there any genuine *cognitive* differences between "S elicits R" and "S is a cue for R"? The fact that one suggests analogies the other does not is inconclusive, for to say that A is analogous to B is only to imply that there is *some* respect in which A resembles B, and not until the point of resemblance is made explicit can we decide whether or not C is also analogous to B in this way. That is, if by "elicit" we mean whatever sort of relation it is that links response to stimulus in a *reflex*, while we also agree (as surely we must) that this relation is not *literally* the same as the connection between doorbell and pushbutton, nor is it a literal jerking, pushing or forcing, then it remains to be seen whether those aspects of jerkings and bell-ringings which make reflexes appear analogous to the latter may not also appear, perhaps more subtly, in cueings and occasion-settings as well. Or turning the point around, what there is about bell-ringings and physical jerks and pushes which does *not* have a suitable parallel in discriminated operants and verbal respondings may not have a proper counterpart in reflexive elicitations either, and should hence not be construed to be implied by "elicits." Now, the most conspicuous formal property of these physical analogies, and the one which surely dominates the thinking of most persons who deny that verbal-association performances or operant respondings are like this, is the near-perfect correlation between antecedent (e.g., button push) and consequent (bell ring) – and as a matter of brute fact, this is *not* an essential or even frequent property of reflexes. The strength of a reflexive association $S \to R$ is maximal when the probability of R, given S, is 1.0, but nothing in reflex theory demands that all reflexes be near maximal strength, and conditioned reflexes in particular usually involve low response probabilities in early formation or late extinction. Hence there is nothing in the concept of "reflex," and thus neither in "elicitation" or "evocation," which *properly* connotes inflexible coupling of R to S.

Even so, there are more subtle meaning ingredients in "elicit," derived from its paradigmatic application to reflex action, which do not quite fit most behaviour-theoretical conceptions of operant (instrumental) responding. In brief, the most important of these are that (*a*) reflex theory makes no provision for motivational determinants of behaviour;[22] (*b*) the reflex-theoretical conception of "stimulus" and "response" envisions these paradigmatically as a pulse of sensory excitation and a pulse of reaction, respectively, to which the notion of "latency" is applicable,[23] whereas the paradigmatic discriminated operant is a response which occurs repetitiously throughout the discriminative stimulus's continuation (i.e. it is the presence of S, not its onset, which is primary); and (*c*) the paradigmatic responses in reflexive elicitation are specific motor discharges, whereas in operant behaviour

22 Pavlov (1928), p. 152, observed that degree of food deprivation influences the strength of conditioned salivation reflexes, but he did not conceptualize this *as* a motivational phenomenon.

23 Sustained reflexive reactions to steady stimuli, as in prolonged pupillary constriction under continuous bright light, may be subsumed under the pulse paradigm by construing them as limiting cases of a rapid sequence of pulses.

they are achievements (i.e., changes in the environment or the organism's relation to it which can usually be brought about by a variety of motor sequences). Thus a psychologist may justly withold the term "elicitation" from an S-R correlation if he thinks motivation is also significantly involved in R's emission, if he doubts that the stimulus action is primarily an onset phenomenon, or if the response is defined as an achievement. On the other hand, if one objects to "elicitation" only because of analogies to invariant succession in mechanical systems, he has not merely failed to distinguish between literal meaning and metaphor in behaviour theory, but has also implicitly ascribed to psychologists who *do* speak of elicitation views which in all probability they do not in fact hold.

(ii) While linguistic style is one feature which usually helps to distinguish one perspectival theory from another, one would like to think that preferences in grammatical phrasing make little difference for a theory's cognitive impact. But such is not the case, as attested by the remarkable increase in conceptual power which accompanies the shift from transitive to intransitive verb-forms. Consider, for example, the contrast between "John sees (perceives) the stopsign" and "John has a perception (percept) of the stopsign." A trivial difference? Far from it. The transitive verb regards perception as a primitive relation between the perceiver and the perceived, whereas the intransitive construction construes perception as mediated by a condition of the perceiver which is what stands more directly in the aboutness relation to the perceived. That is, "s perceives o" has the logical form

$$P_1(s,o),$$

whereas the logical form of "s has a percept of o" is[24]

$$(\exists \phi)[\phi(s) \cdot P_2(\phi,o)].$$

There is no incompatibility between these two formulations. A theory of perception which prefers intransitive constructions can always maintain that "s has a percept of o" is an *analysis* of "s perceives o," while a perspective which prefers transitive verbs concedes the analytic equivalence of the two forms so long as it is agreed – if it is – that when a person perceives something he does so in virtue of certain features of his momentary psychological condition which constitute his perceiving one thing rather than another. Yet a transitive perspective in perception theory is inherently focused upon the objects of perception and has no linguistic resources (except insofar as these are subsequently introduced by deliberate contrivance) with which to think about the *means* of perception, whereas an intransitive perspective has explicit concern for the mechanisms by which perception occurs, and even a rudimentary propositional theory thereof, built into its very grammar.

The difference between transitive and intransitive verbs is, of course, relevant to many other psychological issues besides perception. In fact, a great deal of com-

---

24 More precisely, "s has a percept of o" should perhaps be formalized as $(\exists x)[H(s,x) \cdot P(x) \cdot R(x,o)]$, in which H is whatever relation holds between a percept and the person who has it, P is the attribute of being a percept, and R is a referential relation. However, the nature of H is presumably exemplification, while P can be combined with R to constitute a relation P_2 of perceptual aboutness.

monsense psychology is couched in transitive forms whose replacement in our thinking with more articulated intransitive counterparts is requisite to getting on with technical progress in these areas. But unfortunately, intransitive constructions don't have the same subjective warmth and liveliness as do their transitive precursers. They seem to construe the person as a passive, psychologically demeaned and impoverished thing whose sole function is to provide a point of confluence for such impersonal entities as sounds, smells, twitches, and the like. And a psychological perspective in which human beings appear as colourless containers for what happens to them, rather than the active agents we know ourselves to be, readily provokes rejection and hostility from critics who interpret such a perspective as an attack on human individuality, responsibility and personal worth. Actually, this reaction is without cognitive foundation. The organism's apparent psychological emasculation by intransitive verb constructions is simply an instance of the holistic delusion that analysis is denial of the thing analysed. Yet wherever in past and present psychology the concept of "self" has been esteemed, the noncognitive feeling tones of transitive grammar have been an impediment to the growth of more penetrating theory, while even in areas where there is no fear of devaluating humanity, seduction by transitive grammatical habits continues to procreate conceptually crippled theory.[25]

The preceding two examples are small illustrations of how points of tension between divergent theoretical perspectives can be amorphous fusions of emotion-charged irrelevancies with genuine cognitive issues which may or may not sustain serious interperspectival hostilities or intraperspectival uncertainty when they are examined openly. But metatheoretically problematic quasi-conflicts can be found at all levels of the perspectival/propositional continuum. Even where assertions are most definite in their substantive commitments, it is still not at all uncommon for theories which apparently contradict one another to be in fact perfectly compatible or even to lend each other active support. Some of the most blatant instances of this occur when different patterns of organizing abstractions (theory$_{B3}$) or idealizations (theory$_{B4}$) are contrasted. For example, alternative non-linearly related choices of scale for a given variable lead to different statistical conclusions about its expected value in a given population; while idealized equations of grossly different algebraic form can be virtually indistinguishable over the region of the data to which they are fitted, or, even if the idealizations themselves differ significantly, the residual variance in the data may be no worse under the one than under the other.

Thus two summary statements of what, on the whole, a given body of data is like, especially in regard to the patterns of relationships therein, can appear to disagree even though both are in fact equally true. Or at least they *may* both be true. It is also quite possible that different ways to summarize the same extant data take the form of generalizations which become irreconcilable when extrapolated to predict what would happen if the range of the independent variables were extended, the background constancies shifted, or extraneous variables more tightly

25 E.g., hypotheses about subjects' transitive "use" of mediated associations in verbal behaviour, aptly characterized by Mandler (1963, p. 247) as "homunculus-like."

controlled. Since assertions of empirical regularity (i.e., observation-language theories) are universally vague about the boundary conditions under which they are considered to hold, it is a job for metatheoretical analysis to decipher just where actual disagreement begins in different accounts of the same body of data, and what its nature may be.

To be sure, in these days of relatively enlightened quantitative methodology, few research psychologists are disposed to quarrel over mildly discrepant idealizations treated merely as summaries of extant data, especially when these are described as "models" with all the bland tolerance for inaccuracy and untoward implications this term encourages. Even so, one tends to feel that alternative "models" of the same data are working at cross-purposes in that if each *were* elevated to the status of indicative theory, then they *would* be conflicting hypotheses about the events and regularities underlying these observations. I think it is fair to say that for the most part, the really embattled conflicts about psychological reality concern theoretical entities in sense B1, and that theorists are often disposed to regard non-synonymous B1-type theories over the same empirical domain as logically incompatible. But in fact, there are good abstract-metatheoretical reasons for thinking that two theories about unobservables can be in factual conflict only if they entail an observational disagreement, no matter how contradictory their theoretical$_{B1}$ postulates or theorems may appear (Rozeboom, 1962), and even quite possibly that they must make essentially the *same* theoretical$_{B1}$ commitments to the extent that they are warranted by the same body of data. Thus it may well be that two propositional theories (or the more propositional aspects of two theoretical perspectives) which are thought by their proponents to be at loggerheads actually say pretty much the same thing, though not necessarily so in any *obvious* way.

For example, by far and away the most celebrated controversy in psychology's history has been the running battle between behavioural (S-R) and mentalistic (cognitive) theories. We all know of the agony and outrage with which so many mentalistically oriented psychologists have excoriated S-R theory as a denial of man's inner existence, and how, conversely, S-R accounts of overt actions often seem to be thought by their partisans to render mentalistic interpretations otiose. Yet so long as behaviour theories are not couched entirely in their observation language (and none has ever been, not even Skinner's), then it is altogether possible that the theoretical$_{B1}$ terms introduced by a behavioural hypothesis to account for certain overt regularities *refer to* (designate, are about) the very same internal entities that we know more familiarly in mentalistic terms, even though the behaviour-theoretical terms do not have the same *meanings* as the mentalistic concepts with which they are co-referential. For example, if an S-R theory of motivation finds it necessary to postulate an "intervening variable"[26] D_T which varies as a function of water deprivation and in turn influences, *inter alia*, the intensity of drinking behaviour, D_T may in fact be the very same variable that we introspectively identify as "thirst" even though the meaning given to D_T by its postulated

---

26 Really a hypothetical construct, though since psychologists have refused to use the term "intervening variable" in the sense given to it by MacCorquodale and Meehl (1948), I will not fight the current here.

connections with peripheral Ss and Rs does not logically require that D_T be identical with subjective thirst. Although we are still a long, long way from it today, there is no reason at all why a suitably sophisticated behaviour theory whose theoretical$_{B1}$ terms have only stimulus- and response-conferred meanings cannot nonetheless be *about* all the rich, warm inner experiences that we are now able to address only through the undisciplined conceptual resources of phenomenology and commonsense mentalism.[27]

Moreover, even when the individual theoretical$_{B1}$ terms and propositions of two *prima facie* competing theories do not have a simple one-to-one correspondence in factual reference, they may still be factually equivalent on a larger scale. For example, a good deal of printer's ink has been spilled in inferential factor analysis over how best to solve for common factors, the chief dimensions of controversy having concerned orthogonal *versus* oblique solutions and simple-structure *versus* hierarchical factor patterns. Now, extraction of common factor space by estimating data-variable communalities is an act of ampliative (i.e., not deductive) inference to underlying source variables (see Rozeboom, 1966, p. 252ff.) which is certainly a worthy subject for controversy. But for the most part, the big disputes in factor theory have concerned not the solution for common-factor *space*, but where the source variables lie *within* that space – i.e., communality estimation has generally been treated as a negotiable detail while the battle lines have been drawn over rotation to terminal axes. But if $F_1, ..., F_n$ and $F'_1, ..., F'_n$ are different choices of axes for the same common-factor space, then each F_i is an exact linear combination of the F'_j and conversely, and any hypothesis about the nature and functioning of one or more of the inferred source variables $F_1, ..., F_n$ is true if and only if a corresponding (though quite possibly more complicated) statement about the F'_j is also true. At the root of the rotation controversy is the obscure but compelling notion that since inferential factoring is a hypothesis about underlying (non-observational) reality, it must also be assumed that some of the dimensions (variables) in common-factor space are *more* real than others. This is the very same intuition which causes us to feel, say, that a person's weight-in-pounds and height-in-inches have an existential solidity not possessed by measures such as "whyght," defined as weight-in-pounds plus height-in-inches, analytically abstractable from the former. I am by no means convinced that this feeling is wholly without foundation, but it concerns exceptionally esoteric philosophical issues on which, to my knowledge, no factor analyst has ever *intended* to take a stand. Thus apart from presumably unwanted overtones, it would seem that different styles of inferential factoring disagree more over how the total inference about source variables is to be partitioned conceptually than over what is actually hypothesized to be the case about underlying reality. Or more precisely, while there may well be genuine cognitive issues involved in the rotation problem, it is still highly obscure just what they are.

To summarize the present point, then, if *prima facie* competing theories are pruned of their unintended presumptions and ingenuous metatheoretic denials of

---

27 This is essentially what is known in philosophy as the "identity" solution to the mind-body problem (see Feigl, 1958), except that I am here focusing upon the possible co-reference of mental concepts with behavioral rather than neurophysiological constructs.

rival positions, it may turn out that they all say essentially the same thing or at least supplement, rather than contradict, each other albeit through the media of different conceptual frameworks. Determining the extent to which this is so is hence another task at which technically skilled metatheoretical analysis can be of value. Or is this of value? If we but leave intertheoretic squabbles to those who have nothing better to do, will it not suffice for each theory to take care of its own growth and revision? No; because this idyll of deep down intertheoretical accord I have been suggesting is only a possibility, not a to-be-expected actuality. Competing theories often contain genuine disagreements along with the spurious ones, and there is probably no faster way for theories to evolve than for one to be pitted against another on points of real issue. Or one theory may have developed a concept, solved a problem or recognized a phenomenon which would greatly benefit another were it translated into the other's terms. The encompassing point is that the ways in which contraposed theories supplement, contradict or concur with one another are often very different from the ways in which they *seem* to do so, and it is hardly conceivable that a more veridical perception of their interrelations would not be of immense value for development and application of the theories themselves.

The tasks which I have commended to metapsychology so far may be described generically as an explication of what the cognitive ingredients of a given theory actually are. And arch as this phrase, "explicating cognitive ingredients," may sound, there is a solidly operational way for metatheoretical practice to realize its vision, namely, by laying bare the *logical structure* of the theory's concepts and tenets. As is true of any technical skill, the actual procedures and products of such analysis can be properly appreciated only through observing it at work in serious applications, and since part III of this paper attempts to communicate a modicum of this appreciation through deeds, there is little to be gained at this point by loitering over words. But insomuch as *Problems of Logical Structure* is one of the two primary categories into which metatheoretical issues fall, I would like to say one or two things about what, abstractly, is involved here.

In brief, the logical structure of a theory is the *pattern* by which its concepts and assertions, if any, hang together. The following semi-technical definition will clarify this somewhat. Let $\mathbf{E}^T = \{E_i^T\}$ be the set of all meaningful linguistic expressions – individual terms, sentences, compound predicates, or whatever – contained by a theory T; let $\mathbf{S}^T = \{S_j^T\}$ be the set of all meaningful sentences which can be generated by concatenating expressions in $\mathbf{E}^T$; and let $\Sigma = \{\mathbf{E}^k\}$ be the set of all subsets of *all* meaningful linguistic expressions (not just those found in T) such that each $\mathbf{E}^k$ in Σ also satisfies the following condition: There exists a mapping ϕ^k of expressions in $\mathbf{E}^T$ into expressions in $\mathbf{E}^k$, and derivatively of all concatenations of expressions from $\mathbf{E}^T$ into corresponding concatenations of expressions from $\mathbf{E}^k$, in such fashion that for any S_i^T and S_j^T in $\mathbf{S}^T$, if S_i^T analytically entails S_j^T, then $\phi^k(S_i^T)$ and $\phi^k(S_j^T)$ are meaningful sentences such that $\phi^k(S_i^T)$ analytically entails $\phi^k(S_j^T)$. Then the logical structure of system $\mathbf{E}^T$ (i.e., theory T) is whatever is common to all systems in Σ – i.e., it is whatever is described by a set of rules which tell how to change the meanings of the symbols used by theory T without changing the entailment-relationships among sentences constructed from these symbols.[28] For an ideally precise and explicit theory, this is essentially the syntactic structure abstracted in the logician's concept of "uninterpreted" theory (A2), except that it is the *spirit* of formalization which is vital to applied metatheory, not the typographic accoutrements of logistical or mathematical notation. As it is, the primary goals which mathematicians and logicians have sought to achieve through formalization, namely, consistency, deductive impeccability, and parsimony of postulates and logical machinery in axiomatic development of criterion theorems already well established by informal argument, have only secondary importance for a science like psychology wherein beliefs remain in a flux of emendation and overthrow even where they can be found at all. Deductive accuracy is unquestionably desirable (and rarer than we like to think) in science, as is being able to trace out the implications of a set of premises beyond the point where technically unamplified reason falters. But extant mathematical or logical formalisms which enhance deductive power do so precisely because they suppress all logical structure which is not directly germane to the particular inferential algorithms there exploited, not to mention the distortion which may have to be introduced into the original theory in order to satisfy the formal system's presuppositions. With our present still-primitive awareness of conceptual structure, an approach to theory construction which seeks to promote deductive rigour by *replacing* the half-inarticulate but semantically intricate verbal ventures of a living science with a computer-programmable formal calculus will inevitably freeze out most of the subtle complexities to which the theory owes its perspectival appeal and capacity to evolve.

The most important role of formalization in scientific theory lies not in constructive applications wherein theorems are derived algorithmically, or new belief-systems are created wholesale by tacking meanings onto a pre-existent abstract calculus by means of correspondence rules, but in *re*constructive analysis which brings to light the theory's implicit structure. A given array of semantically linked propositions can usually be formalized in many different ways at different levels of complexity, and their finer logical texture is almost certain to escape us at first. But by formalizing as much of the theory's structure as we are now able to perceive,

---

28 While this definition of "logical structure" is not completely explicit (especially in regard to sentence formation through concatenation), it has been rather carefully worded to avoid any presupposition that theory T has been formalized. To search out logical structure in a living language teeming with synonyms (meaning equivalences not revealed by symbol identity), ellipses and suppressed premises (sources of meaning relations among statements not revealed by their overt grammatical construction), and the like, we need a definition of structure which does not require any initial assistance from the physical properties of the language's sign-vehicles. The entailment cited here is not formal but analytic (semantic), so that a sentence S_i can entail sentence S_j because the meanings of S_i and S_j require that S_j be true if S_i is, even though typographically S_i and S_j may have no formal connection. Weaker forms of implication (i.e., inductive support) are also relevant to disclosure of logical structure, but presumably any structural property which mediates weak implication will also be manifested elsewhere in strict entailment.

we construct templates which, when held against the living reality of the theory's usage, throw into bold relief what the theory has in it *beyond* what we have captured so far. For example, suppose that a certain theory advances a natural-language argument in which conclusion q is held to follow from premise p, but that when p and q are replaced by their *prima facie* formalized equivalents ϕ and ψ, respectively, ψ is not a deductive consequence of ϕ. Three main alternatives now present themselves. The first is to accuse the theory of a logical fallacy, and this would indeed be legitimate if, after the demonstration that ϕ does not formally entail ψ, q no longer seems to follow from p. (In this way it might be discovered, e.g., that the earlier informal argument implicitly assumed a second premise r which is needed to supplement p before q follows.) Secondly we may decide that for any two propositions respectively formalizable by structures ϕ and ψ, the former still counts as good *evidence* for the latter even though the relationship between them is not one of deductive implication. In this case the formalization has isolated a pattern of inductive inference which may or may not have been recognized previously (and if not, we have turned up a new datum for inductive logic to assimilate), but contributes no new powers to a theory which has been using this pattern of inference all along. Finally and most significantly, the natural-language proposition q may still seem to follow from natural-language premise p even after we have recognized that an argument of form "If ϕ, then ψ" has no generic merit. In this case, we must conclude that formalizing p as ϕ and q as ψ fails to capture those logical connections between p and q in virtue of which the former supports the latter, and we are accordingly directed to reanalyse p and q more deeply in search of *why* p is evidence for q, thereby disclosing ingredients in p and q which we had previously overlooked.

Let me give a more concrete illustration of this general point, for it is an important one. Suppose that I say, "John is infatuated with Marsha, but doesn't want to marry her." How is this to be translated into logistical notation? If we write "$I(x,y)$" for the predicate "x is infatuated with y," "$M(x,y)$" for the predicate "x wants to marry y," "a" for "John" and "b" for "Marsha," my statement about John's feelings for Marsha analyses most obviously as

$$I(a,b) \cdot {\sim}M(a,b).$$

However, if we translate this formalization back into everyday English, we have "John is infatuated with Marsha *and* it is not the case that he wants to marry her." That is, "but" passes over into "and" in the formalization. Now, as soon as we recognize this it becomes apparent that the original statement conveyed more than *just* the co-occurrence of two relations, I and $\sim M$, holding between entities a and b. The conjunctive "but" carries an overtone of surprise which softly implies, without actually asserting it, that $\sim M\ (a,b)$ is contrary to expectation given $I(a,b)$. The expectation presumably rests upon some background regularity connecting I and M, though it is not at all clear what relationship is envisioned (e.g. "Almost everyone wants to marry persons with whom they are infatuated" and "John usually wants to marry girls with whom he is infatuated" both support the "but"-surprisal in this case) or how strong it is. In any event, if I am trying to be maximally explicit in what I have to say about John and Marsha, I now have two choices: (*i*) I can abandon "but" for "and" and claim *merely* that John is infatuated with Marsha and doesn't want to marry her, or (*ii*) I can state this and augment it with some generalization linking infatuation and matrimonial desires in virtue of which this particular conjunction is atypical. What I am *not* entitled to do is to remain pat with my original "but"-statement, for this has now been shown to contain a lawlike allegation which has not been expressed in a form amenable to cognitive evaluation. (Of course, no one can *compel* me to make any revision of my original statement, but if I am not willing to do so, then my continued use of "but" in this context is intellectually dishonest.)

And what does the logistical formula "$I(a,b) \cdot \sim M(a,b)$" contribute here? Its virtue lies not in a dehumanizing reduction of John's feelings for Marsha to an inflexible concatenation of meaningless marks in an abstract calculus, but in its precise expression of a plausible paraphrase for my original statement, a paraphrase which I am challenged either to accept or to compare with the original and make explicit the surplus meaning so disclosed. Notice that the full value of the formalization emerges only when we translate it *back* into a semantically familiar form. In principle, we could carry out this comparison without ever leaving ordinary English. The advantage of the logistic mediation is merely (though this is considerably more than just a "mere") that this compels our analytic paraphrasing to emphasize those grammatical forms which are most clearly understood in technical logic. As it is, the present example also serves to illustrate why it is dangerous (or would be were there any appreciable likelihood of this step's being taken) to *work* with one's concepts and hypotheses in logistic format. The predicate "x wants to marry y" contains immensely more logical structure than is represented by the dyadic form "$M(x,y)$". For one, the tensed verb in the original predicate makes a temporal reference which is altogether suppressed in "$M(x,y)$". More important, *wanting w* is most penetratingly analysed as having a want related referentially to w (cf. earlier comments on transitive *versus* intransitive verbs), and the grammar of want-descriptions is on the same level of logical complexity as descriptions of memories, percepts, beliefs and the like[29] – none of which is remotely suggested in the formalization of marriage-wanting as a dyadic relation lacking internal grain. The fine structure of want-concepts is essential to much of the intuitive reasoning we do with them, and can eventually be made explicit by successive attempts to formalize such arguments. But here as in all such cases the original concept or statement is still the onion off which a particular formalization peels only certain restricted layers of structure.

Analysis of logical structure answers questions about what, cognitively, a theory has in it. (It's not the whole answer, of course, since something must also be said

29 In primary occurrences of the grammatical form "Person s wants (remembers, perceives, believes) ———," the blank is filled with an expression whose logical structure is that of a complete sentence, though components of this are frequently suppressed in practice. Thus "x wants *to marry y*" is more accurately written "x wants *that x will marry y*." It may be noted, incidentally, that "John doesn't want to marry Marsha" is not properly formalized as $\sim M(a, b)$ at all if what is intended by the original is not a simple lack of marriage desire in John for Marsha, but rather, John's wanting *that John will not marry Marsha*.

about meaning. But meaning becomes to a surprising degree superfluous once logical structure has been disclosed. E.g., in a science whose concepts were so exhaustively formalized that *all* their meaning relations were syntactically explicit, meanings would make a difference only when raw observations call forth datum assertions.) Moreover, successful explication of a theory's logical structure to any depth desired requires no more than persistent application of concept-analytic routines, even if proficiency in these skills and indeed even appreciation for the ends they serve is still conspicuously lacking in contemporary psychology. But there is a second cluster of metatheoretical problems, just as fundamental as the first, for which no simple resolution routines exist, namely, *Problems of Veridicality*. While straightforward declarative assertions are not nearly so prevalent in psychological theory as traditional metascience would lead one to expect, it is surely the ultimate *goal* of psychology to arrive at true statements about psychological reality. A perspective remains unfulfilled so long as it is merely perspectival, while idealizations (B4) and models (B5) are truth-claims playing it cool. But when *is* a theory true (correct, veridical), anyway?

Now, Truth in all its philosophic splendour is far too involved and ponderous a concept to be invoked here with useful issue. Fortunately the problems of veridicality which confront applied metatheory can be reworded to avoid it. To ask whether or not a proposition p is *true* is for all practical purposes equivalent to asking whether or not we should believe p. Thus the root problem of veridicality may be rephrased as *when is a theory* T *credible*? Or better, since credibility is a matter of degree, to what *extent* is T credible (plausible, warranted, tenable, believable, acceptable), and why? It can, I think, be agreed without much argument that research psychologists are to a man profoundly committed to weighing and altering the credibilities of various psychological "theories" in one sense or another of this term. This is, after all, the definitive process of science: We start with beliefs at the highest level of assurance we can achieve, i.e. datum-convictions, and move from there to (hopefully) appropriate degrees of belief in certain other propositions about which we would like to be certain; and all our most elaborate techniques of experimental design and data collection are simply methods for generating datum-beliefs which drive the tenability of these questioned propositions toward one extreme or another. Since research science is so extensively engaged in the *practice* of assaying theoretical credibility, it is meet that metatheory identify and, ultimately, pass normative judgment on the forms which govern these assessments – except that such norms best arise not by one man's fiat of how another must conduct his thinking, but through so detailed an explication of the patterns by which a theorist *does* transfer credibility from one proposition to another that the theorist himself, given this heightened awareness of his own inferential methodology, can judge whether this procedure still appeals to his reason in quite the same way as before, and if not, what purifications of method now support his conclusions more strongly. Mankind is still very much in the throes of evolving its powers of non-demonstrative inference, and while this has reached its most powerful development in the professionally disciplined construction and evaluation of scientific theories, I shall now show that what makes a theory credible is considerably more problematic than has generally been recognized, and that the region of uncertainty has major operational import for practical theory building.

Extant metatheoretical interpretations of how scientific theories wax and wane in their cognitive respectability may be sorted rather neatly into three primary perspectives, *inductivist*, *hypothetico-deductive*, and *omnitheoretic*. Inductivist views hold that there exist specific patterns of nondemonstrative inference according to which properly organized datum-beliefs project credibility beyond themselves. With respect to Reichenbach's celebrated distinction between the "context of discovery" and the "context of justification," the inductivist outlook substantially equates the two – the data are thought to call their inductive implications to mind as well as to endow them with evidential support. Although the vast majority of practicing scientists probably subscribe to some version of the inductivist position, it is regarded as rather naive and hopelessly inadequate by many contemporary philosophers of science. Instead, most abstract metatheoreticians have until very recently favoured the hypothetico-deductive view. This holds that how a theory originates in imagination is inexplicable by any pattern of formal logic and is, in fact, irrelevant – all that matters for the theory's epistemic stature is subsequent verification or refutation of the theory's testable consequences. And finally, objecting to both inductivist and hypothetico-deductive positions on grounds that they presuppose a theory-free base of observations, is the nascent omnitheoretic development. None of these views are wholly satisfactory in their extreme versions, but I shall argue that the inductivist position is at least *basically* correct in a way that the other two are not.

Actually, the omnitheoretic perspective has not as yet advanced any firm thesis about the determinants of a theory's credibility, though this movement's most dedicated spokesman, Paul Feyerabend, has been explicit in his judgment that traditional hypothetico-deductive and, presumably, inductivist accounts are untenable because they assume datum beliefs to be independent of the theories for or against which they are cited as evidence (Feyerabend, 1963). Hanson (1958) and Kuhn (1962, chap. 10) have proposed that the conceptual onset of a theory is essentially a perceptual phenomenon – i.e. that scientists do not *infer* a theory from the data, but somehow begin to *see* their data *as* an embodiment of the theory, while since these new datum-perceptions contain the theory as a presupposition, they are just not the same as the datum-perceptions which would have been made had the theory not been accepted (perceived therein). *But this is simply to claim that rational judgment does not enter into acceptance or rejection of theories at all.* For rational judgment is above all a process of inference from one proposition to another, and if the theory's acceptance or denial is given in our very basis for inference, then there is nothing further to be done – the theory's status has been settled for us before we can even start to pass judgment on it. In particular, if datum-proposition D entails (presupposes) theory T, then D can imply $\sim T$ only insofar as D is self-contradictory, in which event D is scuttled as a datum-belief and T is no more impugned than before. (Kuhn argues that scientific revolutions replace old theories with new ones when crises and tensions – i.e., data which do not fit comfortably – become too much to bear. But under the omnitheoretic view, tensions should not be able to arise in the first place.) The only way for a theory to be discarded would be for us to undergo a spontaneous (i.e. nonrational) shift of perception. Further, the mere discarding of a theory is not the same as *discomfirming* it, any more than e.g. putting aside our present system of weights and measures in favour of the metric system would be a denial of the numerical readings we took in the old units. Even if our new perceptual theory has the appearance of contradicting the old one, the omnitheoretic contention that observation-language terms change their meanings with changes in theory (cf. Feyerabend's rejection of "meaning invariance") implies that there need be no logical inconsistency between the sentence-complex T when it asserts an accepted theory and the sentence-complex $\sim T$ asserted when the theory previously expressed by T has been abandoned. Hence, not only are we unable to disconfirm accepted theories, we cannot even know that they were wrong after we have relinquished them.

The undeniable fact that scientists and laymen *do* make inferences from datum-beliefs, while any proposition to which inference is made can be construed as a "theory," shows that the omnitheoretic thesis is absurd unless severely attenuated in some way. One mandatory retreat is that datum-beliefs must be conceded neutrality with respect to at least *some* of the theories to which they are cognitively relevant. In the modified omnitheoretic view, then, the datum-perceptions D of a given scientist at a given moment carry certain theoretical commitments T_D, but any theory T whose negation is compatible with T_D can be argued for or against on the basis of D by whatever standards of inference are acceptable on non-omnitheoretic grounds. Given this reformulation, the omnitheoretic thesis becomes generically undeniable (as discussed under B1, perceptual judgments in data collection are never incorrigible in the toughest philosophic sense but always incorporate hypotheses of one sort or another), but the extent to which it advances our metatheoretic understanding of scientific knowledge is highly moot. It was pointed out earlier that when scientific controversy begins to involve questions which differentially bias the datum-perceptions (or at least the verbalized datum-statements) of an area's researchers according to their individual theoretical preconvictions, as signalled by their inability to reach consensus even on datum-statements, strong pressures arise toward development of methods for data collection and description which are, in fact, neutral with respect to the theoretical question at issue, though not necessarily so regarding presuppositions which have not as yet become controversial. Such neutrality is not easily achieved, but its pursuit is one of the primary *technical* phases of science (and hence easily obscured or left incomprehensible in commonsense descriptions of scientific activities) and the history and contemporary practice of the various sciences makes abundantly clear that through sustained effort and professional skill, the observation-language impartiality requisite to *reasoned* judgements on particular points of theoretical issue can be adequately approximated in operational reality.[30] While the omnitheoretic

---

30 I submit that if the many provocative examples of scientific "revolutions" cited by Kuhn (1962) are analysed closely, it will be seen that they either in fact did proceed or, with a little more methodological acumen, readily could have proceeded by argument based upon observational assertions mutually acceptable to all parties concerned.

thesis usefully reminds us that a naive empiricism which considers theoretical neutrality in datum-beliefs to be the natural state of primitive perception is badly misguided, and that one important mode of scientific progress is the liberation of datum-beliefs from presuppositions which have become problematic, it does nothing to illuminate how a science's observational premises support or disconfirm theories which are *not* presupposed by the science's datum basis.

We next turn to the hypothetico-deductive account of theory development. While this is the perspective which has dominated the past several decades of metascientific theory, I shall demonstrate that it fails abjectly to provide any acceptable standards for the confirmation of theory by data. According to the hypothetico-deductive thesis, how a theory T first arises – i.e., what makes its proponents first think of it – is neither relevant to its credibility nor (at least in Popper's extreme views) can be accounted for by any formal inference patterns. Once T has emerged into conscious consideration, however, it can be supported or disconfirmed through testing of its observational consequences. Specifically, let C be some observation-language proposition such that C is a logical consequence of theory T,[31] while the truth of C has not as yet been settled.[32] Then the credibility of T is enhanced if C becomes verified while, of course, T is disproved if C is shown to be false. So far, the hypothetico-deductive thesis is unassailable. Under any acceptable idealization of rational inference, if T entails C, then confirming C even probabilistically likewise increases the credibility of T. But the hypothetico-deductive account also *stops* at this point and, by thus ignoring further analysis of T, invites the inference that verification of T's consequence C increases the credibility of T *throughout* – i.e., of all of T's conjunctive components.

Acceptance of this invitation, however, would bring total disaster to the scientific enterprise. For suppose that T is a theory which entails testable consequence C, while T^* is the conjunction of T with some arbitrary hypothesis H (i.e. $T^* =_{\text{def}} T \cdot H$). Then T^* also entails C, and verification of C increases the credibility of both T and T^*. But if verification of one of a theory's consequences confirms the theory throughout, as the hypothetico-deductive thesis tacitly urges, *then confirmation of* T* *by verification of* C *strengthens the credibility of* T*'s *component* H *even though* H *has no relevance for* C. For example, let T be a theory of celestial mechanics which has as a consequence that the sun will rise tomorrow morning, while T^* is T conjoined with the hypothesis that my wife is unfaithful. Then by the hypothetico-deductive argument, the sun's rising tomorrow morning should confirm my suspicion of my wife's infidelity. By this line of reasoning, the most bizarre hypothesis can be given repeated empirical support by attaching it to a legitimate theory which has many verifiable consequences.

31 The hypothetico-deductive thesis readily extends to cases where T implies C only probabilistically. But deductive consequences are simplest to discuss and quite suffice to make my present point about this position's inadequacy.

32 Discussion of the manner in which theory T derives support from a consequence C whose truth was known prior to its derivation from T involves some technical niceties which, since they add nothing of importance to my main argument, I shall avoid by assuming that C becomes verified only after its deduction from T.

Now, while hypothetico-deductive holism *seems* to imply that affirmation of a theory's consequences indiscriminately confirms all the theory's components, the position does not actually *assert* this, nor could it do so without becoming trapped in a fundamental inconsistency. For suppose that T entails C while $T^* =_{\text{def}} T \cdot H$ and $T^{**} =_{\text{def}} T \cdot \sim H$. Then verification of C confirms both T^* and T^{**}, and if this support were to penetrate to all conjunctive components of the theories confirmed we would have a simultaneous increase in the credibilities of both H and $\sim H$, in violation of the cardinal metatheoretic rule that an increase in the credibility of any proposition must be accompanied by a decrease in the credibility of its negation. The hypothetico-deductive thesis must therefore concur with the following negative principle: *If C_1 and C_2 are both unverified deductive consequences of theory* T, *subsequent verification of C_1 necessarily increases the credibility of* T *as a whole, but need not increase – and in fact may even decrease – the credibility of C_2.* In particular, this holds when C_2 is one of the postulates whose conjunction composes T. We shall look more deeply into this situation in a moment. The immediate point is that the hypothetico-deductive argument provides no basis for distinguishing those of a theory's components which have evidential backing from those which are entirely arbitrary or are perhaps even discredited by the data. It does not help to argue that if we continue to test T's consequences long enough (say by a series of "crucial experiments"), we should eventually find one which is false if anything in T is unsound. When judging a theory's credibility, we are in possession only of these datum-beliefs which *have been* acquired, never those which *will be*, and to have any practical significance a theory of scientific inference must address itself to what can reasonably be inferred from the datum-beliefs which we in fact hold now.[33]

The analytic problem of theory confirmation, which hypothetico-deductive holism simply ignores, is thus: *If theory* T *is equivalent to the conjunction of postulates P_1, ..., P_n while C is a logical consequence of* T, *in what way does verification of C affect the credibility of postulate P_i* ($i = 1, ..., n$)? And our discussion of arbitrary additions to an otherwise sound theory, whereby one might try to confirm his paranoid suspicions of his wife's infidelity by observing the sunrise, makes evident the following descriptive/normative[34] principle: *If theory* T *can be analysed as the conjunction of postulates P_1, ..., P_n, while C is a logical consequence of P_1, ..., P_{n-1}, then the fact that* T *logically entails C is irrelevant to whether or not verification of C confirms P_n.* That is, verification of a theory's consequences can be

---

33 It is noteworthy that while Popper's version of the hypothetico-deductive position advocates bold, highly *confirmable* (corroborable) theories, where the greater the theory's logical content (i.e. factual commitments) the more confirm*able* (corroborable) it is, the degree to which a theory is actually confirm*ed* (corrobor*ated*) at any given stage of testing is inversely related to its logical content even in Popper's account. Specifically, suppose that $T_1, T_2, ..., T_i, ...$ is a series of theories such that T_1 entails C and for each i, T_{i+1} entails but is not entailed by T_i. Then by either of the two confirmation measures proposed by Popper (1959, Appendix ix), confirmation of T_i by verification of C is a decreasing function of i.

34 Descriptive in that it is a pattern by which we *do* find ourselves reasoning; normative in that we also feel that it is *right* for our beliefs to be so patterned.

trusted to confirm at most those components of the theory which actually contribute to the derivation of these consequences.

But can we then salvage the hypothetico-deductive argument by proposing that verification of T's consequence C at least confirms those theory components which are needed to deduce C from T? Even this won't help, as shown by the following partition. Let C be a consequence, or the conjunction of a set of consequences, of theory T (i.e., $\vdash T \supset C$) while R is defined

$$R =_{\text{def}} \sim(C \cdot \sim T)$$

(i.e., R denies that T is false while C is true.) Then it is easily proved that (i) T is equivalent to the conjunction of C and R (i.e., $\vdash T \equiv C \cdot R$); (ii) unless C is logically true, C is *not* a consequence of R (i.e., $\vdash R \supset C$ if and only if $\vdash C$); and (iii) R is the weakest assertion with which C can be supplemented to yield T (i.e., for any sentence S, if $\vdash C \cdot S \equiv T$, then $\vdash S \supset R$).[35] This says that given any consequence C of any theory T, T can be expressed as the conjunction of C with a residual R which is what remains of T when C is factored out. Then confirmation of T by verification of C is a trivial outcome of the fact that this confirms T's component C.[36] The scientifically significant question, however, is not whether verification of C confirms C, but whether it lends support to anything in T over and above C. (For example, if T is the hypothesis that all αs are βs while C is the datum that all αs observed so far have been βs, the problem of statistical inference is not whether C strengthens the credibility of T but whether it increases the plausibility that αs yet unobserved are also βs.) Doubly embarrassing to the hypothetico-deductive thesis is that in the $C \cdot R$ factoring of T, R is *discredited* by C under most any plausible formalization of credibility relationships.[37] Hence not only can a theory T always be conjunctively partitioned in such fashion that its only component needed to deduce its consequence C is C itself, but the credibility of T's remainder under this partition receives no support whatsoever from C's verification and is in fact generally disconfirmed by it. To be sure, this does not imply that

35 (i) and (ii) are obvious consequences of the fact that R is equivalent to $C \supset T$. (iii) follows from the fact that $S \supset R$ is equivalent to $\sim(S \cdot C \cdot \sim T)$ while the latter is equivalent to the tautology $\sim(T \cdot \sim T)$ so long as $\vdash C \cdot S \equiv T$.

36 If credibility can be represented by a probability measure, so that $\Pr(T)$, $\Pr(R)$ and $\Pr(C)$ are the probabilities (credibilities) of theory T and its components R and C, respectively, prior to verification of C, while $\Pr(T|C)$ and $\Pr(R|C)$ are the respective probabilities (credibilities) of T and R upon verification of C, we have $\Pr(T) = \Pr(C \cdot R) = \Pr(C) \times \Pr(R|C)$ while $\Pr(T|C) = \Pr(C \cdot R \mid C) = \Pr(R|C)$. Hence verification of C increases the credibility of T from $\Pr(T)$ to $\Pr(T|C)$ merely by replacing $\Pr(C)$ with unity.

37 Since $\Pr(R) = 1 - \Pr(\sim R) = 1 - \Pr(C \cdot \sim T) = 1 - \Pr(C) \times \Pr(\sim T|C)$ while $\Pr(R|C) = \Pr(R \cdot C \mid C) = \Pr(T|C) = 1 - \Pr(\sim T|C)$, we have $\Pr(R|C) - \Pr(R) = -\Pr(\sim T|C)[1 - \Pr(C)] = -\Pr(\sim C) \times \Pr(\sim T|C) \leq 0$. Hence the probability (credibility) of R, given C, is less than the prior probability (credibility) of C unless either C conclusively verifies T or C's prior probability (credibility) is zero, in which case $\Pr(R|C) = \Pr(R)$.

verifying T's consequence C never confirms anything in T beyond C itself, but it does make clear that so long as C is entailed by T, the confirmation of T by C may well be inferentially misleading. Only when some component P of T has been identified which is confirmed by T's consequence C even though P does *not* entail C – in fact, only when neither C nor P entails an uncertain component of the other[38] – do we have evidence that verification of C gives any epistemically *signficant* support to T. That verification of C is, in fact, often felt to confirm some such P in cases where C and P are ingredients of a tightly knit theory is undeniable, but the hypothetico-deductive account of nondemonstrative inference gives no clue whatsoever about the principles governing this flow of credibility.

The juncture at which we have now arrived is this: Two scientific propositions P and C are often so related that verification of C increases the credibility of P even when C is *not* a logical consequence of P or conversely; and the foremost methatheoretical problem of scientific inference is, for now, simply to *learn* what patterns of propositional relationship effect this sort of credibility coupling. It is altogether possible – perhaps even necessary – that such a connection between P and C involves a mediating theory T of which both P and C are consequences. (That is, while the confirmation of P by C is a *sign* that C confirms T nontrivially, what is given significant confirmation most immediately by C is in all likelihood something in T which implies C and from which P also follows.) However, our preceding argument has shown that for this to occur the relations among C, T and P must be more specific than *merely* the joint entailment of C and P by T. The problem would be obviated if there existed a satisfactory theory of propositional probability (or credibility) which supplied a computable unconditional probability (credibility) number for every proposition constructable in the science's language. We could then compute $\Pr(P|C)$ $(=\Pr(P \cdot C)/\Pr(C))$ and $\Pr(P)$ and know not merely whether or not C confirms P but also, more importantly, exactly how much credence to invest in P upon verification of C. Despite the massive attention which probability theory has received within the past century by statisticians and philosophers, however, the only developments which have come within shouting distance of a practical theory of propositional probability are essentially confined to inferences about probability parameters (and whatever can in turn be inferred from these) based on sample frequency distribution; while to my knowledge no one has even begun to explore probability measures over theories which postulate non-observational entities. Over much – perhaps all – of the domain of non-demonstrative inference it seems less likely that propositional probability theory will furnish the grounds for drawing inferences from datum-beliefs as that will be a purification and unfolding of certain primitive induction patterns which are either themselves presupposed in the theory's axiomatic basis or are taken as criteria against which the theory's adequacy is assessed. That is, if verification of C confirms P, the explanation for this is not likely to be found in a more fundamental fact that $\Pr(P|C) >$

---

38 If both C and P have a common implicate H, each can be written as the conjunction of H with a residual. Hence verification of C includes verification of H, and if $\Pr(H) < 1$, confirmation of P through verification of C may be no more than a trivial result of verifying P's component H.

$\Pr(P)$; instead the latter is most probably *due to* the former while the reason *why* C confirms P must be dug out of the structural relations between P and C. If so, the inductivist thesis has won the day.

The essential tenet of an inductivist interpretation of scientific inference is that there are, in fact, descriptive/normative formal patterns by which belief flows from one proposition (or set of propositions) to others not logically entailed by the former. If such patterns exist, they may be expected to guide datum-beliefs toward conclusions which complete the gestalt; hence inductivists are disposed to admit of a "logic of discovery" as well as of a "logic of confirmation." But the inductivist thesis does not require that all inductive conclusions be called to mind by the evidence which supports them. It insists only that no matter what causes the conclusion to be first thought of, its plausibility follows from recognition (perhaps intuitively, without explicit awareness) of its inductive relation to the evidence. What differentiates this from hypothetico-deductivism is that (*a*) inductivists, unlike hypothetico-deductive partisans, are disposed to look favourably upon the possible existence of a logic of discovery; and (*b*) inductivists are prepared to find that the relation between an inductively justified conclusion and its evidence depends upon logical structure a great deal more specific than mere entailment.

The state of contemporary theory on inductive logic is far too involved for me to say much about it here beyond that we still have a long, long way to go.[39] But it is perhaps not altogether misleading to summarize this work as consisting almost exclusively of attempted justification, reconstruction, and enrichment of the primitive inference schema of *statistical induction*. In brief, statistical induction is a projection of the pattern of things already known upon our expectations about things yet unencountered. Thus if $p\%$ of observed αs have been βs, we infer by statistical induction that probably about $p\%$ of αs still forthcoming will also be βs. So characterized, this inference form is not completely general – in ways which are still distressingly obscure its intuitive applicability depends upon additional features of the projected pattern and the nature of the entities involved, so that artificial examples can easily be constructed in which the formal induction schema yields painfully counterintuitive conclusions (see Goodman, 1955). Even so, until very recently this was the only inductive argument form known to abstract metascience; in fact, throughout much of philosophy and logic the term "induction" is synonymous with "statistical induction." Unfortunately, statistical induction appears hopelessly inadequate to confer credibility upon hypotheses more complex than mere statistical generalizations,[40] which is one reason why the inductivist position has

---

39 For a valuable review of recent developments, see Kyberg (1964).

40 The hypothetico-deductive argument can be construed as a special case of statistical induction if we reason that insomuch as all the consequences of theory T tested so far have been verified, all its remaining consequences are probably also sound. In fact, I suspect that this way of looking at the matter does occasionally have force in real-life theory assessments. However, statistical induction from the truth of tested consequences of T to the truth of yet untested consequences of T is marginal at best with respect to the intuitive restrictions (notably, something akin to "randomness" in the selection of observed cases) requisite for statistical induction to feel convincing.

seemed simple-minded to many philosophers.[41] I have recently been able to show, however, that at least some inferences to unobserved (theoretical$_{B1}$) entities are governed by a standard induction form in which an observed property of a class as a whole is transformed into an inferred attribute ascribed to each member of the class (Rozeboom, 1961) – though again, as in statistical induction, the intuitive acceptability of the argument requires special conditions whose nature is unclear. That this is the only route by which we come to believe in underlying entities is most unlikely (in fact, see Rozeboom, 1966, p. 208ff.); what is metatheoretically funda-mental is that argument forms by which propositions incorporating theoretical$_{B1}$ concepts originate and command observational support – i.e. patterns of *ontological induction* – do, in fact, exist. Hence there is no good reason to discount the possi-bility that *all* varieties of plausible inference, including justification for some of the most recondite and observationally remote components of scientific theories, in-stantiate one or another of certain determinate induction forms.

From this absurdly inadequate survey of the grounds for theory credibility, two implications nonetheless emerge which have major significance for practical theor-izing in psychology. The first is that with the partial exception of inferences about statistical parameters, there still exist no accredited standards of non-demonstra-tive inference to which we can turn for normative assistance when judging the plausibility of a particular psychological theory. Not only are we strictly on our own in this respect, with no sagacious metatheoretical father-figure standing behind us to beam approval for our right thinking and gently correct our inferential errors, we have a double responsibility for special care in our evaluations of theories both to avoid inappropriate belief on the theory's own account *and* to provide instances of inductive arguments which have passed the test of detailed appraisal by profes-sionally polished sensitivities in order that metatheory may eventually abstract from these the patterns which count as sound inference. Secondly, we have seen that a theory cannot properly be accepted or rejected holistically, but that the available evidence gives each of its conjunctive components its own separate degree of credibility. In particular, a detachable component of the theory which has no implications for any of the data upon which the theory rests is unlikely under natural circumstances to draw much support from these data, though neither can this possibility be altogether excluded. This is the situation I had in mind when I contrasted *warranted* theory with *speculative* theory in part I, though the distinc-tion is best conceived as a continuum rather than a dichotomy and applies more usefully to the various components within a given theory rather than to the theory as a whole. To state the point once more, if theory T is analysed as a conjunction of premises $P_1, ..., P_n$ – and it is important to realize that there are many alterna-tive ways to perform such a logical partition, some of which may have little resem-blance to the conjunctive organization in which the theory is first conceived – then even if all the evidence, D, available so far is logically consistent with T and per-haps even includes verification of certain initially implausible consequences of T, the credibility given by D to T's component P_i may range anywhere from near-certainty (a highly *warranted* inference from D) through indifference to D (i.e.,

41 See, e.g. Wisdom (1952), and Bunge (1963).

$\Pr(P_i|D) \simeq \Pr(P_i)$, in which case, unless P_i's prior probability is high, P_i is still *speculative*) down to the possibility that P_i is highly unreasonable in light of D.

Now, a serious danger from theories whose components are not confirmationally homogeneous with respect to present or immediately portending evidence is that unless each component's contribution to the theory's datum-entailments is made explicit, we shall inevitably find our theoretical beliefs grossly misaligned with what our own good judgment would dictate were we but able to apply it. In particular, hypothetico-deductive holism encourages us both to accept untested, irrelevant or implausible components of a theory which has successfully accounted for the major research findings in its area of application so far, especially if the theory has brought off some unexpected predictions, and to scorn theories containing some conspicuously untenable or distasteful ingredient which in fact is no more than a superfluous embellishment on premises which service the theory's actual work load.[42] I contend that most psychological theories *do*, in fact, suffer badly from this intellectual malady, and that those portions of theories which carry the colour, excitement and challenge of a particular psychological perspective seldom have much overlap with those portions which are sustained by evidential support.

If my argument for the credibility partitioning of theories is accepted, what then? Well for one, it goes a long way toward resolving the sometimes bitter metatheoretical polarity which now exists over the role of theory in psychological science. It is no secret that many psychologists who consider the goal of science to be the attainment of *knowledge* deplore theories about the underlying sources of overt behaviour as tantamount to mysticism and fantasy, or disown their own theoretical contributions by characterizing them as "models" whose only function is to describe and perhaps occasionally predict empirical regularities. But the *credibility* contrast between warranted and speculative theory components must not be confused with the observational/theoretical contrast in *perceptual accessibility*. A presumptive empirical generalization can exceed its evidential basis just as wildly as can a speculation about unobservables, whereas the truly relevant components in a theory about the underlying sources of some empirical phenomenon may have as strong an inductive warrant as any statistical generalization at the datum level. On the other hand, insomuch as inquiry which does not seek to replace speculation and surmise with a harder intellectual coinage is unworthy of scientific respect, no theory component is exempt from the harsh credibility tests at which professional scientists, including research psychologists, have become adept, and until a theory has been stripped of its fat and flourishes down to an austere core which is *demanded* (i.e., strongly confirmed) by extant data it well deserves the second-class cognitive status which hard-nosed empiricists are disposed to grant it.[43] This is not to contend that speculative theorizing has no place in science. Quite the opposite – imagination, hunches, and inspired guessing remain a highway to the novel empirical discoveries without which scientific knowledge would remain static. But

---

42 This point has been nicely emphasized by Deutsch (1960), chap. 1.

43 Thus one can wholeheartedly accept the spirit of Turner's (1961) distinction between "Type I" (scientifically respectable) and "Type II" (scientifically disreputable) conjectures while protesting his co-ordination of it with the observational/theoretical distinction.

it still remains essential to distinguish what is, in fact, well confirmed from what *might* possibly be true.

In addition to urging metatheoretical conciliation over the scientific respectability of theories, recognition that a theory is usually a very mixed bag of credibilities calls for an essentially new approach to practical theory development. So far as the theory's initial creation is concerned, anything goes – though statistical and ontological inductions from known data will undoubtedly remain a primary source of inspiration, preoccupation with plausibility in the discovery phase of theory building will only inhibit imagination. But once a set of premises has been found which successfully accommodate the available evidence, it is a waste of time and intellectual energy to take a stance on the global acceptability of these premises, or to set about testing the theory-as-a-whole in traditionally indiscriminate hypothetico-deductive fashion. The efficient procedure is to do a metatheoretical dissection of the theory in order to see what specific function is served by each of its ingredients, both for explaining extant data and for prediction of other phenomena relevant to research interests in this area. I know of no analytic routine which will parse a theory along lines having the greatest epistemic perspicuity, but the separable components disclosed in the theory by skillful factoring should fall roughly into four main categories: (1) Premises which, through statistical or ontological induction, are highly confirmed by present evidence. (2) Premises which entail and in turn are inductively implied by certain tentative empirical regularities whose confirmation by the extant data is still spotty. (3) Premises which have no relevance for the data obtained so far but do have significant implications for (and hence confirmational ties to) potentially demonstrable phenomena lying within this research area's range of concern. (4) Premises which are relevant only to possible phenomena lying outside of this research area's scope. For example, suppose that a theory (or "model") under consideration as a possible interpretation of certain learning phenomena presupposes that all subjects in the population studied have the same value of a certain theoretical parameter τ. If it turns out that only the population mean on τ makes a discernible difference for what the theory implies should happen when background conditions or procedures are standardized as in the experiments conducted so far, but that the population variance on τ is importantly related to how certain alterations in these background conditions should affect the phenomena under study, then the premise that $\mathrm{Var}(\tau) = 0$ is a Class 3 component of this theory. On the other hand, if the theory explains these phenomena in terms of a hypothesized physiological mechanism, the theory's implications for overt behaviour would be unaffected if it were cut back to postulation merely that *something* of unspecified nature is functionally related to the data variables in the manner assumed by the physiological hypothesis. Consequently, the theory's further premise that the underlying mechanism which manifests these functional properties also has such-and-such a physiological constitution has import only for certain types of physiological observation which are of no concern for psychology as such (though of course it is perfectly legitimate for psychologists to have physiological curiosities as well) and is hence a Class 4 component of the theory so long as the latter's intent is only to account for psychological phenomena.

While the various categories of theory components obviously shade off into one another, each has its own distinctive cognitive and methodological status. Classes 1 and 2 compose *warranted* theory, with Class 1 propositions constituting what may be thought of as "scientific knowledge" while Class 2 hypotheses are reasonable but still tentative conclusions which require further substantiation before they can aspire to knowledge stature. Theory components in Classes 3 and 4, on the other hand, are fatty *speculation* deposits within the theory's cognitive muscle. No matter how amusing, provocative, or comforting these may seem in the private meditations of individual scientists, they lay no serious claims to credibility and thus have no place in the science's public pronouncements. However, Class 3 speculations differ importantly from those in Class 4 in that the former generally direct attention to previously unsuspected dimensions of the phenomenon under study (even though research on this new aspect of the problem will more likely than not disprove the conjecture which led to its investigation), whereas Class 4 speculations are a froth of irrelevancies which give the theory spurious bulk. To be sure, as the science broadens the scope of its interests or as new fields of study spring up in interdisciplinary lacunae, a Class 4 hypothesis may receive Class 3 reassignment and acquire an outside chance of eventually graduating to *warranted* status. But it is intellectually fraudulent for a theory to include detachable premises which make a diffference only for some extraneous area in which the theory's proponents undertake no serious research responsibilities.

The practical desirability of identifying the implicative/confirmational status of a theory's assorted components should be evident. Fundamentally, it is simply a matter of keeping possibilities in their proper credibility perspective. Speculative fantasies should not be allowed to usurp assent by riding piggyback on well-confirmed inductions, nor should our recognition of the latter be in turn undermined through implausibility-by-association. In particular, it is unprofessional to bicker over the holistic merits of a given theory when its advocates are justifiably impressed with its Class 1 and Class 2 contents while its critics justifiably distrust its Class 3 assumptions and scorn its Class 4 pretentions. An important corollary for theory-guided research is that only if the theory in question has been analysed in the way here envisioned can we have much assurance that our experimental program to test and correct the theory yields data which are relevant to the points ostensibly at issue – and if not, what they *are* relevant to. Little is to be learned, for example, from continuing to verify consequences of the theory which follow from premises which, upon analysis, can be seen to have already been highly confirmed (though of course there is always a fair chance that soft spots may appear even in Class 1 conclusions); while if the heat of theoretical controversy centres around the Class 4 nature of underlying mechanisms, verification of consequences derived from Class 3 hypotheses fused with the former in the theory's original formulation will not help to resolve the dispute even though these findings may well break open vital new dimensions of warranted theory in this area. Similarly, a perceptive articulation of the inferential relations between a theory's variegated premises and the observations they subsume is essential to effective modification of the theory with accumulating evidence. Contrary to hypothetico-deductive holism, which sees a theory's evolution as a sequence of *de novo* inspirations in which every revision arises from the shambles of its disconfirmed predecessors by a new act of creative discovery, each separate slug of empirical evidence has its own specific target within the theory where it strikes with confirmational or disconfirmational impact, and the growth of scientific knowledge is a continual accretion of local additions and corrections, any one of which leaves the warranted components of theory in this area largely unaltered.[44] It would be most unfortunate if, say, experimental disproof of some of a theory's Class 3 conjectures were to be construed as evidence against Class 2 premises from which the former can be detached, especially if this were to terminate research designed to firm up the inductive basis for the latter. More generally, it is important to know whether a disconfirmatory research outcome conflicts with the theory's Class 1 or Class 2 components and hence violates the pattern of events that seemed to be emerging from previous data, or whether what has been discredited is merely a speculation which was never much more than a cognitively arbitrary if aesthetically appealing guess in the first place.

Of course, the most seemly research attitude is one in which we are aware of the alternative theoretical possibilities hovering behind the known phenomena in the area under investigation, and appreciate their various implications for observations yet unmade, but feel no special partiality toward any particular one of the competing prospects. This has always been the empiricist research ideal, but as attested in our recent history by the emphasis placed upon hypothesis testing in graduate research instruction, it is downgraded[45] by the hypothetico-deductive outlook and often seems to conflict with our felt need for understanding which goes deeper than mere surface generalizations. The contemporary surge of interest in "models," with its repudiation of the personal involvement that "theories" seem to demand, is a commendable move back toward old fashioned open-minded neutrality, but it, too, shirks its intellectual responsibilities by failing to distinguish between what in the model is really true and what is just pretend. Given an appropriate implicative/confirmational factoring of a theory's propositional content, however, the proper balance between commitment and impartiality should emerge more or less automatically upon realization that the speculative components of theory can be manipulated – or ignored – with as much zest, playfulness or disdain as suits one's mood without insult to one's dedicated conviction, if it comes to that, in those aspects of the theory which have genuine evidential support. Class 3 conjectures are then no longer bastions of emotional allegiance to be attacked or defended by all-

---

44 While Kuhn (1962) has argued persuasively for the *revolutionary* character of major advances in scientific theory, I am prepared to argue that genuine upheavals of foundations seldom if ever occur. My contention is that the body of accumulated data inductively determines a logical structure which, within limits, must be embedded within any theory adequate to subsume these data, and that Kuhn-type "revolutions" are for the most part shifts in the Class 3 and Class 4 speculations with which this structure is fleshed out – though such a shift may well require a psychologically revolutionary conceptual overhaul while the pressure to revolution may come from data which undermine the Class 3 components of the old theory even as they support Class 2 components in its successor.

45 For a remarkable exhibition of this attitude, see Medawar (1964). Fortunately, the hypothesis-testing bias in psychological research now appears to be on the wane.

or-none hypothesis-testing experiments, but become expendable roadmaps to parametric studies that enrich, rather than convulse, the explanatory framework within which our research is conceived.

Coda

What should a psychological theory be? It should be *analysed* – exactingly, sensitively, and exhaustively.

III   THE CONCEPTUAL STRUCTURE OF BEHAVIOUR THEORY: SOME FRAGMENTS

In this section, I shall discuss a number of current and recent conceptions of behaviour mechanisms. While these analyses demonstrate at the substantive level the sorts of metatheoretical concerns abstractly advocted above, the significance of each lies foremost in what it says in its own right, and only incidentally in its role as an illustration for the precepts of part II. The particular cases to be examined, none of which will be developed in as much detail as would be desirable in more expansive circumstances, fall into three groups: (A) the now-classic behaviour theories of Hull and Tolman; (B) mediation-response hypotheses; and (C) contemporary theories of response emission.

A1   All behaviour theories contain one or more classes of constructs which hypothesize states of the organism by whose intervention past experience influences present responding. For the sake of theoretical neutrality, let us call such states "experience residues." In Hullian theory the major experience-residue construct category is *habit*, while in Tolmanian theory it is *expectancy*;[46] and it is most instructive to observe how the *structural* differences between Hullian habits and Tolmanian expectancies make a difference for what can be done with them conceptually.

For both Hull and Tolman, a specific experience residue is a variable whose argument (i.e., entity to which it applies) is a particular organism at a particular time, and whose value is a particular degree of strength. That is, the grammatical form (at one level of analysis) of a habit or expectancy ascription is "organism o has experience-residue X in strength s at time t." Moreover, both habits and expectancies are identified in terms of stimuli and responses;[47] where they differ is in

---

46   I describe these as the *major* experience-residue categories in these systems because both contain others as well; conditioned drive and reinforcement dispositions in Hull, and experience-modifiable cathexes (and others?) in Tolman.

47   That the concepts of "stimulus" and "response" are not technically well defined is notorious. I shall here do nothing to alleviate this unclarity, for the present metatheoretical contrasts hold irrespective of *what* stimuli and responses may be. It would of course, be possible for Hullians and Tolmaniacs to disagree over the membership of the S and R categories, but this would be a point of controversy altogether distinct from the structural differences between these two systems in their experience-residue constructs.

the *formal complexity* by which the experience-residue constructs are character-ized. Specifically, let $\mathbf{S} = \{S_i\}$ and $\mathbf{R} = \{R_j\}$ be the sets of all potential stimuli and all potential responses, respectively. (For technical convenience $\mathbf{S}$ and $\mathbf{R}$ are both construed to contain a null-element.) Then in Hullian theory, to each combination of an element S_i in $\mathbf{S}$ with an element R_j in $\mathbf{R}$ there corresponds a "habit" variable S_iR_j (or "$_{s_i}H_{R_j}$" in Hull's notation) which organism o has in some strength s (possibly zero) at time t; whereas in Tolmanian theory, as clarified by MacCorquo-dale and Meehl (1954) with Tolman's (1959) blessing, to each ordered pair of elements S_i and S_k in $\mathbf{S}$ and an element R_j in $\mathbf{R}$ there corresponds an "expectancy" variable $S_iR_jS_k$ which o has in strength s at time t. (Note that habits and expectan-cies are theoretical constructs identified *in terms of* stimuli and responses, not *with* them.) Thus the set of all Hullian habits is in one-one correspondence with the product-set $\mathbf{S} \times \mathbf{R}$, while the set of all Tolmanian expectancies is in one-one cor-respondence with the product-set $\mathbf{S} \times \mathbf{R} \times \mathbf{S}$. Clearly, then, even before a single proposition is framed in these theories and persisting throughout any modifications of specific postulates, Tolmanian expectancies have a more complex formal struc-ture and hence a higher order of conceptual potency than do Hullian habits. For $S_iR_jS_k$ can be made to do anything that S_iR_j can simply by ignoring S_k or letting it be the null-element of $\mathbf{S}$,[48] whereas any principle of behaviour which discrimi-nates between $S_iR_jS_k$ and $S_iR_jS_h$ – i.e. between expectancies which differ only in their third term – is beyond the logical capabilities of formulation in terms of S_iR_j, though, as discussed below, it is possible to *enrich* Hullian theory to the point where it contains a conceptual structure essentially isomorphic to expectancy $S_iR_jS_k$.

To be sure, the extent to which the structural *potential* of a concept is in fact utilized depends upon the particular patterns of inference it is allowed to mediate. E.g. if none of the premises of expectancy theory were to let an expectancy's third term make a difference for how it functions, the formal superiority of expectancies over habits would be lost. Let us, therefore, briefly consider what Tolmanian theory does with expectancies which cannot be done with Hullian habits. As a preliminary, we note that the primary way in which a habit S_iR_j gains strength is for the organ-ism to have experiences in which he does R_j in the presence (or shortly after the occurrence) of stimulus S_i followed by drive reduction, whereas an expectancy $S_iR_jS_k$ is strengthened primarily by the organism's emission of R_j in the presence of S_i followed by an experience of S_k. Then the functional difference between habit S_iR_j and expectancy $S_iR_jS_k$ is that while both Hullian and Tolmanian theories allow S_k to influence what organism o learns from the sequence of events, onset of S_i : emission of R_j : onset of S_k, at the time when learning occurs, notably when S_k produces reinforcement (drive reduction) for habit S_iR_j, expectancy $S_iR_jS_k$, unlike

---

48 Unlike Hullian theory, expectancy theory as formulated by Tolman does not adequately handle reflexive responding. This can, however, be treated as a special case of expectancy behaviour by assuming that reflex $S_i \rightarrow R_j$ corresponds to an expectancy $S_iR_jS_o$ in which S_o is the null-stimulus and has special valence properties. (Combined with the expectancy-integration principle – see below – this line of argument has to be developed delicately if it is to avoid counterintuitive implications, but formally it seems to be workable.)

habit S_iR_j, maintains in o's present state a counterpart of the specific stimulus S_k which followed the co-occurrence of S_i and R_j in o's past and hence provides a mechanism by which the *present* significance of S_k for o can also make a difference for o's present responding to S_i. Tolmanian theory capitalizes upon this potential through two basic assumptions, one of which concerns the specificity of motivation while the other allows for integration of expectancies acquired piecemeal.

The motivational premise is that given a fixed non-zero strength of $S_iR_jS_k$ and stimulation by S_i, the tendency of o to emit R_j is an increasing function of the "valence" S_k now has for o (MacCorquodale and Meehl, 1954, p. 246), where this valence is determined by o's present motivational condition in ways which need not concern us here except for noting that valences generally vary independently of one another. This activation postulate is the counterpart of Hull's premise concerning the effect of drive upon reaction potential (i.e., that given a fixed non-zero strength of S_iR_j and stimulation by S_i, the tendency to do R_j is an increasing function of D) except for the crucial difference that Hullian D activates all habits simultaneously – and it is important to appreciate that even if Hullian theory were to admit more than one kind of drive, as hinted in Postulate V.D. of the 1951–2 system, the habit construct provides no conceptual means by which these could be *selective* in what habits they activate – whereas in Tolmanian theory, present motivational determinants can discriminate one expectancy from another on the basis of their third terms so that, e.g., given fixed non-zero strengths of $S_iR_aS_j$ and $S_iR_bS_k$, the likelihood that o will emit R_a rather than R_b when stimulated by S_i can in principle be made as small or as large as we please by motivational operations which differentially adjust the valences of S_j and S_k.

The Tolmanian learning-integration principle is that o's strength of expectancy $S_iR_aR_bS_k$ (where R_aR_b is the act of doing R_a followed by R_b) is an increasing function of the joint strengths of o's expectancies $S_iR_aS_j$ and $S_jR_bS_k$, regardless of how the latter have been established.[49] Thus if o acquires $S_iR_aS_j$ through experiencing S_j as a result of doing R_a in the presence of S_i, and subsequently, on occasions when S_j arises by means other than o's doing R_a, builds expectancy $S_jR_bS_k$ through experiencing S_k upon emission of R_b, o thereby also derives the integrated expectancy $S_iR_aR_bS_k$ even though he has never had an actual experience in which doing first R_a and then R_b in the presence of S_i was followed by S_k. This is the mechanism[50] by which expectancy theory assimilates the broad class of "latent learning" phenomena which I have elsewhere (Rozeboom, 1958) called *conditioned generalization*. There can be no corresponding habit-integration principle in Hullian theory for the simple reason that a habit system's logical structure does not provide the formal linkages among habits through which their sequential concatenation becomes conceptually possible.

To be sure, it is well known that through liberal application of mediation-

---

49 This is a stronger version of MacCorquodale and Meehl's (1954) Postulate 4, p. 242, in which R_b is needlessly restricted to the null response.

50 Actually, this integration principle is to a large extent redundant in its empirical consequences with MacCorquodale and Meehl's (1954) cathexis-learning Postulates 6–8, p. 244.

response hypotheses, Hullian theory professes to account for the same (alleged) empirical phenomena implied by Tolmanian theory. Instructive as it would be to analyse these arguments in detail, space precludes this here.[51] We can, however, give thought to how closely the formal properties of an expectancy $S_iR_jS_k$ can be approximated by a Hullian mechanism. What is needed is some learnable state of the organism formally isomorphic to a contingency of S_k upon R_j given S_i. Now apart from conditioned drive and reinforcement dispositions, which offer no additional prospects here, the only states of the Hullian organism which correspond to experiential contingencies are S-R habits; hence a Hullian counterpart for expectancy $S_iR_jS_k$ must be a habit whose stimulus term represents the co-occurrence of S_i and R_j while its response term represents stimulus S_k. (At least this is true of the 1943 theory – we shall consider the 1951–2 system later.) This demands first of all an enrichment of Hullian theory which allows stimuli or their surrogates to act like responses, and conversely. However, the means for accomplishing this are familiar to all contemporary behaviour theorists: we hypothesize that (i) every different response, overt or covert, gives rise to distinctive sensory feedback, and that (ii) every different perceived stimulus is accompanied by a distinctive response, the nature of which need not be specified but can if desired be construed as a perceptual orientation unique to that stimulus.[52] Then it may be postulated that when the organism has experiences in which stimulus S_k results from doing R_j in the presence of S_i, the stimulus complex comprising the stimulus concomitants of S_i (including in particular, besides S_i itself, the sensory feedback from S_i's response correlate) together with the sensory feedback from R_j becomes conditioned to the response correlate of S_k – and the resultant habit construct has the same formal structure as Tolmanian expectancy $S_iR_jS_k$.

Even so, there still remains the task of putting the structure of this Hullian expectancy-counterpart to work in principles which do the same job as the Tolmanian activation and integration postulates. The fact that our expectancy-counterpart is a *habit* poses complications here, for it does not automatically follow that entrenched Hullian laws governing the acquisition and behavioural consequences of habits yield, or are even compatible with, the activation and integration principles needed to make an enriched Hullian theory equipollent to Tolmanian expectancy theory. Actually, apart from secondary though by no means trivial complications which will be overlooked here,[53] the integration of Hullian expectancy-counterparts can be managed not too implausibly. In overview, the argument is that if a major part of the total stimulation which consistently accompanies S_k is the sensory feedback s_k from S_k's response correlate r_k, then the effect of S_k on organism o

51 Critical examination of S–R mediational hypotheses has been remarkably scanty in the literature, but significant contributions to this task have been made by Deutsch (1956), Ritchie (1959), and especially Treisman (1960).

52 The word "every" may be dropped from these hypotheses so long as particular instances of them can be adopted at will.

53 These "secondary complications" concern discrimination learning and stimulus patterning, and are too involved for discussion in a few sentences.

should by and large be similar to the effect of s_k even when the peripheral S_k is lacking; hence any habit in which r_k is the response term thereby contains the potential for arousing S_k's effect on o in the absence of the external S_k. Differential activation of Hullian expectancy-counterparts, on the other hand is more difficult to bring off effectively. What is needed is a way for the current motivational significance of a response's conditioned sensory consequences to modulate the organism's tendency to emit that response. There are a variety of mechanisms which can be hypothesized to accomplish this, though none remain very convincing when probed deeply (an action which, however, is not considered good form in S-R theory). One which has some technical interest is the following: Suppose that organism o repeatedly experiences S_k after doing R_j in the presence of S_i, while s_k is the feedback from S_k's response correlate r_k. Then r_k will become conditioned to the stimulus complex comprising S_i plus the feedback s_j from R_j; and if we can get the sequence $S_i + s_j : r_k : s_k$ to run off rapidly enough for s_k to occur while S_i or its trace still persists and R_j is still going on (if needed, we can hypothesize that s_k is conditioned to the feedback from just the beginning of R_j), the connection $S_i + s_k \rightarrow R_j$ should eventually become established – i.e., the compound of S_i plus the feedback from S_k's response correlate should acquire some control over response R_j. Then if an operation which in Tolmanian theory gives positive valence to S_k in expectancy $S_i R_j S_k$ can here be conjectured to maintain a standing activation of s_k, notably when r_k and hence s_k are aroused by stimuli resulting from a distinctive drive condition to which S_k is relevant, this operation will enhance o's tendency to do R_j as soon as he encounters S_i. In particular, if S_1 is a choice-point stimulus in whose presence R_a has previously led o to S_2 while R_b has led to S_3, we can in this way argue for o's acquisition of habits $S_1 + s_2 \rightarrow R_a$ and $S_1 + s_3 \rightarrow R_b$, in virtue of which a drive operation which arouses s_2 but not s_3 (or conversely) should result in o's doing R_a rather than R_b (or conversely) at choice point S_1.[54] It should be added however, that the present activation mechanism is not altogether congruent with the one previously suggested for integration, insomuch as the latter requires a habit $S_i + s_j \rightarrow r_k$ in which S_i plus the feedback s_j from R_j (or from a fractional part of R_j) arouses r_k and hence s_k, whereas for activation we have here proposed that $S_i + s_k$ arouses R_j. An alternative activation mechanism based on $S_i + s_j \rightarrow r_k$ which

54 The activation mechanism considered here is quite similar to one proposed seriously by Hull (1952, p. 138f.) and Spence (1951, p. 278f.), except that the Hull-Spence hypothesis envisions representational goal reactions becoming differentially conditioned to stimuli which arise only after the organism orients toward one or the other of the choice-alternatives, and is hence vulnerable – as the present version is not – to the criticisms raised by Deutsch (1956) and Treisman (1960) concerning why on the test trials the organism should orient one way rather than another to begin with and how he can correct his orientation if he starts with the wrong one. (However, the Deutsch-Treisman difficulty can be surmounted within the Hullian framework by a scanning mechanism of the sort described on p. 133f., below.) The present activation mechanism does not, however, avoid more general difficulties resulting from an awkward overabundance of mediational habits which the Hullian account should have to admit (cf. Ritchie, 1959, p. 4).

has come to the fore in recent developments within the Hullian tradition will be examined in subsection c1, below.

A2 While our reflections on the formal properties of expectancies are still fresh in mind, I shall grasp the opportunity to protest against the prevalent misconception that Tolmanian expectancies are *beliefs*, or dispositions thereto. This way of characterizing his experience residues was certainly congenial to Tolman himself (e.g. Tolman, 1959), and has been emphasized by George and Handlon (1957). Yet in MacCorquodale and Meehl's reconstruction of expectancies, which Tolman accepted with grace and gratitude, it would be grossly misleading to speak of these as being or giving rise to "beliefs" for the simple reason that expectancies and their consequences lack the logical structure required of beliefs.

To begin, it should be mentioned that Tolman, and after him MacCorquodale and Meehl, distinguish between the experience residue $S_iR_jS_k$ (called an "expectancy" by MacCorquodale and Meehl but a "means-ends readiness" by Tolman) which persists in the organism even when stimulus S_i is not actually present, and the activated internal process $s_ir_js_k$ (the actual "expectancy" for Tolman, an "expectant" for MacCorquodale and Meehl) to which a non-zero-strength $S_iR_jS_k$ gives rise when prompted by stimulation from S_i. However, (i) $S_iR_jS_k$ and $s_ir_js_k$ are identified in terms of the very same stimulus and response elements, (ii) MacCorquodale and Meehl do not mention expectant $s_ir_js_k$ at all in their postulates for expectancy theory and hence give it no functional properties, and (iii) it is the enduring $S_iR_jS_k$ which is called a "belief" by Tolman and George and Handlon. Hence I shall concentrate on the possible belief-status of expectancy (means-ends readiness) $S_iR_jS_k$ and mention the activated expectant $s_ir_js_k$ only parenthetically.

The reason why expectancy $S_iR_jS_k$ is so often construed as a "belief" is that it seems to call for translation as the proposition "if R_j when S_i, then S_k." But there are two good reasons why this reading is inacceptable as expectancy theory now stands. The first is that "S_i", "R_j" and "S_k" – e.g., "hearing a buzz," "turning left," and "encountering food" – are *predicate* expressions which designate attributes, not states of affairs (see Rozeboom, 1960). Hence "if R_j when S_i, then S_k" is only a propositional *schema* and cannot become a believable *proposition* until its argument-variables are either replaced by subject terms or are bound by logical quantifiers. Thus it is logically impossible for $S_iR_jS_k$ (and similarly $s_ir_js_k$) to be a belief until further propositional detail is specified. Secondly, expectancy theory has provided no satisfactory way to associate a *propositional attitude* with $S_iR_jS_k$ or $s_ir_js_k$. A person's entertainment of an honest-to-god proposition p is characterized on the one hand by the intensity (i.e., vividness) with which he is thinking p, and on the other by the mode (propositional attitude) in which he is considering it – i.e., believing, disbelieving, wondering about, desiring, contemplating, non-judgmentally appreciating (as when p is encountered in a work of fiction), etc. If, as seems most reasonable, we interpret $s_ir_js_k$'s degree of activation as intensity of thought, while the strength of $S_iR_jS_k$ is what determines the degree to which $s_ir_js_k$ is activated when S_i is presented, extant expectancy theory provides no way to tag $S_iR_jS_k$ or $s_ir_js_k$ with a propositional attitude. On the other hand, if the strength of expectancy $S_iR_jS_k$ is interpreted as degree of belief, we have no provision for the belief's vividness nor for the other dimensions of propositional attitude.[55]

To be sure, Tolmanian theory can be enriched to the point where expectancies or expectants become genuine beliefs. But there are many alternative ways in which this might be done, all compatible with the theory's present state of development. Thus, "the next time I do R_j in circumstances S_i, I will encounter S_k," "whenever I have done R_j in circumstances S_i, I have encountered S_k," "the next time I do R_j in circumstances S_i, S_k will occur somewhere," "whenever I do R_j in circumstances S_i, I encounter S_k," and "whenever someone does R_j in circumstances S_i, S_k occurs there," are some of the many *different* ways in which "if R_j when S_i, then S_k" can be completed to make a meaningful proposition. Any one or more of these might reasonably be believed by an organism who has a strong expectancy $S_iR_jS_k$, and an acceptable theory of belief must be able to say something both about the conditions under which a particular one of these arises in contradistinction to the others and, even more importantly, what differences there are among them in their behavioral implications. In short, to assume that the extant articulation of Tolmanian expectancy theory contains sentences of form "organism o believes p at time t," or the equivalent, is abjectly to fail to provide in one's psychology of cognition for the logically crucial distinction between propositions and predicates.

A3 Whatever lasting value Hullian conceptions of behaviour may hold for psychological theory, Hull's own published systems – the 1943 theory and its 1951–2 revision – are a treasure lode for metapsychological research which has scarcely begun to be worked.[56] In particular, there is a profound – one might almost say cataclysmic – difference between the 1943 and 1951–2 systems in Hull's treatment of *incentive*, and analysis of how this is so greatly illuminates not merely the content

55 Tolman (1959, p. 107) has commented that $S_iR_jS_k$ has two dimensions of magnitude, one being how *probable* S_k is thought to be, given S_i and R_j, while the other is the believer's degree of confidence in this probability judgment. But this merely replaces our "if R_j when S_i, then S_k" reading of $S_iR_jS_k$ with the more complex schema, "If R_j when S_i, then S_k with probability p," and the present argument about expectancy theory's present inadequacy for dealing with vividness of belief and propositional attitude holds precisely as before. It should be added that Tolman offered no suggestions as to how these two dimensions of expectancy magnitude differ in their causal antecedents or behavioural effects.

56 I find it immensely irritating when contemporary surveys of behaviour theory or history and systems of psychology, after acknowledging Hull's historical importance, go on to stress that among Hull's shortcomings were imprecision, inconsistency, inadequacy of definitions, etc., in a tone implying that Hull fell far short of psychology's best standards in these respects. *Of course* Hull was imprecise, inconsistent, and all the rest – but his work is still the finest expression of clarity and explicitness that psychological theory has yet managed to achieve. It is precisely because Hull was so clear about so much that the imperfections in his work are so visible, and why Hullian theory is such valuable material for metatheoretical research and education.

of Hull's own ideas but the formal properties of psychological theory in general. In what follows, I shall ignore details of Hull's formulations, such as the distinction between D and $\overline{D}$, which are irrelevant to present concerns.

In 1943, Hull hypothesized that the growth of habit $_sH_R$ and reaction potential $_sE_R$, as a function of the number (N) of conditioning trials on which presentation of S to organism o is followed by o's emission of R when the physical magnitude of reinforcement (w), delay of reinforcement (t), stimulus-response asynchronism (t'), and drive level (D) are the same on each trial, is governed by the equations

$$_sH_R = m \cdot (1 - e^{-aN})(1 - e^{-bw})e^{-ct}e^{-dt'}, \qquad _sE_R = D \cdot {_sH_R},$$

in which a, b, c and d are empirical constants and m is a constant expressing the physiological maximum which habit can attain.[57] If we introduce the defined physical quantities

$$k =_{\text{def}} f_1(w) =_{\text{def}} 1 - e^{-bw},$$
$$j =_{\text{def}} f_2(t) =_{\text{def}} e^{-ct},$$
$$t'' =_{\text{def}} e^{-dt'},$$

and for notational brevity drop the here-unnecessary subscripts in "$_sH_R$" and "$_sE_R$," the 1943 growth functions for H and E may be written

$$H = m \cdot (1 - e^{-aN}) \cdot k \cdot j \cdot t'', \qquad E = D \cdot H.$$

In 1951, on the other hand, the growth of H and E with drive, magnitude of reinforcement, and delay of reinforcement held constant became

$$H = 1 - e^{-aN}, \qquad E = D \cdot H \cdot K \cdot J \cdot V$$

(Hull, 1951, p. 58), where K is a function of the physical magnitude of reinforcement, namely,

$$K = 1 - e^{-b\sqrt{w}} = f_1(\sqrt{w}),$$

J is a function of reinforcement delay, namely,

$$J = e^{-ct} = f_2(t),$$

and V is a function of stimulus energy.

Let the unit of measurement for H in 1943 be chosen to set $m = 1$, as Hull does in 1951, and for simplicity assume that $t'' = V = 1$. (That is, ignore the difference between the 1943 and 1951 systems introjected by stimulus-response asynchronism in 1943 and stimulus dynamism in 1951). Then Hull's postulated growth of

57 The equation for habit given here is notationally the same as Hull's own (1943, p. 178) except for minor changes in the letters used to denote empirical constants. Hull's algebraic equation for habit is not altogether true to his verbally stated theory, for the amount of need reduction accomplished by receipt of a given magnitude of reinforcement should be a function not merely of w but also of D (or more precisely of the correlated drive condition) and the relevance of the reinforcer's nature (e.g., food *versus* water) to the drive condition. However, since the present discussion will assume D and the nature of the reinforcer to remain constant throughout, we may consider these additional determinants of habit to be assimilated by w's empirical coefficient b.

reaction potential under fixed conditions of drive, reinforcement magnitude and reinforcement delay is

<table>
<tr><td>In 1943
(assuming $t'' = 1$)</td><td>In 1951
(assuming $V = 1$)</td></tr>
</table>

$$E = D \cdot H$$
$$= D \cdot (1 - e^{-aN}) \cdot k \cdot j$$
$$= D \cdot (1 - e^{-aN}) \cdot f_1(w) \cdot f_2(t)$$

$$E = D \cdot H \cdot K \cdot J$$
$$= D \cdot (1 - e^{-aN}) \cdot f_1(\sqrt{w}) \cdot f_2(t)$$

Hence it might appear that apart from the differences in stimulus-response asynchronism and stimulus dynamism, the constitution of reaction potential differs in the two systems only in a trivial substitution of $\sqrt{w}$ for w.

But this apparent similarity only goes to show how misleading – or rather, how poorly communicative – a bare algebraic equation can be. Actually, the difference between Hull's 1943 and 1951–2 treatments of reaction potential is profound, but it cannot be clearly seen until two important methodological distinctions are properly appreciated, namely, that of (i) trajectory laws *versus* dynamic laws *versus* system-constraint laws and of (ii) states of the organism *versus* environmental parameters. By a "trajectory" law, I mean a generalization which traces the values of a variable through a sequence of events which affect it. More specifically, though not in full abstract generality, let X be the value of a given variable at time T for a given system s. (The time coordinate T need not be explicitly chronometric – it may just as well, say, count the number of times a certain operation has been performed on the system.) Then a law which says that $X = \phi(T)$ holds for s under certain fixed background conditions C – i.e., which asserts that the value of X at time T for any system satisfying condition C is a specified function of T – is a trajectory law. For example, the familiar law of falling bodies $S = 1/2 \, g \cdot T^2$ is a trajectory law which says that under a number of rather special circumstances (being released with zero velocity at time $T = 0$, falling without resistance under a constant gravitational force g, etc.), the distance S travelled from the point of release by a falling body at any moment T can be computed from T by the formula given. Such a law envisions no causal influence of T upon X, however. T is simply an index for identifying a particular stage in the system's temporal progression. (In the terminology of Rozeboom, 1961, T is not a scientific variable like X, but only a component of X's argument-place.) Thus while the immediate sources of change in X at time T are presumably the conditions affecting the system at T, the function $X = \phi(T)$ merely describes the time course of these accumulated effects. In contrast, "dynamic" and "system-constraint" laws specify principles which actually govern the system. Specifically, though again without complete generality, a law is dynamic if it tells how the *change* in variable X for system s at time T is determined by the conditions affecting s at T. For "open" systems such as organisms, moreover, the conditions relevant to such changes may conveniently be partitioned between *system states* and *environmental parameters*, the former being system attributes whose alternative possibilities define the dependent variables under study,[58] while

---

58 Elsewhere (Rozeboom, 1965) I have used the term "state" in a narrower sense than here

the latter include everything else, notably, the influences impinging upon the system from without. Then if vector $\mathbf{X} = \langle X_1, ..., X_n \rangle$ lists the state properties of system s at time T while $\mathbf{c} = \langle c_1, ..., c_m \rangle$ is the vector of environmental parameters affecting s at T, the dynamic laws of this system are given by a statement of form

$$\Delta \mathbf{X} = \psi(\mathbf{X}, \mathbf{c}),$$

where $\Delta \mathbf{X} = \langle \Delta X_1, ..., \Delta X_n \rangle$ is the vectorial change in state of s at T, i.e., where

$$\Delta X_i =_{\text{def}} X_i' - X_i,$$

in which X_i' is the value of variable X_i for system s at the time immediately following T.[59] (Dynamic laws can also be probabilistic, but this complication need not be considered here.) System constraints, on the other hand, are laws which impose restrictions on the simultaneous values that the system's state variables can have at any given time.[60] Such laws may not or may not contain environmental parameters, and are generally written as one or more equations of form

$$\phi_i(\mathbf{X}, \mathbf{c}) = 0,$$

where as before $\mathbf{X}$ and $\mathbf{c}$ vectorially describe the values of the system's state variables and environmental parameters at time T. Usually, though not always, system-constraint laws can be solved to express one or more of the system's state variables as a function of the others.

Given a system's dynamic and system-constraint laws, specifying the values of its state variables at time $T = 0$ together with its environmental parameters for all times $T \gtreqless 0$ determines (or at least imposes a probability distribution on) the values of its state variables at every time $T > 0$; hence each such specification generates a particular trajectory law for the system under these environmental conditions. Contrarily, it is hopeless to attempt full description of a system's lawful behaviour in terms of trajectory laws and system constraints alone, for there is an infinitude of the former corresponding to different starting configurations and parameter sequences. The only scientific interest in trajectory laws (other than pragmatic concern for prediction and control) lies in the fact that empirical determination of a few trajectory laws under different parametric constancies may permit inference to the system's dynamic laws, from which it can then be deduced

to distinguish relatively stable attributes of the system from its more transient "process" stages. The present usage of "state" includes both process stages and system states in the more restricted sense.

59 This formulation of dynamic laws in terms of difference equations assumes that T takes discrete values. If T is continuous, dynamic laws are expressed by differential equations. Both my discussion and formulae in this paragraph are much more abbreviated than leaves me comfortable, but they are ellipses, which are conventional (albeit often confusing) for this sort of material, and a fuller development is here impractical.

60 In a more general treatment, wherein *time* disappears in favour of more abstract ordering indices, the distinction between dynamic laws and system constraints tends to blur, though not altogether so.

what the system will do under any arbitrary schedule for the environmental parameters.[61]

Returning now to Hull's equations for the growth of habit and reaction potential
as a function of N, it is evident that these are trajectory laws posited only for the
highly special case of trial-to-trial invariance in the environmental parameters and
are *not* presumed to hold otherwise (cf. Hull, 1951, p. 58n.) In both the 1943
and the 1951–2 systems, N(umber-of-learning trials) is not a causal factor but
only a temporal index defined by treating the organism's history as a sequence of
discrete stages punctuated by successive learning experiences, whereas drive, habit,
and reaction potential are state variables whose respective values at a given time
N for organism o are not only the internal condition of o at time N (i.e., immediately after trial N) but also what o contributes to how he is affected by the
$(N + 1)$th learning trial. The 1943 and 1951–2 systems also agree that physical
magnitude (w) and delay (t) of reinforcement are environmental parameters
which *could* change from trial to trial even though the laws as given assume them
to remain constant. The terms k and j are likewise environmental parameters for
the 1943 system, for these have been explicitly defined here in terms of w and t,
respectively, and are nothing more than non-linear rescalings of the latter. The
1951–2 status of K and J, however, is more interesting. Both are left ambiguous in
Hull's abbreviated 1951 account, but Hull made amply clear in 1952 (p. 140ff.)
that K is a *state* variable, not an environmental parameter. The equation of form
$K = f_2(\sqrt{w})$ postulated to relate incentive to reinforcement (1951, p. 51; 1952,
p. 7) is not a *definition* of K, but is rather the asymptotic value of K under repeated
reinforcement with the physical magnitude thereof held constant at w. A similar
interpretation was presumably intended for J; however, J was eliminated from the
1952 system (wherein Hull treated the delay-of-reinforcement phenomenon as a
derived effect) and to avoid further complication we shall continue to assume that
t, and hence J, remains constant. Finally, we note that Hull's 1943 and 1951–2
equations for the *constitution* of reaction potential (as distinguished from its
growth function) stipulate that the organism's momentary value of E is determined
by his values of the other state variables at that same moment and are hence
system-constraint laws.

While as we have seen, Hull's 1951–2 *trajectory* equation for the growth of reaction potential under fixed environmental parameters is virtually identical with
its 1943 counterpart, conversion of the 1943 environmental parameter k into
the 1951–2 state variable K makes a remarkable difference, clearly visible in the
dynamic equations for E, for how past reinforcement influences present behaviour.
It is easily proved that if the trajectory of a variable X under a discrete temporal

---

61 Dynamic laws made their first appearance in psychology with the advent of statistical
learning theory in 1950, but apart from a brief statement by Estes (1960, p. 140f.), the
technical significance of this development has apparently gone unrecognized in psychological metatheory. As it is, this shift in perspective is so important a methodological advance
that it alone, quite apart from any substantive contribution made in its terms, suffices to
justify the professional energies which have gone into statistical learning theory.

index N has the form $X = m \cdot (1 - e^{-aN})$, where m and a are constants and N progresses in unit steps, then $\Delta X = g \cdot (m - X)$ where g is the growth constant $(1 - e^{-a})$.[62] If for simplicity we assume drive to remain constant, the dynamic laws which underlie Hull's trajectory equations for habit and reaction potential are hence

<table>
<tr><td align="center">In 1943</td><td align="center">In 1951</td></tr>
<tr><td align="center">(assuming $D' = D, t'' = 1$)</td><td align="center">(assuming $D' = D, J' = J, V = 1$)</td></tr>
</table>

In 1943 (assuming $D' = D, t'' = 1$):

$$\Delta H = g \cdot (k \cdot j - H),$$
$$\Delta E = {}_{\text{def}}\, E' - E$$
$$= D' \cdot H' - D \cdot H$$
$$= D \cdot (H' - H)$$
$$= D \cdot \Delta H$$
$$= D \cdot g \cdot (k \cdot j - H)$$

- - - - - - - - - - - - -

$$= D \cdot g \cdot k \cdot j - D \cdot g \cdot H$$
$$= g \cdot (D \cdot k \cdot j - D \cdot H)$$
$$= g \cdot (D \cdot k \cdot j - E),$$

In 1951 (assuming $D' = D, J' = J, V = 1$):

$$\Delta H = g \cdot (1 - H),$$
$$\Delta E = {}_{\text{def}}\, E' - E$$
$$= D' \cdot J' \cdot H' \cdot K' - D \cdot J \cdot H \cdot K$$
$$= D \cdot J \cdot (H + \Delta H) \cdot (K + \Delta K)$$
$$\qquad\qquad - D \cdot J \cdot H \cdot K$$
$$= D \cdot J \cdot [(K + \Delta K) \cdot \Delta H + H \cdot \Delta K]$$
$$= D \cdot J \cdot [(K + \Delta K) \cdot g \cdot (1 - H)$$
$$\qquad\qquad + H \cdot \Delta K]$$

- - - - - - - - - - - - -

$$= g \cdot [D \cdot J \cdot K' - D \cdot J \cdot (K + \Delta K)$$
$$\qquad\qquad \cdot H] + D \cdot J \cdot H \cdot \Delta K$$
$$= g \cdot (D \cdot J \cdot K' - D \cdot J \cdot K \cdot H)$$
$$\qquad\qquad - g \cdot D \cdot J \cdot \Delta K \cdot H$$
$$\qquad\qquad + D \cdot J \cdot H \cdot \Delta K$$
$$= g \cdot (D \cdot J \cdot K' - E)$$
$$\qquad\qquad + D \cdot J \cdot H \cdot \Delta K \cdot (1 - g)$$
$$= g \cdot (D \cdot J \cdot K' - E)$$
$$\qquad\qquad + (1 - g) \cdot E \cdot (\Delta K / K),$$

where g is a growth-constant and $k[= f_1(w)]$ and $j[= f_2(t)]$ are determined by the magnitude (w) and delay (t) of reinforcement, respectively, on the trial producing ΔH.

where g is a growth-constant and ΔK, though left unspecified in 1951, is treated in 1952 (p. 143) as a function of K and w, namely, $\Delta K = .8(m_w - K)$ where $m_w[= f_1(\sqrt{w})]$ is the asymptote of K under constant reinforcement at magnitude w.

The equations above the dotted line express ΔE as a joint function of the organism's independent state variables at the beginning of a learning trial and the environmental parameters operative on that trial. Given these dynamic equations, it is no longer necessary for Hullian theory to assume trial-to-trial constancy in w — one can choose any arbitrary schedule of reinforcements and by iterative application of the dynamic equation determine what value the theory says E should have after N learning trials on this schedule.

The manner in which Hull's 1951–2 version of reaction potential has acquired increased adaptability to changes in reinforcement is maximally conspicuous in the

62 *Proof*: If $X = m \cdot (1 - e^{-aN})$, then $\Delta X = {}_{\text{def}}\, X' - X = m \cdot (1 - e^{-a[N+1]}) - m \cdot (1 - e^{-aN}) = m \cdot e^{-aN} - m \cdot e^{-aN} \cdot e^{-a} = m \cdot e^{-aN} \cdot (1 - e^{-a})$. But $X = m - m \cdot e^{-aN}$, so $m \cdot e^{-aN} = m - X$ and hence $\Delta X = (1 - e^{-a}) \cdot (m - X) = g \cdot (m - X)$. QED

final equations for ΔE below the dotted line. Since by assumption t remains constant, $j = f_2(t) = J$, and the 1951 equation for ΔE (given the restrictions noted) hence differs from the 1943 version in having two major components, one of which is identical to the entire 1943 E-increment except for having K' in place of k. The terms k and K' are not entirely the same, for k is determined wholly by the magnitude of reinforcement on the trial producing ΔE, whereas K' is the value of the incentive state-variable after the trial has had its effect and does not completely accommodate in a single trial to a change in w. However, apart from a mild sluggishness in the adjustment of incentive to altered circumstances, and ignoring the trivial detail that $\sqrt{w}$ occurs in 1951 where w occurs in 1943, K' and k may be thought of as numerically equivalent. The major structural difference between the 1943 and 1951 dynamic equations is then seen to be that in the 1943 system, a change in reinforcement magnitude from w to w' merely changes the rate at which new E accumulates; whereas in the 1951 system, besides the 1943-type increment in the growth of E, the additional term $(1 - g) \cdot E \cdot (\Delta K/K)$ allows a reinforcement change from w to w' *also* to operate through ΔK upon the amount of E accrued from previous trials to move reaction potential rapidly toward the strength it would have been at had the magnitude of reinforcement been w' all along. And thus, by what turns out to be a structurally profound revision of the theory, Hull painlessly assimilates the Blodgett type of latent learning.

It is an instructive methodological lesson to trace down just *how* Hull's 1951–2 system achieves this additional virtuosity, and in particular, to observe that this is not something which could have alternatively been attained simply by modifying details of the component functions relating H or E to w, t, and N in the 1943 trajectory laws. (It is often thought that the flexibility of a system is determined by the number of adjustable parameters it contains. Yet Hull could have added parameters to his 1943 trajectories until he was blue in the face and still not have achieved what he did simply by converting a parameter into a state variable.) Note to begin with that with drive, reinforcement delay, stimulus-response asynchronism, and stimulus dynamism held constant, change in reaction potential as a joint function of intervening state variables and present environmental parameters takes the form $\Delta E = \Phi_1(H, w)$ in 1943, whereas in 1951 the form becomes $\Delta E = \Phi_2 (H, K, w)$. However, the manifest presence of two state variables (counting only those not assumed here to remain constant), rather than merely one, in the 1951 dynamic equation for E does not suffice to account for its additional versatility, for the number of intervening variables in a theory can always be increased at will by stipulative definition without altering the theory's power. In particular, due cognizance must here be given to the fact that H in 1943 is a function jointly of the same empirical variables which determine H and K separately in 1951–2. If we expand the dynamic laws to eliminate intervening variables in favour of their empirical antecedents, we find equations of form $\Delta E = \Psi_1(w, \Sigma_w)$ for 1943 and $\Delta E = \Psi_2(w, \Sigma_w)$ for 1951–2, in which w is reinforcement magnitude on the current trial and Σ_w is a vector stating the magnitude of reinforcement on each of the previous learning trials. That is, given the constancies here assumed, ΔE is ultimately determined by the same reinforcement-history variable Σ_w in both the 1943 and the 1951–2 systems, and the problem remains to show in what significant way these functions, Ψ_1 and Ψ_2, differ. The answer is that although state variable H in the original dynamic law $\Delta E = \Phi_1(H, w)$ and the pair of state variables $\langle H, K \rangle$ in the revised law $\Delta E = \Phi_2(H,K,w)$ are both functions of the organism's previous conditioning history, their mutual dependence on Σw is of such nature as to establish a one-many correspondence between values of H in 1943 and values of the pair $\langle H, K \rangle$ in 1951–2. That is, alternative reinforcement histories which produce different value-pairs for the 1951–2 $\langle H, K \rangle$ may produce the same value for the 1943 H. Thus the 1951–2 system makes more information about the organism's conditioning history accessible, via the state variables, to be operated upon by a new learning experience – i.e., the 1951–2 function Ψ_2 discriminates more of the details of Σw than does the 1943 function Ψ_1.

There are additional illuminating features of Hull's 1943 and 1951–2 systems which the foregoing analysis also positions us to appreciate. For one, while I casually spoke a moment ago about eliminating the "intervening" (i.e., theoreti-cal$_{B1}$) state variables in the dynamic laws for reaction potential in favour of their empirical (observational) antecedents, this cannot actually be done by explicit definition. To be sure, for an organism o which has had exactly N prior learning experiences, we can replace o's present value of E with an explicitly defined quantity Q_N which is a function of, among other observational antecedents, the N-component vector giving the magnitude of reinforcement received by o on each of his past N trials. But in both the 1943 and 1951 systems, the function defining Q_N assumes a different form for each different value of N, and there exists no fixed function f and finite set of observation variables $X_1, ..., X_m$ (including N or not) such that $E = f(X_1, ..., X_m)$ regardless of the number of previous learning trials. Thus *it is not logically possible to eliminate occurrences of the predicate* "the value of variable $_sE_R$ for organism o at time t is ———" *in Hullian theory in favour of a truth-functionally equivalent expression which refers only to a condition, or abstraction from a complex of conditions, external to o.* (The same is true of $_sH_R$ in 1943 and of K in 1951–2.) The belief to the contrary which appeared so often in the "intervening variable" literature undoubtedly resulted from an unthinking assumption that Hull intended his trajectory equations to remain true under all reinforcement histories. But there never was the slightest mathematical possibility that habit (in 1943), reaction potential, or other Hullian "intervening variables" except habit in 1951–2 were intervening variables in MacCorquodale and Meehl's (1948) sense of this term, namely, as explicitly definable out of observation variables. To be sure, Hull himself called $_sH_R$, D, $_sE_R$, etc. "intervening variables" because what he meant by this phrase was roughly what MacCorquodale and Meehl had in mind by "hypothetical constructs." But Hull himself was most explicit that his theoretical variables had an intraorganismic existence altogether distinct from the environmental variables to which they were functionally related (cf. Hull, 1943, p. 109).

Secondly, it is most interesting to note that while Hull at times thought in terms of dynamic laws (e.g., Hull, 1943, p. 119), his failure to make these explicit kept him from realizing *that his 1943 postulate for the modification of habit by reinforcement accounted for extinction fully as much as it did for acquisition.* For if

$\Delta H = g \cdot (k \cdot j - H)$, a trial on which the reinforcement-parameter product $k \cdot j$ $[= f_1(w) \cdot f_2(t)]$ is lower than the level of habit already attained results in a *decrease* of H. In particular, this is true for extinction trials on which $k \cdot j = 0$. Hence Hull's Conditioned Inhibition postulate – which is well known to be one of the most unsatisfactory components of Hullian theory – is formally super-fluous, and in fact the 1943 extinction premise (Postulate 14) is inconsistent with the course of extinction derivable from the 1943 dynamic equation for ΔH. This redundancy is even more striking in the 1951–2 system, for there Hull himself shows (1952, p. 142ff.) how a decrement in reinforcement weakens E through its effect on K without requiring a separate $_sI_R$ variable. To be sure, Hull might have wished to invoke a notion of conditioned inhibition in order to explain *why* habit and/or reaction potential decays under non-reinforcement, as well as, conceivably, to deal with certain secondary phenomena involving reduced reinforcement, but mathematically, primary extinction is already in the dynamic law for E and, in 1943, for H regardless of how it is explained.

Another important and previously unrecognized consequence of Hullian theory emerges when its dynamic reformulation is broadened to include the effect that reinforcement of one habit has, via stimulus generalization, upon another. Let H_i and H_j be the strengths of habits $S_i \rightarrow R$ and $S_j \rightarrow R$, respectively, where the response R is the same in both cases while S_i and S_j are somewhat similar stimuli d_{ij} jnds ("just noticeable differences") apart. Also, for convenience let $r [=_{def} k \cdot j]$ be the product of reinforcement magnitude (k) and reinforcement delay (j) on a given learning trial and called the reinforcement "potency" on that trial. Then we wish to know what increment results in H_i from a learning trial on which H_j is reinforced with potency r. (In the 1951–2 system, r is replaced by unity on all trials.) Now in Hull's own notation (1943, p. 199), "effective habit strength" – i.e. habit strength under generalization – has trajectory "$_s\bar{H}_R = {_sH_R}e^{-j'd}$," in which d is the number of jnds between stimulus S and the stimulus at the point of reinforcement, j' is an empirical constant, and $_sH_R$ is the strength which habit $S \rightarrow R$ would have had R been reinforced directly to S rather than to a stimulus d jnds away from S. For brevity, let quantity h_{ij} be defined

$$h_{ij} =_{def} e^{-j'd_{ij}}$$

and called the "sensory similarity" between stimuli S_i and S_j. Then in present terms, what Hull seems to be saying is that if habit H_j (i.e. $S_j \rightarrow R$) is repeatedly reinforced with potency r, the trajectory equation for the growth of habit generalized to H_i (i.e., $S_i \rightarrow R$) is

$$H_i = (1 - e^{-aN}) \cdot r \cdot h_{ij}$$

(where we let stimulus-response asynchronism and the physiological maximum of habit be unity as before), with a corresponding dynamic equation of

[G1] $$\Delta_{rh}H_i = g \cdot (r \cdot h_{ij} - H_i),$$

in which the difference-operator "Δ_{rh}" denotes change produced by a reinforcement of potency r given h jnds away from the stimulus in question. But equation [G1] will not do at all. In the first place, it violates Hull's own example (1943; pp.

195, 201f.) of how reinforcements at several different points of the stimulus continuum summate in a combined generalization gradient. (Specifically, Hull's illustration and calculations show the combined generalization gradient as independent of the order in which the different stimulus points are reinforced, whereas this is *not* true under dynamic equation [*G1*].) Worse, equation [*G1*] says that if H_i has non-zero strength, and reinforcement is given at a point S_j a sufficiently large number of jnds away from S_i, the resulting change in H_i will be *negative*. That is, according to [*G1*], a habit $S_i \to R$ can be extinguished by reinforcing R to another stimulus highly discriminable from S_i. Thus Hull's own equation for stimulus generalization cannot be taken literally. What Hull apparently intended to hypothesize is that the amount of habit strength "behaviourally added" to habit H_i by reinforcement of habit H_j is the number of habits which would have been behaviourally added to H_i had the reinforcement been given directly to H_i, attenuated by the sensory similarity factor. If so, then Hull's dynamic law for habit increments under stimulus generalization is

[G2] $$\Delta_{rh}H_i = g \cdot h_{ij} \cdot (r - H_i).$$

Unlike [*G1*], equation [*G2*] agrees with Hull's numerical example,[63] and is the only interpretation I can find for Hull's statements about stimulus generalization which makes any mathematical and behavioural sense. It will be observed, however, that sensory similarity measure h_{ij} appears in [*G2*] as a factor in growth *rate*, not in growth *limit*. Hence according to Hullian theory, *if habit* $S_j \to R$ *is repeatedly reinforced with constant potency, then through stimulus generalization other habits* $S_i \to R$ *will increase to the same asymptote as does habit* $S_j \to R$ *but will do so at a slower rate, the rapidity of growth being an increasing function of the sensory similarity between* S_i *and* S_j. That is, under repeated reinforcement (with fixed potency) at a given point on a sensory continuum, the generalization gradient will become flatter and flatter until eventually all stimuli on that continuum have habit strengths to the reinforced response equal to that at the point of reinforcement.

Finally, it should be pointed out that while K is by far and away the most pivotal concept in Hull's 1951–2 system, Hull left its formal behaviour highly obscure and in fact did not apparently realize the extent to which it had taken over the function of other mechanisms in the older system. If one studies the 1951–2 postulates for the role they confer upon reinforcement in the determination of behaviour, it is found that all reinforcement phenomena (and by rights extinction phenomena as well) are mediated entirely by K – i.e., reinforcement history makes a difference for present behaviour only insofar as this makes a difference for present incentive. But Hull makes *use* of K only for deriving Blodgett-type latent learning. Everywhere else in the 1951–2 system's accounts of reinforcement effects, secondary reinforcement through r_g-mechanisms is the dominant motif, with nothing whatsoever said about K – whereas insomuch as K is a postulated function only of the

---

63 Specifically, it can be shown that if variable X undergoes n changes of form $\Delta_i X = a_i \cdot (m - X)$ in which m is constant but a_i varies from change to change according to the series $a_1, a_2, ..., a_n$, then the value of X after change Δ_n is invariant under any permutation of the a_i.

physical magnitude of primary reward, the system contains no provision for secondary-reinforcement phenomena at all. The inconsistencies and oversights which result from failure to take K seriously could be remedied readily enough if the formal properties of K were sufficiently clear. This, however, is emphatically not the case, as revealed by the following simple but fundamental question: is K a single variable like D, or is it a *class* of variables like $_sH_R$? Hull himself does not say. His notation suggests the former; but if so, then K would energize all habits simultaneously, with the result that, e.g., increasing the quantity of food reward received by the organism for doing R_a in circumstances S_1 would increase not merely his tendency to do R_a in circumstances S_1, but also his tendency in other circumstances S_2 to make a different response R_b which had previously been followed in S_2 by water reward. If K were really intended to be this indiscriminately promiscuous, its formal behaviour would be essentially like drive, and the product $D \cdot K$ would play virtually the same role in the 1951–2 system that D alone served in 1943. Clearly, then, there must be a multiplicity of K-variables, differentially associated with different habits. But if so, how are the different incentive variables distinguished from one another, and how is formal provision to be made in the theory for telling which incentive operates upon what habit? Most noncommitally, we can identify a particular incentive variable by affixing a subscript – e.g., K_k – and leave open K_k's more detailed formal character; but in order to connect K_k with the proper habit(s), a class of *coupling* variables C_{ijk} must be invoked to specify how strongly habit $S_i \rightarrow R_j$ is acted upon by incentive K_k. The triplet of variables $\langle _{s_i}H_{R_j}, C_{ijk}, K_k \rangle$ is then an experience-residue vector which represents in the organism's present state the effect of previous experiences wherein doing R_j in the presence of S_i was followed by reinforcement of a kind corresponding to incentive k, while the effect of this particular experience-residue vector on present behaviour is that for nonzero values of $_{s_i}H_{R_j}$ and C_{ijk}, the organism's tendency to do R_j in the presence of S_i is an increasing function of the present magnitude of K_k, Formally, this is very close to a valenced Tolmanian expectancy, except that Hullian incentive theory need not assume that to every different stimulus which can follow a response there corresponds a different incentive, nor that the organism's present value of K_k is influenced by his present motivational condition. If it *were* to be postulated, however, that (i) every different stimulus S_k corresponds to a different incentive variable K_k, that (ii) conditioning trials on which R_j in the presence of S_i is followed by S_k produces a strengthening of C_{ijk}, and that (iii) the present strength of K_k is determined by the organism's present motives in the same way that Tolmanian valences are so determined, then Hullian state-vector $\langle _{s_i}H_{R_j}, C_{ijk}, K_k \rangle$ becomes virtually identical in logical structure and functional properties with the valenced expectancy $S_iR_jS_k$. (More precisely, what is formally equivalent to expectancy $S_iR_jS_k$ is $\langle _{s_i}H_{R_j}, C_{ijk} \rangle$, while K_k corresponds to the Tolmanian valence of S_k.)

So much for classical behaviour theory. We now turn to another facet of S-R speculation, the use of hypothetical mediation responses as explanatory mechanisms.

B1 Until S-R theorists overran the fortress of cognitive processes with mediation-response armament a decade or two ago, one of the primary issues in behaviour theory concerned whether learned associations were basically stimulus-response (S-R) or sensory-sensory (S-S) in nature (cf. Spence, 1950). For example, the well-known empirical phenomenon of classical conditioning, somewhat oversimplified, is that if a stimulus S_u elicits a response R from organism o while S_u is repeatedly paired in o's experience with another stimulus S_c, then S_c will also come to elicit R from o. But *why*, after such experienced contingencies, does o do R when stimulated by S_c? The commonsense explanation is that S_c now makes o think of S_u – i.e., that o has learned an association of ideas – which is also what is implied when classical conditioning is described as S_c's coming to be a *sign of* S_u for o. But as Thorndike argued (for instrumental rather than classical conditioning) as early as 1898, it is altogether possible that the conditioned elicitation of R by S_c is simply a linkage of S_c directly to R without any intervening sensory or ideational event corresponding to S_u at all. These two alternative interpretations of classical conditioning are illustrated in Fig. 2.1, where the learned linkages presumed by S-R and S-S hypotheses are shown by arrows ① and ②, respectively.

Now at first impression, Fig. 2.1 would seem to imply a simple experimental test between S-S and S-R views of classical conditioning. For suppose that after response R has been conditioned to stimulus S_c, the elicitation of R by S_u is extinguished (with S_c omitted) and a new response $R*$ is conditioned to S_u in its place, as shown by the dotted lines in Fig. 2.2. According to S-R theory, S_c should continue to evoke R, whereas by S-S theory, S_c should now elicit $R*$ instead. But of course, with mediation-response mechanisms at its disposal, S-R theory would never allow itself to be discredited this simply. If such a reconditioning experiment were to yield transfer of $R*$ to S_c, S-R theory would explain the results as follows. (i) Stimulus S_u, in addition to evoking R initially, also elicits another response component r_m which in turn produces stimulus feedback s_m. Since stimulation by S_u thus evokes both s_m and R, R becomes conditioned to s_m. (ii) When a neutral stimulus S_c is paired with S_u, r_m becomes conditioned to S_c which hence comes to evoke R (Fig. 2.3a). (iii) When R is extinguished to S_u, S_u continues to elicit r_m so that the extinction procedure also serves to extinguish R to s_m; and when S_u is conditioned to a new response $R*$, s_m similarly becomes conditioned to $R*$ (Fig. 2.3b). (iv) Finally, since r_m still remains conditioned to S_c while s_m now elicits $R*$, S_c will be found to evoke $R*$ (Fig. 2.3c), the same result that is predicted by S-S theory.

Now, the capacity of both S-S and S-R perspectives to account for positive results in a transfer experiment of this sort does not, as might at first be thought, imply that such data would tell us nothing about the internal mechanisms which underlie conditioning. Note to begin with that quite apart from theoretical interpretations, the experiment of Fig. 2.2 addresses an important *empirical* question, namely, the extent to which pairings of S_c with S_u in a classical conditioning operation establish generalization from S_u to S_c rather than an $S_c \rightarrow R$ linkage which is independent of subsequent modifications in the effect of S_u (cf. Rozeboom, 1958). Given that conditioning of generalization does, in fact, occur (the extant evidence is scanty, but suggests that conditioned generalization is a genuine if not necessarily common phenomenon), neither S-S nor S-R theories are at a loss to explain it – but what is more significant is that *both of these prima facie alternative explanations have a*

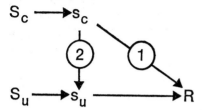

FIGURE 2.1
Stimulus-response (arrow 1) and sensory-sensory (arrow 2) interpretations of classical conditioning. S_u and S_o are external stimuli which activate sensory (or ideational) processes s_u and s_o, respectively, within the organism.

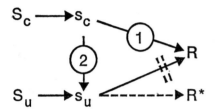

FIGURE 2.2
The mediation experiment for classical conditioning. The dotted lines indicate operations performed upon stimulus S_u after stimulus S_o has been conditioned to R through pairings with S_u, namely, substituting R^* for R as the response elicited by s_u.

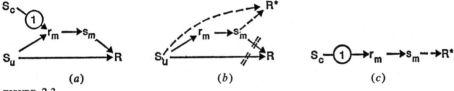

| (a) | (b) | (c) |

FIGURE 2.3
An S-R interpretation of positive results in the mediation experiment of Fig. 2.2.

common conceptual structure. For if we replace "s_u" by "m" in the S-S version of Fig. 2.2, while "m" is similarly substituted for "$r_m \rightarrow s_m$" in the S-R transfer model (Fig. 2.3), both accounts are seen to embody the very same logical form, namely, that there exists some mediational element m such that: (i) unconditioned stimulus S_u elicits m which in turn elicits unconditioned response R; that (ii) when neutral stimulus S_c is classically paired with S_u, S_c acquires the ability to elicit m which, in turn, continues to elicit R; that (iii) an operation which substitutes R^* for R as the response to S_u does so by leaving the $S_u \rightarrow m$ connection intact, but replaces $m \rightarrow R$ with $m \rightarrow R^*$; and hence that (iv) S_c continues to elicit m which now gives rise to R^* rather than R, so that empirically, the reconditioning of S_u is generalized to S_c. Where the S-S and S-R accounts diverge is in their further premises about the nature of m, the former assuming that m is some sort of cognitive "idea" corresponding to S_u while the latter hypothesizes that m is a feedback-producing response intimately associated with S_u. But the only known behavioural data which bear on the mediation question are instances of conditioned generalization or closely allied phenomena.[64] Thus while postulation of underlying (i.e., theoretical$_{B1}$) entities of unspecified nature which mediate transfer of conditioning is a Class 2 hypothesis (see p. 100 above) inductively warranted by conditioned generalization data, the additional assumption *either* that this mediator is a stimulus-producing response *or* that it is a sensory-like idea is a Class 3 or Class 4 speculation (depending on just what this further premise is construed to imply) for which there exists no present evidence and concerning which no behaviour theorist is intellectually entitled to have strong convictions. In particular, it is absurd to pretend that $r_m \rightarrow s_m$ mediational hypotheses are any more scientific or tough-minded than are frankly mentalistic interpretations of mediation – one is just as arbitrary a padding on the mediational structure so far backed by evidence as is the other.

To be sure, conjecture that mediators of conditioned generalization are stimulus-producing responses is not wholly without behavioural import. For one, if r_m in Fig. 2.3 is really a peripheral (even if covert) effector action, then the mediated sequence $S_c \rightarrow r_m \rightarrow s_m \rightarrow R^*$ should require a longer reaction time from S_c to R^* than would the sequence $S_c \rightarrow m \rightarrow R^*$ if m occurs wholly in the brain. More importantly, according to S-R principles the operation envisioned in Fig. 2.3a should condition R directly to stimulus S_c as well as to s_m; hence, since the reconditioning operation of Fig. 2.3b should not weaken the $S_c \rightarrow R$ connection, the transfer test of Fig. 2.3c should show S_c eliciting R together with R^*. That is, the $r_m \rightarrow s_m$ interpretation of m should not allow for a *clean* conditioned generalization effect.[65] No evidence exists for or against these implications, so surmise that conditioned-generalization mediators have a peripheral response component is a Class 3 conjecture. Moreover, even these S-R commitments are weakened by the view that r_m and s_m may be wholly central processes, involving no stimuli or responses in the usual sense of these terms (e.g., Miller, 1959, p. 239ff.). To the extent that this internalization gambit is a way of recognizing our lack of warranted opinion about the more detailed nature of mediators, it well merits commendation. But its intent is then largely thwarted by continuing to symbolize the mediational element in "$r \rightarrow s$" terms; for not merely does this notation formally structure the mediator as a two-stage process whose termini differ in kind, conceptualizing its first stage as a "response" and its second stage as a "stimulus" implicitly or even explicitly hypothesizes that s and r follow the same laws as do peripheral stimuli and responses (cf. Miller, 1959, p.243), so that, e.g. if S_u elicits both r_m and R while S_c is repeatedly paired with S_u in a classical conditioning procedure, S_c should in principle become

64 A few neurophysiological experiments also have marginal relevance here, but before such data have psychological implications, additional assumptions must be made about the neurophysiological nature of the psychological processes at issue (e.g., what and where "ideas" are in the brain.)

65 This is altogether typical: in *all* S-R explanations of expectancy-type phenomena (or hypothetical phenomena), even if the argument is taken at face value without probing its weaknesses, the best the proposed mechanism can come up with is a *slight* tendency for the organism to favour expectancy-manifesting behaviour over the non-expectant response.

conditioned to R in the same way it becomes conditioned to r_m.[66] But if mediation theory attempts to *account for* empirical S-R relationships rather than merely hypothesize covert S-R relations which run *parallel to* (i.e., on the same systemic level as) observable relations, then to treat mediators or their components as falling under the very same law-generalizations that cover overt behavioural regularities is to commit a monumental logical blunder.[67]

B2 A phenomenon which is profoundly important for many aspects of complex behaviour and which proves to be unexpectedly resistant to theoretical explanation is that of precise discrimination. Specifically, *if two stimuli have sufficient sensory similarity that appreciable stimulus generalization initially obtains between them, how is it possible for the organism to learn to discriminate between them with – as we know empirically often occurs – virtually 100% accuracy?* Despite the considerable attention that other aspects of discrimination learning have received, theoretical analysis of precise discrimination has been surprisingly meager, possibly due to a mistaken impression that extant behaviour-theoretical treatments of this have successfully accounted for it.

According to Hull's classic theory of precise discrimination learning (1943, p. 266f.),[68] if an organism is given repeated reinforcements of response R to a stimulus S_i while R is repeatedly extinguished to another stimulus S_j at a different point on the same sensory continuum, then the gradient of habit generalization (to R) built up on this continuum around S_i will eventually be counteracted by the gradient of conditioned inhibition (to R) built up around S_j in such fashion that the effective reaction potential at S_j will lie below response threshold while it still remains appreciably above threshold at S_i. The trouble with this treatment in its original form is that Hull's conception of conditioned inhibition has proved to be thoroughly unsatisfactory (cf. Gleitman, Nachmias, and Neisser, 1954); hence a theory of discrimination learning which rests upon it must be similarly untenable. Even so, we saw above (p. 116f.) that when Hullian theory is rephrased dynamically, the conditioned inhibition postulate becomes superfluous and it is thus also possible that Hull's dynamic laws of learning will suffice for precise discrimination. As will now be shown, however, this is not so – at least not to the extent needed.

66 I say "in principle" because there might be details of the case (e.g., different response latencies) in virtue of which pairing S_c with S_u conditions S_c more effectively to r_m than to R, or conversely.

67 Since this point is somewhat subtle, an extreme example may help to clarify it. There is surely little disagreement that when an overt unconditional stimulus S elicits an unconditioned response R, the relation is mediated by an afferent process s such that S arouses s while s, more immediately, is what activates R. If sensory process s were to be construed as a "stimulus" on a par with S, however, we should then infer from the principles of classical conditioning that the constant occurrence of s immediately following presentations of S should establish a conditioned connection directly from S to R in virtue of which presentations of S should elicit R even when s is prevented from occurring.

68 The fundamentals of this argument originate with Spence (1936).

Suppose that on trial t of an indefinitely long series of learning trials, habit variable H undergoes increment $\Delta_t H = a(m - H)$, where a and m are values of random variables whose joint probability distribution may be a function of both trial number and the value of H on that trial. H is then a random variable whose expected value changes on trial t by the amount

[G3]
$$\begin{aligned}
\Delta_t \mathrm{E}(H) &= \mathrm{E}_t(H + \Delta H) - \mathrm{E}_t(H) \\
&= \mathrm{E}_t(\Delta H) \\
&= \mathrm{E}_t[a(m - H)] \\
&= \mathrm{E}_t(am) - \mathrm{E}_t(aH) \\
&= \mathrm{E}_t(am) - \mathrm{E}_t(a) \cdot \mathrm{E}_t(H) \cdot (1 + v_a v_H r_{aH}) \\
&= \frac{\mathrm{E}_t(a)}{1 - \epsilon} \left[\frac{\mathrm{E}_t(am)}{\mathrm{E}_t(a)} (1 - \epsilon) - \mathrm{E}_t(H) \right],
\end{aligned}$$

where "$\mathrm{E}_t(x)$" denotes the expected value of random variable x on trial t, r_{aH} is the linear correlation between random variables a and H on trial t, v_a and v_H are the coefficients of variation – i.e., standard deviation divided by expected value – for a and H, respectively, on trial t, and where for simplicity we write

$$\epsilon \underset{\text{def}}{=} \frac{v_a v_H r_{aH}}{1 + v_a v_H r_{aH}}$$

for the second-order quantity contributed to [G3] by whatever tendency there may be for the value of H to influence the growth constant for H's increment on a given trial. (For the transition from line 4 to line 5 of [G3], see Rozeboom, 1966, equation 7.200.) Assuming only that the probability parameters in [G3] are asymptotically stable, the asymptotic expected value, $\mathrm{E}_\infty(H)$, of H is thus

[G4]
$$\mathrm{E}_\infty(H) = \frac{\mathrm{E}_\infty(am)}{\mathrm{E}_\infty(a)} (1 - \epsilon) \simeq \frac{\mathrm{E}_\infty(am)}{\mathrm{E}_\infty(a)}.$$

To appreciate how minutely ϵ generally differs from zero in [G4], and hence how good the right-hand approximation should be, observe that unless the joint asymptotic distribution of a and H is extraordinarily bizarre, each of the quantities v_a, v_H, and r_{aH} will have a magnitude of the order of 10^{-1} or less, whence the order of magnitude for ϵ should be at most 10^{-2}.

Now let an organism o be given a long series of discrimination trials on which response R is reinforced with potency r to stimulus S_a and extinguished (i.e., reinforced with potency zero) to stimulus S_b. If we wish, we may further assume that the conditioning procedure also reinforces S_b and extinguishes S_a to a competing or inhibitory response R^*; this affects only the values of parameters p_a and p_b, below, unless there is appreciable response generalization between R and R^*. On each trial, o then has one of the following conditioning experiences.

A_1: o is presented with S_a and makes reinforced response R.
A_2: o is presented with S_a but does not make response R.
B_1: o is presented with S_b and makes unreinforced response R.
B_2: o is presented with S_b but does not make response R.

Since o does not make response R on trials of types A_2 and B_2, Hullian habits in which R is the response term are unchanged by such trials even if (presuming no response generalization) habits with response terms other than R are reinforced or extinguished on these occasions.[69] Consequently, if H_i designates the strength of habit $S_i \rightarrow R$ for organism o, where S_i is any stimulus whose sensory similarities to training stimuli S_a and S_b are h_{ia} and h_{ib}, respectively, it follows from [G2] (p. 118, above) that the change in H_i respectively produced by each of these experiences is

$$A_1: \Delta H_i = gh_{ia}(r - H_i); \quad A_2: \Delta H_i = 0 = 0 \cdot (r - H_i);$$
$$B_1: \Delta H_i = gh_{ib}(0 - H_i); \quad B_2: \Delta H_i = 0 = 0 \cdot (0 - H_i).$$

Now, the asymptotic probabilities of experiences A_1, A_2, B_1, and B_2 on a given conditioning trial are $\pi_a p_a$, $\pi_a(1-p_a)$, $\pi_b p_b$, and $\pi_b(1 - p_b)$, respectively, where

$\pi_a =_{\text{def}}$ asymptotic probability that stimulus S_a is presented;
$p_a =_{\text{def}}$ asymptotic probability that o makes response R given stimulus S_a;
$\pi_b =_{\text{def}}$ asymptotic probability that stimulus S_b is presented;
$p_b =_{\text{def}}$ asymptotic probability that o makes response R given stimulus S_b.

Summing across each experience type's probability times its growth constant for ΔH_i yields the asymptotic expected growth constant for ΔH_i, while the corresponding expected growth-constant-times-reinforcement-potency is similarly obtained. Substituting these quantities into [G4] then reveals the asymptotically expected strength of generalized habit $S_i \rightarrow R$ to be

$$[G5] \qquad E_\infty(H_i) = r\left[\frac{\pi_a p_a h_{ia}}{(\pi_a p_a h_{ia} + \pi_b p_b h_{ib})}\right](1 - \epsilon_i).$$

While the quantity ϵ_i is difficult to evaluate analytically, qualitative arguments can be adduced to strengthen our general expectation (see above) that it should be negligible. If for simplicity we let stimuli S_a and S_b be presented with asymptotically equal probabilities, [G5] then reduces to

$$[G6] \qquad E_\infty(H_i) = r\left[\frac{p_a h_{ia}}{(p_a h_{ia} + p_b h_{ib})}\right](1 - \epsilon_i)$$
$$\simeq r\left[\frac{p_a h_{ia}}{(p_a h_{ia} + p_b h_{ib})}\right].$$

In particular, since $h_{aa} = h_{bb} = e^0 = 1$, the asymptotically expected strengths of habits $S_a \rightarrow R$ and $S_b \rightarrow R$ (i.e. the ones respectively reinforced and extinguished during the discrimination training) are then

$$[G7] \qquad E_\infty(H_a) \simeq r\left[\frac{p_a}{(p_a + p_b h_{ab})}\right], \quad E_\infty(H_b) \simeq r\left[\frac{p_a h_{ab}}{(p_a h_{ab} + p_b)}\right].$$

69 Although a case can be made from Hull's 1943 treatment of stimulus-response a synchronism for treating A_2 and B_2 as extinction trials, it is questionable whether Hull intended this

Extracting from [G7] the Hullian limitations on precise discrimination is complicated by the fact that the numerical values of response probabilities p_a and p_b are importantly dependent in Hullian theory on parameters and state variables additional to habit strengths H_a and H_b, as well as upon further details of the training procedure, notably, whether or not discrimination training strengthens a competing or inhibitory response R^* to S_b as well as extinguishing R to it,[70] and whether a correction or non-correction procedure is used.[71] Even so, it is clear from [G7] that o's asymptotic discrimination between S_a and S_b approaches perfection only as the sensory similarity, h_{ab}, between S_a and S_b approaches zero. In fact, it follows from [G7] that

[G8][72]
$$\frac{\mathrm{E}_\infty(H_b)}{\mathrm{E}_\infty(H_a)} \geq h_{ab}.$$

That is, the asymptotic expected strength of extinguished habit $S_b \rightarrow R$, expressed as a proportion of the expected strength of reinforced habit $S_a \rightarrow R$, remains at least as great as the sensory similarity between S_a and S_b. To be sure, a near-zero probability of R to S_b can be made compatible with appreciable strength of habit $S_b \rightarrow R$ by adroit juggling of the other Hullian parameters and state variables, notably, by assuming strong conditioning of S_b to a competing response R^*. But boundary conditions which minimize the probability of R to S_b under given nonzero H_b also attenuate the probability of R to S_a for a given value of H_a (e.g., generalization of $S_b \rightarrow R^*$ to $S_a \rightarrow R^*$), and the capacity of Hullian theory to reconcile [G8] with probabilities of R to S_b and S_a of near-zero and near-unity, respectively, is rapidly exhausted as h_{ab} becomes greater than zero. Thus the sensory similarity between two stimuli establishes an inflexible limit to the accuracy with which a Hullian

interpretation and we shall hence construe trials on which o does not make response R to leave habits in which R is the response term unchanged in strength. The present argument can easily be amended to assume the alternative, however, and the reader who does so will see that it makes little difference for the argument's conclusion.

70 If training modifies the strengths of both habits $S_i \rightarrow R$ and $S_i \rightarrow R^*$, the probability of R given S_i depends not merely upon the momentary effective reaction potential of R but also upon how this compares to the simultaneously aroused momentary effective reaction potential of R^* (Hull, 1943, p. 341). Alternatively, if R^* is construed as "conditioned inhibition," it attenuates the relation between habit strength and response probability at a more central stage of the arousal process (Hull, 1943, p. 281ff.)

71 In a "correction" procedure, each trial persists until o makes the reinforced response. In this case, presentation of S_a is not terminated until o does R, whence $p_a = 1$ though of course p_a is then no longer the probability that o's *first* response to S_a is R.

72 *Derivation*: Treating the approximations as essentially exact, the ratio of $\mathrm{E}_\infty (H_b)$ to $\mathrm{E}_\infty (H_a)$ in [G7] is a decreasing function of the ratio p_b/p_a. When the latter ratio equals 1, the former equals h_{ab}; hence $\mathrm{E}_\infty(H_b)/\mathrm{E}_\infty(H_a)$ is less than h_{ab} if and only if $p_b > p_a$. But whatever the detailed relation between habit strength and response probability, $p_b > p_a$ requires $\mathrm{E}_\infty(H_b) > \mathrm{E}_\infty(H_a)$ and (since $h_{ab} \leq 1$) is hence inconsistent with [G7] – whence [G8] holds unconditionally, given [G7].

organism can differentiate between them in his behaviour. For Hullian theory to permit perfect discrimination between two stimuli S_a and S_b which initially have appreciable sensory similarity, a mechanism must be found by which discrimination training causes h_{ab} to decrease toward zero.

Hull took a further step toward solution of the discrimination problem when, in 1952 (p. 64ff.), he analysed the to-be-discriminated stimuli S_a and S_b as consisting really of these stimuli plus the complex S_c of background stimuli which accompany all the stimulus alternatives which the experimenter might present in this particular setting, so that what the organism really learns to discriminate is $S_a + S_c$ from $S_b + S_c$. Hull's 1952 contention is that early in discrimination training comprising reinforcement of R to $S_a + S_c$ and extinction of R (or reinforcement of a competing response R^*) to $S_b + S_c$, R is partially conditioned to S_c and hence causes the generalization gradient around S_a to be broad (since presentation of any stimulus, no matter how dissimilar to S_a, will also be accompanied by S_c); but that as discrimination training progresses, the background stimuli become neutralized to where they no longer contribute any reaction potential to the response situation, thereby allowing the generalization gradient around the point of reinforcement to become steeper. Given such a neutralization phenomenon, it might then be hypothesized that any two stimuli S_a and S_b whose sensory similarity h_{ab} is greater than zero may be construed as aggregates of highly dissimilar microstimuli, some of which are common to both S_a and S_b, and that neutralization of the common elements through discrimination training between S_a and S_b leaves only the dissimilar elements effective for response elicitation, thus functionally reducing h_{ab} to zero. Now, I have little doubt that any adequate theory of discrimination will need to recognize a *phenomenon* wherein the organism comes through experience to disregard irrelevant cues, and in fact a number of recent mathematical models for discrimination learning have included a barefaced premise to this effect. Of deeper theoretical significance, however, is to show *how* this can occur. For if $S_i + S_c \rightarrow R$ is consistently reinforced while $S_j + S_c \rightarrow R$ goes consistently unreinforced, $S_c \rightarrow R$ receives partial reinforcement and by the primary principles of most any associationistic theory of learning should persist at some intermediate level of strength. In particular, since the dynamic reformulations of both the earlier and later Hullian systems do, in fact, imply that partial reinforcement maintains moderate habit (or habit-times-incentive) strength, Hull's assumption that discrimination training neutralizes background stimuli was in violation of his own learning postulates.

An alternative approach to the discrimination problem has developed in S-R mediation theory through the hypothesis that the discriminability of stimuli can be enhanced by attaching distinctive responses to them. The contemporary version of this notion, known in the literature as "the acquired distinctiveness of cues,"[73]

---

73 Sometimes this phrase is used to denote the empirical fact that discrimination training between stimuli with respect to one set of responses facilitates subsequent discrimination training on these stimuli with respect to other responses, and at other times to refer to the S-R mediational explanation of this phenomenon. It is the latter sense which is understood here. For a useful historical review of this concept, see Tighe and Tighe (1966).

apparently originated with Miller and Dollard (1941, p. 73), received its major development at the hands of Lawrence (1949, *et seq.*), and has been a major ingredient in recent theorizing about perceptual "coding" (e.g., Lawrence, 1963). Briefly, the idea is as follows: let S_1 and S_2 be two stimuli whose sensory similarity is appreciable, while L_1 and L_2 are "labelling" or "coding" responses whose sensory feedbacks s_{L1} and s_{L2}, respectively, are highly dissimilar. Then reinforcing L_1 to S_1 and L_2 to S_2 will develop conditioned associations whereby presentation of stimulus S_i ($i = 1,2$) elicits label L_i and adds s_{Li} to S_i in the organism's sensorium. In this way stimuli S_1 and S_2 become functionally replaced by $S_1 + s_{L1}$ and $S_2 + s_{L2}$, respectively, and if s_{L1} and s_{L2} are sufficiently distinctive, the sensory similarity of the two complexes $S_1 + s_{L1}$ and $S_2 + s_{L2}$ is less than the original sensory similarity between S_1 and S_2.[74] If stimuli S_1 and S_2 can be perfectly discriminated by the organism *prior* to label training, then the acquired-distinctiveness hypothesis does indeed conceive of a way in which the effective sensory similarity between S_1 and S_2 might be further decreased. It does not, however, help to make perfect discrimination possible in the first place. For if S_1 and S_2 are imperfectly discriminable in themselves, it will be impossible to condition L_1 to S_2 and L_2 to S_2 without establishing $S_1 \rightarrow L_2$ and $S_2 \rightarrow L_1$ in some strength as well, and the latter unwanted associations will cause the feedback from the labelling responses to decrease, rather than to increase, the effective discriminability of S_1 and S_2.

Let me show by a rather condensed argument how this works out quantitatively in a particular mathematical model. (There are innumerable alternatives to the specific case here examined, but any reasonable version which does not contain provision for the acquisition of perfect discrimination *without* introduction of labelling responses or their equivalent should have about the same mathematical structure as the present one.) We make the standard stimulus-sampling assumptions that each stimulus S_i controlled by the experimenter is actually a population of microstimuli from which a particular presentation of S_i draws a random subset; that each response R_j (including labelling responses) occurs in all-or-none fashion; that each microstimulus is either conditioned or not conditioned to R_j; that any operation which conditions a given microstimulus to R_j also simultaneously extinguishes it to any other response R_k with which R_j is incompatible, while a microstimulus once conditioned stays so until extinguished by counterconditioning; that the probability $\Pr(R_j|S_i)$ that a presentation of S_i elicits R_j is equal to the proportion of S_i's microstimuli which are conditioned to R_j at the start of that trial; and that all microstimuli present on a given learning trial become conditioned to the response which is reinforced on that trial. Now let S_1 and S_2 be two stimuli which for simplicity comprise the same number of microstimuli and which contain a subset of microstimuli in common. Then it is easily seen that if L_1 and L_2 are incompatible labelling responses, and a sufficiently long series of conditioning trials is given wherein L_i ($i = 1, 2$) is always reinforced to S_i while both types of trials

---

74 Note that we are *not* here considering the "observing response" concept (cf. Wyckoff, 1952), which envisions the organism's learning to make the *same* response R to both S_1 and S_2, where R in the presence of S_i ($i = 1,2$) produces a new stimulus S^*_i such that S^*_1 and S^*_2 are sharply discriminable.

occur equally often in random alternation, then all the microstimuli unique to stimulus S_i become conditioned to L_i while half the microstimuli common to S_1 and S_2 are conditioned to L_1 and the other half to L_2. Hence asymptotically under label training,

$$\left. \begin{array}{l} \Pr(L_1|S_1) = \\ \Pr(L_2|S_2) = \end{array} \right\} 1 - \alpha \qquad\qquad \left. \begin{array}{l} \Pr(L_2|S_1) = \\ \Pr(L_1|S_2) = \end{array} \right\} \alpha$$

where α ($0 \leq \alpha \leq 0.5$) is half the proportion of microstimuli in S_1 or S_2 which are common to both. Next, after having carried label training to asymptote, we give our subject a series of trials in which discrimination responses R_1 and R_2 are always reinforced to S_1 and S_2, respectively, where R_1 and R_2 are incompatible with each other but not with L_1 and L_2. On the R_1-to-S_1 trials, S_1 will elicit L_1 with probability $1 - \alpha$ and L_2 with probability α, while on the R_2-to-S_2 trials, S_2 will similarly elicit L_2 and L_1 with probabilities $1 - \alpha$ and α, respectively. Hence if the two kinds of discrimination trials are given equally often, the stimuli which arise from L_1's sensory feedback will be reinforced to R_1 on $100(1 - \alpha)\%$ of the trials and to R_2 on $100\,\alpha\%$ of the trials, and similarly for L_2 to R_2 and R_1; so assuming there to be no overlap between the feedbacks from the two labelling responses, the proportions of the microstimuli produced by L_1 which are conditioned to R_1 and to R_2 are asymptotically $1 - \alpha$ and α, respectively, and similarly for L_2. Meanwhile, the proportion of S_i's microstimuli ($i = 1, 2$) conditioned to R_i goes asymptotically to $1 - \alpha$ for the same reason that $\Pr(L_i|S_i)$ went to $1 - \alpha$ under label training, while the proportion of S_i's microstimuli conditioned to the other R-response similarly goes to α.

Now, the probability that R_1 is elicited when S_1 is presented is

$$\begin{aligned} \Pr(R_1|S_1) = {} & \Pr(L_1|S_1) \cdot \Pr(R_1|S_1L_1) + \Pr(L_2|S_1) \cdot \Pr(R_1|S_1L_2) \\ & + \Pr(\bar{L}_1\bar{L}_2|S_1) \cdot \Pr(R_1|S_1\bar{L}_1\bar{L}_2) \\ = {} & (1 - \alpha) \cdot \Pr(R_1|S_1L_1) + \alpha \cdot \Pr(R_1|S_1L_2) + 0, \end{aligned}$$

where $\Pr(R_1|S_1L_i)$ ($i = 1, 2$) is the probability that R_1 is elicited on an S_1-trial on which labelling response L_i is also evoked, and the probability $\Pr(\bar{L}_1\bar{L}_2|S_1)$ that S_1 evokes neither labelling response is zero because label training was carried to asymptote. Further, the probability $\Pr(R_1|S_1L_i)$ that R_1 is elicited on an S_1-trial on which L_i is also evoked is a weighted average of the proportions of microstimuli constituting S_1 and the feedback from L_i, respectively, conditioned to R_1, this weighting being determined by the relative sizes of the microstimulus populations corresponding to S_1 and L_i-feedback. Thus asymptotically,

$$\begin{aligned} \Pr(R_1|S_1L_1) &= (1 - w)(1 - \alpha) + w(1 - \alpha) = 1 - \alpha, \\ \Pr(R_1|S_1L_2) &= (1 - w)(1 - \alpha) + w\alpha, \end{aligned}$$

where w ($0 \leq w \leq 1$) is the weight of label feedback when conjoined with S_1; whence substituting above yields

$$\begin{aligned} \Pr(R_1|S_1) &= (1 - \alpha)(1 - \alpha) + \alpha[(1 - w)(1 - \alpha) + w\alpha] \\ &= (1 - \alpha) - w\alpha(1 - 2\alpha). \end{aligned}$$

The asymptotic probability of a correct discrimination response to S_2 is similarly

$$\Pr(R_2|S_2) = (1 - \alpha) - w\alpha(1 - 2\alpha)$$

while the asymptotic probability of a wrong discrimination response is

$$\left.\begin{array}{l} \Pr(R_2|S_1) = 1 - \Pr(R_1|S_1) = \\ \Pr(R_1|S_2) = 1 - \Pr(R_2|S_2) = \end{array}\right\} \alpha + w\alpha(1 - 2\alpha).$$

Since $\alpha(1 - 2\alpha) > 0$ if $\alpha > 0$, discrimination between S_1 and S_2 with respect to R_1 and R_2 is hence maximal when $w = 0$ – i.e., when feedback from the labelling responses contributes nothing to elicitation of the discrimination responses – and becomes *poorer* as the sensory contribution of the labelling responses increases in importance. Moreover, the model assumes that the two sets of label-feedback stimuli contain no common elements. If the labels were imperfectly discriminable, their impairment of discrimination between S_1 and S_2 would be even worse.

We derive the very same asymptotic equations for $\Pr(R_i|S_j)$ ($i = 1, 2; j = 1, 2$) if, instead of assuming that labelling response L_i occurs probabilistically in all-or-none fashion, we think of L_i as an ensemble of microresponse from which particular elicitations of L_i draw random subsets.[75] (This allows our subject to make the same labelling response to each occurrance of S_j, though that response will be a mixture of correct and incorrect microlabels.) Moreover, conceiving of the labels as stimulus-producing responses is quite unnecessary – the mathematics proceeds in precisely the same way as above if we admit direct sensory-sensory associations and replace L_i, or the microresponses constituting L_i, with sensory elements unmediated by responses. While it is always risky to make inferences from what doesn't work to what can't work, it would appear that *precise discrimination among stimuli containing common elements or having appreciable sensory similarity to one another cannot be explained by principles of association learning alone, whether the associations appealed to be S-S or S-R in nature.* The facts of discrimination implicate the existence of some means by which irrelevant input is suppressed and effectiveness enhanced, but this apparently calls for its own laws, for principles of perceptual processing that involve something more than just evocation bonds among psychological atoms.

Finally, let us consider how some of the structural themes sounded above are embodied in current behaviour-theoretical conceptions of response processes.

c1 The most advanced formulations of systematic behaviour theory in the S-R tradition appear in the recent work of Spence and Mowrer. Both similarly envision an effect of reinforcement upon responding which is very different from older conceptions of instrumental behaviour and which, with a little more tinkering, nearly achieves the formal horsepower of a Tolmanian expectancy.

According to Spence (1956, chap. 5), some components of the response R_g

---

75 In this model we assume that the microresponses in L_1 are respectively paired with those in L_2 in such fashion that microresponses are incompatible with their pair-mates but not otherwise. Alternative assumptions about microresponse incompatibilities lead to somewhat different quantitative results, but the qualitative conclusion remains the same.

made by the organism in a primary reward situation S_g can also be made in the absence of S_g and without interfering with other responses. These detachable components, r_g, of R_g are assumed to be classically conditionable to cues upon which S_g is contingent, while the sensory feedback, s_g, produced by r_g is hypothesized to energize responses which occur in its presence, the degree of such activation being an increasing function of the intensity of s_g. Specifically, if organism o has repeated experiences in which doing R_j in the presence of S_i is followed by primary reward S_g, then both R_j and r_g will become classically conditioned to S_i, the strength of habit $S_i \rightarrow R_j$ being a function of the number of conditioning trials but not of the magnitude of reward supplied by S_g. However, since the intensity of R_g aroused by S_g varies with the latter's reward value, the vigor of r_g and hence the intensity of s_g which becomes conditioned to S_i is a function of primary reward magnitude as well as of number of conditioning trials. Hence when o subsequently encounters cue S_i, the vigour of r_g (or more precisely, the intensity of s_g) thus aroused combines with drive level to multiply the strength of habit $S_i \rightarrow R_j$ into the reaction potential with which S_i elicits R_j from o.[76] Spence (1960, p. 91ff.) has also suggested that extinction of R_j might similarly be explained by an anticipatory frustration response r_f which becomes conditioned to S_i and which inhibits other responses with which it is compresent.

In an independent but remarkably parallel development, Mowrer (1960a, 1960b) has proposed that when organism o has experiences of drive reduction following response R_j, the sensory feedback s_j from R_i will become classically conditioned to a process r_h which Mowrer calls "hope" (or, if the drive reduced is a secondary drive, "relief"). Mowrer is not entirely explicit about the nature of r_h, but it either is or gives rise to a reduction in the organism's drive level and "facilitates" – i.e., intensifies, prolongs or otherwise enhances – the behaviour which it accompanies, the degree of this facilitation presumably being an increasing function of how strong the "hope" is while the latter, in turn, is presumably determined by the magnitude of reward previously received for R_j. Conversely, when R_j has led in the organism's experience to an increment in drive, the feedback from R_j becomes conditioned to a "fear" (or "disappointment") process r_f which increases drive and acts as a behavioural suppressant.

If we consider Spence's fractional goal reaction r_g and Mowrer's "hope" r_h to be functionally equivalent, the most conspicuous difference between these two proposals is that given an organism which has received reward S_g for doing R_j in circumstances S_i, Spence would argue for the conditioning of r_g to S_i, whereas Mowrer envisions r_h becoming attached to the feedback s_j from R_j. Each side of this contrast remedies a defect in the other: in Spence's account, the anticipatory r_g aroused by stimulus S_i should intensify all responses cued to S_i irrespective of whether they have previously been followed by reward S_g or not. Thus if the organism has done R_a and R_b equally often in the presence of S_1, and R_a has always been followed by positive reward S_2 whereas R_b has always produced aversive

---

76 The vigour with which o is engaging in r_g at time t plays essentially the same role in Spence's system as does the value of K for o at t in Hull's 1951–2 theory, and Spence makes clear that he regards his r_g-activation mechanism to be an interpretation of Hull's more abstract incentive concept.

stimulus S_3, the two habits $S_1 \rightarrow R_a$ and $S_1 \rightarrow R_b$ will be at equal strength while the incentive responses elicited by S_1 will be a mixture of r_g from S_2 and r_f from S_3 – a combination which then operates simultaneously on both $S_1 \rightarrow$ and $S_1 \rightarrow R_b$ with the result that S_1 elicits R_a to the very same degree it elicits R_b. It may, however, be argued that the organism should learn a discrimination between stimulus $S_i + s_j$ (where s_j is the feedback from R_j as before) and S_i without s_j, insomuch as it is the former but not the latter which is classically paired with S_g, so that it should be primarily $S_i + s_j$ which elicits the Spencian r_g or r_f, not just S_i by itself. (Spence himself comes very close to making this move when he invokes the idea of a goal-gradient for elicitation of r_g.) Similarly, while Mowrer makes explicit the conditioning of r_h or r_f only to s_j, which as it stands would imply that once the organism emits a response R_j whose feedback arouses r_h he should persevere in doing R_j until $s_j \rightarrow r_h$ extinguishes, it can better be argued that what becomes conditioned to "hope" or "fear" is not just s_j alone but whatever stimulus compound is consistently associated with primary reward or punishment – which compound will generally contain not merely s_j but also the antecedent condition S_i which is discriminative for whether or not R_j results in the reinforcement in question. Hence after minor adjustments to which neither theorist should object, we may say that Mowrer and Spence both propose that *when organism o has experiences in which doing* R_j *in circumstances* S_i *leads to consequence* S_k, *there is a certain effect* e_k *of* S_k *upon o which becomes classically conditioned to* S_i *plus the feedback* s_j *from* R_j, *and which, when evoked, facilitates or inhibits o's ongoing behaviour in a manner appropriate to the motivational value of* S_k *for o.*

It is obvious that the Spence-Mowrer habit construct $S_i + s_j \rightarrow e_k$ has, with one qualification, the same formal structure as Tolmanian expectancy $S_iR_jS_k$. The qualification is that neither Spence nor Mowrer authorize the claim that to every different S_k there corresponds a unique e_k. Spence admits of different es (i.e. different fractional consummatory behaviours) for different primary reward substances (e.g. water versus food) but has suggested no way to differentiate between the es – or even to say that there are any – for stimulus settings which do not call forth consummatory or frustration reactions. Mowrer's original version of hope theory is in even worse shape here, for he speaks of only four kinds of es, namely, hope, relief, fear and disappointment. With no more e-resources than these, giving a hungry and thirsty organism water for doing R_j in the presence of cue S_i should develop the very same expectoid $S_i + s_j \rightarrow r_h$ as would reinforcing him with food, so that after water reinforcement for R_j in S_i, if the organism is put at S_i when hungry but not thirsty, he should feel just as much hope upon starting to do R_j as he would feel were he thirsty but not hungry. Mowrer's hope mechanism will not begin to do the mediational things expected of it (Mowrer, 1960b, chap. 2) unless it is able to tell the organism *what* he is hoping for, and for this reason, Mowrer (1960b, chap. 5) has gone on to add sensory images to the list of what can be elicited by conditional stimuli. Since it does no great violence to Spence's views to broaden his concept of anticipatory goal reactions to include anticipatory perceptual reactions of all sorts, while Mowrer has already made essentially this move, we may conclude that e_k in the Spence-Mowrer expectoid $S_i + s_j \rightarrow e_k$ is in principle distinctive to the particular stimulus outcome S_k experienced by the organism after doing R_j in circumstances S_i.

In formal potential, then, the Spence-Mowrer experience residue $S_i + s_j \to e_k$ acquired by organisms which encounter S_k upon doing R_j in circumstances S_i is equivalent to the Hullian expectancy-counterpart discussed on p. 106, above, and it only remains to see how effectively this structure can be mobilized within the Spence-Mowrer framework to yield expectancy-type phenomena. Most critical is the activation principle: given that organism o is in stimulus situation S_i with non-zero strength of $S_i + s_j \to e_k$, to what extent is o's tendency to do R_j controlled by the motivational significance of S_k for o? This question has three primary facets: (i) activation of R_j given S_i, considering just $S_i + s_j \to e_k$ by itself; (ii) motivationally appropriate selection among two or more competing activations; and (iii) cases where the present motivational value of S_k for o is different from its value when $S_i + s_j \to e_k$ was laid down. With respect to (i), Spence is in excellent health: presentation of S_i with some drive present elicits a modicum of R_j without assistance from e_k, whereupon the partially or weakly aroused R_j adds its feedback s_j to S_i and evokes e_k, which then intensifies or suppresses R_j according to its wont. Mowrer, however, has for some reason eschewed all evocation bonds except those by which hope, fear and images are elicited, so that given a presentation of S_i, Mowrer's organism must sit there until some random process gets R_j started, whereupon $S_i + s_j$ then calls forth e_k to govern the intensity or persistence with which R_j gets completed. (Mowrer's organism would operate much more efficiently were it to regain classically conditioned S-R connections whose R, once aroused by S, is then further facilitated or suppressed by its associated hope or fear.)

With respect to (ii), on the other hand, both Spence and Mowrer have troubles. Suppose that S_1 is a choice-point stimulus at which R_a has led to outcome S_2 while R_b has led to S_3, so that organism o has acquired both $S_1 + s_a \to e_2$ and $S_1 + s_b \to e_3$, and let us suppose also that S_2 is much more valuable to o than is S_3. (E.g. S_2 might be a full food tray while S_3 is an empty one.) Then if the Spence-Mowrer mechanism is to behave expectantly, o must favor R_a over R_b when placed at S_1. However, neither Spence nor Mowrer provide a means by which an elicited e can be *selectively* activating or inhibiting – i.e. e exerts its modulating effect indiscriminately upon whatever behaviours are concurrent with its arousal. Thus if o arrives at S_1 and this elicits compatable fractional components r_a and r_b of R_a and R_b, respectively, S_1 plus the feedback from r_a will tend to arouse e_2 while S_1 plus the feedback from r_b will tend to arouse e_3; but the combined activational effect $e_2 + e_3$ will operate upon both R_a and R_b and whichever response wins out will not be determined by the fact that it is $S_1 + s_a$ which elicits e_2 and $S_1 + s_b$ which elicits e_3 rather than conversely. Whereas if R_a and R_b are completely incompatible, the fact that with S_1 present, arousal of R_a activates strong energizer e_2 while arousal of R_b activates weak energizer e_3, does not help determine which of the two responses R_a or R_b will be the first to get started in S_1's presence – and there is no particular reason why whichever one begins first should not run to completion so long as its consequent e is facilitative. What is needed here is some way for the choice-poised organism to scan the alternative responses he might emit and give each a propensity of occurrence commensurate with the incentive value of its associated e. One mechanism for accomplishing this is the following: we assume that the organism's emission of overt response R_j begins with an incipient component r_j, but that unless r_j exceeds a certain vigour it does not go to its completion R_j; that only one such r_j

can occur at a time but if the one aroused at any given moment does not exceed its completion threshold within a brief time interval Δt, it dies away and is replaced by some other incipient response in the habit-hierarchy cued by the persisting stimuli present; that the response feedback s_j in the stimulus complex $S_i + s_j$ which gets conditioned to incentive effect e_k when the organism encounters S_k upon doing R_j in situation S_i is produced by the incipient beginning r_j of R_j; and that when r_j is elicited by S_j, the likelihood that r_j will achieve the vigour required to reach fruition in R_j before Δt elapses is a function of the enhancement or inhibition produced by the e_k elicited by $S_i + s_j$. Then an organism with nonzero expectoids $S_1 + s_a \rightarrow e_2$ and $S_1 + s_b \rightarrow e_3$, when placed at choice point S_1, will engage in an oscillation (a Tolmanish "vicarious trial and error") between incipient response components r_a and r_b until one of them exceeds the threshold for completion, while the probability that r_a exceeds threshold before r_b does is determined by how much more energizing e_2 is than e_3.[77]

Where both Spence and Mowrer leave the structural potential of expectoid $S_i + s_j \rightarrow e_k$ most unfulfilled, however, is in (iii) its sensitivity to motivational changes. Given that organism o has acquired $S_i + s_j \rightarrow e_k$ through past contingencies of S_k upon R_j in the presence of S_i, neither Spence nor Mowrer provide grounds on which the activational properties of e_k can accommodate to the *current* motivational significance of S_k for o if this differs from S_k's value at the time when $S_i + s_j \rightarrow e_k$ was learned. For example, suppose that S_i is the choice point in a T-maze, R_a is the left-turn response which leads to goal box S_2 containing food, and R_b is the right-turn response which leads to goal box S_3 containing water. Also, suppose that o, while mildly hungry and thirsty, is run through the maze an equal number of times to each goal box, building expectoids $S_1 + s_a \rightarrow e_2$ and $S_1 + s_b \rightarrow e_3$ in which for Spence e_2 and e_3 are fractional anticipatory eating and drinking, respectively, while for Mowrer they are hope-of-food and hope-of-water (or perhaps hope-of-S_2 and hope-of-S_3). If o is now satiated on water but made ravenously hungry, $S_1 + s_a$ and $S_1 + s_b$ will still elicit, respectively, the same degree of anticipatory eating and drinking, or hope-of-food and hope-of-water, that they would were o run under moderate hunger and thirst as before;[78] hence the Spence-Mowrer choice-point expectoids do not help o to make the response which is most suitable to his present needs. Or if, after the T-maze training just stipulated, o's drives remain the same as during training but he is now placed directly in the left goal box and

---

77 A scanning mechanism rather similar to this has already been proposed by Spence (1960, p. 380f.), except that Spence's conception requires feedback from the external environment.

78 We here disregard the important Hullian argument that changing o's drive conditions, and hence the drive stimuli operative within o, also alters the total stimulus complex present at the choice point. Even if the change in drives makes a difference for the relative degrees to which e_2 and e_3 are active prior to the choice-point responses – say by partially arousing e_2 but not e_3 – the only way this should affect response *selection* at choice point S_1 is by making e_2 *less* subject to further arousal by $S_1 + s_a$ than before (presuming that arousal of e_2 has an upper limit), while e_3 becomes *more* available to arousal by $S_1 + s_b$, with the maladaptive result that making o hungry but not thirsty increases the likelihood that he will make the water-side rather than the food-side response.

shocked, thereby making the stimulus complex there (S_2) secondarily aversive to him, incipient left-turning at the choice point will still elicit the same anticipatory eating or hope-of-food (or hope-of-S_2) as before, and his punishment directly in S_2 should not diminish his propensity to turn left (R_2) the next time he reaches the choice point. However, if Spence and Mowrer are willing (as Mowrer has already indicated himself to be) to let the e_k attached to $S_i + s_j$ by the past outcome S_k of doing R_j in circumstances S_i be not energizing or inhibiting in itself, but to correspond to the sensory character of S_k in such fashion that it in turn gives rise to whatever facilitation or suppression S_k would itself produce, then the operation of expectoid $S_i + s_j \rightarrow e_k$ will show proper concern for the organism's present motivational condition. Thus in our T-maze example, if e_2 is not merely anticipatory eating or hope-of-food (or better, anticipatory S_2-reacting or hope-of-S_2), but is a surrogate of food (or of S_2) whose hopefulness or anticipatory consumption arousal depends on how presently attractive food (or S_2) is to o, then when o's interest in food (or in S_2) has been satiated, or the value of food (or S_2) has become more dubious in virtue of its recent traumatic associations, the effect of e_2's evocation by $S_1 + s_a$ at choice point S_1 will be less facilitative of R_a than before and o will most likely make what we consider to be the "correct" response.

I don't think for a minute that the Spence-Mowrer activation hypotheses, with or without my suggested modifications, have much detailed plausibility in their present form, especially in their peripheralistic emphases. But then I hardly imagine that their authors expected them to prove spotlessly veridical. Of greater significance is the remarkable degree to which the most advanced S-R interpretations of instrumental behaviour have uniformly moved toward the same formal structure as found in reconstructed expectancy theory.[79] That this structure is the primary form of many experience residues in higher organisms may, I think, be fairly well accepted as a Class 2 conclusion of behavioural research, though the empirical data which justify it are nowhere near as abundant as is often presupposed. On the other hand, most if not all specific embodiments which have been proposed for this structure, whether cognitive or S-R, have no evidential backing whatsoever and in many cases (especially the S-R models) imply no end of complications which are unwanted, unneeded, and are hence conveniently ignored by their partisans. It is high time to lay aside irrelevant perspectival preconvictions and to get on with parametric studies which will disclose the functional properties of experience residues by inductive argument. Or as Ritchie has appropriately concluded in a similar context:

This marks the end of the controversy between the S-R and cognitive theories. ... I do not mean that all the theoretical differences which have divided these two groups of

---

79 It is worth noting that this structure proposed for *instrumental* conditioning and behaviour has substantially greater complexity than the S-S or S-R mediational account of *classical* conditioning (cf. subsection B1, above). What gives this observation special poignancy is that the currently dominant themes in behaviouristic psychology – statistical learning models, verbal association theory, concept formation, and the like, which in the past few years have gained ascendancy over the behaviour-theoretic tradition – are based exclusively on associationistic structures.

psychologists are now resolved. Nor do I mean that we now have a final analysis of purposive behaviour. All I mean is that on this one issue of the difference between an "expectancy" interpretation and an "r_g" interpretation of purposive behaviour, there can no longer be any basic difference. What must now be done is to devise a more precise mediational analysis of such behaviour, and here I foresee future controversies even more exciting than the old one. (Ritchie, 1959, p. 12)

c2 One of the most important recurrent concerns of behaviour theory has been the nature of responses, notably, whether a "response" is best conceived as a configuration of muscle movements (a "molecular" or "proximal" interpretation), or as an achievement defined without specification of how the organism brings it about (a "molar" or "distal" approach). That there is room in psychology's conceptual pantheon for both muscle movements and achievements, and indeed, that a behaviour theorist can ill afford to ignore either, is widely recognized today. What is perhaps not quite so well appreciated, however, is that the bare question of how the organism is *able* to behave distally (i.e., achievement-wise) raises some exceedingly penetrating problems about the formal structure of the psychological machinery underlying response emission. As the grand finale to this overbloated opus, I shall proffer some thoughts on this matter, taking as my point of departure some recent reflections by Donald Campbell and Neal Miller, and closing (subsection c3) with a formal appraisal of Miller (Geo.), Galanter & Pribram's influential concept of "plan."

However jaundicedly one may view the increasing contamination of psychological theory by cybernetics jargon, it must be conceded that in a few areas, at least, this has stimulated new thinking on long neglected details of old problems. This influence is conspicuous in Miller's (1963, p. 86f.) provocative distinction between "ballistic" responding and "cybernetic" responding, the latter being Miller's proposed mechanism for generating goal-oriented behaviour through reinforcement feedback from the organism's immediate environment. Campbell (1963, p. 135ff.), too, has risen to the cybernetics challenge, though his description of the contrast here at issue as "muscle-consistent" *versus* "object-consistent" modes of responding is free of cybernetic taint. Campbell's proposal is that the organism is enabled to make an object-consistent response by having in his CNS a "template" or "image" of the to-be-achieved goal against which sensory input is matched and behaviour adjusted appropriately. I am quite willing to agree that both Miller and Campbell have envisioned mechanisms which do indeed play a role in achievement behaviour. As will be seen, however, neither account presents either necessary or sufficient conditions for an organism's being able to behave object-consistently, nor do they lay bare the most significant formal aspects of the movement/achievement issue.

Speaking as loosely as conscience will allow, we may consider achievement, molar, distal, or object-consistent responses to be those behaviours which are conceived as *the bringing about of some given environmental condition*, where this "environmental condition" may or may not require the organism's own involvement therein in some specified way. (E.g., when Mother has finally persuaded Junior to eat his carrots, both Mother and Junior have accomplished the very same achievement of *getting-the-carrots-into-Junior*, but in Junior's case, unlike Mother's, a particular relation between responder and environment is a necessary ingredient in the response's completion.) That is, an achievement may be characterized as a distal stimulus configuration (where a "distal stimulus" is a feature of the environment, in contrast to a "proximal-stimulus" pattern of sense-receptor activation), the bringing about of which constitutes the response; while the strength of this response for the organism in a given molar (environmental) situation may be defined in terms of how rapidly, dependably and/or persistently he tends to bring about this distal outcome in this situation.[80] Conversely, a molecular, proximal, muscle-consistent, or movement response is characterized in terms of the organism's limb motions or other bodily adjustments without specification of any particular environmental consequence which may result from these. Then the definitive problem of object-consistent behaviour is to explain how the organism brings about distal stimulus (i.e., environmental outcome) S^G with some degree of dependability, given that he is in situation S^a within which attainment of S^G is physically possible. To keep discussion as simple as possible for now, let us assume that S^a is a certain region of space whose physical contents include a distinctive object A, and that we are studying the approach response *getting-to*-A.[81] Environmental situation S^a may be formally regarded as a set $S^a = \{S^a_i\}$ of proximal stimulus configurations, each element S^a_i of which is the totality of sense-receptor impingements received by organism o when he assumes a particular locus and posture in this setting. Similarly, the achievement *being-at*-A may be identified with a subset S^A of S^a, namely, those S^a_i one of which impinges upon o when he has assumed some posture and location which satisfy our criterion for *being-at-A*. Now when organism o is introduced into situation S^a, if he is not placed at A to begin with, he can get there only by emitting a series of specific movements, albeit there are innumerably many different movement sequences which will produce this result. Let $\mathbf{r} = \{r_j\}$ be the set of all alternative configurations of effector-organ actions – i.e. proximal responses – which o is in principle able to emit at any given moment. Then o makes distal achievement response $R^A =_{\text{def}}$ *getting-to*-A if and only if he puts together a string of proximal responses from $\mathbf{r}$ which terminate in his receiving a proximal stimulus in S^A. The strength of distal response R^A for o in this situation may be measured by how rapidly or effectively o succeeds in emittting an S^A-terminating movement sequence irrespective of the proximal stimulus in S^a with whose impingement o begins responding, while if the strength of R^A for o in S^a is to be high, the determinants of o's movements must be such that for every proximal

80 I am here deliberately evading an honest attempt at acuity in this description of achievement-response concepts in order to stay clear of certain fundamental conceptual problems about which, regrettably, contemporary psychology is as yet ill prepared to think. Some hints concerning the nature of these problems may be found in Rozeboom (1961).

81 Of all object-consistent behaviours, *approach* is both the simplest and the one which has been most prominent in behavioural research and theory. For example, the "place" behaviour in the "place *versus* response" learning experiments (cf. Kimble, 1961, p. 223f.) is an approach response, while Spence's (1937, *et seq.*) account of "relational" responding makes sense only if the response being generalized and inhibited is approach.

stimulus S^a_i in $\mathbf{S}^a$, o's proximal-response sequence initiated at S^a_i soon eventuates in an element of $\mathbf{S}^4$.

According to Miller (1963), an organism's approach to A in situation $\mathbf{S}^a$ is "cybernetic" when the sequence of proximal responses by which R^4 goes to completion is guided throughout by reinforcement feedback from the proximal stimuli encountered in the course of getting to A. I am not entirely clear whether Miller intends his concept of "cybernetic responding" to subsume all behaviours directed by environmental feedback, or whether it is restricted to special cases of this in which control is effected specifically through the motivational properties of the feedback stimuli. The generic notion of cybernetic feedback control would seem to give priority to the first of these alternatives. But if this were all that is envisioned by "cybernetic responding," the concept would be empty; for *all* movement sequences, no matter how arbitrary, are feedback governed in that each proximal response carries the organism into a new stimulus impingement – i.e., the response's feedback – which then elicits, cues, or otherwise regulates whatever responses are in turn influenced by it. Thus the running off of a Watsonian reflex chain qualifies as cybernetically guided behaviour in the broadest sense of this notion, regardless of whether this particular cluster of reflexes produces object-consistent results. What Miller appears to have in mind by "cybernetic guidance," however, is a more specific mechanism by which *going-to*-A is brought about not through a series of reflexive elicitations but by the moment-to-moment motivational effects of successive proximal stimulation. Just how this mechanism is to work, Miller leaves somewhat obscure. He cites with approval Mowrer's activation hypothesis, which holds that present stimulation facilitates or suppresses ongoing behaviour according to the reinforcement value of that stimulus; but even granting that the proximal stimuli projected by object A are positively reinforcing in such fashion that the closer to and/or more accurately aimed at A the organism is, the more valuable (i.e., activating) is the proximal stimulation thereby received, it still remains to show how this will get the organism to A. For example, if the organism orients toward A by head turning while the more frontal is a retinal projection of A the more facilitatively reinforcing it is, then head turning will be given maximal activation as A passes through frontal projection and it will be exceedingly difficult to get the organism's head *stopped* in the frontal-A position. In general, the Miller-Mowrer activation mechanism is highly inefficient in that if proximal stimulus S^a_i is positively reinforcing, it intensifies whatever movement the organism is making when S^a_i arrives, and this may not at all resemble the movement which maximizes immediate reinforcement once S^a_i is present. I suspect that what Miller is really surmising is the existence of some means by which the organism scans the alternative responses available to him at a given moment and selects the one which produces the most valuable feedback. But there can be no such mechanism for the simple reason that the organism must actually *make* a response before he can receive its feedback. The closest approximation to it would be some procedure by which the organism makes several brief response forays followed by return to the starting point, the various reinforcement consequences of these being then somehow compared and the most successful of these forays repeated unconditionally, its outcome then becoming the anchor position for a new set of explorations. That some human and animal behaviour (e.g., the oscillatory head turning of VTEing rats) is like this seems very plausible to me, but it is surely a special and complex process which requires explanation in terms of more fundamental mechanisms, not one which is a satisfying *basis* for behavioural explanation. Regardless of how it is accomplished, moreover, if the organism's responses in a given situation progress by successively maximizing (or roughly so) the reinforcement value of immediate feedback, what is object-consistent about his behaviour in this setting is that he generally ends up where the most rewarding stimulation happens to be (or at least at a local peak of reinforcement), and his achievement is properly described not as *getting-to*-A but as *getting-to-the-most-valuable-place-around-here*. To be sure, if the stimuli in S^A are the most valuable ones for organism o which occur in situation S^a, then o will go to A in the process of getting to the most valuable place in S^a; but if at all possible, we should like to be able to conceive of o's being able to emit the achievement-response *getting-to*-A in situation S^a even when A is *not* in fact the most rewarding place in S^a for o, so that, e.g., o can behave in a fashion commonsense would describe as o's deciding to go to A, and doing so, because o mistakenly thinks this is the most valuable place for him around here.[82] Moreover, Miller suggests that the organism may also eventually learn how to achieve *getting-to-A* by "ballistic" – i.e. elicitational – responding which does not depend upon motivational feedback, thus implying that cybernetic guidance in his sense is only one of alternative means by which an organism can produce a consistent distal outcome. Consequently, while Miller's ballistic/cybernetic contrast raises some interesting speculations about what the flux of reinforcement throughout a sequence of proximal responses contributes to approach behaviour, it does little to clarify what significant theoretical differences, if any, there may be between movements and achievements.

Campbell, on the other hand, plunges into the movement/achievement issue off the deep end when he asserts that "every molar, object-consistent act is purposive or goal-oriented" (Campbell, 1963, p. 145), and proposes that the organism achieves goals by having a "template" or "image" of the desired outcome against which he matches present stimulation and behaves to reduce the discrepancy. The trouble with this account is that its second part is fragmentary while its first part is altogether unacceptable. Let us agree that when organisms have purposes, these do indeed act to bring about realization of their intended goals, though of course not all purposes are successful. To hold that *all* object-consistent behaviour is purposive, however, is either to make a fantastically implausible assumption about the extent to which cognition controls even the most primitive forms of behaviour, or to redefine the word "purpose" with imperial disdain for what is ordinarily meant by this term. The essential ingredient of a *purpose* (i.e., want, desire, intention) is a cognitive conception of a valued but not-yet-existent state of affairs. That is, purposes are here-and-now internal conditions of the organism which are cognitively *about* (i.e. designate, refer to, signify) the future goals they help the organism to attain. To date, scientific psychology has learned little if anything

---

82 What I have in mind here is a rather subtle but extremely important point about the possible formal structure of achievement responding which will become clarified on p. 148f.

about the nature and functioning of purposes – our knowledge on this score is pretty well confined to the lore of commonsense mentalistic psychology. Nor shall we acquire any scientific understanding of purposes as a distinctive class of psychological processes until we begin, oh so carefully, to tease out the technical differences between purpose-directed and non-purposive behaviour. And we have no good reason whatsoever to think that all object-consistent actions are purposeful. Rainwater usually ends up in the lowest depression accessible to it, and a rivulet breaking a fresh course down a shallow slope often conveys a vivid impression of search behaviour, yet shall we say that free-running water is possessed of *desire* to reach a lower level? Or consider the moth who is drawn to the streetlight with remarkable object-consistent repetitiveness – is his molar approach-to-light achieved *on purpose*? I suspect that Campbell has allowed himself to be beguiled by the ambiguity of the expression "goal-oriented," which is often used metaphorically to signify that there is a certain outcome – the "goal" – which the system in question consistently brings about despite variations in the route by which this outcome is reached, whereas the primary meaning of this phrase is that the system (organism) is directed toward the goal by his present desirous conception of it. Few educated persons today – surely not Campbell – would seriously suspect that anthropomorphic *intentions* govern the actions of inanimate servomechanisms, the homeostatic adjustments of bodily maintenance mechanisms, the tropisms of plants and taxes of primitive animals, and the like. But they *do* underlie much human behaviour and probably that of other higher animals as well. So, to equate "purposive" with "goal-directed" and then to interpret the latter in its metaphorically extended sense of "different conditions, different movements, same outcome," as apparently favoured by Campbell and others (e.g., Rosenblueth and Wiener, 1950; Churchman and Ackoff, 1950), is at the very least to ravage our conceptual resources for differentiating cognitive purposes from more primitive sources of object-consistent behaviour, and is more likely to have the force of denial that the distinction is worth preserving at all.

As for Campbell's suggestion that distal achieving is controlled by "templates" or "images" of desired outcomes, this is a tempting enough description of our own introspected purposes, but it is surely not a *necessary* condition for object-consistent behaviour – tropisms and taxes will suffice as counterexamples. Moreover, when Campbell cites thermostats and engine governors as paradigm instances of template-controlled systems, it is clear that his templates cannot be equated with "images" in any ordinary sense of the term (does a thermostat have an "image," mental or otherwise, of a to-be-sought temperature?), and it yet remains for the performance characteristics of a "template" to be identified. I conclude that while Campbell's account mobilizes some important intuitions about the nature of object-consistent behaviour, its value lies more in its powerful evocation of questions than in any sense of closure supplied by its answers.

I shall now set forth what seem to me to be the most salient dimensions of the movement/achievement issue. I make no pretense at comprehensiveness or technical depth; my intent is only to sketch with a few bold strokes the oversimplified essentials of a structure whose details are bound to vary considerably from one specific instance of distal behaviour to another.

Our guiding problem, it will be recalled, is to say what is involved in an organism's being able to emit an achievement (object-consistent) response R^G in a molar situation (distal environment) $\mathbf{S}^a$ regardless of how he is initially positioned therein. As before, we may think of situation $\mathbf{S}^a$ as formally equivalent to the set $\{S^a{}_i\}$ of alternative proximal stimulus configurations which might conceivably confront the organism in this environment, except that to avoid needless limitations we shall adopt an importantly broader conception of "proximal stimulus configuration" than suggested previously. Specifically, the proximal stimulation S_i acting upon organism o at any given moment t will be considered to include not merely the total input from o's sense receptors at time t, but also decaying traces of the stimuli and movements respectively received and emitted by o just prior to t to the extent that these, too, make a difference for what o does at time t. We shall also continue to assume that an achievement response R^G consists in the bringing about of some environmental conditions $\mathbf{S}^G$ which corresponds to a set $\{S^G{}_i\}$ of possible proximal stimulus configurations, one of which confronts o when he succeeds in attaining $\mathbf{S}^G$.[83] Then o emits achievement response R^G on a given trial in situation $\mathbf{S}^a$ if and only if he manages to encounter one of the proximal stimuli in $\mathbf{S}^G$ on that trial. (This does not require, as was assumed in our previous example of approach behaviour, that $\mathbf{S}^G$ is a subset of $\mathbf{S}^a$. However, if it is possible for o to do R^G in situation $\mathbf{S}^a$, sets $\mathbf{S}^a$ and $\mathbf{S}^G$ cannot be fully disjoint.)

Now, it is an obvious but fundamental fact about molar behaviour that organisms can accomplish distal achievements only *by means of* their proximal movements, while similarly the distal environment regulates the organism's movements only through the mediation of proximal stimulus impingements. Moreover, if $\mathbf{r} = \{r_i\}$ is the set of all alternative movement configurations possible to organism o, which element of $\mathbf{r}$ is emitted by o at any given moment is determined jointly by o's proximal-response dispositions to the various proximal stimuli which he *might* have received at that moment and the proximal stimulation which he *in fact* then encountered. That is, the habits, motives, abilities and other psychological attributes which o brings with him to his stimulus encounter at time t determine for each possible stimulus totality S_i a distribution of potential response probabilities for o at t, namely, the probabilities for what o *would* do if o *were* to receive stimulation S_i at time t; while which of these potential response-probability distributions becomes actual is selected by the stimulation which o does in fact receive at time t.[84] We may thus characterize o's proximal response dispositions in situation $\mathbf{S}^a$ at any

---

83 Simple identification of distal achievements with sets of proximal stimuli is one of the more significant ways in which the present discussion of object-consistent behaviour is an oversimplification, since this fails, e.g., to distinguish between *accomplishing* $\mathbf{S}^G$ and *perceiving that* $\mathbf{S}^G$ *is accomplished*. However, a more penetrating analysis is impractical here and would in any event affect the argument only in technical details which are irrelevant to the points here at issue.

84 Analysis of response tendencies in terms of *probabilities*, as adopted here, presupposes that all responses are emitted in all-or-none fashion. This is not quite so serious a limitation as it might first appear, since if a given response can occur in varying degrees, these degree-alternatives may be formally treated as a set of alternative all-or-none responses.

given moment by a matrix $\mathbf{P_{Sr}}^a = \{Pr(r_j|S_i^a)\}$ whose rows and columns correspond respectively to the proximal stimulus configurations in $\mathbf{S}^a$ and proximal movement configurations in $\mathbf{r}$, and whose entry at row i and column j is the probability that o would respond to S_i^a by movement r_j. The array of probabilities $\mathbf{P_{Sr}}^a$ may be called o's "proximal responsivity matrix in situation $\mathbf{S}^{a\prime\prime}$" or, more briefly, o's *responsivity* to $\mathbf{S}^a$. The extent to which o is disposed to achieve distal outcome $\mathbf{S}^G$ in situation $\mathbf{S}^a$ is then an analytic consequence of o's responsivity to $\mathbf{S}^a$ together with the manner in which the physical properties of the situation cause one proximal stimulus in $\mathbf{S}^a$ to be followed by another, contingent upon o's proximal behavior. Specifically, let $\mathbf{P_{SrS}}^a$ be the 3-dimensional array whose element $Pr(S_k^a|S_i^a r_j)$ is the probability that organism o receives proximal stimulation S_k^a upon emitting proximal movement r_j in the presence of proximal stimulus S_i^a. $\mathbf{P_{SrS}}^a$ may be called the *reactivity* of situation $\mathbf{S}^a$ to o. Then o's first-order transition matrix $\mathbf{P_{SS}}^a = \{Pr(S_j^a|S_i^a)\}$ in $\mathbf{S}^a$, whose element $Pr(S_j^a|S_i^a)$ is the probability that when o is confronted with proximal stimulus S_i^a the next proximal stimulation he receives is S_j^a, follows from $\mathbf{P_{Sr}}^a$ and $\mathbf{P_{SrS}}^a$ by the relation

$$Pr(S_j^a|S_i^a) = \sum^k Pr(r_k|S_i^a) \cdot Pr(S_j^a|S_i^a r_k).$$

Assuming that o's responsivity to $\mathbf{S}^a$ and $\mathbf{S}^a$'s reactivity to o remain essentially constant throughout a given trial (we shall consider changes in $\mathbf{P_{Sr}}^a$ later), the probability that a sequence of n movements by o in situation $\mathbf{S}^a$ starting with proximal stimulus S_i^a deposits him at proximal stimulation S_j^a is given by the element in row i and column j of matrix $(\mathbf{P_{SS}}^a)^n$ (i.e., matrix $\mathbf{P_{SS}}^a$ multiplied times itself n times), which is o's nth-order transition matrix in $\mathbf{S}^a$. Let $\mathbf{p_S}^a$ be a row vector of starting probabilities for o in $\mathbf{S}^a$ – i.e. the ith element in $\mathbf{p_S}^a$ is the probability that S_i^a is the first proximal stimulation to confront o when he is introduced into situation $\mathbf{S}^a$. Then the ith element of vector $\mathbf{p_S}^a(\mathbf{P_{SS}}^a)^n$ (i.e., the product of o's starting vector and nth order transition matrix in $\mathbf{S}^a$) is the probability that o's nth movement after his introduction into situation $\mathbf{S}^a$ carries him into proximal stimulus position S_i^a. The probability $Pr(S^G|S^a, n)$ that o accomplishes distal achievement $\mathbf{S}^G$ within his first n movements in $\mathbf{S}^a$ is hence

$$Pr(S^G|S^a, n) = 1 - \prod_{k=1}^{n} [\sum^{\bar{g}} \mathbf{p_S}^a(\mathbf{P_{SS}}^a)^k],$$

where $\sum^{\bar{g}} \mathbf{p_S}^a(\mathbf{P_{SS}}^a)^k$ is the sum of probability elements in vector $\mathbf{p_S}^a(\mathbf{P_{SS}}^a)^k$ corresponding to those proximal stimuli in $\mathbf{S}^a$ which are *not* also set $\mathbf{S}^G$, while the strength of o's propensity to achieve $\mathbf{S}^G$ in situation $\mathbf{S}^a$ is shown by the asymptote of $Pr(S^G|S^a, n)$ with increasing n and the rapidity with which this is approached.

The mathematical details of the preceding paragraph (which are but finitary approximations to a continuous reality) are not crucial for present purposes and have been developed only to convey some technical appreciation for the relation between proximal and distal responses. What is fundamental here is that whatever distal achievement tendencies an organism may have in a given situation, these are analytic abstractions from his proximal responsivity to that situation together with the latter's reactivity to the organism. This was, to be sure, evident from the outset;

yet frequently the obvious does not assume its proper significance until it has been thought through in some depth. As it is, the movement/achievement distinction is often discussed in terms which misleadingly imply an *opposition* between movements and achievements, or which confound this difference in level of analysis with the contrast between outcome-divergent and outcome-convergent patterns of molar behaviour. For example, we have here concurred with Campbell's apparent equating of "muscle-consistent" responses with proximal movements and "object-consistent" responses with distal achievements; yet the main thrust of Campbell's argument is that muscle-consistency and object-consistency are *rival* hypotheses about a given bit of behaviour (Campbell, 1963, p. 138). Now, when the muscle-consistency/object consistency distinction is aligned with the movement/achievement, proximal/distal or molecular/molar contrast, muscle-consistent responding at the proximal level is a prerequisite for distal object-consistency rather than an alternative to it, insomuch as an organism can consistently produce achievement S^G in situation S^a only if he consistently makes the appropriate muscle movements in response to the various proximal stimuli he encounters on his way to the goal. That is, an organism with a high strength of S^G-achievement in situation S^a shows flexibility in his trial-to-trial behaviour in S^a *not* (in general) because there is any special lack of consistency in his proximal response to a given element S^a_i of S^a, but because on different trials he passes through different sequences of proximal stimuli in S^a. (While consistent achievement of S^G in situation S^a will usually tolerate some degree of variability in the organism's proximal response to each S^a_i – i.e., an S^G-achieving responsivity matrix $\mathbf{P_{sr}}^a$ does not have to contain only zeros and unities – the lower the probability that o makes the optimal movement at each proximal stimulus position S^a_i, the more inefficient will be o's achievement of S^G.) When Campbell conceives of "muscle-consistent" behaviour as an alternative to object-consistency, he has in mind cases where the organism's responsivity matrix in S^a makes likely the same proximal response to *different* proximal stimuli in S^a even when consistency in distal outcome requires that appropriately different movements be made to these. For example, in a "transposition" experiment of the type which has been paradigmatic for Campbell's thinking on this matter (cf. Campbell, 1954), organism o learns to choose the west alley at a maze choice point approached from the south and is then given a trial on which he enters the choice point from the north. If on the test trial o again goes west at the choice point, his behaviour is "object consistent" in that he gets to the same environmental destination as before; whereas if he continues to turn left, which is the movement a west turn required previously, his distal accomplishment at the choice point is now to go eastward and his behaviour shows "muscle consistency" rather than object consistency. But the proximal stimulus configurations presented by the two directions of choice-point entry, say S_s for approach-from-south and S_n for approach-from-north, must be discriminably different if object-consistent responding is here possible at all, so the difference between "muscle-consistency" and "object-consistency" here comes to whether o has acquired a high probability of left-turning to *both* S_s and S_n or, alternatively, a high probability of right-turning to S_n along with his left-turning to S_s. When discussing response processes, we must thus be careful not to confuse issues pertaining to level of analysis (e.g., molecular study of individual cells in proximal responsivity matrix $\mathbf{P_{Sr}}^a$ *versus* molar study of properties abstracted from the sequential unfolding into $\mathbf{P_S}^a(\mathbf{P_{SS}}^a)^n$ of $\mathbf{P_{Sr}}^a$ as a whole) with issues concerning differences among response patterns at the same level. In particular, the extent to which an organism is consistent in his proximal responses to individual proximal stimuli in situation $\mathbf{S}^a$ must not be confused with the extent to which his responsivity to $\mathbf{S}^a$ generates a muscle-consistent *molar* pattern rather than an object-consistent one.

Insomuch as distal behaviours are unfoldings of proximal responsivities, any behavioural principle (e.g. laws of learning) or distinction (e.g. manifestly goal-oriented *versus* manifestly aimless actions) at the molar level of analysis has a counterpart on the level of proximal movements as well. It does not, however, follow that a given principle or distinction presents the same appearance or emphasizes the same problems in molar form as it does when recast in terms of its proximal underpinnings. In my judgment, much past discussion of goal-directedness in behaviour has been subtly distorted and misdirected by insufficient attention to differences in level – not so much in that what has been said is obviously wrong, but because what seems most significant at the molar level turns out under molecular analysis to have only secondary importance for the major points at issue, or to have relevance in a way which is quite different from the way in which it appears to matter. The persistent attempts which have been made to equate purposiveness with cybernetic guidance (and I am not thinking especially of Miller or Campbell here) are a good illustration of this. As observed previously, *all* molar behaviour, object-consistent or not, is cybernetically governed in the broad sense of feedback control, insomuch as each movement of the organism revises the proximal stimulation bearing upon his responsivity matrix and thus actualizes a different set of proximal response probabilities. Since this is true fully as much for outcome-divergent responsivities as it is for outcome-convergent ones, the generic concept of cybernetic guidance does nothing to illuminate the difference between molar behaviour which is object-consistent and molar behaviour which is not. Neither is the "feedback" notion particularly helpful at the molecular level of analysis. The organism's proximal behaviour at any given instant is probabilistically selected by the proximal stimulation which precedes that movement, not by the stimulation which results from it; and once we appreciate that molar behaviour is contained in the sequential unfolding of proximal responsivities, there is nothing more we can learn from cybernetic feedback concepts about what particular molar patterns may be contained in a given $\mathbf{P_{Sr}}^a$ or why the numerical probabilities in $\mathbf{P_{Sr}}^a$ are what they are for a particular organism on a particular occasion. As will be noted, this charge of irrelevancy does not apply to the guidance hypotheses of Miller and Campbell, but the latter have value because they propose specific molecular processes which might generate an object-consistent molar pattern, and what is of interest about them is not that they illuminate the difference between object-consistent and response-consistent modes of responding but that they touch upon issues much more fundamental to the problem of purposiveness than is the mere presence or absence of manifest goal-directedness in behaviour.

For there are two classes of problems which emerge from study of the constitution of achievement behaviour: (i) those concerning the nature of object-consistent responding as such, which turns out to be a matter with little behaviour-theoretical significance however important it may be for cybernetic engineering; and (ii) questions about the dynamic and system-constraint laws which govern the probabilities in proximal responsivity matrices, such questions being generally indifferent to whether these responsivities have outcome-convergent or outcome-divergent molar unfoldings even though they are critical for differentiating purposeful from purposeless behaviour. By problems of the first kind, I mean those which are basically of form, "How is it possible for organism o consistently to achieve distal outcome S^G in situation S^a?" The reason why this is ultimately unimportant, despite its well-intentioned concern for underlying causes, is that the necessary and sufficient answer to this question is given by the proximal responsivity matrix $\mathbf{P}_{Sr}{}^a$ (and the situation's reactivity $\mathbf{P}_{Srs}{}^a$) in virtue of which o's behaviour in S^a consistently attains S^g; while once the probabilities in $\mathbf{P}_{Sr}{}^a$ are specified, the particular mechanism which generates them makes no further difference for o's behaviour in S^a. For example, if proximal stimulus configuration $S_i{}^a$ includes sense-organ activity s together with the fresh trace of movement r, the probability $\Pr(r|S_i{}^a)$ that o does r given stimulus $S_i{}^a$ could be high either, $inter$ $alia$, because input s is positively reinforcing to o and facilitates the trace of r in $S_i{}^a$ according to Miller's motivational-feedback mechanism, because o has acquired an expectancy $S_i{}^a r S_j{}^a$ whose third term, $S_j{}^a$, is highly valenced by o, or because stimulus complex $S_i{}^a$ elicits r reflex-wise in virtue of o's having previously experienced classical contingencies between $S_i{}^a$ and an unconditioned elicitor of r – and which of these alternatives, if any, happens to be the source of $\Pr(r|S_i{}^a)$ is irrelevant to o's molar behaviour in S^a. To be sure, it is an interesting intellectual exercise, and of considerable value for cybernetic technology, to design responsivities which confer a reliable disposition to produce distal outcome S^G in a given environmental setting S^a, especially when essentially the same molar achievement can be produced by many different responsivity matrices differing greatly in efficiency and complexity. Also, further insight into the management of distal behaviour by real organisms will soon require research techniques for discovering what proximal responsivities are, in fact, responsible for an organism's achievements on a given experimental occasion. But the responsivity matrix which explains a particular pattern of molar behaviour in itself reveals little about this action's psychological genesis – as may be appreciated by reflecting that if we know the numerical probabilities in $\mathbf{P}_{Sr}{}^a$ for a given o, we can in principle always wire them into a robot which will then behave just as object-consistently as o in situation S^a, even though to infer a significant parallel between the inner workings of o and the circuitry of our robot would be to succumb to the crudest sort of analogical thinking. In fact, we can (again in principle) build a robot whose circuitry allows us to give any configuration of values in $\mathbf{P}_{Sr}{}^a$ that we please, whether the molar behaviour so generated be outcome-convergent or outcome-divergent, simply by setting a dial for each cell in $\mathbf{P}_{Sr}{}^a$. It must be concluded, therefore, that the difference between object-consistent and response-consistent responsivity patterns has little significance as $such$ for behaviour theory.

Even so, the special features of object-consistent behaviour reappear with transfigured thrust when one begins to question how, in the normal course of real-life behavioural events, organisms ever manage to acquire responsivities which have this character. Consider again the proximal movements of an organism who, in a reversible-stem T-maze $\mathbf{S}^m$, has learned to turn into the west goal-alley rather than into the east one, irrespective of the direction from which he arrives at the choice point. If $S_s{}^m$ and $S_n{}^m$ are the proximal stimulus configurations which confront o as he reaches the choice point from the south and from the north, respectively, while r_L and r_R are respectively the proximal movements of turning left and turning right, then o's molar disposition at the choice point in $\mathbf{S}^m$ is properly characterized as *turning into the west goal-alley* if and only if o's responsivity matrix for this situation has r_L as the high-probability response to $S_s{}^m$ and r_R as the high-probability response to $S_n{}^m$.[85] If o's T-maze training has consisted of repeated rewards in the west goal box culminating trials from both south and north starting positions, then o's acquisition of a responsivity to $\mathbf{S}^a$ which unfolds into consistent $\mathbf{S}^G$-achievement consistency is fully to be expected on traditional grounds, insomuch as o has then been reinforced for doing r_L in the presence of $S_s{}^m$ and for r_R in the presence of $S_n{}^m$. Immensely more challenging, however – and this has been found experimentally not merely to occur but to prevail – is for o to acquire a turn-westward-at-choice-point pattern just from training on a single direction of choice-point entry, as demonstrated by o's later turning, after a number of approach-from south trials, into the west goal alley the very first time he is allowed to enter the choice point from the north. That is, reinforcement of r_L in the presence of $S_s{}^m$ generally increases not merely $\Pr(r_L|S_s{}^m)$ but $\Pr(r_R|S_n{}^m)$ as well. Insomuch as stimulus configuration $S_s{}^m$ and $S_n{}^m$ are certain to share a great many features which should induce primary stimulus generalization between them, whereas r_L and r_R are opposing responses, this is a transfer phenomenon altogether inexplicable under any orthodox theory of learning.[86]

85 This is, of course, an enormous simplification of the choice-point situation, since in reality there are many different proximal stimulus configurations available to the organism through arrival at the choice point from either direction, while turning either right or left is actually the outcome of a sequence of more molecular movements.

86 Note that expectancy theory is no better off than any other in this regard. Even if o acquires expectancy $S^m{}_s\ r_L\ S_w$ from experiences in which left-turn r_L in the presence of choice-point stimulus $S^m{}_s$ leads to west goal-box S_w while S_w becomes highly valenced through its association with primary reward, the theory provides no reason why this should also lead o to expect S_w from turning right in the presence of the altered choice-point stimulus $S_n{}^m$.

In their sophisticated and inexcusably neglected analysis of achievement behaviour, MacCorquodale and Meehl (1954, p. 218ff.) have likewise called attention to the appearance in achievement learning of puzzling generalizations across incompatible responses, and later (1954, p. 251ff.) suggest an expectancy postulate which might cover them. Unfortunately, MacCorquodale and Meehl interpret the "multiple trackness" of object-consistent behaviour to be cases wherein (*a*) several different (i.e. incompatible) responses to the *same* stimulus S will achieve the same molar outcome and (*b*) reinforcement of one of these responses to S also strengthens some of the other, alternatively goal-effective, responses to S as well. We observed above (p. 143), however, that while goal attainment in a given molar situation *may* allow alternative movements to the same proximal stimulus,

The general point illustrated by the foregoing example is the following. Suppose that situation S^a is one in which achievement of molar outcome S^G, and only this, is strongly rewarding to organism o. If o were to have repeated experiences with each proximal stimulus configuration S_i^a in S^a (or at least with a sufficiently large proportion of the more critical ones), then o should eventually learn to emit at S_i^a the proximal movement which most efficiently eventuates in reinforcement, and o's acquisition of a responsivity to S^a which unfolds into consistent S^G-achievement is in this case theoretically uninteresting. But in fact, mature organisms frequently seem to develop object-consistent responsivity to a new situation from experience with only a few of the proximal stimuli therein. That is, the organism's probability distribution in row i of $\mathbf{P}_{Sr}{}^a$ usually arises not from any learning involving S_i^a directly, but through generalization or transfer from what has been learned from experience with certain other stimuli in S^a – except that the patterns of proximal-stimulus/proximal-response "generalization" which yield object-consistent molar behaviour seem often to be wildly at variance with the forms of generalization and transfer with which we have become familiar in past research on learning. This, then, is the behaviour-theoretical significance of achievement responses: not that there is anything inherently interesting about an organism's bare *having* of the ability to behave object-consistently in a given situation, but that the dynamics of that ability's *acquisition*, when examined at the proximal level, is likely to reveal patterns of covariation among responsivity elements which are not adequately accounted for by known behavioural principles. (Note, moreover, that if $\Pr(r_j|S_i^a)$ and $\Pr(r_k|S_h^a)$ show trial-to-trial covariation in a manner alien to accepted laws of transfer, the theoretical challenge of this phenomenon is in no way diminished if the behaviour to which these probabilities contribute does *not* show any special propensity to bring about a consistent distal outcome.) When we become able to determine empirically what transfer patterns do in fact hold among responsivity elements during the course of molar learning, we shall also be in position to infer inductively what sorts of internal conditions underlie an organism's manifestly goal-directed actions, and the laws by which these under-lying determinants are governed. Meanwhile, we can develop some notions about what forms of responsivity organization to look for by imaginative creation, as in Miller's motivational feedback hypothesis and Campbell's "template" proposal, of guidance mechanisms which generate object-consistent responsivities acquirable through a relatively small number of learning experiences.[87]

the fundamental methodological problem of object-consistent behaviour is getting the organism to make appropriately different movements to the *different* proximal stimuli which arise for him in this situation.

87 Miller's activation mechanism, reviewed above, implies a highly distinctive and specific set of dynamic and system-constraint laws to govern the probabilities in $\mathbf{P}^a_{Sr}$, though for reasons given earlier it is highly questionable whether this would produce the molar behaviour which Miller expects of it. (What Miller really wants is a responsivity matrix which maximizes the reinforcement value of the input feedback from each proximal movement, but a mechanism for accomplishing this has not yet been proposed.) Campbell's template hypothesis, on the other hand, has no specific responsivity-pattern implications

Before plunging into serious research on how responsivities are modified by experience, however, we need also to consider a further important question about the dynamics of responsivity matrices. Are responsivities themselves *learned*, akin to habits, expectancies and associations, or are they *aroused*, like responses and ideas, by stimulus-like antecedents which operate upon something else which has been learned. I have discussed the generic difference between learnable and arousable psychological attributes elsewhere (Rozeboom, 1965) and will not review the analysis here, but the distinction is largely a matter of temporal stability. Do the numerical probabilities in $\mathbf{P}_{Sr}{}^a$ for organism o, while modifiable by experience and motivation, nevertheless have the same degree of *relative* constancy as do habits and expectancies (or at least habits-times-drive and valenced expectancies), or do they have the moment-to-moment variability of actions and ideational processes? To take a concrete example, suppose that environment $\mathbf{S}^a$ contains, among other things, objects A and B. Let us say that an organism o in situation $\mathbf{S}^a$ is *going-to-A* at moment t if the numerical pattern in o's responsivity to $\mathbf{S}^a$ (together with the reactivity of $\mathbf{S}^a$ to o) at moment t has the molar property that with these probabilities held constant, o is almost certain to get to A but not to B within a short time irrespective of where he is started in $\mathbf{S}^a$, while conversely, o is *going-to-B* at moment t if o's numerical probabilities in $\mathbf{P}_{Sr}{}^a$ at t, if held constant, are fairly sure to get him quickly to B rather than to A. Then if the immediate determinants of $\mathbf{P}_{Sr}{}^a$ are experience residues (i.e., habits, expectancies and the like) alone, or experience residues coupled with motivational factors, the numerical values in $\mathbf{P}_{Sr}{}^a$ for o should remain essentially constant throughout a given trial in situation $\mathbf{S}^a$ and, with motivation held constant, should show the gradual and regular trial-to-trial changes characteristic of learning (including, of course, the asymptotic possibility of no change at all). But real-life observations of molar behaviour in mature organisms often convey a very different impression of $\mathbf{P}_{Sr}{}^a$'s temporal stability. It is not uncommon to see apparent shifts in $\mathbf{P}_{Sr}{}^a$ from one distal-achievement pattern to another in the course of a single trial – e.g., o may start going-to-A and then change over to going-to-B or even alternate between these several times before letting one unfold to completion. Even if $\mathbf{P}_{Sr}{}^a$ remains for the most part constant for o throughout any one trial in $\mathbf{S}^a$, if o is taught to go-to-B in $\mathbf{S}^a$ (say by making reinforcement contingent upon o's getting to B) when o starts training with a high going-to-A strength, learning will most likely be shown not by passage of $\mathbf{P}_{Sr}{}^a$ through a transition series of molar intermediaries between going-to-A and going-to-B, but by trial-to-trial oscillation between going-to-A and going-to-B with the probability of the latter increasing as learning progresses. In short, organisms frequently appear to shift from one object-consistent responsivity pattern to another in pretty much the same way, if not quite so rapidly, as they shift from one proximal

---

at all, since even if o's response to proximal stimulus $S^a{}_i$ is based on the discrepancy between $S^a{}_i$ and a goal image, there is a different discrepancy for each different proximal stimulus in $\mathbf{S}^a$ and it still remains to say how o learns to make an appropriate movement – and what this may be – to each one of these. Even so, as will be seen later, the "template" notion makes an important contribution to explaining the rapidity of responsivity acquisitions by older organisms.

movement to another. Only when responsivity matrices show this sort of holistic, quantum-jump adjustability, as though the organism were able to determine by an act of choice the distal outcome at which his proximal response dispositions are aimed, have we any reason to think that the behaviour so produced is *purposive*.

It is by no means the case that the responsivities of all organisms at all times behave like response processes, not even – as shown by tropisms and taxes – all which have object-consistent unfoldings; but those which do plunge us into behaviour-theoretical depths which have scarcely begun to be fathomed. For one, when o switches from one molar pattern of probabilities in $\mathbf{P}_{Sr}{}^a$ to another, how has o actually changed? Since the elements in $\mathbf{P}_{Sr}{}^a$ are only dispositional measures (i.e., $\Pr(r_j|S_i{}^a)$ is the conditional probability that o *would* do r_j if o *were* now to experience $S_i{}^a$), there must be occurrant properties of o which are the basis for these potentialities. In particular, when o operantly reorients his responsivity pattern from one distal target $\mathbf{S}^G$ to another $\mathbf{S}^{G'}$, he can do this only by replacing in himself one response-like condition g by another, g', such that which condition, g or g', o is in makes a difference for the probability that o would make movement r_j were o to be confronted with proximal stimulation $S^a{}_i$. But what sorts of psychological conditions are these gs, anyway? The answer to date is that we simply don't know, anymore than we know the detailed nature of the response-like mediators which conditioned generalization phenomena seem to require (cf. subsection B1, above). All that we can now say about the gs is that their existence is implicated by the apparent temporal dynamics of many responsivities; that they arise and subside in a manner akin to actions, ideas and other psychological attributes which come and go with the passing circumstances; and that each g modulates the organism's proximal reactions to proximal stimuli in such fashion as to make likely o's achievement of a particular distal outcome to which g corresponds. In view of this last property of the gs, and for want of a better name, we may call them *goal surrogates*. It would be highly premature simply to equate goal surrogates with the "purposes" we know introspectively to direct our own goal-oriented behaviour; in fact, we may well expect to find that a number of importantly distinct species of psychological processes qualify as "goal surrogates" in the present sense. Even so, the generic class of goal surrogates surely includes purposes (wants, desires, intentions) wherever these exist, while such goal surrogates as may lack the full credentials of a genuine cognitive purpose are still a good first approximation to the latter in their systemic behaviour.

Actually, it is somewhat specious to ask bluntly what the "nature" of goal surrogates may be, since as is true for any theoretical$_{B1}$ entity, this is a question which can be answered only by an exhaustive compilation of functional properties. How to learn these, or even what we should be looking for, is a nice methodological problem indeed, one which is far too vast to be comprehensively addressed here. But two lines of inquiry which clamour for immediate attention are (i) what are the principles which determine what goal surrogates are active in the organism at any given moment, and (ii) how does a goal surrogate manage to instate responsivities which are likely to attain its corresponding goal? The first of these is a matter on which we already happen to have a fair amount of relevant data, albeit not wholly uncontaminated by factors relating to question (ii). Roughly speaking, goal surrogate g is dominant in organism o on a given trial situation $\mathbf{S}^a$ if and only if o's predominant responsivity pattern during that trial makes probable o's achievement of the distal outcome to which g corresponds. Thus a reasonably reliable criterion for whether or not o has goal surrogate g on a given trial should be whether or not o makes achievement response R^G on that trial. A great deal of past research and theory on the determinants of overt behaviour in which the studied responses have been distal achievements may consequently be reinterpreted as applying more immediately to the determinants of goal surrogates. There are, however, two important ways in which an experimenter-defined achievement may not adequately reflect an underlying goal surrogate. In the first place, o's molar accomplishment on a given trial as identified by an outside observer need not be the actual distal target of o's responsivity matrix then, either because the probability of success failed to pay off that time or because the outcome noted by the experimenter was only an accidental concomitant to some other achievement which was the real aim of o's behaviour. That is, in cognitive terms, what the organism actually does is not necessarily what he is *trying* to do. And secondly, the molar unfoldings of an organism's responsivities do not always manifest the character of his underlying goal surrogates: temporally stable outcome-convergent responsivities do not warrant inference to corresponding goal surrogates at all, while on the other hand a goal surrogate g may be active in o even when the responsivity matrix it selects confers little if any likelihood upon o's attaining the goal, $\mathbf{S}^G$, to which it corresponds. That is, o may want $\mathbf{S}^G$ without knowing how to bring it about. Which brings us once again to the role of learning in goal-oriented behaviour.

We have hesitated to describe an organism's responsivities as *learned* on grounds that in many cases, $\Pr(r_j|S_i)$ appears to depend in o upon a goal-surrogate condition which varies from one occasion to another as though reset by o through an act of choice. But this only pushes the problem of learning back a step, for now we need to ask what determines o's responsivities given his goal surrogates. Specifically, for organism o, time t, goal surrogate g_i, proximal stimulus configuration S_j and proximal movement r_k, there is a dispositional probability that o would make movement r_k were he to experience S_j at t while being possessed of goal-surrogate g_i. The 3-dimensional array $\mathbf{P_{gSr}} = \{\Pr(r_k|g_iS_j)\}$ of these probabilities may be called o's *goal-mannerism* complex at time t,[88] and our problem then becomes: where do the organism's goal-mannerism probabilities come from? Presumably, they are a result of o's past experience (or past experience plus motivation[89]) and to some extent innate factors. If so, the principles which govern these acquisitions pose an immediate challenge to behaviour theory, for it is not at all obvious what relevance the findings of past learning research may have for the learning of goal

---

88 An organism's "goal-mannerisms" may be thought of as dispositional responsivities (i.e., second-order movement dispositions) which are actualized (i.e., converted into actual responsivities, which are first-order movement dispositions) by the organism's choice of goal-surrogate.

89 It is a moot question whether motivation operates upon responsivities entirely through the mediation of goal-surrogates, or whether motivational factors also affect proximal movement probabilities in ways additional to this.

mannerisms. Most work on operant (instrumental, voluntary) behaviour has studied simple achievements in reasonably mature organisms who had undoubtedly already acquired most of the goal mannerisms requisite for success at the experimental task and needed only to learn what goal surrogates to activate at the right places and times. (E.g., an adult rat mastering a complex maze needs to learn which direction to choose at each intersection, but not, in addition, how to execute his choice once it is made.) Whereas the other main branch of behaviour-theoretical research, on respondent (reflexive, unvoluntary) behaviour, has for the most part examined processes (notably, autonomic adjustments) which in all likelihood are not appreciably influenced by goal-surrogate variables. While this is no occasion for a detailed analysis of goal-mannerism learning even if I were prepared to make one, I shall conclude with a brace of speculations which seem to me to have some importance for this matter.

In the first place, while an organism's learning of an achievement differing only in minor details from others at which o is already skilled (e.g., learning to approach or avoid a new location) may not require much of o in the way of new goal mannerisms, this should be much less true when the demanded achievement is highly novel to o, especially if o is very young and hence inexperienced at most everything. Conseqently, study of the differences in instrumental learning between mature and immature organisms, and between achievements of familiar and unfamiliar types, should help us to distinguish phenomena of goal-mannerism learning from the goal-surrogate learnings with which the former are usually confounded. It would come as no great surprise to me were it to turn out that classical S-R reinforcement theories (notably, Thorndike and early Hull), which now seem so inadequate as an explanation of molar behaviour, will serve quite nicely, at least in outline, as an account of goal-mannerism acquisitions. If an aroused goal surrogate operates in response determination like an internal stimulus, or more precisely as one ingredient in a total stimulus complex, then $\Pr(r_k|g_iS_j)$ may well be no more than the strength of a reflexive or habit-wise association $g_iS_j \to r_k$. (Reasons: unlike molar response probabilities to distal stimuli, there is no behavioural benefit in having $\Pr(r_k|g_iS_j)$ sensitive to motivational variables, insomuch as motivation is already accommodated by the goal-surrogate component of stimulus complex g_iS_j. Moreover, the speed at which movement sequences are often run off requires proximal S-R latencies which are shorter than what seems reasonable for a process more complex than reflexive elicitation.) Adaptive learning of such goal-mannerism reflexes would seem to require a reinforcement principle according to which emission of r_k in the presence of stimulus complex g_iS_j causes $g_iS_j \to r_k$ to be strengthened or weakened according to whether or not this movement is soon followed by attainment of the goal corresponding to g_i. How such reinforcement is brought about (whatever the source, it can scarcely be drive reduction) and the extent to which g_iS_j may require secondary reinforcement properties through its temporal proximity to goal attainment are additional questions far too conjectural to be pursued here.

Secondly, my surmise that simple instrumental learning by experienced organisms probably does not require much learning of new goal mannerisms presupposes an answer to our previous puzzle of how, after experience with no more than a few proximal stimuli in a new situation S^a, o can acquire an object-consistent responsivity matrix for S^a by generalizing to the rest of S^a in patterns inexplicable by ordinary standards. If the proximal stimulation acting upon o at a given moment is actually but part of a larger stimulus complex in which a goal surrogate is also an important ingredient, then goal-surrogate similarity should be a major dimension along which previous learning generalizes to new situations. More precisely, if o has previously learned to make movement r_k in response to proximal stimulus S_j when under the guidance of goal surrogate g_i, then $g_i S_j \rightarrow r_k$ may well generalize to $g'_i S'_j \rightarrow r_k$ in more or less orthodox fashion if complex $g'_i S'_j$ is sufficiently similar in critical respects to $g_i S_j$, even if S'_j arises in a situation with which o has had no previous experience while g'_i is a goal-surrogate never before aroused in o. In this way, the organism's early learnings, clumsy, tedious and fragmentary as they might appear from our accustomed molar viewpoint, would consist first and foremost in assembling a repertoire of goal mannerisms which then generalize to new situations as soon as o has learned what goal surrogates to activate in the latter. Moreover, while the expression "similar in critical respects" is horrendously programmatic, an especially important development of this program is implicit in Campbell's template hypothesis. Campbell's "templates" or "images" are clearly his conception of what have here been identified, more noncommittally, as "goal surrogates,"[90] and his proposal that behaviour is directed by the match between template and sensory input alerts us to the strong possibility that the most critical feature of the stimulus complex $g_i S_j$ in o's goal mannerism $g_i S_j \rightarrow r_k$ may be the *relation* between g_i and S_j. If so, even when g'_i and S'_j are very different in "absolute" respects from g_i and S_j, respectively, if the relation between g'_i and S'_j is the same as that between g_i and S_j, then whatever movement o has learned to make to $g_i S_j$ should readily generalize to $g'_i S'_j$ as well. (E.g. if o has learned from long experience with a distal target A what muscle twitches it takes to shift A's retinal projection to the fovea from any initial peripheral position, then o should also, through relational generalization, know how to foveate any new object B whose projection now appears in his retinal periphery.) In any event, the theory of goal-mannerism acquisition depends crucially upon the principles of generalization and discrimination among complex configurations. And considering that behaviour theory is still struggling to get free of the hopelessly inadequate thesis that an organism's reaction to a compound stimulus is an algebraic resultant of his reactions to the compound's elements, our knowledge in this area has scarcely entered its postpartum infancy.

c3 Outrageously schematic as the ideas invoked in the preceding subsection admittedly are, they nonetheless usefully explicate the theoretical significance of Miller, Galanter and Pribram's (M., G., and P.) (1960) imaginative treatise on psychological organization, *Plans and the Structure of Behaviour* (*PSB*). Our concern with *PSB* here is not to give it a balanced appraisal, but only to examine

90 Except for the important difference that in postulating "templates" to underlie *all* object-consistent behaviours, Campbell fails to distinguish between *aroused* object-consistent responsivity matrices, which call for correspondingly aroused goal surrogates, and *learned* (or innate) ones which do not.

the logical structure of its thesis and see how this differs formally from more traditional conceptions of responding.

PSB is erected upon two major theoretical concepts, the "TOTE unit" and the "Plan," with occasional decorative shoring from a perversely ambiguous notion of "Image." Of these, the TOTE (for "Test-Operate-Test Exit") is primary, since a Plan is a multi-levelled concatenation of TOTE units while the Image somehow works to give each TOTE its distinctive character. TOTEs on the lowest level are *PSB*'s machinery for getting overt behaviour out of the organism. The "Operate" phase of a first-level TOTE is some specific muscle movement, while what movement is made depends on the prior Test, this being a comparison between the organism's sensory input and a normative standard or "image" of a target outcome.[91] The particular TOTE in charge of behaviour at a given moment keeps Testing and Operating until sensory input matches the unit's norm (or until a "stop" order is sent to it), whereupon the unit Exits by passing "control" to another TOTE unit built around a different norm. Which first-level TOTE is put into control following a first-level Exit is decided by the second-level TOTE operative at that moment, namely, by comparing input to its own norm and selecting a first-level TOTE accordingly. Similarly, which one of the available second-level TOTEs is in charge of first-level TOTE selection at a given moment is chosen by a third-level TOTE, and so on for a finite but open-ended number of TOTE levels. The totality of this hierarchical organization of TOTEs is the organism's Plan, while any substructure in the total Plan defined by a particular nth-level TOTE and the hierarchy descending from it is a "subplan."

When a first-level TOTE unit is scrubbed clean of its cybernetic flow-diagram cosmetics, it is easily recognized as just a device for getting the organism to output a distal achievement. Moreover, as M., G., and P. leave it, TOTE theory offers no explanation of *how* this is accomplished beyond saying that different stimuli give rise to different movements which should eventuate in the achievement's realization, and that different first-level TOTEs are characterized by different patterns of stimulus/movement coordination. (There is nothing in the TOTE concept to suggest how a particular TOTE ever manages to output *appropriate* responses to its Tests, nor have M., G., and P. given the norm-comparison aspect of input assessment any functional role beyond allowing the organism to move differently when stimulated differently and to switch to a different stimulus/movement pattern in response to certain higher-order cues.[92]) Thus if T^G is a TOTE unit whose norm corresponds

91 The "image" incorporated in a particular TOTE (*PSB*, p. 38) cannot be the same as the Image, since the latter is officially defined (*PSB*, p. 17f.) to be "all the accumulated knowledge that the organism has about itself and its world" and – inconsistently or naively, depending on what M., G., and P. think that "knowledge" is – also includes values and "everything the organism has learned."

92 To appreciate how little *use* M., G., and P. make of a TOTE's "image," recall that the possibility of an organism's responsivity under a particular goal surrogate g (i.e., the input/output coordination of a particular TOTE unit) being mediated by comparison between input and g proved relevant in our earlier discussion of goal attainment (subsection c2) only for the acquisition of adaptive responding under g by generalization from previous learning under other goal surrogates.

to stimulation from distal outcome S^G, assertion that T^G has control in organism o says no more than that o is in the process of emitting achievement response R^G through the unfolding of an arousable responsivity matrix under which attainment of S^G is at least modestly probable. Insomuch as the overwhelming majority of instrumental responses studied by behavioural research over the past quarter century have been defined environmentally – i.e. are achievement responses – it may be concluded that the idea of a first-level TOTE in itself introduces no insights or conceptual resources which have not already been available in behaviour theory for some time.

The parallel between *PSB* and orthodox behavioural conceptions of responding breaks down, however, with the introduction of TOTE-hierarchies with an indefinite number of levels. The operative character of a second-level TOTE is a particular coordination of alternative achievement responses with the various sensory inputs the organism might receive, where this input is registered as perception of the state of o's distal, rather than proximal, environment, and this too is found in traditional behaviour theory as o's set of all Hullian habits or Tolmanian expectancies in which the R-terms are achievements. But a third-level TOTE is able to switch from one pattern of input/achievement coordinations to another in response to still higher-level molar assessments of input, while *what* input/achievement coordination is instated as a result of this assessment is itself selected by the action of a fourth-level TOTE, and so on up to the Plan's pinnacle. Nothing at all like this appears in orthodox behaviour theory, for there the organism's input/achievement couplings are not considered to be operantly adjustable by o himself, but are determined for o by the theory's general laws as a function of motivation, past experience, heredity and other non-input factors.[93] That is, no behaviour-theoretical provisions have so far appeared for a possible hierarchical determination of achievement responding.

But there is nothing inherently alien to behaviour theory in multiple-level Plans, as is shown by the ease with which the logical structure of M., G., and P.'s computer-flow analogy (which, plus the proposal that *something* like this goes on inside the skins of real-life organisms, is all that PSB gives us) can be accommodated by our previous goal-surrogate analysis of object-consistent behaviour. It is obvious that a goal surrogate g guides proximal movements to a corresponding distal outcome S^G in precisely the manner envisioned by M., G., and P. for a first-level TOTE,

---

93 The sensitivity of input/achievement coordination to motivational changes (e.g., from hunger to thirst) in Tolmanian and, to a lesser extent, in Hullian theory bears a certain resemblance to the action of a third-level TOTE, except that these changes are not there construed as a reaction to present input cues and are hence more properly assimilated along with past experience and heredity into the class of phenomena governing the wiring and rewiring of a particular second-level TOTE rather than to third-level selection among different second-level TOTEs. It is also possible for S-R theory to coax mediation-response mechanisms to function very much like third-level TOTEs, but discussion of this lies beyond the present scope. (These and many other points in subsections c2 and c3 clamour for a more thorough treatment, but before this becomes possible it will be necessary to develop in considerable technical detail certain methodological concepts which are not yet familiar in the literature, notably the state/process distinction introduced in Rozeboom (1965).)

even (though the action of g does not *have* to proceed in this way) to response selection through comparison of sensory input to g as norm. While M., G., and P.'s implied model of "control" as an abstract particle rolling around the flow diagram like a marble in a pin-ball game cannot be taken literally, the goal-surrogate counterpart of "control" being passed from one first-level TOTE to another is simply a change in what goal surrogate is currently active in the organism. Moreover, while nothing in subsection c2 suggested that goal surrogates partake of a Planlike hierarchy, this was only because we did not there speculate about the mechanics of goal-surrogate arousal. Since g-activation is something the organism operantly *does*, like making a movement except for its taking place (presumably) within the central nervous system, nothing[94] could be easier than to iterate responsivity theory by substituting first-level goal surrogates (i.e., the gs discussed so far) for proximal responses and replacing proximal stimulus configurations by abstractions therefrom corresponding to perceptions of the external world at about the same distality distance from o as his first-level goal-surrogate targets. This gives us the concept of a second-level responsivity matrix $\mathbf{P}_{\mathrm{Sg}}^{(2)} = \{\Pr(g_j^{(1)}|S_i^{(1)})\}$ whose element in row i and column j is the probability that o activates first-level goal surrogate $g_j^{(1)}$ in response to stimulation containing first-level abstraction $S_i^{(1)}$. And since there is no particular reason why second-level responsivities cannot be operantly adjustable in the same way as are first-level responsivities, we then also admit the possibility of second-level goal surrogates such that o's pattern of probabilities in $\mathbf{P}_{\mathrm{Sg}}^{(2)}$ at a given moment is selected by the particular $g^{(2)}$ active in o at that time. Further iteration of this schema generates, for each $k \geqslant 1$, the prospect of a kth-level responsivity matrix $\mathbf{P}_{\mathrm{Sg}}^{(k)}$ whose ijth element is the probability that $(k-1)$th-level goal surrogate $g_j^{(k-1)}$ is aroused in o by $(k-1)$th-level stimulus abstraction $S_i^{(k-1)}$, while the numerical entries in $\mathbf{P}_{\mathrm{Sg}}^{(k)}$ are a cross section of the kth-level goal-mannerism matrix $\{\Pr(g_j^{(k-1)}|S_i^{(k-1)}g_h^{(k)})\}$ selected by whatever $g_h^{(k)}$ is o's currently active kth-level goal surrogate. (For $k = 1$, $g_j^{(0)}$ is r_j and $\mathbf{P}_{\mathrm{Sg}}^{(1)}$ is $\mathbf{P}_{\mathrm{Sr}}$.) Then each $g_j^{(k)}$ together with its associated kth-level responsivity matrix have all the formal properties of a kth-level TOTE unit, and the totality of this goal-surrogate/goal-mannerism structure is a Plan voluptuously hierarchical enough to satisfy M., G., and P.'s most libertine desires.

Actually, there is good reason to suspect that control of overt responding by hierarchical processes of the sort just described is not just a logical possibility, but may be not far from the real thing, at least for organisms with a CNS worthy of the name. For one, it corresponds to the organization that often seems to characterize complex actions, wherein elementary achievements are concatenated into fancier accomplishments which in turn are integrated into still more elaborate outcomes. For example, even so simple a distal action as *going-to-A* can be analysed as the interweaving of (at least) two distinct sub-acts, bodily orientation and forward locomotion, while each of these, in turn, is built out of more local achievements such as extending a previously flexed limb until it presses against the ground. Moreover, the goal-surrogate hierarchy makes a great deal of evolutionary and neuroanatomical sense, at least as a simplified ideal. A kth-level goal surrogate

94 Well, hardly anything.

behaves efferently like a response emitted by the system's $(k+1)$th level of organization, but has the effect of a discriminative stimulus for the pattern of input/output coordination at the kth level. But this is exactly what is to be expected of a nervous system laid down in successive strata, each layer maintaining the basic afferent/associational/efferent horizontal flow but sending its output into the association areas of the level just below it to modulate the latter's action. It is likewise what should be found if psychological development, both of species and of individuals, proceeds through successive stages of increased complexity in which each new stage is not so much a revision of the patterns of functioning developed previously as it is an imposition of superordinate controls which integrate the lower functions to achieve a higher end.

To be sure, the only evidence which I – or M., G., and P. – have offered in support of this hierarchical structure is soft, impressionistic stuff which carries little technical weight. Even if the organization of behaviour is *something* like this, it is certain to be more noisily complicated than the tidy stratification suggested here. More importantly, any multi-levelled substructure in a Plan or goal-surrogate hierarchy can be transformed on purely formal grounds into a single-level array of input/output relationships, and vice versa; so if the hierarchical model is not to be an arbitrary word-game, we need to think through rather carefully just what empirical patterns of response phenomena would inductively urge that the underlying determinants we infer from them be conceived in ascending strata. But this is research of the future. For now, it is enough that we begin to *think* about hierarchical possibilities in psychological organization, with clear appreciation that herein lies not repudiation of past behaviour-theoretical conceptions of responding, but fulfillment of them.

SUMMARY AND CONCLUSION

Rather than attempting to review my paper, I will try to point up its relevance for the unification of psychology.

When we address ourselves to the "unification of psychology," what is it that we are bothered about? The empirical source of our concern, it seems to me, is simply that different people who call themselves psychologists don't all say the same things; for if all psychologists made the same verbal utterances or written statements, no problem of unification would presumably exist. Now, there are three primary categories into which a pair of discrepant psychological assertions P and Q may fall. First of all, P and Q may actually *agree* with one another in that they express essentially the same thought albeit in different words. Secondly, P and Q may *contradict* one another. And thirdly, P and Q may *complement* each other in that they say different but compatible things. (Still a fourth possibility which I prefer to repress is that one or both are empty sounds which contain no substance at all.) What prospects for unification arise here? In the first case, where P and Q agree, we have unity already and it only remains to make this explicit. In the case where P and Q are contradictory, unification requires resolution of the points of disagreement. And if P and Q are complementary, unification would consist in finding some significant connection between them in virtue of which our awareness of the one enriches our understanding of the subject addressed by the other.

Before unification can be sought along any of the lines just cited, however, some prior preparation is certain to be needed. For the cognitive connections among statements made by different psychologists are usually obscure. It is often *very* uncertain whether these agree, disagree or complement each other, and if the last, whether they are talking about the same or different things. Making clear what various psychologists have in fact said, or have intended to say, in contrast to the fuzz and fury of what they may have seemed to say, and spelling out the logical relations among these propositions, is conceptual analysis of the sort which I have advocated in my paper; and I would argue not merely that this is essential to any program of unification in psychology, but that it has major importance for learning where psychology stands as an intellectual discipline irrespective of what this does for "unification." For example, there has been an awful lot of unnecessary controversy in which psychologists have shouted at each other without having any substantive bone of contention – what is likely to emerge under analysis is that each combatant is outraged (perhaps with some justice) by the other's metaphors, doesn't think that the other is concerned with the right issues, and has grossly distorted the content of the other's position. Conversely, I strongly suspect that there is considerably more substantive agreement among manifestly conflicting psychologies than is generally realized. I have argued in part II of my paper that any given theory is usually a heterogeneous mixture of warranted and speculative components which are seldom properly distinguished by either its adherents or its opponents. When the warranted bases of rival theories over the same empirical domain are stripped of their cognitively arbitrary speculative trimmings and compared dispassionately, I venture that substantial agreement will be found in most instances. The conceptual convergence of S-R and "cognitive" theories of learning, discussed in part III of my paper, illustrates this metatheoretical phenomenon nicely.

Finally, I want to emphasize again that metapsychological analysis, if it is to have any value for serious psychology, must look carefully at the fine details of specific propositions in the professional research literature, not at loose, overview ideas of the sort found in chapter summaries of introductory texts. Too much of what has passed for metatheory in psychology has consisted in global massings of grandiose concepts which are never put into any definite, grammatically well-formed sentences or examined for what role, if any, they have actually played in technical description and interpretation of research findings.

References

AYER, A. J., *Language, truth and logic*, 2nd ed. London: Gollancz, 1946

BORING, E. G., "When is human behavior predetermined?" *Science Monthly,* **84** (1957) 189–96

BUNGE, M., *The myth of simplicity*. Englewood Cliffs, NJ: Prentice-Hall, 1963

CAMPBELL, D. T., "Operational delineation of 'what is learned' via the transposition experiment." *Psychological Review,* **61** (1954) 167–74

CAMPBELL, D. T., "Social attitudes and other acquired behavioral dispositions." In *Psychology: a study of a science*, edited by S. Koch, vol. 6. New York: McGraw-Hill, 1963

CAMPBELL, N. R., *Physics: the elements*. Cambridge: Cambridge University Press, 1920

CARNAP, R., "The methodological character of theoretical concepts," in *Minnesota studies in the philosophy of science*, edited by H. Feigl and M. Scriven, vol. 1. Minneapolis: University of Minnesota Press, 1956

CARNAP, R., "On the use of Hilbert's ε-operator in scientific theories." In *Essays in the foundations of mathematics*, edited by A. Robinson. Jerusalem: Manes Press, 1961

CHAPANIS, A., "Men, machines, and models." *American Psychologist*, 16 (1961) 113–310

CHURCHMAN, C. W. and ACKOFF, R. L., "Purposive behaviour and cybernetics." *Social Forces*, 29 (1950) 32–9

DEUTSCH, J. A., "The inadequacy of the Hullian derivations of reasoning and latent learning." *Psychological Review*, 63 (1956) 389–99

DEUTSCH, J. A., *"The structural basis of behaviour*. Chicago: University of Chicago Press, 1960

FEIGL, H., "Operationism and scientific method." *Psychological Review*, 52 (1945) 250–9

FEIGL, H., "Some major issues and developments in the philosophy of science of logical empiricism," in *Minnesota studies in the philosophy of science*, edited by H. Feigl and M. Scriven, vol. 1. Minneapolis: University of Minnesota Press, 1956

FEIGL, H., "The 'mental' and the 'physical'," in *Minnesota studies in the philosophy of science*, edited by H. Feigl, M. Scriven, and G. Maxwell, vol. 2. Minneapolis: University of Minnesota Press, 1958

FEYERABEND, P. K., "How to be a good empiricist – a plea for tolerance in matters epistemological," in *Philosophy of science: the Delaware seminar*, edited by B. Baumrin, vol. 2. New York: Wiley, 1963

GEORGE, F. H. and HANDLON, J. H., "A language for perceptual analysis." *Psychological Review*, 64 (1957) 14–25

GLEITMAN, H., NACHMIAS, J., and NEISSER, U., "The S–R reinforcement theory of extinction." *Psychological Review*, 61 (1954) 23–33

GOODMAN, N., *Fact, fiction, and forecast*. Cambridge, Mass.: Harvard University Press, 1955

HANSON, N. R., *Patterns of discovery*. Cambridge: Cambridge University Press, 1958

HULL, C. L., *Principles of behavior*. New York: Appleton-Century, 1943

HULL, C. L., *Essentials of behavior*. New Haven: Yale University Press, 1951

HULL, C. L., *A behavior system*. New Haven: Yale University Press, 1952

KAPLAN, A., *The conduct of inquiry*. San Francisco: Chandler, 1964

KIMBLE, G. A., *Hilgard and Marquis' Conditioning and Learning*. New York: Appleton-Century, 1961

KOCH, S. and HULL, C. L., in *Modern learning theory*, edited by W. K. Estes *et al.*, New York: Appleton-Century, 1954

KOCH, S., "Epilog," in *Psychology: a study of a science*, edited by S. Koch, vol. 3. New York: McGraw-Hill, 1959

KUHN, T. S., *The structure of scientific revolutions*. Chicago: University of Chicago Press, 1962

KYBERG, H. E., "Recent work in inductive logic." *American Philosophical Quarterly*, 1 (1964) 249–87

LAWRENCE, D. H., "Acquired distinctiveness of cues: I. Transfer between discriminations on the basis of familiarity with the stimulus." *Journal of Experimental Psychology*, 39 (1949) 770–84

LAWRENCE, D. H., "The nature of a stimulus: some relationships between learning and perception," in *Psychology: a study of a science*, edited by S. Koch, vol. 5. New York: McGraw-Hill, 1963

MACCORQUODALE, K. and MEEHL, P. E., "On a distinction between hypothetical constructs and intervening variables." *Psychological Review*, 55 (1948) 95–107

MACCORQUODALE, K., MEEHL, P. E., and TOLMAN, E. C., in *Modern Learning Theory*, edited by W. K. Estes *et al*. New York: Appleton-Century, 1954

MANDLER, G., "Comments on Professor Jenkins' paper," in *Verbal behavior and learning*, edited by C. N. Cofer and B. S. Musgrave. New York: McGraw-Hill, 1963

MAXWELL, G., "The ontological status of theoretical entities," in *Minnesota studies in the philosophy of science*, edited by H. Feigl and G. Maxwell, vol. 3. Minneapolis: University of Minnesota Press, 1962

MEDAWAR, P. B., "Is the scientific paper fraudulent?" *Saturday Review*, Aug. 1, 1964

MILLER, G., GALANTER, E., and PRIBRAM, K. H., *Plans and the structure of behavior*. New York: Holt, Rinehart & Winston, 1960

MILLER, N. E., "Liberalization of basic R–R concepts: extensions to conflict behavior, motivation and social learning," in *Psychology: a study of a science*, edited by S. Koch, vol. 2. New York: McGraw-Hill, 1959

MILLER, N. E., "Some reflections on the law of effect produce a new alternative to drive reduction," in *Nebraska symposium on motivation, 1963*, edited by M. R. Jones. Lincoln: University of Nebraska Press, 1963

MILLER, N. E. and DOLLARD, J. C., *Social learning and imitation*. New Haven: Yale University Press, 1941

MOWRER, O. H., *Learning theory and behavior*. New York: Wiley, 1960 (a)

MOWRER, O. H., *Learning theory and symbolic processes*. New York: Wiley, 1960 (b)

NAGEL, E., *The structure of science*. New York: Harcourt, Brace & World, 1961

PAVLOV, I. P., *Lectures on conditioned reflexes*. New York: Liveright, 1928

POPPER, K. R., *The logic of scientific discovery*. London: Hutchinson, 1959 (original German publication, 1939)

RITCHIE, B. F., "Explanatory powers of the fractional antedating response mechanism." *British Journal of Psychology*, 50 (1959) 1–15

ROSENBLUETH, A. and WIENER, N., "Purposeful and non-purposeful behavior." *Philosophy of Science*, 17 (1950) 318–26

ROZEBOOM, W. W., " 'What is learned?' – an empirical enigma." *Psychological Review*, 65 (1958) 22–33

ROZEBOOM, W. W., "Do stimuli elicit behavior? – a study in the logical foundations of behavioristics." *Philosophy of Science*, 27 (1960) 159–70

ROZEBOOM, W. W., "Ontological induction and the logical typology of scientific variables." *Philosophy of Science*, 28 (1961) 337–77

ROZEBOOM, W. W., "The factual content of theoretical concepts," in *Minnesota studies in the philosophy of science*, edited by H. Feigl and G. Maxwell, vol. 3. Minneapolis: University of Minnesota Press, 1962

ROZEBOOM, W. W., "Of selection operators and semanticists." *Philosophy of Science*, 31 (1964) 282–5

ROZEBOOM, W. W., *Foundations of the theory of prediction*. Homewood, Ill.: Dorsey Press, 1966

ROZEBOOM, W. W., "The concept of memory." *Psychological Record*, 15 (1965) 329–68

ROZEBOOM, W. W., "Scaling theory and the nature of measurement." *Synthese*, 16 (1966) 170–233

SEWARD, J. P., "The constancy of the I–V: a critique of intervening variables." *Psychological Review*, 62 (1955) 155–68

SPENCE, K. W., "The nature of discrimination learning in animals." *Psychological Review*, 43 (1936) 427–49

SPENCE, K. W., "The differential response in animals to stimuli varying within a single dimension." *Psychological Review*, 44 (1937) 430–44

SPENCE, K. W., "Cognitive versus stimulus-response theories of learning." *Psychological Review*, 57 (1950) 159–72

SPENCE, K. W., "Theoretical interpretations of learning," in *Comparative psychology*, edited by C. P. Stone. New York: Prentice-Hall, 1951

SPENCE, K. W., *Behavior theory and conditioning*. New Haven: Yale University Press, 1956

SPENCE, K. W., *Behavior theory and learning*. New York: Prentice-Hall, 1960

TIGHE, L. S. and TIGHE, T. J., "Discrimination learning: two views in historical perspective." *Psychological Bulletin*, **66** (1966) 353–70

TOLMAN, E. C., "Principles of purposive behavior," in *Psychology: a study of a science*, edited by S. Koch, vol. 2. New York: McGraw-Hill, 1959

TOULMIN, S., *Foresight and understanding*. London: Hutchinson, 1961

TREISMAN, M., "Stimulus-response theory and expectancy." *British Journal of Psychology*, **51** (1960) 49–60

TURNER, W. S., "A re-examination of the two kinds of scientific conjecture." *Psychological Record*, **11** (1961) 279–98

WISDOM, J. W., *Foundations of inference in natural science*. London: Methuen, 1952

WORKMAN, R. W., "What makes an explanation." *Philosophy of Science*, **31** (1964) 241–54

WYCKOFF JR., L. B., "The role of observing responses in discrimination learning, Part I." *Psychological Review*, **95** (1952) 431–42

Comments: David Krech

Professor Rozeboom's paper is a most impressive attempt to set down some house-rules under which to play the games of Theory-Examining and Unification-Striving. These house-rules abjure and rule out-of-bounds reliance on word-magic. Professor Rozeboom's paper (and this becomes even more explicit from his summary remarks this morning) makes it quite clear that we must restrict ourselves to the examination of sets of detailed technical propositions – not glittering generalities or Empty Concepts. I suspect that if we hew to Professor Rozeboom's line, even the paper-and-pencil theoretician might help us all eventually achieve something which might be called unification. What Professor Rozeboom seeks is a good thing. But I suspect that whatever unification may come from this, it will be quite different from what is usually meant by "unification." In the first place, we will find that we have not achieved *intra*psychological unification (among the numerous candidates for psychological theories or theorettes) but *inter*disciplinary unification (theories of thinking with theories of linguistics, theories of learning with theories of trans-synaptic mediation). Of course, such unification (derived from the examination of detailed technical propositions à la Rozeboom) would have to be preceded by actual interdisciplinary work – psychologists with linguists, psychologists with biochemists. In the second place, however, such unification may be self-defeating. Interdisciplinary work on specific problems, *precisely when it is successful in unifying across disciplines*, very frequently leads to the further *dis-unification* of science. Let me give you one such instance in which I am involved. Over the last several years there has been a very active interest on the part of neurologists, physiologists, psychologists, biochemists, and pharmacologists in making joint attacks on the problem of the physiological foundations of behaviour. These interdisciplinary efforts have led to many forms of unification across these disciplines. One of the outcomes of this unification-urge was the creation of the *American College of Neuropsychopharmacology*. The creation of this organization was a good and helpful thing, of course. It brought us all together under one roof as brothers-in-the-bond. But not what has happened: fission has taken place; still another new science has come into being. We have our own meetings, we are gradually developing our own specialized language, and we hope eventually to have our own journals. Then, *if* we prosper and multiply and do good, we will have our own differentiated growths and splits and perhaps even a conference – or even an Institute – dedicated to unifying the science of Neuropsychopharmacology.

Discussion: W. W. Rozeboom

THEORIES, STRUCTURE, AND CONCEPTUAL ANALYSIS

AUDITOR   In your paper, you pointed out that through the hypothetico-deductive method, the axioms of a theory may receive spurious confirmation by empirical tests. To someone like me who is rigid about science and believes that science should be content with nothing less than ideal knowledge, this is a horrible state of affairs. Could not the notion of "hypothetico-deductive theory" be limited to theories which have axioms such that if any one of them is wrong, then nothing that the theory predicts will be observed? This would mean that we would have no strongly confirmed misleading axioms, or myths.

ROZEBOOM   If I understand you correctly, you are asking if we can't design theories which are unable to have a true empirical consequence if the theory itself is false. Unfortunately, the only theories which have this property take the form of a single atomic proposition – the theory would consist only of its empirical consequent itself. In short, the ideal theory that you are seeking doesn't exist, except trivially.

AUDITOR   You made some remarks about psychological "structure" which I would like to hear amplified.

ROZEBOOM   The trouble with "structure" for me is that I don't know the right way to talk about it, and I doubt that anyone else does either. That we need to deal with it somehow has become very clear to me, however. I found myself grappling with it for the first time in my "Do stimuli elicit behaviour?" paper. I had no intention of talking about "structure" there, but when I began to discuss the logical difference between stimuli and eliciting events, there it was. The foremost problem of "structure" is to get clear on just what it is that demands this concept's use. What are we trying to talk about in this way that can't be dealt with just as effectively without it? To make any headway on this we shall have to get down to concrete research problems. To date, discussions of structure and organization have been largely holistic pieties in which people say "things are complex and we've got to talk about structure," but where nobody spells out what, specifically, it is that's hurting.

AUDITOR   Isn't this a case where we have conflict between finding a precise, reliable way of talking about something and trying to encompass the subject matter in the area?

ROZEBOOM   Yes, this is always a nasty problem.

AUDITOR   It's a nasty problem, and it seems to me that it is what we are up against in this "structure" business. We have a feeling that by ignoring "structure" we aren't getting at the validity of the subject at issue. We can talk about it reliably without getting at "structure," but then we lose validity. Whereas if we stress validity, then we don't have reliability.

ROZEBOOM   I'm not sure what "reliability" would mean in this context.

AUDITOR   Well, I'm not either.

ROZEBOOM   Incidentally, this is a perfectly legitimate thing to do, to use ideas like "reliability" in obscure ways such as this, if you feel somehow that it says something; for once you have said it, you can then try to take your thought apart and see what was really in it. The odds are that its actual content was pretty trivial, but then again maybe not.

AUDITOR   This is like the point in your paper about going back and forth from the formal conceptual analysis to the informal. The formal treatment gives precision and in that sense reliability, while going back to the informal shows if anything has been left out.

ROZEBOOM   Yes. If you lay down a rigorous formalization, and stay strictly within it from there on, there's a good chance that you have omitted some of the most important things that you initially intended to deal with. Whereas if you concern yourself only with the Big Picture, and never try to look at its precise details, you'll never come to grips with anything serious, either.

SCIENCE AND METAPHOR

AUDITOR   I want to raise a point about your comments on "intervening variables," which disturbed me a little. As an example of intervening variable, suppose that I shock a rat in a box and say that height jumped is equal to the amount of fear, which is equal to the number of volts. You say that this is not an intervening variable because it's not really expressing a relationship; it's partaking of a relationship. Isn't this a quibble? We use this kind of thing as a condensed statement of relation – it is a metaphorism, which, however, can be elevated by empirical checks.

ROZEBOOM   That's not quite what I said about "intervening variables," but the important point in this particular case is: if you want to talk about the relationship between voltage and height jumped, talk about the relationship. If you want to talk about something which happens between application of voltage and jumping, talk about that, but don't get the relation itself confused with what mediates it.

AUDITOR   But man, by his nature, has to use these metaphoric ways of thinking and communicating.

ROZEBOOM   Nonsense! If you want to do science, don't talk metaphors. Thinking metaphorically may possibly give you some initial ideas, but if you never say anything but metaphors, you're not engaged in serious intellectual functioning. Actually, I don't think you really mean metaphor here at all. What's metaphorical about hypothesizing that the relation between voltage and height jumped is mediated by fear?

AUDITOR   Aren't many scientific terms metaphorical?

ROZEBOOM   They don't have to be. In practice, most technical vocabularies develop by starting with some commonsensical word that seems to have some – well, all right–metaphorical relevance to the use which is intended for it, and then giving it a technical redefinition. This is a perfectly respectable procedure; the words have got to come from somewhere, and if a technical term can be made more intuitively accessible by introducing it in this way, fine. But we can't leave scientific concepts at the level of metaphor. We must make precise what we intend them to mean, and to strip away their excess metaphorical baggage when we put them to serious work.

AUDITOR   Then you disagree with Dr Royce's thesis that the symbol is a useful thing, in terms of humanistic psychology, because a symbol is one-to-many; whereas in scientific discussion we need signs, that is, one-to-one relationships.

ROZEBOOM   Yes, and I also object to the use of the terms "sign" and "symbol" in this way. If Royce wants to give "sign" versus "symbol" a technical sense of "single meaning" versus "multiple meanings," I'll try to play his game as far as I can, but I don't like this terminology.

AUDITOR   Why do you object to this?

ROZEBOOM   The word "sign" gets used in a variety of ways, but its most common sense is a non-semantic one. That is, the connection between a "sign" in the usual sense of the word and what it is a sign of isn't a cognitive meaning relation, as is the relation between a symbol and what it stands for. By his treatment of "signs" as semantic designators, Royce is referring to a special case of what philosophers of language recognize as symbols. The concept of "symbol" is not ordinarily restricted to the multiple-meanings case – in fact, in philosophical semantics, "symbol" usually denotes what Royce calls "signs."

3
On the Nature of Laws
in Psychology

Eugene Galanter
COLUMBIA UNIVERSITY

3
On the Nature of Laws
in Psychology*

Eugene Galanter
COLUMBIA UNIVERSITY

DR GALANTER received his undergraduate degree in philosophy from Swarthmore College in 1950, and went on to a M.S. and PH.D. in psychology at the University of Pennsylvania, receiving the latter in 1953. His early interest in philosophy led to the study of the formal aspects of psychological problems, and as a result, he studied mathematics at the first Social Science Research Council Mathematics Program in the Behavioral Sciences.

From 1953 until 1962 Dr Galanter was a faculty member of the University of Pennsylvania, where he was appointed Professor in 1960. During that time he took two leaves of absence, one to Harvard University and another to the Center for Advanced Study in the Behavioral Sciences. In 1962 he accepted an appointment as Professor and Chairman of the Department of Psychology at the University of Washington. He was the Joseph Klingenstein Visiting Professor of Social Psychology at Columbia University during 1966–7, and in 1967 was appointed Professor of Psychology at Columbia.

Dr Galanter is the author of the *Textbook of elementary psychology* (San Francisco: Holden-Day, rev. ed., 1970). With R. D. Luce and Robert R. Bush, he is co-editor of the *Handbook of mathematical psychology* (New York: Wiley, 1963–5). He is co-author with George A. Miller and Karl H. Pribram of *Plans and the structure of behavior* (New York: Holt, 1960). His other articles and monographs reveal his wide ranging interests and his concern with the teaching of psychology.

The development of the philosophy of science by British philosophers from Hume to Whewell has resulted in a peculiar conception by psychologists of the goals of the scientific enterprise. The simplest statement of this conception is that science is the search for causal laws. For one reason or another psychologists have adopted this creed as their own. It shall be my thesis that the weakness of psychological science, *qua* science, is a consequence of this direction of the scientific effort. I hope to convince you that the search for causal laws is the purpose behind engineering, technology, and other practical pursuits of man's affairs. It is not and has never been the guiding principle of the scientist. Rather, scientists investigate the *nature* of things; they do not investigate the cause of things. I shall claim further that modern psychology is almost entirely concerned with causal questions, and therefore the great body of psychological knowledge, practical though it may be, is often irrelevant to the science of psychology.

These are strong words, and in what follows I shall try to soften them. But even treading softly it is important to strengthen the subject matter of our science, because unless we do we will lose our subject matter – the nature of the human and animal mind – to other disciplines. We shall discover that the neurophysiologist and the bio-chemist have occupied our niche, and that psychology has finally become (and the path is lined with roses) a practical discipline serving auxiliary roles in medicine, business and government. These remarks are intended to convey an urgency to our consideration of theoretical issues in psychology not only at the level of the research psychologist, but even in respect to the way we educate our students.

Now what can it mean to say that an interest in causes is unscientific? Surely, Everyman expects the scientist to tell him what causes the things he sees. The scientist is unwilling to disappoint him because the layman's questions about causes are indeed the only questions with any utilitarian value. When the farmer is told that the cause of his stunted corn is inappropriate fertilization he apprehends directly the value of "science." But we all know very well that no biological scientist can tell him what to do about his corn. It takes a sophisticated agricultural engineer to provide the solution to this practical problem. But surely, you say, the causal laws of the biological scientist were what the engineer used to arrive at his practical prescription. Phooey. The laws of science are scientific laws, the laws of engineering are causal laws. Let us turn to the question of what these two kinds of laws are

*Portions of this research were supported by Contract NONR 477(34) between the University of Washington and the Office of Naval Research.

like, and examine the distinction between them for the implications they may suggest.

The position put forth here is that causal laws are *pre*-scientific, and *post*-scientific, that is, they encircle science. They promote scientific enquiry in the early stages of study, and derive from scientific knowledge in the mature phase of a science. That is to say, "causal" assertions are a pre-scientific description and compression of a class of pre-experimental hypotheses that constitute the engineering basis on which the scientist works. They provide a necessary ground for the study of scientific laws. The scientific laws then may suggest new and fruitful causal conjectures which the engineering communities may adopt, and which the scientist himself may use to refine his search. Notice that the first implication of the distinction is the primacy of engineering over science. Any reasonable examination of scientific history justifies this order of affairs.

The knowledge of combustion of our primitive ancestors made possible the prediction and control of the effects of fire. Elaborate causal principles that provided a set of reasonable rules for building fires, containing them, and extinguishing them were used. I suppose that if modern psychology and its statistical paraphernalia had been available, great "scientific experiments" would have been performed. An analysis of variance would have shown an interaction between the size of the sticks used for fuel, and the elapsed time since the fire had been started, or the amount of water that was heated. Wind velocity may have been introduced as a third variable when real sophistication was achieved. And we would have learned that large kindling early in the game cause failures, as do high winds. You can elaborate on this fable as easily as I, and can also recognize that no amount of behavioural research on the nature of fire would have provided any insight into the oxidation and reduction theory of combustion. At the same time, chemical theory has added very little to the repertoire of the boy scout, the primitive, or the suburbanite who wants to build a fire. The practical knowledge of fire building replete with causal laws is oceanically separated from the scientific laws of chemistry.

If a causal law is a statement of the form "if this happened then that will happen," then what is a scientific law? Obviously a statement of the same form. If this is the case, then how are we to distinguish between these ostensibly different theoretical structures? To get to this problem we must make more precise what is meant by a scientific law and then show its connection to causal laws. I shall begin with an example taken from Newtonian mechanics only because the model is transparent. I would then like to explore in more detail examples in psychology from which some general principles may be extracted.

When Newton observed that a detached apple fell to the ground, he may have formed a causal conjecture that there is some "force" that operates to "attract" objects toward the earth. Like all sensible effects it was given a name – this invention of the human mind – and "gravity" became the cause of falling objects. As a result of this causal explanation we can make statements such as, "the apple falls because the gravity of the earth exerts a force upon it." It is about as scientifically valuable as the assertion that nature abhors a vacuum. Where then is the scientific law? The insight that yields an answer to this question depends on the recognition of which variables are basic or fundamental to the science.

If forces act on objects to move them, and we wish to understand the interplay of forces and movements, then the relevant features of the science are invented abstractions like position and time. The question becomes: how do forces act on objects to move them? And the answer of the scientist is that it constrains the connections between the scientific variables. Thus we conjecture a scientific law connecting position and time:

$$s = gt^2/2$$

Observe that the scientific law is a power function relating position and time with the coefficient g, a free parameter. g, of course, is our old friend the cause of the motion: gravity. The scientist's interest in its numerical value is exactly nil. As far as the scientist is concerned, g may be any positive real number. It is merely a multiplier whose value depends on the boundary conditions under which the experiment is performed. The scientist expects the law to hold everywhere. He expects to have to estimate g for every new condition of the experiment. Of course it would be convenient to be able to predict the value of g on the basis of independent measurement, but this ability is a luxury, not a requirement for the acceptance of the law.

If, on the other hand, a rocket engineer were concerned with landing a rocket on a new planet, the value of g for that planet would be an empirical estimation problem that he would want solved. Every scientific law gives rise to engineering information. Indeed, the engineering knowledge of the scientist is often his most valuable asset in conjecturing scientific laws. So-called heuristic principles by which scientists work in their routine treks to discovery are just such engineering insights.

And so we arrive at our characterization. Scientific laws are explicit relations between the postulated variables of a science. Causal factors are represented in a science by the free or empirically determined parameters of a scientific law. Considered abstractly, suppose we conjecture, derive, hallucinate, or copy from another discipline, a "scientific law" in linear form:

$$y = ax + b$$

The "dependent" variable y, and the "independent" variable x, are the representations of the obvious events of scientific interest. The parameters (or in an earlier age "constants") are, to the scientist, the to-be-estimated statistics of the experiment; what have here been called the "causal" factors. But, someone asks, if we re-write and solve for a, have we changed the causes into the events of scientific interest? Of course not, because we cannot, as scientists, re-write the equation. The mathematical equivalence of

$$b = y - ax$$

to the previous equation in no way guarantees that the structure of the phenomena represented by the first expression is capable of this, possibly outlandish, description.

Sometimes, as in the case of axiomatic statements in a science, the distinction is less than obvious. For example, the fact that force is the product of mass and acceleration leads one to believe that there are no causal parameters in the expression, but only scientific variables. Re-write it, however, as $F = gm$ and you recognize that acceleration is indeed the equivalent of our gravitational constant, expressed in Newton's law not as a fixed parameter but as an experimentally manipulatable boundary condition. But who is to decide which expression is the parameter or boundary condition and which are the scientific variables? The answer depends, of course, on judgment and sensitivity. Sometimes quasi-empirical considerations such as simplicity may impose limitations, but usually it is scientific elegance and axiomatic coherence that wins the day.

Let us turn now to our own field and see how the argument fares. Unlike physicists and chemists, psychologists are lucky because it is fairly simple to distinguish between psychological variables and variables outside the domain of psychology. Certainly we would all agree that a measure of behaviour, say response latency or relative frequency, is a number that represents or is symptomatic of a psychological variable. On the other hand, the intensity of a stimulus or the degree of deprivation of an organism is a manipulation of a non-psychological variable, intensity or time, which although they have psychological effects are surely the *causes* of behavioural modification and therefore are appropriately considered as parameters.

Let us review this point again, because it contains a great deal of destructive power. I am here announcing what is psychology and what is not psychology. I am trying to gull you by selecting examples with some obvious basis for shared agreement. Let us go further, because things get fuzzy at the edges and I would like you to be really convinced. After all, if you are convinced, which I truly consider an unlikely event, we will have agreed on the characterization of psychological science, a highly personal notion. But even if you are not convinced, you may better understand some of the reasons for the interests of a new clique of psychologists, who often appear to dabble with minutiae, and who play the numbers game for apparently low stakes.

The heart of the matter is that the variables in psychology – the things that the laws of psychology connect – should represent psychological events. The constants or parameters of the laws – the boundary conditions of the experiment – may represent any event that affects the psychology.

If this analysis is at all appropriate it leads to the wholesale rejection of "scientific" laws in psychology of the form $R = f(S)$, so called stimulus-response laws, and replaces them with what have been called R-R Laws. The distinction between these kinds of laws is here elevated to a place of importance; a place not previously considered as warranted by the distinction. Indeed, R-R Laws, if they are mentioned at all, are thought of as stepchildren that belong to the psychometrist. Here, of course, the pendulum has swung over and we hold the R-R Law in high esteem, a justifiable position for a principle long given short shrift.

But, the carping critics carp, how can you reject the role of the stimulus in the evocation, control, and modulation of behaviour? Of course the stimulus causes the response, just as gravity causes motion. But the scientific question is: how does this causal aspect of the science enter as a parameter into the scientific law? Let us consider some examples to see how the answer may be expressed, first in the field of learning, and then in the field of perception.

The classical concern of psychologists who study the process of learning can be diagnosed by an examination of the graphs they draw. Without question the pre-ponderance of learning data are plotted to show the time course of behaviour. Certain abstractions are made, e.g. real time may be quantized to form "trials," but the fundamental concern remains the learning curve. It would be more just to the data to say learning curves, because the candidates for this ostensible scientific law are many and varied. Do a new experiment and you get a new curve: S-shaped, concave upward, concave downward, linear, autocatalytic and so on. The different curves are widely applauded, because dear to the heart of the psychologist is the discovery of differences. And the rationalization of the difference revolves around the clever suggestion of causes. For no matter how it is sliced, a plot of behaviour as a function of trials is a mixed metaphor: one axis a physical variable and the other a psychological variable. It is for this reason that I have elsewhere included learning experiments, in which a physical variable forms the abscissa, as members of the class of "psychophysical experiments."

But damning the learning curve is an old game. What is the appropriate alterna-tive? Skinner had already suggested the answer in his use of the cumulative response function of time. What he pointed to was the structure among the responses. In fact, he never even bothered with numbers along the axes, which suggests his belief in the strong underlying invariance of the shapes of those data. His critics pointed rightly to the fact that these weren't an exhibition of learning at all, rather they were asymptotically stable post-learning performance. Learning, the transient aspect of behaviour, was suppressed in the Skinner method and called "shaping." This is truly the scientific way. Discard the complicated aspects that reveal too many dif-ferences and work on a repeatable and reliable phenomenon.

But does this position then leave learning adrift as a psychological process? Not necessarily, if we form reasonable causal conjectures about the nature of practice periods and examine the behaviour itself on the assumption that the practice period in question, i.e., the trial number, is not really relevant. Trial numbers, like differ-ent values of g, give rise to different behavioural measures, but the inescapable hope is that the behavioural measures are lawfully related to each other independ-ent of the value of the trial number. Fig. 3.1 shows a collection of classical learning curves (Galanter and Bush, 1959). All of them are different because all of the "treatments" were different. But look at Fig. 3.2. Here, the particular trial and the particular experimental treatments are smeared to reveal the invariant dependence of the responses of the succeeding trial on the preceding trial.

Such an exercise in replotting data can, in this context, be justifiably denigrated as the artistry of the graph paper compulsive. The criticism is justified because the data are, indeed, meager. It would certainly be a waste to propose that Fig. 3.2 displays a psychological law of any real power. It does, however, provide us with the basis for a conjecture that can lead to a new kind of experiment in the study of learning. By indicating that trial succession gives rise, as a first approximation, to a linear function among successive responses, we are led to a difference equation of the form

$$P(r_{t+1}) = \alpha P(r_t) + \beta ,$$

as a reasonable representation of the phenomenon, where $P(r_t)$ is the probability

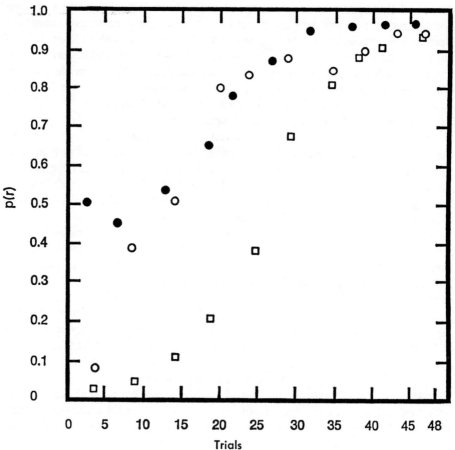

of the response to be learned on the tth trial, and α and β are parameters. The stochastic learning theories of Bush and Mosteller, and Estes, derive immediately from this representation.

These plots suggest that other things besides succession may interlock responses in interesting ways. Thus we can take the next step and suppress trials as a variable. We are then led to invent, as Estes did, the two-trial experiment. The second trial contains all the information relevant to what has been learned. And so we direct our attention to the behavioural connections on the second trial of a learning experiment.

Consider now what kind of behaviour could be interconnected. In the simplest form of experiment two response alternatives are allowed, of which, one is deemed "correct," "reinforcement worthy," or some other such appellation, and the other not. We can then examine the relation between two conditional probabilities generated by the same organism: the conditional probability that correct learning has occurred, and the conditional probability that incorrect learning has occurred. If we plot these two probabilities for a single organism when we vary some causal

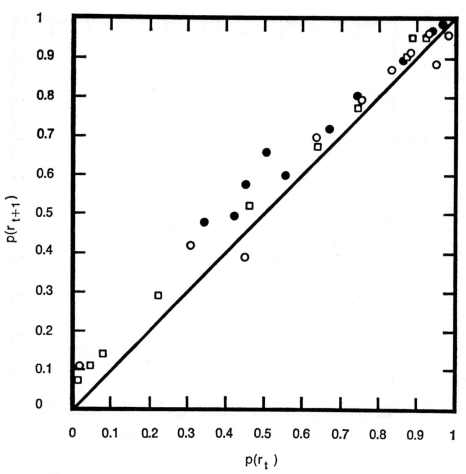

FIGURE 3.2

factor that changes one or the other of them, the results look like Fig. 3.3 (Pollack, Norman, and Galanter, 1964). Here, the parameter that has been altered is
the probability that the stimulus presented to the organism should give rise to a
particular response, here called r_1. The conditional probabilities that make up the
function are $p(r_1|s)$ and $p(r_1|\bar{s})$. These two probabilities can be interpreted as "cor-
rectly remembering the stimulus" and "reporting a stimulus as remembered when it
had not been presented." The analogy of "hits," and "false alarms," in the field of
perception will be elaborated upon subsequently.

This lawful relation, that we have named an "iso-mnemonic function," reveals
an interlock between two distinct sorts of behaviour that is merely parameterized
by a physically manipulatable variable. The law emerges as an invariant of the
memorial process. It is constrained by the independent variables dear to the heart
of the experimenter but is not altered by them. This law demonstrates that the
same person may indeed do different things under different conditions but behind
those different things is a thread of coherence that would never have been seen

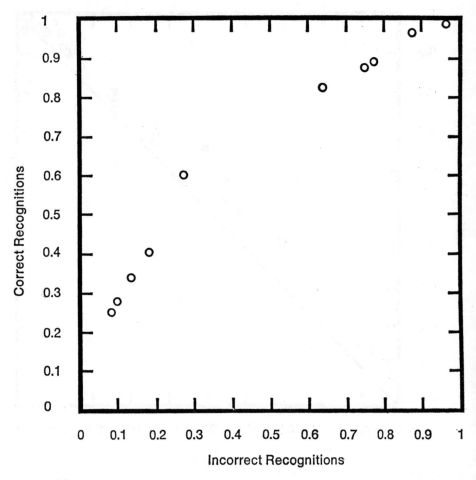

FIGURE 3.3

from a simple catalogue of the effects of experimental manipulations – causal changes – on behaviour. These analyses of learning demonstrate the feasibility of invariant behavioural laws that may be concealed by an interest in manipulating experimental variables in order to study their causal effect.

The strongest case for this point of view in psychology is seen best, of course, in that area of perception classically called psychophysics. Here, because of the unlucky reliability of the relation between stimulus and response, psychologists have searched for and proposed psychophysical laws in the same tradition of causal search that we saw in the field of learning. One axis plots a physical variable, the other a psychological variable, and the laws presumably show the effects of stimulus changes on specific and well-defined responses. By the middle nineteen thirties the breakdown of the invariance of many psychophysical functions had brought the entire field to disrepute; the similar condition in learning theory has, unhappily, not had much effect on that field.

Once again the problem arises through a failure to treat the causal basis of psy-

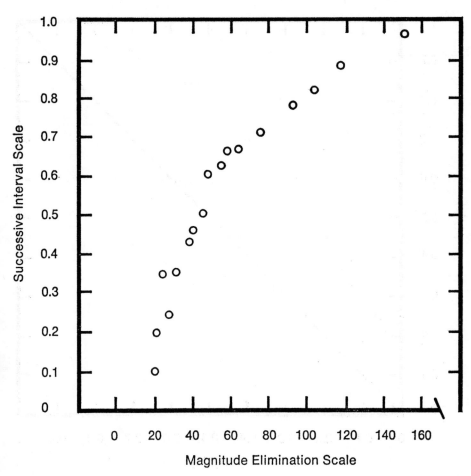

FIGURE 3.4

chophysical judgments as a parameter. In 1956, Stevens and I explored the relation between category and magnitude scales of sensation on a dozen perceptual continua. The most important result, unexplained to this day, is the striking invariance of the two forms of behaviour in the face of the most disparate stimulating conditions. Regardless of the stimuli that are used, regardless of their intensity levels, relative frequency, and spacings, regardless of the environmental conditions under which the data are collected, the two forms of judgment, those giving rise to the magnitude scale and those giving rise to a Thurstonian category scale, display the invariant relation shown in Fig. 3.4 (Galanter and Messick, 1962). The relation connecting the two scales has been conjectured, by Torgerson (1958), and by Messick and myself as $T = a \log M + b$. No one has yet examined the experimental variables that determine the parameters. Thus the causes of the connection are unknown to us and probably multitudinous.

This psychological law has a counterpart at the level of detection and discrimination in the iso-sensitivity function derived from various modern detection

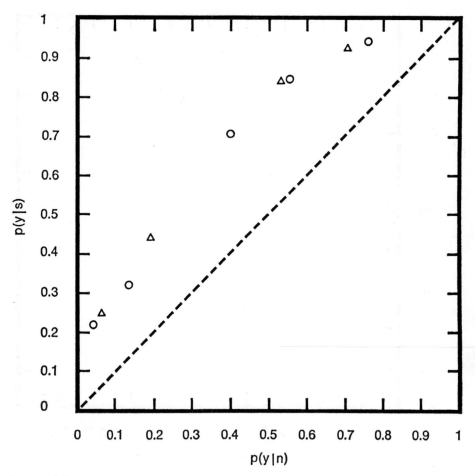

FIGURE 3.5

theories (Luce, 1962). In these experiments the subject reports the presence or absence of a signal. The conditional probability of the report of the signals' presence when in fact it is (a hit) and when in fact it is not (a false alarm) make up the data shown in Fig. 3.5 (Galanter and Holman, 1967). Once again we see that the same subject responding to the same signal intensity may range in his reports from rarely hearing the signal to always hearing the signal. But underneath this observed variability is the coherent mind that drags his false alarms along the curve.

In this area of research the psychological law is fairly well understood. Two causal effects seem to operate. First and obviously, the signal strength changes the behaviour. The behaviour is changed not by affecting the form of the curve, but rather in how high the curve arches in its progress across the square. That is to say, the signal strength selects a member of a family of formally identical curves. The second causal factor, the willingness of the subject to report the signal, has been shown experimentally to depend upon at least two kinds of experimental

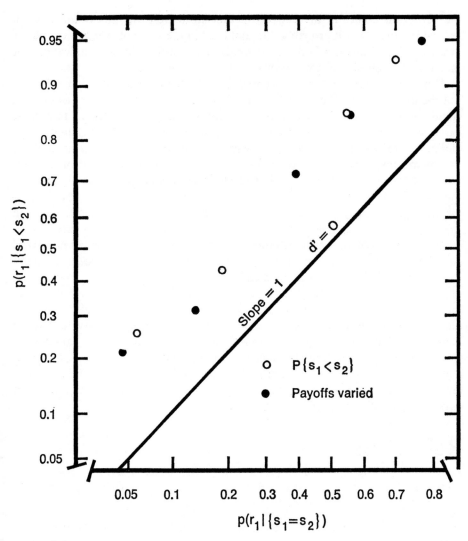

FIGURE 3.6

manipulation. We can change the position of a point on the curve by changing the signal presentation probability. We can also change the position of a point by changing the pay-off to the subject for hits and false alarm. But the causal factor is the subject's criterion. We know how to change it, but like gravity we cannot point to it. Thus we see here a case in which one causal factor – stimulus intensity – has the simple, and therefore acceptable, property of localizability, direct measurement, and a form of intuitive "connection" to the behaviour. On the other hand, the second parameter, equally causal in our sense, is ghostly, immaterial, and not obviously "connected" to the behaviour. Such a cause is best described as a "state of mind," and as such it shares its properties with many other scientifically acceptable causes in many fields. It would be pleasant, of course, to locate the "criterion point" in the chemico-neural structures, but this is unlikely for several reasons. First it probably does not exist in the sense of being pointable to, and second, and this is a fairly sad commentary on scientific communication, the biochemist or physiologist will probably not hear about it.

This second causal factor is presumed to reflect the subject's criterion point and not the direct effects of pay-offs, presentation probabilities, or other factors that could influence the criterion. We have only recently demonstrated that these experimental manipulations produce the same effect. Fig. 3.6 (Galanter and Holman, 1967) shows two different manipulations of the environment, and the parametric invariance of the data. This constitutes a demonstration of a rarely observed principle in psychological research. If a law contains one free parameter, there is no guarantee that only one experimental manipulation will effect that parameter. If many manipulations do affect the same parameter, one is led to question the nature of the psychological similarity of the two independent causes.

As laws of psychology become more clearly enunciated in the form of numerical equations, the parameters of these equations become an object of study in themselves. These studies – sophisticated engineering research – may lead to the kinds of contributions people want from us for the solution of the mundane but incredibly important problems of daily life. How can we know if the mentally ill behave differently in some subtle sense if we do not have any laws of behaviour? When people do behave differently are those differences ones of form or of parameters? If they are parametric changes can we associate empirical variables with the parameters? Only when we place scientific psychology in a context that gives us some leverage on questions of this kind, can we expect the growth of the practice of psychology to exhibit the maturity that it deserves.

References

GALANTER, E. and BUSH, R. R., "Some T-maze experiments," in *Studies in mathematical learning theory*, edited by R. R. Bush and W. K. Estes. Stanford: Stanford University Press, 1959, pp. 265–92

GALANTER, E. and HOLMAN, G. L., "Some invariances of the isosensitivity function and their implications for the utility function of money." *Journal of Experimental Psychology*, **73** (1967) 333–9

GALANTER, E. and MESSICK, S., "The relation between category and magnitude scales of loudness." *Psychological Review*, **68** (1961) 363–72

LUCE, R. D., "Detection and recognition," in *Handbook of mathematical psychology*, edited by R. D. Luce, R. R. Bush, and E. Galanter. New York: Wiley, 1963

POLLACK, I., NORMAN, D., and GALANTER, E., "An efficient non-parametric analysis of recognition memory." *Psychonomic Science*, **1** (1964) 327–8

TORGERSON, W. S., *Theory and methods of scaling*. New York: Wiley, 1958

Comments:
W. W. Rozeboom

I shall begin with a recap of what I consider to be the main theme of Galanter's paper, and the extent to which, in my judgment, this is sound and important, and then go on to criticize several specific points which seem to me to be inconsistent or untenable.

Galanter opens with the strong, provocative claim that science is not concerned with the *causes* of things, but only with the *nature* of things. If this is interpreted the way I think it is intended, in an engineering sense of "cause," there is an important truth in this which I would reconstruct as follows: whenever we are dealing with a behavioural system, it is convenient to think of the relevant variables as divided into two classes; on the one hand, those which characterize the properties of the system itself, which I call "state variables" in part III of my own paper (p. 111), and on the other hand, "environmental parameters" which characterize properties of the system's external surround. (The latter should not really be thought of as "parameters," but I had a special reason for this terminology which is probably not far from Galanter's reason for also calling them this.) As engineers, our interests lie in what we can do to the external surround that will throw the system into states we desire of it. And this, it seems to me, is what Galanter the scientist holds in low esteem. In his view, what is scientifically illuminating is not laws which tell how to control the system through environmental manipulations, but laws which show how the system is itself put together, i.e., which describe interrelations among the system's state variables.

Now, as Galanter has made clear in his summary remarks, those psychological laws which he would countenance as scientifically worthwhile are simply R-R laws. And while the R-R concept as such is hardly a new idea in psychology, more significant is that Galanter's specific examples illustrate the two fundamental law-types which I have labelled "dynamic" and "system-constraint" laws, respectively see p. 111 ff.). Laws of form $R_{t+2} = f(R_t)$ where R_t is a response measure at time t, as illustrated in Galanter's Fig. 3.2, are dynamic laws which express how the system changes as a function of its present condition (though these are best written in difference-equation form – if R_{t+1} is replaced in Fig. 3.2 by ΔR [$=_{\text{def}} R_{t+1} - R_t$], Galanter's graphs tell a rather different story from what they now seem to show); while the relationships exhibited in Figs. 3.3 to 3.5 are system-constraint laws specifying limitations on what state conditions the system can simultaneously realise. It is only within recent years that psychologists have begun to search for laws at this basic level, and I wholeheartedly concur with Galanter on the methodological importance of this development, even if I am not overly awed by what it has so far accomplished substantively.

However, when Galanter contrasts dynamic and system-constraint laws in which environmental parameters are held constant with engineering laws which focus upon how environmental parameters control the system, and then equates the latter with scientifically unimportant "causal" laws, he goes far beyond the relatively modest advocacy of R-R research which I think is his real intent. To begin with, the word "cause" is troublesome here. It would be helpful to have at least a rough specification of what Galanter means by this. I won't try to define it either, but as I understand this concept it extends far beyond the action just of environmenal factors. In particular, I would insist that dynamic laws such as $R_{t+1} = f(R_t)$ (or better, $\Delta R = f(R)$) must be included as instances of "causal" laws. In any event, after his opening denigration of causes, Galanter goes on to state that causal factors appear in scientific laws as parameters (this is a highly important technical point with all sorts of interesting ramifications which unfortunately can't be explored here); and finally, at the very end of his paper, concludes that these parameters eventually become an object of study in themselves, this being scientific maturity. I quite agree with this conclusion, but since Galanter's initial contention was that concern for such parameters was unscientific and of interest just to Boy Scouts, it seems to me to be something of an inconsistency.

A more serious inconsistency appears when Galanter admires the law of falling bodies, $s = \frac{1}{2} gt^2$, as a paradigm instance of genuine science, and then goes on to sneer at the traditional learning curve as being an $R = f(S)$ law. But learning curves are not S-R laws at all – the character of the subject's response (e.g., its latency or probability) to a given stimulus presentation is interpreted as a measure of an underlying state condition H (e.g., a habit, an association, or an expectancy, perhaps, but *not* a response), which the learning curve then plots as a function $H = f(T)$ of learning trials. And $H = f(T)$ has exactly the same methodological status as $s = \frac{1}{2} gt^2$: both are trajectory laws (see p. 111, above) which follow a state variable (H and s respectively) through a series of changes by means of a temporal index (T and t, respectively) which itself has no causal efficacy. To be sure, neither the traditional law of falling bodies nor the traditional learning curve is nearly so powerful as the underlying dynamic law or laws into which, as in Galanter's re-working of Fig. 3.1 into Fig. 3.2, it can be analysed. But whatever degree of scientific merit we attach to $s = \frac{1}{2} gt^2$ must logically be acceeded to the old-fashioned learning curve as well.

Finally, I had intended to protest that Galanter's identification of the gravitational constant with acceleration (p. 170) confuses the theoretical entity g (a force) with one of its observable effects. But since this is an issue in physics, not psychology, I think that we can forego that point.

J. R. Royce

A brief portion of my comment has to do with semantics, but the remainder is of more basic importance. Let me focus on the equation cited by Galanter, $s = gt^2/2$. First of all my preference regarding terminology is for use of the word parameter as a more general term – that is, in my usage it includes both constants (such as g) and variables (such as s and t) – whereas Galanter equates the term parameter with constants.

Perhaps more importantly, I'm troubled by referring to g determinations as engineering feats parallel to S inputs, from which it presumably follows that S-R statements are henceforth to be regarded as pre-scientific or engineering, with R-R statements now becoming the only ones of any value. I object to this position because *all* the parameters s, g, and t in the equation $s = gt^2/2$ are of potential *scientific* interest. That is, *any* of the three parameters could be held constant in a given experiment so that we can determine the lawful relationship between the remaining two. In short, as scientists we are simply interested in the lawful relationships between variables. Thus, the particular engineering-science distinction suggested by Galanter seems to be a spurious one.

David Krech

Professor Galanter's approach to problems psychological intrigues me as much as it worries me. His proposals for dealing with certain kinds of data – his kind of data – are sophisticated and ingenious, and I applaud and am impressed with his achievement. His work merits study. But Professor Galanter, in his paper, and even more so in his comments this afternoon, goes on to assert that the operations he uses in dealing with his data are *the* operations every psychologist *must* use – and this is scientific *hubris*! For one thing, I am convinced that there are *many* roads to Rome, and, therefore, no one of us should assert that unless we travel on his road (presumably El Camino Real) we will end up as (ugh!) Engineers! For another thing, to make the proposal that all "psychological laws" must conform to a specified form (and deal with specified kinds of data) can easily lead to an encapsulated, isolated concern with an artificially restricted category of problems. And this – at least to me – is abhorrent because I refuse to dedicate my days and spend my substance on a limited set of problems defined as "psychology" by Professor Galanter or anyone else. I am not, I suppose, a dedicated "psychologist" of any stripe. What I think I am is a dedicated scientist – someone who finds mental and spiritual sustenance in asking questions about life and matter, and seeking for the answers to these questions wherever he lists. I seek for my answers in stimulus-response relations, and within the organism and perhaps, now, within the kinds of relations suggested by Professor Galanter. And let no one say that I am a lesser scientist because I seek my answers in unapproved manners or places. Judge me by my answers.

I want to make one final – and perhaps minor – point. Professor Galanter this afternoon seemed to be mounting an attack on a little straw man who wasn't there – the physiological psychologist who believes that stimuli impinging on a passive organism elicit responses in a reflexive manner. There does not exist and never has existed such physiological psychologists. In the first place, those who sometimes write to that effect, the rather simple-minded S-R psychologists (and they are still among us), never were *physiological* psychologists. In the second place, I know of no *practicing* physiological psychologist who assumes that organisms are passive recipients of stimuli and reflexive emitters of responses. What Professor Galanter seems to be attacking, then, is *not* physiological psychology, or physiological psychologists, but textbook chapters (in introductory books) on "physiological psychology" written twenty years ago by certified and approved S-R psychologists who had never peered into the little insides of the organism.

4
Psychology as a
Biological Science

S. Howard Bartley
MICHIGAN STATE UNIVERSITY

4
Psychology as a
Biological Science

S. Howard Bartley
MICHIGAN STATE UNIVERSITY

DR BARTLEY received his undergraduate degree from Greenville College in 1923 and his M.A. and PH.D. from the University of Kansas in 1928 and 1931, respectively. He is known as a psychologist, neurophysiologist, and biological theorist, and as a person devoted to the theoretical consideration of man and his place in Nature.

Dr Bartley was a National Research Council Fellow from 1931–3 at Washington University Medical School in St Louis, and a Research Associate in the Neurophysiology Laboratory there from 1933–42. From 1942–7 he served on the staff of the Dartmouth Eye Institute. In 1947 he came to Michigan State University as Professor of Psychology, and in 1966 was appointed the first Director of The Laboratory for the Study of Vision and Related Sensory Processes.

Dr Bartley is the author of several books: *Vision: a study of its basis* (New York: Van Nostrand, 1941; reprinted, New York: Hafner, 1963); *Fatigue and impairment in man*, with Eloise Chute (New York: McGraw-Hill, 1947; reprinted, New York: Johnson Reprint Corporation, 1969); *Beginning experimental psychology* (New York: McGraw-Hill, 1950); *Principles of perception* (New York: Harper & Row, 1958; 2nd edition, 1969); *The mechanism and management of fatigue* (Springfield, Ill.: Thomas, 1965); *The human organism as a person* (Philadelphia: Chilton Books, 1967). In addition, he has contributed over 200 articles to journals, handbooks, and encyclopedias on such topics as the neurophysiology of the optic pathway, visual perception, systematic psychology and psychological theory, and fatigue.

At its best, psychology is not simply a collection of independent or unrelated inter-pretations of behaviour phenomena. It should not be regarded, as some define it, simply as whatever psychologists study. This is to be satisfied with a hodge-podge.

A look at almost any general textbook in psychology seems to demonstrate a lack of concern with system. It seems that most psychologists take it for granted that system is impossible. Perhaps it is assumed by many psychologists that system building has been tried again and again and has failed, and that the job by its very nature is too big to achieve, or that we are not ready to undertake it. The apparent prevalence of this view should not inhibit an attempt on the part of those who are convinced otherwise. I believe in the possibility of a systematic psychology. This means that I believe in the fruitfulness of providing psychology with the following. (i) A comprehensive scheme having to do with the nature of the psychological task. (ii) A considered conclusion concerning the relation of psychology to science in general. (iii) A statement of the relations between the major rubrics in the dis-cipline. But I must say that in the prevailing context one feels almost too timid to conceive of making a start, even though his convictions would indicate its advisability.

My intention in this paper is not to sketch the outlines of a system of psychology. Rather I shall first ask whether psychologists envision psychology as a branch of basic science or as some other form of inquiry. If it is to be a basic science, it will surely fall within the framework of biological science, and this seems to indicate several kinds of reform. Therefore, I will secondly undertake to describe several things that might be done to make it more consistent and respectable. Finally, I will attempt to give examples of the kind of information one can obtain once theorizing has been built within a systematic framework.

PRELIMINARY PROBLEMS

Man has been studied in many ways as a biological organism with no distinction between concepts applied to him and those applied to lower animal forms. This is amazing, for it has occurred despite centuries of belief that man is somehow apart from Nature rather than a part of it. But the biologically oriented studies of man have had to do with anatomy and part-functions, beginning with cells and cellular function, to tissues and organ systems. Never yet has the *total organism as a biological system* been consistently and persistently studied. It seems that our understanding of animal, including human, behaviour has come to a point and stopped. No more than lip service has gone beyond the point. Definitions of psychology run something like the following: "Psychology is the science of behaviour," "Psychology is the science of the organism as a unit," etc. Sound sentiments, no doubt of it. But the implications of such definitions have never been systematically carried out.

In some quarters it does not yet seem to be clear that the difference between cytology, histology, general physiology, and psychology is only a matter of the level of organization that is studied. If one talks about *muscle contraction* all will agree to the possibility of studying it as biological science. But if one speaks of studying the *organism reaching for something*, then the climate changes, the possibility of this being an object of science seems dubious, or the approach puzzling, to the same people. Psychology has instead tended to separate psychological concepts from cells, tissues, and organs. A basis of behavioural significance that lies far from biology is sought. Too often the social aspect of behaviour is seized upon as the encompassing problem. And from this vantage those who study and deal with body process are looked upon as outside the pale.

It is dismaying to witness what appears these days to be a resistance against the very term *biological*. Instead of envisaging psychology as a biological science, other terms have been corralled for the purpose of giving psychology a membership in something beyond itself. These terms are *life science* and *behavioural science*. Look critically at the flavour and the characteristic of these so-called life sciences and behavioural sciences. It appears that anything solidly biological about life is given the minimum of attention or ignored. Life sciences in the universities are in fact a cluster of disciplines that deal with human affairs in a way different from that established by biology. One cannot easily legislate against this. It is clearly, however, a concept of psychology countering the notion that biology is an acceptable context for it.

Unfortunate as I consider this new identification, I cannot say that the re-identification is unjustified. Psychology has simply not so far turned out to be a biological science. It has taken its origins from theology, various other abstract systems, workaday considerations, and personal problems.

Psychology: A Science Guided by Intellectual Considerations
I would seek to reconstruct psychology from a purely intellectual though empirical origin. What I shall have to say further will be guided solely in this way. This would not mean that it would sidestep any sort of behaviour that is particularly human and about which psychologists are rightly curious and concerned. It would mean, however, that psychology would get its cue neither from the words we have in our language, nor from considerations outside of science. I believe there is a tendency to suppose that for every word in the language (barring full synonyms) there ought to be a behaviour mechanism that psychologists could possibly study. This – along with the misuse of operationism, whereby a person may simply define his operations, describe the response, attach a name to it, and thereby be in business – must be abandoned. Nowhere are there nearly so many possibilities for this curious proliferation as in what is called social behaviour. And it is apparent that an overabundance of such possibilities have been seized upon.

Definition of Psychology
We do not essentially need to change the words in the definition of psychology. It is the science of animal behaviour, but with the implications I have already suggested. I have called it the science of the behaviour of the organism as a person. This means it deals with orders of body process which describe the total organism in action. As I have just said, we have done everything but reach the study of the organism at this level. All levels up to this have been studied. But we have stopped there.

Biological Causation is Energistic
The causal scheme of biological psychology is energistic. That is, its explanations must be made in energistic terms. There is no place for any item in the causal sequence that lies outside energistics. Thus, the scheme is a monism. One cannot introduce mental items as links in any causal scheme or explanation. For example, emotion defined as a feeling cannot be said to cause anything. Cause and effect must run in an energistic track just as in physics and chemistry. Body processes are only special cases of physico-chemical events. *Man is a part of Nature, not apart from it.*

This is not to preclude dealing with phenomenological terms. These are the shorthand of human communication and can still have their place, if by some means it can always be meant that it is body-process and not experience, consciousness, etc., that is causal. So don't misunderstand my suggestion, and infer that I would discard the phenomenological (experiential) terms from our vocabulary. It is simply that somewhere along the line we failed to develop the connotations for these terms that make it clear that the causal scheme lies in body process.

Cue Theory
In this connection, I should like to call attention to a common error – the error of explaining phenomena in terms of themselves. This must be recognized and not tolerated under any guise. Common cue theory is a case of explaining one aspect of a response in terms of another, a case of using response to cause response. For example, one sometimes reads of size perception being accounted for by distance perception, or colour perception. For explanation to occur one must deal with the causal sequence. It is presumed that these conditions will not be described in response terms but in neural and other body-process terms and the impingement itself. Colour is not a cue for size, or size for colour, or any such thing. So long as we cannot discern what it takes to account for an effect, i.e. what categories are involved, and what are not involved as cause, we have not begun to have a science. Cue theory is evidence that a true biological conceptualization of the human and his behaviour is still absent.

Multiple Meanings; Multiple Labels
Another issue in reconstructing psychology as a satisfactory science has to do with another piece of housekeeping. The customary language used in technical and scientific discourse is not appropriate for what we are trying to do: the way we use language has serious faults which should be immediately obvious once they are

pointed out. One of them allows a technical or scientific term to possess more than one meaning; another permits a concept to possess several labels. Let it be granted that it is characteristic in social conversation for words to derive their meaning largely from context. However, in technical and scientific language, words should be given their meaning by definition, and this rules out multiple meanings for each word and multiple labels for each thing or idea. If this were not the case it would still be context that would have to decide between alternatives. This dictates that words like stimulus, response, etc., should be strictly defined. J. J. Gibson recently pointed out that there are eight issues that have arisen in connection with the use of the word stimulus, and that these issues remain largely unresolved. Depending upon one's decision on each issue, just so will be his definition of stimulus. With eight issues, and some possibility of combining these choices in various ways, there is obviously much left unstructured.

A Separate Vocabulary for Each Category of Phenomena
An appropriate use of language as a tool and expression of our understanding of behaviour requires another step. We must decide how many categories of phenomena are being involved in a discourse, and provide a vocabulary for each. The words used to describe the stimulus are certainly not those used to describe activities of sense organs, neural pathways and other body tissues, and the words used to describe these two separate categories are not those appropriate for describing sensory end results, and other behaviour, which lie in a third category. Despite this, we still describe stimuli in response terms. Is this partly because we have never bothered to make the distinctions just specified? Is this to say we do not know when we are committing this error? These misplaced descriptions are, for example, the cases in which we talk about a photic spectrum in terms of colours, when we use light as a word for both photic radiation, and for what we see, when we use the word sound for the acoustic stimulus, etc.

The use of separate words for corresponding items in several categories may be exemplified by my use of *edge* to label an element of a visual object, i.e. something seen, *border* for what I call the visual target, and *contour process* for the immediately underlying neural activity responsible for seeing the edge. If we actually were in a position to indicate the corresponding feature of the optical array (Gibson's term for the energistic impingement), we would have to find still an additional term. Other examples are my use of *photic pulse* for the stimulus, and *flash* for the response, *photic radiation* for the stimulus and *light* for what is seen. This may sound at first like a needless redundancy, but it is anything but that. If this policy were followed, the listener would always know which category was being referred to and communication would be kept much clearer and more effective.

The Task of the Psychologist Helps Determine the Structure of
the Psychological System
The task of the psychologist in any and all cases is the discovery of relations between the organism and its surrounds, including the body processes that structure that relationship. This task can be carried out not only in perception, but also in learning and thinking. The first step is to discover the nature of the phenomena. It

is only then that there is something to explain, something to be understood. However, phenomena are almost endless in variety, and so their mere discovery cannot continue forever without direction and selection. This limitation calls for some kind of conceptual orientation as early as possible. Since facts are not equally useful and relevant in developing understanding, selection must be considered. This first occurs on a broad basis and then becomes more particularized. For example, I have said that psychology is a biological science. This is an example of one of the first clear choices that must be made. I have pointed out that organisms may be studied at various levels of organization and description and that the focal concern of the psychologist is with the highest level. This reflects another type of selection in orientation.

Whatever they may be, it may be assumed that a limited number of major problem areas can be indicated as rubrics in attempting to understand behaviour. For example, we may consider them to be the following: (a) the contact of the organism with its surroundings; (b) activation, direction, and goals; (c) development; (d) internal organization, unity and conflict; (e) demand and the ability to meet it. The mere making of choices such as these constitutes a beginning in the emergence of structure and system.

The Organism as a Reference in Defining, etc.

Another step is becoming aware that there are two reference points for making definitions and in regarding features of behaviour, namely the *environment* and the *organism*. Consistent with the stated purpose of our endeavour, I would say that, in general, the organism, and not the environment, should be used as a reference in a system of psychology. It is the organism we are attempting to characterize, to find out about. We must, therefore, focus our attention on it rather than anything that lies outside of it, even though it be groups of people.

All too often in psychology, the environment is used as the reference. Whether this is only unwitting or not, I do not know. For example, organism instead of environment-centred, definitions of, e.g., frustration, should be used. In animal (white rat) studies it is too easy to define frustration as the blocking of the animal's progress in a maze. This turns out to be a very blatant environment-centred definition of the term frustration, and an environment-centred procedure. Frustration is simply an *operation* performed by the experimenter, not really what pertains to the rat.

Even though this operation may make a difference to the rat, one still is not focusing on it. If blocking the maze does not seem to make any difference to the rat, the conventional remark is that it manifests *frustration-tolerance*. I would rather say simply that the rat is not frustrated. Why suppose frustration and frustration-tolerance in the same animal at the same time? When one avoids defining psychological concepts in terms of the environment, he obviates the conventional redundancy of the co-existence of frustration and frustration-tolerance. Once one gives up the common policy of shaping his thinking with the environment as the reference, it makes a great difference to his conception of the problems of psychology, to the nature of the problems he studies, and to his method of solving them.

Learning ceases to be an abstraction which is apart from the organism, but becomes a question of how animal and human organisms change in behaviour, and under what circumstances. To solve this, one will go to tissue studies, instead of forever remodelling learning experiments simply under the guidance of mathematical concepts which at times become more focal to the theorist than does the concern for how learning is defined.

Reductionism to be Avoided

It will have been noted again and again that I have referred to body-process, or to tissue study. This sounds to some people like forthright departure from the study of behaviour. Let me remind you of what I shall say later, namely, that whatever set of facts is actually required to solve a psychological problem is psychology in that case.

Reductionism, the pitfall of today's novice and yesterday's veteran, is not to be read into my suggestions. Reductionism is to be excluded in all cases. You are to be reminded that each level of description and organization has its own existence and no level is to be either reduced to another one or in any way to be taken as identical to it. A is *always* A, B is *always* B. Some sort of relation may be spoken of, but one can never be transmuted into the other.

DEFINITION OF THE STIMULUS

Let us see how the general position I have suggested operates with regard to Gibson's eight issues involved in defining the stimulus.

Issue One: Stimulus a Motivator?

Firstly, does a stimulus motivate an individual, or does it merely trigger a response? If the issue must be stated in this way, one would say that the stimulus triggers the response. Motivation is a term referring to the dynamics of the organism, not the stimulus. The term stimulus is a loaded or implicative term. That is, it implies that a response is produced, although it does not carry in it any predetermination of what the response will be. One discovers this from species to species, and to some extent from individual to individual.

Issue Two: Stimulus as Sufficient Cause of Response?

This leads immediately into the second issue pointed out by Gibson, i.e. whether or not a stimulus can be taken as the sufficient cause of a response. He quotes Pavlov as saying that "a stimulus appears to be connected with a given response as cause with effect." Watson also took a similar position. Woodworth and many other psychologists have held to the idea that the stimulus does not constitute the total set of conditions to account for the response, the behavioural act. With this I would agree; but my basis for agreeing goes beyond the usual one: my insistence that psychology is a biological science leads immediately to studying body process just as focally or assiduously as one would anything that might be called the stimulus. Such study makes one far more aware of the many things that go into producing the response than does the simple statement that many body processes are involved. One studies what I call the *contribution of the organism* as a natural and unavoidable class of data.

Issue Three: Is the Stimulus Defined Independently of Response?
Whether or not the stimulus must be defined independently of its response, i.e. in energistic terms rather than behaviour or sensory end result, constitutes the third issue. I have already pointed out that items should be labelled in keeping with their category. This implies that they are defined according to the same principle. In physiology, the stimulus is always dealt with (described) in energy terms. Likewise, it should be in psychology. As yet there are, unfortunately, some gaps in the possibility of doing this. Not all features of all impingements are neatly specifiable in energistic terms. This is no fault of the psychologist, but it does not, however, release us from the obligation of working toward this end. For example, while one can specify intensity of a photic stimulus in energistic terms, and, one can indicate wavelength, and duration, there are other features such as the distribution of the input that are not easily described in that way. This, I suppose, is what induces some workers to deal in quantal terms, specifying the probability of certain numbers of quanta reaching certain receptors per unit time.

Distinction Between Impingement and Stimulus
Probably this is as good a place as any to introduce my distinction between a stimulus and an impingement. One would suppose, in simple-minded literalness, that a stimulus is that which stimulates. That means a stimulus should always stimulate; that which does not stimulate is not a stimulus. But as a matter of course, we find that the energy that is described as reaching a receptor or the sense organ as a whole, does not always prove effective in producing the particular event which is called the response. This introduces a dilemma. I suggest labelling the energy that reaches sense organs an *impingement*. Some impingements stimulate, some do not. It is only when a response is produced that the impingement can be called a stimulus. As we all know, the customary way that this dilemma is met is to call the ineffective impingement a subthreshold stimulus. The effectiveness of an impingement depends upon what is taken to be a response. A response for a physiologist is the body process produced. A response for the psychologist, is a behavioural end result, an act of the organism as a total.

It appears that Skinner has pointed out this business of defining the stimulus in terms of the ability to elicit response, and recognizes it as a sin without a suggested way of salvation. What I have just said would be a means of redemption if we simply substitute the term such as impingement for the word stimulus. It would clear up the hidden error in talking partly about the intrinsic nature of the input and partly about its effectiveness in producing a result. By using the word impingement, we can thus describe the energistic input events in their own terms, and come to the relation between them and their consequences by a language that makes clear this distinction. One can still speak of internal stimuli, for we know that there are internal receptors and/or sense organs. When these are activated some form of specifiable energy is also involved. But to imply that an idea, or even the process that underlies an idea, is a stimulus is a misuse of the term. We had better simply use a generic term such as *origin* unless we can agree on another uncommitted one.

When we define stimulus as an effective impingement, we remove stimulus from the energistic category and make it something else. It is not a generic label for causal origin regardless of categories. A stimulus is always an energistic event. Stimulus and cause, or stimulus and origin, should not be made synonymous where cause and origin are broadly generic.

Issue Four: Are Stimuli in the Environment or at Receptors?

The fourth issue of Gibson is the question of the existence of stimuli in the environment or at the receptors. This question can be answered very quickly because the answer is clearly implied in what we have already said. Impingements, and thus stimuli, exist only at the receptors, or at the sense organ. This dispels the old pair of terms, *distal* and *proximal* stimuli. When these terms are used, it is implied that stimuli are simply chosen origins of what one wishes to consider. If one wishes to start at some distance from the organism, he may do so; if he wants to start at the sense organ, he may do so. In a strictly biological system he does not have that liberty, at least in the way it has been customarily exercised.

Issue Five: Is a Stimulus that which Reaches a Single Receptor?

The next issue is whether or not a stimulus is that which reaches a single receptor, or that which reaches a number, forming, as it were, a pattern. This issue has little import when we are dealing with input as impingement, but when we deal with the question of an input producing a response, i.e., constituting a stimulus, it is likely that the pattern-notion of the stimulus would be chosen. This would (in some cases) be saying that the reason for the ineffectiveness of an impingement reaching a single receptor (i.e., it is not a stimulus) is that it is not a pattern, or perhaps, not quantitatively sufficient.

Issue Six: How Shall the Temporal Aspect of Impingement be Regarded?

The sixth issue has to do with the temporal aspect of impingement. When is an impingement sequence or an extended impingement a single stimulus, and when a number of stimuli? The sequence, if continuous, is all one impingement, although possibly varying in intensity. If it varies as to the inclusion of more or fewer receptors from time to time during its existence, it is an intermittent impingement for some receptors. That is, it is a series of impingements. There are two issues. What is a single impingement and what is a series? What is a single stimulus and what is a series?

The first issue has to do with the variation in inclusion or exclusion of individual receptors, the second with what the organism is able to do as a consequence of any variation in the impingement. The second depends upon one's ability to divide the behavioural end results. Can they be segmented, or not? Let us say that the act is one of reaching. Some reaching is almost ballistic and some is guided as it occurs. If it is guided by feed-back, for example, one would have to say the number of stimuli are involved during the act. One could determine the guiding factors from instant to instant.

This brings up an issue which Gibson does not state, but may imply: do stimuli and responses bear a one-to-one relation, or may a response be produced by a series of stimuli? Gibson asks whether or not a "single enduring stimulus can exist throughout a changing sequence." It would be consistent with my position to say that a series of stimuli can produce a response, but not that a single stimulus could produce more than one response. For a continuing impingement to be a single stimulus it would have to be of such a character as to preclude use by the organism in making more than one discrimination.

Definition of Perception and Perceptual Response

This brings up my definition of perceptual response. Perceptual response (perception) is the immediate discrimination evoked by impingement (energy applied) upon sense organs. How fine and in what way is the organism able to *discriminate* is the question. Thus, if a continuing but variable impingement enables the organism, from instant to instant, to change (vary) its relation to the environment (modify its behaviour) then, in effect, the impingement can be said to constitute a series of stimuli, for a series of discriminations are made.

Issue Seven: How is the Structure of a Stimulus Specified?

Gibson's seventh question is: "How do we specify the structure of a stimulus?" To the extent that one can specify the structure of impingement, one can specify the structure of the stimulus. This brings us to the distinction between the *stimulus* (specified in energistic terms) and *stimulation* (specified in terms of the result). The specification of the stimulus is in energistic terms. The specification of stimulation is given in the results (the response).

Issue Eight: Do Impingements or Stimuli Carry Information? And/or How?

The eighth and last issue is whether or not stimuli "carry information about their sources in the world, and how do they specify such sources?" Impingements carry information partly by reason of the nature of the organism, and partly by reason of the dynamics of the energistic environment. People lift weights. This requires energy, involves muscles, etc., which in turn activate kinesthetic sense organs. There is a lawful, approximately invariant, relation between input and what is fed into the central nervous system. The higher order body processes using this input give rise to cognitive consequences. Certain orders of invariance, including more factors in the complex, come to be involved, and it is by reason of this lawfulness that it can be said that information is "conveyed". It is in a sense a "vicarious" result, rather than a result that stems from some inherent property of limited events in Nature.

DISTINCTION BETWEEN PSYCHOLOGY AND PHYSIOLOGY

Another consideration must be injected here. It is the answer to what informational items are to be called physiological and what are to be called psychological. All too often, the mention of body process is interpreted as the use of physiological fact, never is it called psychological fact.

The conventional view of factual information is that certain items belong to one discipline and others to others; that these facts are borrowed for various reasons by various disciplines from others. The fact that they are borrowed and used is not supposed to change the categories (disciplines) to which they belong. Thus, the basis of assignment of category for informational facts is always discipline, never some other consideration.

My position is that it is not *facts* that set disciplines apart from each other, but rather it is *problems*, *objectives*, etc., that do. The set of problems about Nature that constitutes physiology is *not* the set that constitutes psychology. If the two sets of problems were identical, there would rightfully be only one, not two, disciplines.

All the information, regardless of its nature, that is required to solve the problems of a given discipline, is a part of that discipline when the information is involved in this way. The same information may play a role in helping to solve problems in another discipline, and when it does, it is part of that discipline. This is a *functional* concept of the role of observational fact, in contrast to the old *ownership* or *copyright* notion of where fact belongs, or what categorization is to be put upon it. Let us use this functional position with regard to fact throughout the rest of this presentation.

With this much decided about the stimulus and stimulation, we are ready to move to other sorts of consideration, other decisions regarding the structuring of psychology, and the types of theorizing involved.

PREDICTION AND UNDERSTANDING

There is a tendency in certain quarters to use prediction as a criterion for determining whether or not an endeavour is a part of science. If one uses prediction in a narrow sense, one can possibly conceive of building a psychology that by-passes the study of body process. For all one needs is to discover the relationship between certain events, without concern for knowing about the mechanism which brings about the apparent relationships. This is possibly why so many psychologists pay no attention to sensory mechanisms, and body processes underlying learning. These workers are able, up to a certain point, to discover the superficial type of relations between various pairs or groups of events. Men outside experimental laboratories as well have long been doing just that. Understanding is the knowledge of broad sets of functional relationships, including knowledge of mechanisms whereby the consequences are produced. Increase in understanding involves grasping interrelationships between larger and larger groups of events and the mechanisms at work. The distinction between prediction and understanding is something like the difference between *knowing* that a result usually *happens* when certain restricted factors are controlled and *knowing why* it happens by reason of knowing about a large cluster of functional relationships and mechanisms.

The old streetcar motor-man could, generally, *predict* pretty well what would happen in relation to his operation of the crank on the control box. The evidence that he only predicted and did not *understand*, was the fact that when the car would not run, he had no idea why. He did not have a grasp on a broad enough array of facts and principles for us to say that he had an understanding of the dynamics of the propelling system of the streetcar.

Psychology studied as a biological science is the only way that the *whys* are disclosed and thus, the only way that pervasive understanding is developed. If it is understanding that is required, body mechanisms must be studied.

Hence, a great bulk of psychological theory should deal with picturing body mechanisms. Of course, this kind of theory is not for its own sake, but for its role in helping to provide the over-all organization that produces behaviour. In fact, a great deal of fundamental theory, the kind of theory that should be developed *first*, ought to concern itself with body process. Nothing precedes this except discovering the behavioural phenomena for which theory is needed in the first place.

SCIENCE, TECHNOLOGY AND PRIVATE CURIOSITY

The concern with facts is possessed in common by three classes of people. (*a*) Single individuals whose curiosity has been aroused by something or other. This curiosity is not necessarily or clearly related to a body of related facts that one can point to, and may be quite transient. (*b*) Organizations or individuals who must know the best way to produce an end result. This end result is generally a product to be manufactured or a specific emergency to be handled. Such people are, of course, dealing with Nature and the precision of the information they must have may be extremely great. This is to be known as *technology*. *Science* is a structured attempt to understand Nature. It develops by having due regard for already accumulated knowledge, and the kinds of interpretation of phenomena that make the most consistent and comprehensive sense. It is not meant to be mere encyclopaedic storage of the results of all of man's efforts to satisfy personal curiosity, but rather a set of principles, laws, etc., that provide what I have already suggested as an understanding of Nature.

One must always keep in mind the distinctions between these three concerns and forms of interrogation. While the precision and experimental controls in technology may be as great as those in major and crucial scientific experiments, the purposes are vastly different and the uses to which the information gained is put are totally unlike. The scientist chooses questions and experiments from which he can maximally generalize. This is not a procedural criterion in technology.

Much of what interests man is the gaining of knowledge for technological rather than for scientific reasons, i.e., to improve manufacture, improve transportation, improve labour and industrial relations; yet these get confused with the affairs of science. If we apply the distinctions I have just set down, it can be seen that many of the endeavours and findings that now are taken seriously as parts of psychology are not potential elements of a systematic psychology.

Science, then, is a set of tested generalities, or principles, and not an endless group of specific phenomena regardless of their importance to commerce, industry, politics, theology, and social welfare. In this light, it might be better to modify the definition of psychology I first suggested. Accordingly, I can say that psychology is the study of the *principles* of the behaviour of the organism as a unit, or a person.

As soon as principles are discovered and related to each other, there is then a science of psychology. Beyond principles, the endeavour of psychologists consists in activity guided by the desire to know more and more details about something, generally for some restricted purpose, which often lies outside what I have already defined as science. Wheeler's old dichotomy of *dynamics* versus *phenomenology* seems to apply here. The dynamics of Nature are quite general, and phenomena are endless in form. When one sets his attention on dynamics, he is doing a very different thing than when itemizing phenomena.

This definition and view of psychology helps to contract psychology to something manageable and reasonable. Without it, there would seem to be no limit to the bounds of psychology. It has become all things to all people and has swallowed up many other endeavours that deserve labels in their own right. If exclusion on the grounds just suggested is used, a very great deal of what is now called psychology will be ejected from psychology as a science, and the goal of unifying psychology will be much more nearly thinkable. Disregard for this distinction makes any unification an empty dream.

THE FOUR GENERAL CLASSES OF CONTEMPORARY PSYCHOLOGY

Perhaps a more pragmatic and earth-bound way of surveying psychology is to examine the classes on the scene today, asking what they offer, what principles are involved, and whether or not they are redundant when combined. We can ask whether they are parts of biological science, or whether the kinds of questions they ask and the data they gather are consistent with, or contributory to, biological science. For example, we have today the following kinds of psychology. (i) *Stimulus-response psychology*. Here there is a close connection between some external event and a consequent behaviour. This kind of psychology ranges from the strict sensory psychology to studies of learning. (ii) *Trait psychology*. This includes the kind of studies that enumerate traits, whether they be expressed as enduring attitudes, aptitudes, or other personality characteristics. (iii) *Social interaction psychology*. This studies various "power" or influence relations between people. The study of personality lies partly in this form of psychology and partly in trait psychology. Whether certain of the clinical varieties of psychology, such as Freudianism and its companions, are to be classified as social interaction or trait psychology, or a type of their own, is a question. If the latter, I would simply call them instinct psychologies for want of a better term. (iv) *Energy mobilization psychology*. This is represented by G. L. Freeman's psychology and the "activation" psychology of Elizabeth Duffy. There is a sense in which each of these classes of psychology pretends to be complete or adequate in itself and thus implies that the others are hardly necessary. There is another sense in which many people nowadays take the eclectic path and choose fragments from each in order to feel satisfied that they are handling behaviour comprehensively enough.

I feel bound to examine these psychologies in the light of my repeated affirmations that psychology should be recognized as a biological science. Do all these types of psychology fit into biological science? Obviously not, at least in the form in which they manifest themselves. Do these psychologies deal with essentially the same subject material or the same types of data? Obviously not, even though there may be considerable overlap. Do they ignore types of data that should be included in a fully comprehensive and adequate system of psychology? Or is it to be taken for granted that some of these psychologies need not be considered? When we talk about the unification of psychology, it is these psychologies that we must be referring to. They form the stock-in-trade we have today. Let us see what each of these psychologies has to offer.

Stimulus-response psychology might be thought to be *ipso facto* biological science. However, some of it is biology, and some of it is not. Whether or not any particular example is biological depends largely on the particular definition of stimulus. If the stimulus is defined in energistic terms, it is natural science, and thus biology. If the stimulus is simply any imputed causal origin of an effect, lying in any category whatsoever outside of energistics, it is not a natural science. I have already spoken at length about the various definitions of stimulus. This should have made obvious the many possible positions considering the characteristics that systems may have, and whether or not they are forms of biology.

Typical learning theory by-passes biology since it is not rightly concerned with the definition of the stimulus, nor concerned with the body-process basis for learning. Typical learning theory is not stated as a behaviour change based on body process and does not model its study on such an assumption.

What does trait psychology offer? It assumes there must be certain *natural modes* of reacting which are sufficiently different from each other to be distinct, and that these can be discovered. If this form of psychology is to be considered as a part of biology in the first place, these would form natural objectives of body process isolation and study. The trait is, in effect, a kind of intervening variable. If so, this psychology is saying that this is the kind of intervening variable that explains behaviour. A knowledge of body process is not necessary.

The existence of traits, according to certain definitions is still in doubt. Were there natural fixed units or modes of behaviour, it might be that some underlying body processes for them could be found. Then trait psychology could be a biological science. The existence of traits rises or falls on the same logic and evidence as the existence of instincts, etc.

What can be said about social interaction psychology? Keep in mind that all of its entities and dynamics are expressed in non-biological terms. The only meaningful terms in this psychology are social. Its language is, to a large extent, the language of the man outside of natural science. Furthermore, there is not much agreement among the workers as to what is important to study, or how to study it. Entities emerge largely in terms of the varied insights and conceptualizations of each of the great host of workers in the field. At present most of this endeavour is pretty far from fitting into biological science. Furthermore, we have here some of the best examples of proceeding beyond the discovery principle. There are exceptions, however, and the study of belief systems by Rokeach is an arch example.

Energy mobilization psychology is quite an appropriate aspect of biological study and little needs to be said here to characterize it. It probably has many shortcomings, but they do not exclude it as a type of biological endeavour.

Thus, we have surveyed the various types of current psychology and have found that not all of them have anything to do with biology, and that some that might possibly be a part of biology are not structured appropriately to be useful there. Biological science is explicitly represented only in genetic psychology, pharmacological psychology, "self-stimulation" experimentation, ablation experiments, and the study of the sensory processes.

A Limited Number of Psychological Processes or Behaviours to be Identified
When the "kinds of psychology" problem is settled from the standpoint of the general systematist, then the process rubrics can be dealt with. It is to be taken for granted that a system of psychology does not need to contain all the behaviour terms that are found in the dictionary of a language such as English. More than that, it is to be assumed that the student of psychology is not at liberty to choose at his leisure various words to label the response or activity elicited by the experimental situations he presents to his subjects. A number of years ago what is known as *operationism* was set forth, principally by Bridgman in physics. From it, the tendency to set up restricted sets of conditions or operations, and to give labels to the behaviour results without regard to how these labels are used elsewhere, has developed in psychology. Other experimenters set up other operations which likewise are restricted rather than broadly representative, and use the same labels for the responses as the first experimenter. This has gone on without any implied or expressed rule to limit it, under the excuse that it does not matter what one calls anything so long as he reports the conditions for obtaining it.

For example, some writers report on *coping behaviour*, some on *problem-solving behaviour*, and others on *adaptive behaviour*. There may be other similar terms used. Offhand one might suppose some overlapping, or even nearly full identity to what is being studied, if one judges by the prevalent meanings of the three terms, and one wonders if so many terms are necessary.

HOW VARIOUS CONVENTIONAL FEATURES OF BEHAVIOUR ARE TO BE STUDIED

Obviously the study of sensory response yields best to demonstrating the study of behaviour as a form of biological science. Here one can make close connections between energistic input, body process, and behavioural end result. Other aspects of behaviour are more remotely connected with something which can be pinpointed in Nature. The body processes are so tremendously complicated, and produce such varied outcomes, that tracing the relationships between them is as yet largely impossible. Many people are not interested enough in finding out about them to help make the study of them eventually possible. What is more, they assume one need not know about such interrelations in order to know all that is needed about behaviour.

A few remarks about dealing with complex "higher order" processes will be included here before saying anything about work and theories in the sensory area.

A Model for Defining the Various Facets of Behaviour
The paradigm for the study of many features of behaviour is the manner in which I deal with emotion and its associated body processes. Here I proceed as in all cases, to determine what the personalistic behaviour is, and then to name it, and to distinguish it from the many sub-processes that one may find associated with it, and which in the ordinary way of dealing with matters, become entangled with it, so as to result in language, thinking and experimental confusion, forestalling a systematic end result. I define *emotion*, for example, *as the cognitive-feeling complex aroused when response to a situation cannot be fully acted out.* To provide a basis

for understanding the various phenomena that collectively are conventionally called emotion, I point out that all behaviour is evaluative. It is evaluative in two ways. First, the organism takes each encounter to be one or the other of three sorts: (*a*) something calling for indifference; (*b*) something to be accepted and reacted to positively; or (*c*) something to be rejected, retreated from, or fought (reacted to negatively). Naturally, the encounters with indifference evoke nothing for us to consider. The other two types call for the organism's action and thus, our consideration. The organism, in addition to evaluating external circumstance, evaluates how well it itself acts. It evaluates its own reactions in light of what it takes to be the needed reactions.[1] Generally, complete overt action is not possible and, as a substitute, certain activities *within* the organism take its place. This action is not only a substitute action but it involves various distortions and disruptions in ongoing body activity.

Students of emotion, both in psychology and physiology, recognize the many forms of body-process disruption and disorganization associated with feelings of various sorts and tend simply to include those under the term emotion. Thus, either the whole complex or any part of it is likely to be called emotion, so that it is not clear to the speaker or to the listener, just what is meant. Emotion thus has turned out to be a term combining phenomena of several unlike categories, the result hardly yielding to a very clear and singular definition.

It will be noted here that what I have called emotion is the historical item, the *experience*, the *cognition*, and *feeling*. This experience is about the best representation of the individual's orientation to a situation that we have access to at present. It symbolizes the personalistic behaviour of the organism. The separate body processes that can be identified as associated with or concurrent with the feeling (emotion) are each but part-processes – thus, activities below the personalistic level. Hence, there is a constant need to distinguish what is emotion and what are simply some of the concomitants or items associated with it in various ways.

The example just given is a model for almost any feature of behaviour that one may wish to deal with, whether it be emotion, fatigue, anxiety, believing, or thinking. In dealing with any of these, one must first be clear in distinguishing what the activity at the personalistic level is, and name it. Then one can proceed to identify part-activities that are observable as separate body processes. The names for these, and that for the activity at the personalistic (total organism) level should not be identical. It must be further recognized that part of what is personalistic may be articulate and conscious, and part may not be. Actually two separate names may be necessary here, as for example, when Nelson suggests *tiredness* for what one is aware of, and *fatigue* for the over-all inability to perform. The big issue is the distinction between the organism as a unit, and its separate body processes (the phenomena that physiologists are focally concerned with).

If one is very careful to concern himself with the identification of those phenomena which are examples of personalistic behaviour and those which are simply part-functions, he will go a long way toward avoiding confusion which will plague

1 This description may sound like imputing that conscious "thinking" is involved in all cases. Such an interpretation would seem to stem from the habit of defining words mentalistically.

his progress later on. This distinction is not always easily made. Convention often injects the distinction between conscious and unconscious phenomena as its prime concern and infers that all personalistic behaviour emerges as something the person is aware of. However, in instances in which this restriction is not made, various mentalistic notions about the unconscious or subconscious get entwined in the thinking about what must go on that is not conscious. The unconscious "mind" is talked about. It would seem to the conventionalist that to talk about body processes at this point would be out of the question. This is to say he assumes that thinking must be mental, else it is not psychological, or as I would say, not personalistic.

I would venture to say that the personalistic category that I have been talking about would include a number of features that might now be thought of as subpersonalistic. This is to say that the organism at the personalistic level is possibly truly involved in combating infectious disease, or in surviving in extreme circumstances in ways that transcend the strictly homeostatic. We often speak of the great *resistance* some individuals have, or to their *"will to live."* Whatever these things are, if anything, it would seem that they are a function of the total organism, and not simply a product of certain subsystems. If they are this, they constitute a part of psychology – a part of what goes on in ways outside our present mode of verbal expression, but no less functions of the total organism.

It will be noted that I have just made reference to *homeostasis*. A few cautions with regard to its position as a concept are in order here. It has been too easy for various non-biologists to extend the idea of *homeostasis* far beyond the originally intended use. The criticism I would level against this is not against the broad idea of an organism's adjusting to impacts made against it, but rather that the term homeostasis was chosen originally as a label for a specific form of balance maintenance within a system. It described maintenance of equilibrium at a level below the personalistic. I do not believe Cannon had in mind the actual behaviour of the total organism, but was referring only to a lower level of body organization. The form of organization to be found at the personalistic level, although an example of the same principles, is so different as to deserve a name of its own. It is just as inappropriate to use the term homeostasis here, as it would be to take it out of biology altogether and use it as a label in thermodynamics.

For the personalistic level let us use some other term. This is not to multiply terms or coin new words for their own sakes, but to keep communication clear and to preclude wasting time arguing whether or not homeostasis is exemplified in overall human behaviour. *We are all supposing that it is characteristic for all energy systems to resist disintegration and to maintain equilibrium.* Homeostasis is certainly not the word used in thermodynamics, where the fully generic term belongs when chosen.

To make homeostasis cover the human organism's behaviour when it commits suicide is to bring into the situation various concepts and considerations that a physiologist, by no stretch of the imagination, would consent to include. And yet if, as I have just said, the same general principles of maintenance of equilibrium are involved at the personalistic level as in homeostasis, one must find a rationale for understanding suicide, the very opposite behaviour from maintenance of biological existence. I think I have that rationale, but I consider its presentation here somewhat more of a digression than is warranted.

THEORIES REGARDING THE MECHANISM OF SENSORY RESPONSE

Various theories to account for sensory response are among the best examples of biological psychology. Notwithstanding, they must, however, look irrelevant to a great many psychologists. The enticing field for concern seems to lie in contriving notions about behaviour starting from some arbitrarily chosen origin, or phenomenon of personal interest. As one views the field of social psychology, he finds almost as many starting points as there are men at work.

Sensory phenomena seem to constitute only a trivial aspect of all behaviour. If one were to consider what the organism is doing in seeing, hearing, tasting, and touching, this attitude might disappear. If one realizes that, in these acts, the organism is making *discriminations*, and if one supposes that when the organism (a person) is making decisions that are social, intellectual or whatever, it is also discriminating, then a great deal of psychology's task would be to discover how the organism operates so as to make discriminations at various levels of complexity or abstractness. Conceptualizing behaviour as discriminatory activity (detecting differences, and selecting among them) is a considerable help in setting the stage for behavioural study.

The workers in sensory discrimination are surely setting the stage for studying discriminations of other sorts. More and more we are coming to see that the behaviour in psycho-physical laboratory situations and social situations in or outside the laboratory have a great deal in common. To wit, we now have the theoretical work of Helson in his adaptation level theory which seems to function not only in psycho-physical experimentation but elsewhere as well.

If we discover the discrimination paradigm in the nervous system and the organism's method of "storage" and "retrieval", we shall have gone a long way in structuring a science of behaviour. It may well be that the concept of storage is not appropriate to describe what makes the organism take present selective advantage of past influences, but by use of the term I wish simply to indicate that I am alluding to what has long been called memory and recall.

SENSORY DATA ENABLING THEORETICAL INTERPRETATION

The Response of the Kinesthetic Sensory System
Echlin and Fessard (1938) studying the discharge of single, and groups of stretch receptors in frog preparations in relation to the impingement frequency have obtained very clear evidence that these receptors can discharge at submultiples of the impingement rate. They made this interpretation from the findings and it is exactly the interpretation I would make. They say that "stretch receptors will respond at submultiples of the stimulus frequency and that the composite discharge from a number of these receptors will, at the same time, reproduce the stimulus frequency through a process of alternations." Interestingly enough, these findings and this in-

terpretation were made independently, almost concurrently with the findings of Bishop and Bartley in vision which led to the same interpretation. This interpretation of Echlin and Fessard contained the possibility of yielding a program of research relating in detail the temporal relations of input to neural activity and over-all response of a muscle group in addition to providing a picture of kinesthetic function.

The Response of the Auditory System

The response of the kinesthetic sensory system is reminiscent of the findings and interpretations made by Wever and Bray (1930) in regard to the action of the auditory mechanism. It will be remembered that records from the eighth nerve show waves tallying with an input of 1000 cycles a second. It was doubted that any single axon could conduct quite up to that frequency. Hence, the well-known Wever-Bray *volley theory* was formulated to account for the over-all result in the record. It was supposed that individual fibres conducted at frequencies lower than 1000 cycles per second, and that this over-all result was due to some fibres responding to one cycle of the input, and others to others, in what they called volleys. In essence it was the alternation spoken of by Echlin and Fessard.

Factual Basis for Theory in the Tactile System

Rose and Montcastle in studying the tactile system by paired stimuli and trains, found that the results obtained by using pairs did not "specify the capacity of the system to respond when trains of stimuli are used." Studying the behaviour of a single neuron, it was found that it follows the input rate until the range of 30 to 70 inputs per second is reached. When higher input rates are used, the single neuron continues to respond at about the same rate, but response to every input is produced supposedly by having some inputs, randomly distributed throughout the train, fail to evoke responses. This state they call *equilibration*. Records of responses to trains of inputs show that the first input evokes a response, and then several following it do not. Finally, succeeding stimuli again elicit responses. This relativity in responsive period is called the *silent period*. Note that what I am doing here is indicating that the study of various sensory systems yields data that can form the basis of a kind of interpretation that has enough inherent implications in it to warrant a whole program of both sensory and neuro-physiological research covering a number of years. Note also, as we go into the description of the visual system, that the findings in the already mentioned systems have been essentially similar to those in the visual system, and that I, and later those who have worked with me, have conducted the type of programmatic research just suggested. This has extended over the past thirty-two years and is still in progress without diminishing returns having set in.

Some of the Facts Leading to a Theory of the Central Visual Mechanism

Bishop and I, in recording the electrical response of the visual cortex (elicited by stimulating the stump of the optic nerve) found that a train of equal-sized impingements did not elicit a series of equal-sized cortical responses. Making due allowance for the undulations in the record due to incidental brain waves, we suspected that the inequalities in size of cortical responses to these stimuli might be an expression of some sort of periodicity inherent in the brain. We checked on this idea by varying the separation of the members of the input train to see whether some separation could be found that would produce the same sized responses to all members of the input train. Were such to be found it would tell what this periodicity consisted in. A separation of about one-fifth second accomplished this in the rabbit. Hence, we had evidence of periodicity. A second step in checking upon the idea of periodicity was to shift the input train back and forth. This should continue to produce series of equal-sized responses, but in accord with the phase into which the input entered, just so would the response series be all small waves, or all medium sized, or all large ones. This second phase of timing was also successful. I then tried pairs of impingements to study the relationship between the temporal separation of the members of the pair to the size of the response to the second member of the pair. I found that aside from a very brief separation during which the two members would summate, no response was elicited when the two inputs were close together. As separation was lengthened beyond a certain point, the second input elicited a progressively bigger response. This size reached a maximum, and then if the separation were increased still further, the response to the second input began to diminish. Thus, if separation were made still greater, a second cycle could be demonstrated. In both experiments (Bishop's and mine, and then mine) the separations were the same; and in both, these results were produced with supramaximal inputs, but not with weak inputs. Following general physiological understandings, it was supposed that with maximal inputs, all channels in the optic pathway were activated together. Maximal response to a second input could only be obtained when the temporal separation between inputs was great enough for all channels to recover. With lesser separations, only those channels which had recovered earlier than the rest could be activated. Still smaller separations found no channels ready to be re-activated. These facts and inferences began to go together to form a theory of what was happening in the optic pathway and to imply various consequences if still other manipulations were made in the timing of the members in an input train. I pursued the matter further and, at about the same time, in some of my perceptual experimentation using intermittent photic inputs, human subjects found that intermittent stimulation (a series or train of photic pulses) would produce greater brightness than a steady continuous photic input of the same intensity. There seemed to be a connection between these results and the findings and interpretations in the electrophysiological experiments. The first assumption made was that the input conditions for producing maximal amplitude of cortical response were essentially the same conditions for producing visual brightness in the human experiments. The theory was named the *alternation-of-response theory* and, as you can see, it is essentially the kind of supposition that was made by the workers on the other senses just mentioned. These workers have, to my knowledge, not pursued their work further and excepting Wever and Bray, have not named their interpretation nor stated any further expectations which could be tested. Those possibilities still lie open.

A little further description of the alternation-of-response theory is necessary, not only to show the extent to which a theory may be detailed, but also to indicate what some of the expectations inherent in it have been, and then to describe how these were tested and confirmed. I believe it is difficult to find a more detailed example of theorizing and hypothesizing in the psycho-physiological literature anywhere. Work on this theory and its expectations has been in progress for thirty-two years. It is still not well understood by those who should be its best critics, for somehow it has come to be believed in some quarters that this theory and what has been found out about how the *neuroretina* operates are in conflict. This is not the case, for the theory is based upon the findings from the stimulation of the stump of the optic nerve with the eye removed, and from stimulation of the eye with photic inputs. Under the basic conditions used, and incidentally those adequate for building the theory, the results were essentially the same with both kinds of inputs. They did not depend upon the retina producing the periodicities found. They are a function of the central end of the optic pathway and not of the retina or periphery.

The alternation-of-response theory is psychological theory in the ultimate sense, and not simply physiological, since it is theory that accounts for sensory end results, the kind of phenomena that are psychological data. I am able to say this largely on account of the systematic position expressed earlier regarding what is psychological and what is physiological, or what belongs to any other discipline. It is probable that for those unaware of or not espousing the position I described, this theory would not belong in psychology. It is, however, one of the many that must be structured to account for how body process and sensory or other behavioural end results are related.

THE ALTERNATION OF RESPONSE THEORY

This is a combination of facts and interpretations describing the kinds of events and the principles of operation in the central end of the optic pathway (visual system) in connection with the variations in temporal distribution of input into the optic nerve, or with photic impingements on the retina. The theory does not indicate anything about retina function, but it does imply that, whatever the retinal activity may be, it does not obviate the type of activity described in the theory. In fact, whatever the retina does to produce and temporally distribute the flow of impulses up the optic nerve along its various fibres (pathway channels), it cannot nullify or obliterate the functional principles described in the theory; for the theory, as you will see by what is to follow, is merely a statement of *how the central end of the pathway utilizes all forms of temporal distribution* of discharge ranging from a uniform discharge to various forms of bunching of discharge in which there are burst and null periods in between.

Thus, the theory consists of a time-intensity description of the activity in the central end of the pathway. It predicts what to expect both in cortical response and in sensory end-result when known forms of photic input are provided.

The theory may be stated in the following manner.

(i) The optic pathway consists in a number of parallel chains of neurons, called channels. The fibres of the optic nerve illustrate what is meant by channels in that segment of the pathway. In the peripheral and central ends of the pathway inter-lacings of axons complicate the pathway structure but, in effect, do not annihilate the pathway concept in a functional sense.

(ii) The number of channels is fixed and the only alteration in function has to do with which channels fire at any time.

(iii) Each channel can be repeatedly activated at a maximum rate, for example, about 10 per second in the human, and about 5 per second in the rabbit. Following an activation there is a period during which re-activation is not possible. This is a recovery period, or "rest" period.

(iv) As was said earlier, the channels may be made to act in any distribution ranging from an even rotation or alternation wherein as many channels are going into action as going into rest at any and all instants (continuous, uniform illumination produces this result) to a distribution in which a maximal number fire almost together and then cannot re-fire until a tenth second has elapsed. This then is the condition of maximal bunching, called *synchrony*, whereas the uniform distribution is called *asynchrony*.

(v) Brief intense inputs produce this maximal synchrony when delivered in accord with the one-tenth second periodicity. Channels set into action together tend to recover together, although this recovery may vary some from one channel to another.

(vi) When one takes advantage of the known time required for recovery, and stimulates in accord with it, one is, in effect, dealing as if with a single channel. It was on the basis of this reasoning that the nature of the single channel was deduced.

(vii) When a train of inputs is delivered to the system at rates above the one at which any single channel can repeatedly respond (respond to succeeding members of the train), the following result ensues. The first input (photic pulse) elicits a huge response, the second, and possibly several more, elicit no response, and then various succeeding pulses elicit responses of various sizes. Finally, when 12 to 15 or more inputs are delivered, all inputs begin to have responses. This is not by reason of any change in the properties of the responding channels, but because the channels are so temporally distributed in their respective cycles of activity and recovery that some are always ready to respond to the next pulse regardless of how soon it is delivered. This is what is meant by alternation of response. This provides for over-all continuous response to continuous uniform illumination, but at a lower "intensity" level than when momentary inputs cause a burst of activity (a temporal cluster). This period during which over-all response is irregular and before all inputs of a train elicit responses, I have called the *reorganization period*. It is paralleled by what the workers in at least two of the other modalities describe for the phenomena they studied.

By the use of this conceptualization of what is happening in the pathway, one can predict what ought to happen if one varies intermittency rate from pattern to pattern, and also other factors such as intensity. The theory is consistent with the facts of the reorganization period, with the size of responses obtained at various rates and distributions of input, and tells what to expect under all conditions yet conceived of and tested. While the theory first emerged as an attempt to account for the amplitudes of the cortical responses, and corresponding brightness seen by the human observer, it did not stop there. Temporal manifestations of input have varied other aspects of sensory end result.

Remembering that various workers over many decades have obtained colour effects from whole-spectrum intermittent inputs, it was supposed that our intermittent inputs might alter perceived colour. This was tried, and was found to be the case. A spectrum analysis of the effects of part-spectrum inputs was made, and it was shown that intermittency produced changes in hue, saturation, and brightness. So it can be said that brightness is not the only sensory quality that is temporally controlled. In fact, spectral inputs doubtless have effects on the *temporal* characteristics of retinal ganglion cell discharges, and it is their temporal features that go a long way toward producing the different sensory end results we have already found. The role of the timing of different spectral inputs is what we are presently trying to determine.

In delineating the alternation of response theory, I have given you an example of how empiricism both with regard to behaviour phenomena, and body mechanism can furnish copious material for developing a step by step understanding of why the human being is as he is and how he relates to his surroundings. This same empiricism, guided by basic considerations rather than by the more usual restrictive and personal starting points, can be put to work in dealing with higher orders of discrimination and thus come to cope with the problems that are nearer to the hearts and interests of a great number of psychologists. I have put the matter this way to express a belief that the matters I have talked about are not so far as might be thought from dealing with problems that most psychologists see as psychology.

A GENERAL THEORY REGARDING SENSORY MECHANISMS

I have indicated that information regarding the mechanisms of each of four sensory modalities has led, independently, to kinds of inference which seem to be parallel forms of a single interpretation. It is possible this will enable one to build a unitary theory of sensory mechanisms.

You may have noted that the alternation of response theory, the description of how the visual system operates in utilizing peripheral input, is a fully general statement for one modality, although detailed and concrete enough to produce predictions for a host of situations. While it so far has only been applied to brightness, visual acuity, colour, size, and perceived duration, it gives every evidence of being the kind of understanding for dealing with other visual qualities.

Less is known about the other sense modalities, and they are not all as complexly related to the environment, but what has been disclosed in neurophysiological investigations on the mechanisms of audition, touch and kinesthesis has already shown that these all manifest some of the same essential properties as the optic pathway. Hence, we can already state a few generalities which would form a beginning of a general theory of sensory mechanisms. This theory will have two aspects, of course: (*a*) what the mechanisms accomplish and (*b*) how they accomplish it.

In the following, I want to suggest some features of a theory pertaining to the four, if not to all the senses. In case this may seem premature, let it be remembered that the venture can be profitable in pointing investigators to what to look for and how to regard findings. It can form the basis of extended programs of body-process investigation. Some of the items in what I shall have to say will have been already obvious and some not.

(i) All sensory systems consist in three parts: (*a*) the peripheral part, the sense organ or organs; (*b*) the conductor part; and (*c*) the central utilization mechanism.

(ii) The several sense modalities vary quite considerably in the structure of their peripheral segment and, of course, are sensitive to various kinds of energy. These factors determine to a great extent what is to be literally expected of the body mechanisms.

(iii) A sense organ, in effect, is made up of two portions (two essentially different kinds of tissue, the one is non-neural, the other is neural).

(iv) The non-neural is involved in receiving the energistic impingement, and undergoes some sort of reversible modification as a result. Hence, it is to be taken into account in explaining the setting up of the sensory message. The neural portion is elaborated to various degrees depending upon the modality involved. In vision, this is a complex neural system (an actual embryological outgrowth of the brain).

This range in elaboration of structure, and hence, finer articulation with environmental impingements, does not alter in principle the factors determining the periphery's contribution to the conductor segment of the sensory pathway.

(v) In any case, all that the periphery has to offer is some sort of grouping of impulses carried by a set of parallel circuits, which I have already called channels. This means that two factors are involved in any and all cases: (*a*) the channels that are active at a given time, and (*b*) the temporal distribution of the activity cycles of the channels that make up the population. These are the variables within a given modality, and in accord with the temporal pattern of discharge that results, a message is coded in the form usable by the centre.

(vi) The pathways from the several modalities feed into the central nervous system at different points and this determines to a great extent many of the qualitative and quantitative features of the sensory end results that constitute the particular modality, since the brain is far from a homogeneous structure.

(vii) Since the sensory pathway up to the central utilization mechanism is essentially a set of parallel channels which function as a pattern of temporal discharge relationships, one might expect that the *means* whereby this selectivity is brought about would be the key to the operation of the system. This has been found true, particularly as has been worked out in the alternation of response theory in vision.

(viii) The determiners of how selection (sorting) works are: (*a*) the temporal, intensive, and other energistic characteristics of the impingement (stimulus), (*b*) the intrinsic temporal discharge properties of the individual channels, and (*c*) temporal characteristics of the central segment as regards the utilization of the input it receives.

Both ends of the pathway (sensory system) thus play a role in the selective or sorting process. At the peripheral end, the intrinsic activity-rest cycles and the threshold ranges of the neurons there play a considerable role. In modalities lacking the structural complications found in the eye (in particular), the intrinsic characteristics of individual neurons may be the only factors at work. In the eye, temporal interactions between the retinal layers and transverse portions of them, cooperate to set up the temporal discharge pattern in the optic nerve.

The central end of the pathway utilizes the channel inputs in accord with certain temporal characteristics of its own. This is manifested as a periodicity. That is, whether what arrives over the channels is used to a maximum, only to a degree, or not at all depends upon where in the temporal cycle the input arrives. This makes some channels of little or no effect at given times but of maximal effect at others, which helps to *temporally re-distribute the firing of the channels*, thus changing the input to the centre. *This may be viewed as, in effect, a specific kind of feedback.*

(ix) In all cases, there is a distinction between the rate at which a single channel can fire and be re-activated, and the rate at which the system as a whole can respond differentially to temporal variations in the impingement. For example, in vision, the sensory end result and the underlying response of the system as a whole may be continuous and uniform, while the activity of the separate channels of the sensory pathway is always an alternation between activity (firing) and rest (recovery).

From here on, much specific exploratory work must be done to determine what can be said that characterizes all the modalities and what constitutes something special in each. This will lead to a set of underlying principles that hold true regardless of the unique ways these are exemplified in the various modalities.

Furthermore, the principles here will have a far more general significance. It has long been an unwritten working supposition among neurophysiologists that many things discovered about nervous activity demonstrated in some restricted tissue mass are illustrative of how neurons and/or neuron systems work in general and thus will explain other phenomena. The discovery of more detailed information about sensory mechanisms is the discovery of the kind of information which, when perceptively interpreted, will describe the working principles of neural principles underlying other behaviour functions such as thinking. You may recall my earlier suggestion that many other forms of behaviour which have been given a variety of names are probably in essence only various higher order forms of *discrimination*, the function that characterizes the sensory processes. So the study of sensory discrimination processes will provide understanding beyond perception itself.

SUMMARY AND CONCLUSIONS

In this paper I have defined psychology and indicated that the psychology I am concerned with is a biological science, but is at the same time ultimately concerned with the human as a person. I have pointed out some of the problems naturally encountered in making psychology a consistent and effective scientific endeavour. By implication, if not by detailed discussion, I have asserted that not all that presently is taken to be scientific psychology qualifies as such, and thus attention must be given to what should be included and what to eliminate.

One of the major concerns has been the definition of the stimulus. This term has been used in so many ways that it has ceased to be a technical term. The idea of something external influencing the organism, and as a result, the organism reacting, can scarcely be eliminated from the study of the organism's behaviour. Hence a definitive and restrictive position with regard to stimulus and response is necessary. I have sought to define this position so as to place psychology among the natural sciences.

Another concern has pertained to the use of terms throughout the discipline. No term should be used in more than one way and no concept should possess more than one label.

Since psychology involves study of the organism, definitions in psychology should be organism-centred rather than environment-centred, and since the experiential category is involved, attention should be paid to deciding which words are to refer to the experiential, which words to body process, and which words to other categories, such as the energies that impinge upon sense organs ("stimuli"). Classification of such a matter as this goes a long way to structuring psychology, since we already have the terms and the concepts, but without the classification just mentioned.

Finally, an example of an extended experiential program of studying the relation between energies impinging on sense organs, body processes, and sensory end results was given from my own work in vision. With this a few suggestions regarding the nature of sensory response in general were included.

The paper was intended to be more of an alerting device than a complete and well rounded statement of position. It was meant, therefore, to be one facet of a discussion regarding the unification of psychology.

References

BARTLEY, S. H., "Temporal and spatial summation of extrinsic impulses with the intrinsic activity of the cortex." *Journal of Cellular and Comparative Physiology*, 8 (1936) 41–62

BARTLEY, S. H., "Visual sensation and its dependence upon the neuro-physiology of the optic pathway." *Biological Symposia*, 8 (1942) 87–106

BARTLEY, S. H., "Some facts and concepts regarding the neurophysiology of the optic pathway." *American Medical Association Archives of Ophthalmology* (Part II), 60 (1958) 775–91

BARTLEY, S. H., "Some relations between sensory end results and neural activity in the optic pathway." *Journal of Psychology*, 55 (1963) 121–43

BARTLEY, S. H. and BISHOP, G. H., "The cortical response to stimulation of the optic nerve in the rabbit." *American Journal of Physiology*, 103 (1933) 159–72

BARTLEY, S. H., and BISHOP, G. H., "Factors determining the form of the electrical response from the optic cortex of the rabbit." *Ibid.*, 173–84

BISHOP, G. H., "Cyclic changes in excitability of the optic pathway of the rabbit." *Ibid.*, 213–24

DUFFY, E., "The concept of energy mobilization." *Psychological Review*, 58 (1951) 30–40

ECHLIN, F. and FESSARD, A., "Synchronized impulse discharges from receptors in the deep tissues in response to a vibrating stimulus." *Journal of Physiology*, 93 (1938) 312–34

FREEMAN, G. L., *The energetics of human behavior*. Ithaca, NY: Cornell University Press, 1948

GIBSON, J. J., "The concept of stimulus in psychology." *American Psychologist*, 15 (1960) 694–703

NELSON, T. M., personal communication, 1963

ROSE, J. E., and MOUNTCASTLE, V. B., "Touch and kinesthesis," in *Handbook of physiology*, edited by H. W. Magoun. Washington, DC: American Physiological Society, 1959, section I, chap. XVII

WEVER, E. G., and BRAY, C. W., "Present possibilities for auditory theory." *Psychological Review*, 37 (1930) 365–80

Comments:
E. Galanter

To discuss Bartley's paper within the context of the possible unity of at least experimental psychology I would like to distinguish between two kinds of enterprises that occur in that restricted field. The first is what I shall call Experimental Revelation: the workers in this genre try to discover the actual workings of the organism, whether it is of behaviour or of blood and tissue. They do this by a search process, based on the hypothesis that careful observation will reveal the nature of the beast, whether the beast is a man or a mouse. The other line is what I will call the Constructionistic Venture. I number myself in this somewhat smaller group. I believe that there is very little to be understood by observation, but that one must invent or construct the object of his inquiry. Observations are then used to examine the quality of the construction, but the construction itself is the fundamental quest. I assign Bartley to the revelationists, and my strongest disagreement is, therefore, one of strategy.

The trouble with these two views is that they sound as if they are very close together. Both groups respect the data of the science in some sense, but one side believes that by examining the data they will make certain kinds of discoveries, the other believes that the examination will rarely if ever reveal anything without some prior construction. In its most reprehensible (pure?) form the constructionist argues that there is nothing to discover except the nature of one's own intuitions. It is the formalization of those intuitions that constitute the scientific enterprise. Among revelationists the model of science for psychology is the biologist, whose microscope and dissecting instruments reveal the stuff of life, while among the constructionists the model is the activity of the mathematical physicist.

Let me then turn to Professor Bartley's paper, and state my contextual agreements and disagreements, trusting that you are aware that the general disagreement is of a very special kind. Bartley made a strong point that biological causation is energistic. Now of course there is a sense in which this cannot be denied. But even Bartley does not hew completely to this line, because subsequently he says things that must be taken to imply that the causal sequence occasionally lies outside of energistics. In my own somewhat stilted terminology, any expression in which there are free parameters contains causal links that may indeed not exist except as mathematical inventions. One is forced to make a tremendous enlargement of his ontology by ascribing material existence to these parameters so necessary to complete the description of an experiment. Gravity, an overworked example, constitutes such a parameter, certainly causal but also non-material (read "energistic").

Other points that Bartley makes, such as the careful selection of the set of possible observations, is something with which all of us can agree. Bartley's excellent choice of the analysis of discrimination promotes further agreement, because here is indeed a behavioural phenomenon central to the characterization of all actions of both animals and men. Bartley's deep comprehension of the distinction between science and engineering so closely parallels my own that I must say that his late arrival has saved me from what I felt was going to be a very lonely outpost.

J. R. Royce

Since the psychologist is focused on behaving organisms I agree with Bartley that we cannot ignore those biological processes which intervene between S inputs and R outputs. However, to the extent that he argues for biological reductionism, and in spite of his disclaimer it seems to me he does, I disagree with his position. Knowledge of biopsychological processes increases our ability to understand, predict, and control behaviour. It does not follow from this that all behaviour can be or should be analysed in terms of underlying biological mechanisms, nor does it follow that psychology will eventually be replaced by an all pervading, more mature biology.

David Krech

I find it a bit discouraging that some of us here feel that Professor Bartley's position *re* psychology as a biological science may give rise to grave and fundamental heresies. I so completely agree with Professor Bartley that I find it a bit nonsensical to talk about "the relationship between biology and psychology." In my scientific lexicon, that is equivalent to talking about "the relationship between biology and biology." I find it difficult to accept Professor Galanter's very comforting "A Blessing on Both Your Houses!" position. I have reached the stage – in my dotage – where the issue of "dualism" *versus* "monism" is but an ancient bore. Psychologists have wasted a lot of time on the raising of such pseudo-problems and on the writing of many polemics about various and sundry pseudo-solutions which have been put forth for these pseudo-problems. And I would like to reassure Professor Galanter that most (if indeed not all) physiological psychologists know full well that the study of the "mind" can be fruitful and valuable for the most physiological of physiological psychologists. It is the physiological psychologist who is much more apt, for example, to make recourse to the phenomenological method (when working with human beings) than the non-physiological behaviourist. Of all the experimental psychologists, I suspect that it is the physiological psychologist who listens most attentively to the report of his O's state of awareness, perceptions, and feelings.

Rebuttal: S. H. Bartley

Professor Galanter has chosen to use the dichotomy of Experimental Revelation and The Constructionist Venture as a framework for commenting on my paper on the unity of psychology. The dichotomy has the power of bringing out some very useful points regarding what men do, or may do, in the name of science. But, for anyone to say that there "is very little to be understood by observation" doesn't sound sensible to me. It is to be admitted that one does "invent or construct the object of inquiry," but this is not made possible in a pure, experienceless vacuum.

The closer to a complete vacuum one comes, the further away from science one operates.

I would point out, to begin with, that the two forms of enterprise Dr Galanter describes do not always exist apart, but are intermingled in the activities of one individual. Hence, the relevant issue seems to be the purposes for which each endeavour is utilized. If we suppose that science is based on direct experience (observation), this may play two roles, one to provide a form of knowledge and data and guide what we do in connection with it. It is observation that instigates ideas. As soon as we became *homo sapiens* we seemed to be endowed with a tremendous ability to imagine, and to construct our own realities. Demons, and all forms of sensorially undetected creatures were invented, and invention has never stopped. The question to be asked is how fully and consistently does any invention tally with direct observation, and what can one do with it. How well does one man's invention interrelate with those of others who have devoted themselves to considering the same observations? How well do one's inventions provide consistency to the widest possible variety of observations? I agree with Galanter that observations are not, in themselves, revelations; although I would say that it is revelation or, to put it more aptly, *discovery* that is our business. To say this, is to emphasize the idea of achievement connected with observation, rather than achievement as a form of sheer construction.

It does not pay to be too proud of one's constructions, at least, to the point of misapplying our models. It seems that, after all, most of the constructions called models these days are often quite restricted in nature, and are assumed to be what they are not. That is, they are transposed from one category of data to another often by force, rather than in line with appropriate background knowledge. This is true in many cases in which engineering models, conventions, and mathematical models are applied to the human organism in lieu of direct study of it as a biological system. Many prefer to build an imaginary nervous system rather than examining actual nervous systems. Here is where the dichotomy of the revelationist and the constructionist comes out in its clearest form and best demonstrates the danger and inappropriateness of pure Constructionism. I agree with Galanter only in that science is not simply a plodding and unimaginative job of data collection. Data *are* collected for a purpose.

I do not see that this was the central issue in the content and purpose of my paper. In it, I wished to indicate the central theme and locus of the psychologist's endeavour. I characterized it as an attempt to understand the human organism as a person and to locate the endeavour in the context of biology instead of allowing it to be a coordinate of theology, political "science," and other endeavours decidedly foreign to natural science.

There are several remarks I should like to make in regard to Krech's comments on my paper. I am pleased to see that he also views psychology as a form of biology. I take what he says as also disagreeing with Galanter's espoused old-fashioned dualism. When Galanter defends the study of mind he is not supporting what he thinks he is. If people who use the term *mind* were only doing what people who use *gravitation* are doing, then there would be nothing to criticize or even comment upon. Mind has always been an essential something belonging to a category defined apart from the category of concrete items and processes. It has always belonged to the category of the gods, demons, and spirits, which operated on principles other than those discoverable for material objects. If mind were only a word to cover behaviour of the organism as a whole (or a person), it would be divested of many of its objectionable features. But, since the word has so long contained the medieval connotations to which I have just alluded, a more fortunate way of talking about personalistic phenomena (human behaviour) should be invented. Let the constructionist exercise his talents in this direction.

One of the main objections to mind is that it is the name for something in a separate *causal system*. To explain mental events in the usual way is to avoid descriptions of body process. Mind not only refers to a separate causal system, but a system whose principles are actually unrelatable to those pertaining to body processes. Were it to be admitted or declared or demonstrated that these principles are not at all different from biological principles, then the dualism would be obliterated and there would be no grounds for Galanter or anyone else saying that he is a dualist.

I think Krech and I agree completely.

Professor Royce has misinterpreted what I have said when he declares that I have described a reductionism in my paper. There is a vast difference between saying that certain things stem from biological processes and that certain phenomena can be reduced to biological processes or, to the activity of molecules and atoms. Royce admits that knowledge of biological processes increases our ability to understand, predict, and control behaviour but, somehow, he refuses to admit that all behaviour can or should be analysed in terms of underlying biological mechanisms. Why shouldn't this analysis be performed? Perhaps it is because he believes dealing with biological processes is unavoidably a form of reductionism. I am no reductionist and would fight it, too. But here is not a case that calls for such a war.

The behaviour phenomena that Royce includes in psychology are real and do not need to be *reduced* to anything else. They simply need to be accounted for by the same rationale and with the same scheme as accounting for any natural phenomenon. To have one scheme for psychology and another for the rest of natural phenomena – those expressed by body processes – is to perpetuate the old dualism found in earlier philosophy, religion, and in the non-scientific thinking of today.

The all-pervading, more mature biology that Royce fears is, I suggest, the very thing to be wished for. It will have as one of its components the study of human behaviour, but it will be a unitary system containing much of what is fragmented and disconnected today. It would neither pervert nor de-throne psychology, but would make it a natural science.

Discussion: S. H. Bartley

RELATION OF BIOLOGICAL PSYCHOLOGY TO SOCIAL PSYCHOLOGY, ETC.

AUDITOR   I think you define the relationship of the biologically oriented scientist to sociology or social psychology by saying that he is not claiming social phenomena to be unimportant, but that he is just not concerned with them. What is the biologically oriented psychologist's relation to biochemistry?

BARTLEY   Well, there seems to be a cleavage in thinking among psychologists. All natural sciences, up to a point at least, have something in common; common tenets, common basic viewpoints, certain common principles of methodology. But when psychology is considered – even as a science – a change in outlook seems to be involved in the thinking of some. They seem to use a new set of assumptions and start psychology off on a path of its own. This is not acceptable. I expect psychology to be co-ordinate with its sibling sciences, if it is to be a science at all. Hence, it has natural, logical relations to all other disciplines, including, of course, biochemistry.

AUDITOR   One often hears the criticism that a physiological psychologist is merely a poor physiologist.

BARTLEY   I would often make the same criticism.

AUDITOR   Now, this means then that somehow he isn't fulfilling his role.

BARTLEY   I don't think he is the physiologist, and I don't think he is the psychologist I would expect him to be. He is not the person who is attempting to account for human behaviour by the use of body-process information. He is too likely to be someone simply concentrating on the study of certain limited body-processes without too much training in physiology. Thus, he does not play the role of psychologist adequately nor is he an expert on body-process to the extent of a physiologist.

AUDITOR   The way I understand you, if you were dealing with the social sciences you would consider it more important to have explanations in terms of biological sciences than to have explanations at the more nolar level.

BARTLEY   No, all I want of psychology is the kind of study that promises to contribute to the understandings of behaviour. It must be free from the present thinking that pervades the market place and the political arena. The example of Rokeach's study of belief systems is a case in which a respectable approach to a social problem was made. Rokeach, as a social (personality) psychologist, and I, as a biological psychologist, are quite in agreement.

AUDITOR   Surely both approaches are valid. In *Systems and Theories in Psychology* the authors, Marx and Hillix, discuss this problem from a slightly different perspective by taking an analogy from physics. They say it is difficult to describe the characteristics of water from the molecular components of water. And so, for a long time, the best way to do it was just to deal with water as such. Maybe this is the counterpart of what is happening in social psychology today, or in personality theory. It is difficult to deal with the more molecular components of what would probably be considered personality and social psychology, so we deal with the intact organism. What's happened (and I guess this is the point that would have to be conceded to you) is that wave mechanics has now made it possible to predict most of the characteristics of water from a totally molecular point of view. So, maybe we do get back to your point.

BARTLEY   We have to recognize that there are emergent phenomena. As you say, if you're talking about hydrogen and oxygen only and you think you're talking about water, you are a reductionist. It is a mistake to think that one can reduce *a* to *b*. But whether one is dealing with something in chemistry or with the so-called mind-body problem, he faces some of the same underlying principles of procedure.

UNIFICATION OR SPLITTING OF PSYCHOLOGY

AUDITOR 1   I think your thesis is an agreeable one, but how does it work out on the following very mundane practical matter? In a department of psychology it would seem that the division you would suggest is into a group dealing with the effect of energistic impingements on the biological organism, a group which deals with social phenomena, personality and industrial affairs, and possibly a clinical group. How would these groups work together?

BARTLEY   I think there are serious difficulties in getting these three groups to work together. As soon as practical as well as theoretical considerations are allowed to guide the selection of personnel and other departmental considerations, the clash begins. What I am saying does not mean that social behaviour is to be excluded from psychology. It is only that such phenomena should be studied with the same rigour, and from the same standpoint as other matters. The investigator must be able to detach himself from his object of study. Social affairs are too often loaded with dynamite for the investigator, or too often he is, in effect, one of the partisans.

AUDITOR 1   I gain from your writings that you would not like to see people interested in social phenomena detached from the body of investigators studying the human as a biological organism.

BARTLEY   The only person I would want to see separated is somebody who is enough a part of the everyday world that he uses these as his origins in thinking and structuring what he calls science. Such people get into psychology as a means of furthering non-scientific ambitions, and then contend that their endeavours help to make up the body of science.

AUDITOR 1   Part of Dr Krech's thesis is that if psychology were to just fractionate into various combinations of neurophysiology or neurology, etc., it would lose something; it would disappear.

BARTLEY   Well, something is bound to be lost. Philosophy, once upon a time, had that same feeling, I suppose.

AUDITOR   Professor Tennessen would say that philosophy is no more. The things that it has spawned have become what philosophy was. Well, Dr Krech is one of these people who is fractionating. He seems content to become part of a group which is setting up a separate institute, separate language, separate journals. Would you say that this is indicative of a weakness in psychology that these things happen?

BARTLEY   How genuinely separate? Problems rather than fixed disciplines often rightfully determine outcomes.

AUDITOR 1   He did strongly emphasize interaction between these groups.

AUDITOR 2   That doesn't make any difference. There will certainly be interaction, but we see how little there is in actuality, even though everyone pays lip service to psychology. When does one commit the physical act of separating? None of the psychologists will read this neurophysical brain chemistry journal that they'll put out, perhaps.

AUDITOR 3   That's what they said about Skinner, too. They're reading Skinner, now.

BARTLEY   Some people are. The fact that we are discussing this topic is an illustration that some people realize that "we'd better take stock and better clean house." Housekeeping is involved all the way along. Periodically, you do it in your own homes, your offices and labs. You try to produce internal consistency and mutual compatability between elements. I think there's been all too little collective effort in psychology in taking stock of itself, although there are times when you find prophets and critics making outcries. If one can get as many people as we have here seriously considering the various things we've been discussing, I think it's almost a marvel. I'm really delighted.

AUDITOR 1   Going back to weeding out certain things, you'd have to be very careful not to throw out the baby with the bath.

BARTLEY   Yes. My criticism of colleagues here and there is not that they are imperfect in their achievements; it's that they don't try to achieve this rhyme and reason. I don't see the weeding process going on. I don't see them talking seriously about this matter. They're annoyed by anyone asking them to inspect their own psychologies.

AUDITOR 1   If I understand your thesis correctly, it's not that you would have us do anything differently when we all go home and go our separate ways. You wouldn't have us study different problems, but you would have us study the problems from a different perspective.

BARTLEY   Well, that would be largely it. I would want to think that you would have concern for being members of the most sophisticated group in society, members of a true, natural science geneology, let's say. It used to be thought good for humans to have curiosity. Science was then thought to be simply a product of highly individual curiosity. It didn't matter what you wanted to know about, just so you got busy and asked questions. One question was as good as another. I believe the concern now should be more particularly with *what* one wants to know – whether what one wants to know has some connection with the ongoing development of knowledge and understandings of the better minds and leading thinkers down through the ages. If all I want to know is, whether to plant sweet peas or some other thing in my back yard this year, that's all right, but one should not thereby regard himself as engaged in scientific endeavours. So I think some things can collectively be called science, some superficially similar things cannot. I think of curiosity being involved in three quite different ways – in science, in technology and engineering, and in private affairs. Curiosity has to have some relationship to the body of sophisticated knowledge and insight of the times to be called scientific.

INFORMATION CONTENT OF IMPINGEMENTS

AUDITOR   Would you say a few words about the information carrying quality of impingements, and discrimination?

BARTLEY   What is inherent in an input can be looked at in different ways. Information is something that depends upon a source, something transmitted and/or received, and a receiver, doesn't it? If one wants to call anything information, one must consider what the receiver makes of what was sent and/or received. There are, however, two senses of the word; that which it is possible to make out of what was sent or received, and what is actually made out of it. The study of sensory systems is an important link in trying to understand the matter of information. One of the concepts used in sensory response is the concept of discrimination – the ability to respond to a configuration and to respond in terms of the history of the responder.

AUDITOR   What I am most interested in is your statement that impingements carry information partly by reason of the nature of the organism, partly by reason of the dynamics of the energistic environment. I'm curious about the energistic environment. Does energistic environment refer to the physical qualities of energy, for example?

BARTLEY   There are two things we must look at – what is involved in the neurophysiological principles inherent in the organism, and what has occurred in the particular learning history of the organism dealt with. The energistic environment has to do with the physical qualities of the energy reaching sense organs.

AUDITOR   Is information actually the interpretation that Mr X develops?

BARTLEY   That's what information consists of – what the receiver makes of it. He's always making something out of it. Our everyday language and the language we find in textbooks are not quite adequate. They don't inherently imply these ideas. They are somewhat figurative. Something might have been included this morning about the figurative or the idiomatic nature of would-be scientific language. I would like to see figures of speech eliminated from our scientific language and the language of engineering.

AUDITOR   In Dr Royce's terms, you'd like to replace symbolic elements of the language with sign elements, with a one-to-one ratio.

BARTLEY   I suppose that's part of it. The point is, we don't always realize how many steps of inference we use in arriving at various positions. I don't know what all our meanderings amount to, but they are pretty indirect, complicated, and stepwise.

5a
General System Theory and Psychology

Ludwig von Bertalanffy
UNIVERSITY OF ALBERTA

5a
General System Theory and Psychology

Ludwig von Bertalanffy

UNIVERSITY OF ALBERTA

DR VON BERTALANFFY was born in Vienna (Austria) in 1901, and received his PH.D. (Vienna) in 1926. He was Dozent, then Professor at the University of Vienna from 1934 to 1948, afterwards Professor and Director of Biological Research at the University of Ottawa, Director of Biological Research at Mount Sinai Hospital, and Visiting Professor of the University of Southern California in Los Angeles, and Professor of Theoretical Biology (later University Professor) and member of the Center for Advanced Study in Theoretical Psychology at the University of Alberta. In the fall of 1969, he joined the State University of New York at Buffalo as Faculty Professor.

Dr von Bertalanffy was a Fellow of the Rockefeller Foundation (1937–8), a founding Fellow of the Center for Advanced Study in the Behavioral Sciences (Stanford) in the year of its inception (1949–55), Sloan Visiting Professor of the Menninger Foundation (1958–9). He is an Honorary Fellow of the American Psychiatric Association, member of the Deutsche Akademie der Naturforscher, Fellow of the International Academy of Cytology and the AAAS, and founder and life member (past-president) of the Society for General Systems Research.

von Bertalanffy's work is known in the foundation of theoretical and organismic biology, in biophysics, cancer diagnosis, general systems theory, and behavioral science. He is author of 12 books (partly published in the English, French, German, Italian, Spanish, Dutch, Czech and Japanese languages) and some 250 scientific papers and monographs. His main works include *Modern theories of development* (published in 1928 in German; last English edition New York: Harper Torchbooks, 1962); *Theoretische Biologie*, 2 vols. (Berlin: Borntraeger, 1932, 1941; Bern: Francke, 1951); *Problems of life* (1949; New York: Harper Torchbooks, 1960); *Robots, men and minds* (New York: Braziller, 1968); *General System Theory* (New York: Braziller, 1968); he is editor of *Handbuch der Biologie* (Frankfurt a.M.: Alhenaion), and *General Systems* (Society for General Systems Research, Washington, DC).

The idea of general system theory originated from the recognition of the limitations of the mechanistic approach in science, i.e. the one-sided emphasis on analysis into supposedly isolable, elementary parts, processes and causal chains which ignores, bypasses, or even denies the properties of organized wholes. The latter, however, present the fundamental problems in the biological, psychological and social sciences. For a more adequate approach, essentially new categories are required, transcending those of mechanistic science, which were essentially modelled after the paragon of classical physics and, by now, are found inadequate not only in the life sciences, but in important aspects and fields of physics itself. General system theory had its precursors in Gestalt theory and organismic biology, but has far transcended these in scope and elaboration.

The modern systems approach developed essentially in two lines, theoretical and applied. The first is in the development of general system theory, i.e., a discipline concerned with properties and principles of "wholes" or systems in general. The system aspect applies to problems such as those of multivariable interaction, organization, hierarchical order, differentiation, negentropic trends, goal-directed processes, and so forth. Such concepts did not occur in physics, but are of fundamental nature in the biological, behavioural and social realms (and even in certain fields of recent physics). Because these and related aspects are of a very general nature, they occur in systems different in their nature, components, acting forces, etc. Hence systems may be isomorphic with respect to such general properties and principles; consequently, general system theory and its models may be applied in different fields and are widely interdisciplinary.

System problems can be approached by a variety of partly powerful, mathematical tools, such as "classical" system theory (i.e. based on classical calculus and including, e.g., the theory of closed and open systems), computer technics and simulation, axiomatization in terms of set theory, graph, net, compartment theories, cybernetics (based on the principles of feed-back control and information), and others. There are necessarily many problems which presently cannot be expressed in mathematical language and models, but have to be formulated in ordinary language. However, development of general system theory is steadily proceeding, and finds its expression in numerous textbooks and investigations, journals (*General Systems, Journal of Mathematical Systems Theory*), scientific associations (*Society for General Systems Research*, an associate of the American Association for Advancement of Science, with many Chapters in America, and similar groups and workshops in Europe), etc.

Owing to modern exigencies, another, essentially practical, development took place in the form of the systems approach to many problems arising in technology, industry, commerce, defence, and society in general. Thus systems analysis, systems engineering, and similar denominations have become new technological disciplines and professions. Here, too, the central problem is in interactions within complex systems, questions of organization, planning, etc. This development is closely connected with the progress of computer technics, self-steering machines, servomechanisms and automation. Developments originally stemming from technology proved to have far-reaching theoretical value (e.g. the cybernetic feedback model in its application to biological homeostasis and many other phenomena), although it is incorrect to identify cybernetics and systems theory; cybernetic or feedback systems are an important but special class of "general systems."

The application of systems thinking in psychology resulted from a problem situation corresponding to that mentioned in the beginning. The mechanistic approach found its expression in the "robot model" of behaviour which was germane to otherwise different theories such as classical and neobehaviourism, psychoanalysis, the brain as computer, etc. It was characterized by such general concepts as the S-R scheme, behaviour as "passive" reaction to stimuli, conditioning as the only formative factor, outer-directedness of human behaviour, etc. It neglected or did not provide a theoretical basis for obvious aspects of behaviour such as immanent activity from exploration and play to cultural creativity, the wholeness and organization of personality, meaning, symbolism, and others.

It is hardly an exaggeration to say that most of the recent developments in theoretical psychology are intended to overcome the mechanistic scheme, and are system-oriented, with the central concept of an "active system." This is true whether or not there is a formal connection with, or acknowledgement of, the movement known as general system theory. It applies to theories otherwise so different as, for example, neo-Freudian schools, ego-psychology, personality theories (Murray, G. Allport), the "new look" in perception, Gibson's "senses as perceptual systems," Pribram's TOTE system and hologram model in neurophysiology, self-realization (Goldstein, Maslow), client-centred therapy (Rogers), Koestler's open hierarchical systems in psychology, and others. The "system" in question has, of course, to be defined in every individual case, problem, or field. But the general formal framework is that of general system theory which is strong enough and capable of development so as to provide basic categories applicable to special cases. This has often been stated as, for example, by Piaget, who expressly related his conceptions to the general system theory of Bertalanffy.

The impact of the system idea was even stronger in psychiatry. The line of organismic or systems thinking in psychiatry goes back to Goldstein and even Adolf Meyer, but insight into the limits of current theories has called for explicit acceptance of the systems movement which found its expression in the establishment of a Committee and annual sessions on general systems theory in the American Psychiatric Association. In the words of Grinker, "if there be a third revolution (i.e. after the psychoanalytic and behavioristic), it is in the development of general system theory."

It appears, therefore, that (*a*) the systems approach is an essential factor in recent developments of theoretical psychology used in various ways in the respective fields; and (*b*) that general system theory as a doctrine of the properties and principles common to systems, organized wholes, etc. increasingly proves itself as the conceptual framework for such research, models and theory.

References

LITERATURE INTRODUCTORY TO GENERAL SYSTEM THEORY AND ITS USE IN PSYCHOLOGY

VON BERTALANFFY, L., *Robots, men and minds*. New York: Braziller, 1967

VON BERTALANFFY, L., *General system theory. Foundations, development, applications*. New York: Braziller, 1968

BUCKLEY, W. (editor), *Modern systems research for the behavioral scientist. A sourcebook*. Chicago: Aldine, 1968

GRAY, W., RIZZO, N. D., and DUHL, F. D., (editors), *General systems theory and psychiatry*. Boston: Little, Brown, 1968

VON BERTALANFFY, L. and RAPOPORT, A., (editors), *General systems*. Bedford, Mass.: Society for General Systems Research, 12 vols. since 1956

GRINKER, ROY R. (editor), *Toward a unified theory of human behavior*, 2nd edition. New York: Basic Books, 1967

MESAROVIČ, M. D., *Systems research and design; views on general systems theory*. New York: Wiley, 1961 and 1964

MESAROVIČ, M. D., *Systems theory and biology*. New York: Springer-Verlag, 1968

5b
Organized Complexities

Lawrence K. Frank

BELMONT

5b
Organized Complexities

Lawrence K. Frank

BELMONT

DR FRANK (1890–1968) received his undergraduate degree from Columbia in 1912 and an honorary LL.D. from Wayne State University in 1959. His commitment to an inter-disciplinary, eclectic approach to solving problems in the social sciences is revealed when one surveys his affiliations with such organizations as the New York Telephone Co. as a systems analyst, Laura Spelman Rockefeller Memorial Foundation as a staff member, the Josiah Macy Jr Foundation as a vice-president, the Natural Resources Planning Board as a consultant during World War II, as a director of the Caroline Zachry Institute of Human Development, and as chairman of the International Pre-paratory Commission on Mental Health in 1948.

His official retirement in 1955 was certainly not the culmination of his ideas, as they were ever changing and he was always incorporating new concepts and ideas from several disciplines to better his understanding of the phenomenon of man. His syn-thesizing mind pervaded the atmosphere about him, and he reacted reflexively to situations using this *modus operandi* whether he was alone, with friends, or at the conference table.

L. K. Frank is the author of *Projective methods* (Springfield, Ill.: Thomas, 1948), *Nature and human nature* (1951), and *On the importance of infancy* (Gloucester, Mass.: Peter Smith, 1966). He also co-authored five semi-popular books on develop-mental and personality psychology with his wife, Mary Hughes Frank. His contribution to this volume is one of two completed manuscripts which were on hand at the time of his death in September, 1968.

The development of a more unified, integrated framework for the development of psychology calls for the formation of new concepts and assumptions that will be fruitful, if not essential, for this purpose.

This paper presents a concept of organized complexities for consideration as a promising enlargement of the presently accepted ways of thinking and as a proposal of new problems and methods which might foster such unification.

The term "organized complexities" was first used by Warren Weaver[1] in 1948 when, after reviewing the scientific advances on problems of simplicity and of disorganized complexity, he stated:

These problems (of organized complexity) – and a wide range of similar problems, in the biological, medical, psychological, economical and political science – are just too complicated to yield to the old nineteenth century techniques which were so dramatically successful on two-three, or four variable problems of simplicity. These new problems, moreover, cannot be handled with the statistical techniques so effective in describing average behaviour in problems of disorganized complexity.

These new problems, and the future of the world depends on many of them, require science to make a third great advance, an advance that must be even greater than the nineteenth century conquest of problems of simplicity or the twentieth century victory over problems of disorganized complexity. Science must, over the next fifty years, learn to deal with these problems of organized complexity.

Clearly psychology, which studies the behaviour of organisms, animal and human, must deal with organized complexities. But, like biology, faced with the activities of organisms, psychology has focused its efforts upon the analytic fractionation of its subjects in order to study selected variables, factors and other units which it can isolate and measure to establish relations of various kinds among these units or to demonstrate the operation of specific mechanisms. Only research that conforms to the rigid designs now accepted as scientific and that yield statistical findings are accepted as legitimate psychological inquiries. The clinical psychologists are barely tolerated and their work is dismissed as lacking any scientific validity.

The goal in biology and psychology is to disclose order and regularity and to formulate generalizations from studies which will permit prediction and can be replicated. These practices have been immensely productive of what may be called

1 Weaver, Warren, "Science and Complexity." *American Scientist*, **36** 4 (1948) 536–44.

"laboratory artifacts," since these variable, factors and mechanisms appear only in the closed systems which have been established for investigation and in which all but the selected inputs are excluded and the focus is on what has been abstracted from the open systems in which they occur.

This proposal is not to criticize such analytic studies nor to suggest that they be curtailed or eliminated, but rather to point out that, as many biologists have remarked, the more these reductionist studies are carried on, the further are biology and psychology removed from the basic problem of the organism-personality.

Organized complexities are multi-dimensional configurations, open systems which persist by continually changing, exhibiting not only *inter*-individual variation, but more significantly, *intra*-individual variability, of changing states which enables them to cope flexibly and purposely, as is not possible for determinate cause and effect or stimulus and response or linear mechanisms. In the organism the many variables, and specific mechanisms that are attributed to them, do not operate in isolation, but are all coupled and entrained and operate in sequentially ordered processes that generate the dynamics of the organism.

Unlike cause and effect and mechanisms, a process can and does produce different products according to when, where and in what quantity it operates. Thus, the process of mammalian fertilization and gestation produces the immense variety of mammalian cubs. Moreover, as Bertalanffy has pointed out, different processes can produce similar or equivalent products, in what he calls equifinality.

Organized complexities call for a recognition of organization as distinguished from the orderliness and regularity exhibited by inanimate events and also recognition of process as a non-linear operation or functioning which differs from that of simple linear mechanisms. The order and regularity of events disclosed by scientific investigation are found in homogenous arrays or series that can be ordered to and by the dimensions of space, time and magnitude. Organization appears in heterogenous configurations with specialized differentiated components that are multi-dimensional and, as will be discussed later, appear as the product of a process. These processes differ from mechanisms as indicated above, and may be conceived as operating through the coupling of so-called mechanisms and the articulation and synchrony of processes within the open system of an organism.

Some years ago Irving Langmuir[2] proposed a distinction that seems highly appropriate here. He said:

We must recognize two types of natural phenomena. *First*, those in which the behavior of the system can be determined from the average behavior of its component parts and, *second*, those in which a single discontinuous event (which may depend upon a single quantum change) becomes magnified in its effect so that the behavior of the whole aggregate does depend upon something that started from a small beginning. The first class of phenomena I want to call *convergent* phenomena, because all the fluctuating details of the individual atoms average out, giving a result that converges to a definite state. The second class we call *divergent* phenomena, where from a small beginning increasingly large effects are produced.

2 Langmuir, Irving, "The American Association for the Advancement of Science: Science, Common Sense and Decency." *Science.* 97 1 (1943) 1–7.

Organized complexities do exhibit convergent events that average out in the performance of their various constituent electrons, atoms and molecules, but more significantly they operate by divergent events which give rise to an immense variety and variability in their functioning and their performances and make it difficult if not impossible to predict what they will individually do, although they may display as a group predictable uniformities when averaged out.

Organized complexities may be approached not in terms of specific hypotheses about relations of specific variables, but through a series of models for the basic processes by which they function continuously and produce the variety of products which we can observe and sometimes measure. More specifically, organized complexities may be conceived as dynamic configurations arising from six basic processes operating as a closely coupled system in which every component and its functioning is continuously related, directly or indirectly, immediately or with various time lags, to all other components and functions. Every performance of an organized complexity arises from the operation of the total organism. Here we may invoke the recently formulated and increasingly accepted conceptions of a self-organizing system that is self-stabilizing, self-repairing and self-directing and capable of goal-seeking purposive behaviour, none of which implies any mystical or vitalistic assumptions, but are being given rigorous statement and treatment by knowledgeable investigators. Clearly such a system can be understood only in terms of dynamic operations and flexible functioning for which the term process seems appropriate. Paul Weiss of the Rockefeller Institute recently pointed out that we have been so intent upon measuring the product that the process by which it is produced is past by the time that product becomes observable. Process appears as a sequence of perishing events which are difficult to record and to measure, although we are developing instruments, like the oscilloscope, for this purpose.

An initial and tentative formulation of the basic process which may be assumed to be operating in organized complexities is offered here with the hope that it will be revised, elaborated and refined and be presented in some conceptual models that will enable us to understand what we cannot readily grasp or immediately observe nor precisely measure, but what we need for advancing our thinking and for guiding our research.

The six processes here proposed may be briefly labelled as: (i) the Growth Process; (ii) the Organizing Process; (iii) the Communicating Process; (iv) the Stabilizing Process; (v) the Directing Process; and (vi) the Creative Process. These are all functioning concurrently, but our language compels us to describe them sequentially.[3]

(i) The Growth Process is obviously operating since all organisms, starting with a seed or egg, increase in size and weight by incremental growth – successive enlargements and additions at varying rates of increase. This occurs through division and multiplication of cells which, after an initial period of rapid growth, begin to differentiate, giving rise to the specialized cells, organ systems and other distin-

---

3 These have been described in detail in the chapter on human development – an emerging discipline appearing in *Modern Perspectives in Child Development*, edited by A. J. Solnit and S. A. Provence. New York: International Universities Press, 1963.

guishable components of the emerging organism. This development occurs as self-organization which is directed by the heredity of the new organism, but always subject to the context, the changing conditions and especially the vicissitudes of early development.

The Growth Process operates not only as incremental growth, but also as replacement growth whereby the organism continually replaces different cells and the solid, liquid, and gaseous constituents of many cells and tissues at different rates of turn-over. Organisms have a continual input, taking in and incorporating some of these inputs to maintain the organism which has a variety of outputs, including the elimination of discarded cells and their constituents and the end products of metabolism. An organism, therefore, may be viewed as a persistent configuration through which the universe is ebbing and flowing as the functioning processes utilizes what it captures, stores and releases in its environment. The Growth Process varies with successive epochs in the life cycle of an organism and always operates in concert with the other five processes, being especially governed by the Organizing Process.

(ii) The Organizing Process operates in the initial self-organization when the Growth Process becomes patterned to produce the differentiated components that are coupled to what is already existing and operating. Organization is not an entity imposed on passive constituents, nor is it a hierarchical arrangement as in organization charts. Organization arises as a continual process of closely coupled and interdependent operations whereby every constituent participates in circular, reciprocal operations; each functions autonomously but in concert with all other functioning, to give rise to the organization which reciprocally patterns and regulates their functioning and accordingly creates and maintains the organization.

We have no adequate conception of a dynamic organization and our language lacks capacity for communicating this coupled, interrelated transactional process whereby a multitude of highly differentiated and autonomous operations become reciprocally related. A crude model is that of a football team of eleven players, each of whom has an assigned role and an allocated position in the team; in every line-up and however deployed in active play, each player continually communicates with, and relates his activities to, the other ten and they likewise to him; these autonomous but concerted performances give rise to the team organization as a dynamic process. Thus, organization is created and carried on by the components which are governed by what they themselves have established – a truly non-linear, circular operation, highly variable and adjustable, capable of coping with a wide variety of requirements and often unpredictable events. Obviously, such an organizing process requires continuous communication among all its components.

(iii) The Communication Process operates through a communication network with various channels for the messages which flow without ceasing and with ever varying signals. Such a communication network operates effectively because each component sends messages to evoke what it requires from other components and, likewise, replies to such messages from other components, through the nervous system, the circulation of the blood and of the lymph, plus the more immediate direct communications among adjacent components.

But organisms are also communicating with the surroundings, receiving sensory messages, visual, auditory, tactile, olfactory and gustatory, plus the changing atmospheric pressures, temperature alterations, gravity and various radiations. These inputs are all filtered, amplified or reduced, mingled and patterned and translated into internal messages. The air, food and drink taken in, and the various other messages, aesthetic, sexual and, in man, symbolic, are communications to which the organism responds overtly or internally through these basic processes.

The many relations of man to his environment may be viewed in terms of communications, some of which he deals with as an organism, but others as a personality who has learned to recognize and use symbols and to respond to them in terms of the prescribed conduct expected in his culture.

The communication process operates through a variety of feedbacks, both positive and negative, enabling an organism to change his physiological state and to adapt its varied functioning operations to changing needs, loads and opportunities. The communication process makes possible the organization of the many highly differentiated but autonomous components in an organism by articulating and synchronizing their operation and by accelerating and retarding, enlarging and diminishing their functioning. This involves continual stabilization by the Stabilizing Process.

(iv) Stabilizing Process. If an open system with continual inputs and outputs, with unceasing replacement growth and exposure to rapidly changing external demands, is to survive, it must be able not only to regulate its inputs and outputs but also to regulate the amplitude of the fluctuations and deviations in functioning provoked by these changing inputs and impacts. The Stabilizing Process maintains the integrity and functional effectiveness of an organism through regulation of its varied operations in concert with the other basic processes.

The Stabilizing Process maintains a dynamic stability as shown by the ever-changing physiological states of an organism and involves more than the homeostasis described by Cannon for the stability of the organic fluids. This dynamic stabilization involves all components and their functioning as each participates in the organization and contributes what is required for its functioning as an organism.

As Ashby has suggested, a system is composed of a number of sub-systems, each of which has its own range of variable functioning. When the system is under strain or receives an impact, one or more of these sub-systems will respond, buffering or protecting the whole system, "rolling with the punches," and thus enabling the system to survive and continue to operate. Thus, an emotional reaction, an acute illness, shivering and sweating, eating, drinking, eliminating and sleeping are stabilizing operations. Likewise, chronic anxiety and resentful hostility operate as persistent states of vigilance which individuals develop from experiences that have made them wary and on guard as ways of maintaining their integrity.

Much of what an organism-personality does and refrains from doing may be viewed as learned operations for maintaining a dynamic stability vis-à-vis the world. Each individual develops his own pattern of intra-individual variability expressive of his efforts to maintain a dynamic stability, and this variability modifies his awareness, his perceptions and his responsiveness and become observable in his goal-seeking purposive conduct.

(v) The Directive Process. It is being increasingly recognized that organisms exhibit goal-seeking, purposive striving which does not require any teleological explanations or animistic assumptions, but arises from their inherited patterns of awareness and behaviour, their capacity to scan and evaluate situations and to evoke from the surround both positive and negative feedbacks for orienting their activities. Much of this process has been programmed by evolution, but in man is subject to learning called enculturation and socialization. Through these early experiences the individual personality emerges and becomes observable through the operation of the Directive Process.

The deterministic control of events in most physical and chemical operations has been superseded in the evolution of organisms in which the operation of these basic processes has made possible a high degree of autonomy and a purposive striving for changing goals. Indeed, it may be said that organized complexities have demonstrated the immense potentialities of nature to go beyond the orderliness and regularity of inanimate events, and give rise to organizations capable of the Directive and also the Creative Process.

(vi) The Creative Process appears in the evolution of organisms of which species arose as a creative approach to the task of living existence, some of which flourished but later disappeared, as indicated by many extinct species while others were able to cope with the urgent problems of survival and have evolved into ever more highly organized complexities.

The Creative Process is displayed in the initial growth and development of the plant or animal organism, each of which is more or less true to ancestral type, but nevertheless is different from all others. The Creative Process is also displayed in replacement growth as new cells and tissues are developed from the unorganized components which are made available through the blood stream from the nutrients consumed by the organism. The often highly organized food stuffs must first be randomized into their simpler components and then are incorporated into cells and tissues and complex fluids, a truly amazing Creative Process which we may also observe in the growth and development of plants which, likewise, create their structures from inorganic materials.

It is especially important for psychology to note that man did not adapt to nature as did other organisms which became specialized in body structure and ways of living; man remained plastic and flexible, unspecialized, except for his central nervous system. Instead of adapting to the environment, man relied upon ideas, tools and weapons to create a human environment, a symbolic cultural world of meanings and significance by which he transformed the actual world of nature into the cultural world of his own invention. He imposed upon nature and human nature his three basic symbol systems, of art, science, and theology, according to the creative concepts and assumptions, the beliefs and convictions, the hopes and fears which have given rise to the many different cultural worlds all over the earth as products of human creative imagination.

The individual human personality emerges as a creative product of the individual's idiosyncratic attempts to cope with the requirements and opportunities of his culture. The young human organism is transformed into a personality, but as long as he lives, he must function as an organism exposed to all the biological impacts and inputs and subject to the ever-changing impulses and emotional reactions of his organism, but he is also expected to display the patterned conduct and to meet the expected performances of a personality living in his cultural world and participating in his social order.

This dual, co-existence gives rise to the human predicament and is reflected in the divergent aims and purposes of psychological study. The focus may be upon the organism and its varied responsiveness to specific provocation or upon the personality and its varied expression of action, speech, belief and feelings. The various specialized sub-divisions of the psychological discipline and the numerous conflicting schools and theoretical positions await clarification and resolution of these many issues. This paper, it is hoped, will indicate how a conception of organized complexities may serve to evoke some creative, imaginative thinking to formulate the new problem and to devise models and methods for their study. The recognition of six basic processes, as offering a dynamic approach to this problem, may indicate the direction in which this thinking may be focused.[4]

SUMMARY

This paper assumes that the advancement of psychology, especially a humanistic psychology, calls for a conceptual reformulation to replace the many assumptions and methods that are no longer relevant or fruitful for this task. For such a reorientation it is suggested that the focus be put on the dynamic processes operating in the organism-personality. This unique individual is an organized complexity who should be approached, not in terms of selected variables and linear, determinate sequences, but rather as one who continually exists and functions as an organism. He strives to live as a personality in this symbolic world of meanings and evaluations and to participate in his social order. This involves organization, conceived, not as an entity, but as a number of closely coupled, entrained processes with nonlinear relations and many feedbacks. This individual undergoes continual change, growth, development and ageing with an unceasing internal variability (as contrasted with individual variation from group norms). These processes are "perishing events" which we have not learned adequately to observe and record. They involve continuous "inner speech" as the personality talks to himself and develops what we call consciousness. (What has not been verbalized is the so called "unconscious".)

An institute for humanistic psychology, not limited to studies of overt behaviour and the assumptions and methods of physical science, will embrace the fields of political, economic, social and family living, religious and recreational activities in which the individual is immersed. It will recognize that, while the individual carries on his life career in the public world, he lives in his "life space", and unceasingly guards his private world with his image of the self, the me, my and mine, derived from his experiences with others as he strives to attain and uphold his identity.

We urgently need a humanistic psychology for renewing our disintegrating culture and reorienting our demoralized social order. This calls for new insights and sensibilities, and more reliance upon the various arts to help us renew our courage for carrying on the endless search for human fulfillment.

4 For example, see my chapter on human development – an emerging discipline in *Modern Perspectives in Child Development*, edited by A. J. Solnit and S. A. Provence. New York: International Universities Press, 1963.

Comments on Papers 5a and 5b: T. Weckowicz

I shall start my discussion by comparing what an ordinary man does in the everyday business of life when he tries to understand the surrounding universe with what the scientist does. Both of them, to follow Professor Galanter, reduce the flux of observed events to some matrix of relationship so that they will be able to understand the occuring events and they use, following Professor Frank or Professor von Bertalanffy, a system of symbols by which they interpret this reality. But I think there is one important difference between what an ordinary man does and what a scientist does. The basic difference is that a scientist is trying to make this symbolic system which we apply to reality much more explicit in meaning than the kind of symbolic system which an ordinary person uses. An ordinary person uses ordinary language to explain the experienced phenomena. Ordinary language is a tool, a symbolic tool, exteremely rich in meaning, but unfortunately most of its meaning is implicit, not explicit. Of course there's a lot of work being done by philosophers and by psycholinguists to make the meanings explicit. Psycholinguists are building mathematical models of language structure, language philosophers are trying to analyse using common sense, the meaning implied by ordinary language. Scientists, particularly physicists and chemists, prefer a language which is not so rich in meaning, a language in which all the meaning is explicit; therefore, they prefer the language of mathematics or the language of symbolic logic. Now, I think this is the crux of the matter. The scientist abstracts certain aspects of reality and also tries, as it were, to simplify them by using a system of symbols where all the meanings are as explicit as possible, anyway much more explicit than they are in ordinary language.

If the structure of our language reflects the structure of external reality, as Wittgenstein believes it does, we can understand the "organized complexity" of external events by making the implicit meaning of our language explicit. This is a slow and painful process. In most cases of organized complexity we grasp its implicit meaning, but we cannot make it explicit. We can recognize it, but we cannot explain it. In this connection the distinction made by the famous German philosopher Dilthey is particularly useful. He introduced the concepts of "verstehen" (understanding) and "erklarung" (clarification). "Verstehen" means grasping the implicit meaning while "erklarung" means explicit understanding of the relations of the symbols by which we describe and try to understand the phenomena. I personally prefer the English terms and shall therefore refer to them respectively as implicit understanding and explicit understanding. The trouble is that when we try to understand the complexity of organized phenomena we are only able to understand them implicitly, that is, use an "e.g." or programmatic type of theorizing, rather than some kind of propositional theory in which we can understand the phenomena explicitly. Previous scientists and scholars have reacted in a variety of ways to this difficulty. Some scholars in Germany despaired of ever having an explicit understanding of organized complexities, particularly in the humanities where this level of organization is prevalent. They introduced the concept of "Kulturwissenschaften". According to them, the phenomena occurring at the social and cultural level are so complex that they can be dealt with only by the "verstehen" approach and not the "erklarung" approach. Moreover, any attempt to understand these phenomena analytically would destroy the organized complexity and would defeat its purpose. The same problem has cropped up in dealing with a lower level of organization – namely the biological level. Here, we had vitalists who also despaired of being able to understand this organization, and said that we cannot really understand it explicitly, but can only recognize it in a living organism, which is obviously something different from the same organism after death. We can call it "élan vital" or some kind of vital principle, but we cannot really understand it by an explication of relationships.

There is another approach to this problem of organized complexity diametrically opposed to the previous approach. This approach, or group of approaches, is the type of which both Professor Frank and Professor von Bertalanffy are quite rightly very critical. This is the reductionistic way of dealing with the problem of organized complexity. This approach uses the explicit relationships encountered in the description of much simpler phenomena, as for instance that of Newtonian physics, and applies them both to the explanation of living organisms and of social and cultural phenomena. This method of dealing with the problem is an attempt to atomize the complexities which are being described into some kind of simple elements, and to combine these elements by adding them up algebraically. This mechanistic-reductionistic approach was quite prevalent in nineteenth century biology and psychology, and now seems to be on its way out.

There is a third attempt to deal with the problem of organized complexities, and it is the most promising one. This approach does not try to explain organized complexities by using a metaphor, a "verstehen" type of explanation, and at the same time it does not try to reduce these organized complexities to a simple type of phenomenon (i.e. to atomize them). This third attempt was made to find a new conceptual model, preferably a mathematical one, which would somehow explain the organized complexities explicitly instead of just talking about them in a vague way. It proved to be extremely difficult to find a suitable conceptual, particularly mathematical, model. It has to be a new kind of model, not taken from Newtonian mechanics. There have been many attempts made to deal with this problem. The first attempt in psychology was made by the Gestaltists. They went back to observing phenomena without the assumptions made by the traditional introspective psychologists, such as Wundt and Titchener. They then bracketed their experience, to use Professor MacLeod's language. They rejected the assumptions of associationistic psychology, which were taken from nineteenth century physics, and its mechanistic model, and they looked on the observable world in a new way. After observing the phenomena carefully, they made a different set of assumptions from that made by the associationists. Their method was phenomenological, although I wouldn't equate Gestalt psychology with phenomenology. They rejected the assumptions of associationism and arrived, as a result of their phenomenal analysis, at a set of qualitative, phenomenal laws of complexity. Of course, we have to remember a notable attempt by Köhler himself, in which he tried to objectify these laws of organization, to extend them to physics and to quantify them. I am referring to Köhler's book, *Die physischen Gestalten in Ruhe und im Stationaren zustand* (1920), a book which has never been translated into English. There were some other attempts. One notable attempt was the application of topology to psychology by Kurt Lewin. Nothing very much came out of it because it invoked *post hoc* theorizing (i.e. he really did not attempt to make any predictions). Of the other attempts which were made to apply mathematical models to the problem of organized complexity, one should mention information theory and factor analysis. Both these models tend to oversimplify the problem. The most important contribution to our understanding of the problem of structure and organization is, I think, Professor von Bertalanffy's theory of open systems which perhaps is not a type of "i.e." theory as far as psychology is concerned, but definitely is an "i.e." type of theory as far as biology, or at least certain aspects of biology, is concerned. In developing his theory of open systems Professor von Bertalanffy offered a closely reasoned, and at some points completely quantified, conceptual framework for describing the type of phenomena which previously had been talked about only vaguely by the organismic biologists such as, for instance, Kurt Goldstein. For example, Professor von Bertalanffy's theory of open systems as applied to metabolism is quite explicit as far as its meanings are concerned. This theory is based on the generalization of classical thermodynamics into a more general theory called irreversible thermodynamics. I think a very important step forward made by open system theory was a realization that models which came from classical physics, such as the Newtonian model or even the model of classical thermodynamics, do not apply to living organisms, and even more so, do not apply to psychological phenomena, and that they should be replaced by different types of models. An example of a more rigorous amplification of open system theorizing is Julian Huxley's theory of allometry. It predicts a precise type of mathematical relationship between the rate of growth for different parts of the organism, and even predicts that this type of relationship is a power function (the exponent of which depends on the environmental conditions). The function itself remains the same irrespective of the conditions, and according to Professor von Bertalanffy (to quote from one of his previous papers), it is "an expression of inter-dependence, organization, and harmonization of physiological processes". Only because processes are harmonized does the organism remain alive and in a steady state. Incidentally, the mathematical model Professor von Bertalanffy uses appears to be almost identical with that of Professor Galanter. Another thing, which is very gratifying and which makes Professor von Bertalanffy's theory much more explicit than that of other organismic theorists, is the fact that the constants in the equations can be arrived at quite independently by different experiments. So his theory is completely different from, for instance, Hullian theory, where these constants are not known. The predictions from this theory, such as equifinality, false starts, and overshooting, can be confirmed by the behaviour of various physiological systems. Although the open system model is still programmatic as far as psychology is concerned, there are great possibilities for testing it experimentally. For instance, the allometric model can be tested by investigating relationships in the rate of development of various functions in children, particularly functions which are relatively independent of the environment, like, shall we say, size constancy or sensory thresholds.

We have simpler models of organized systems, such as an ordinary machine. A steam engine is an organized system which depends for its function on a supply of external energy. However, I think the basic difference between the machine model and Professor von Bertalanffy's model is that, while the machine depends on the input of energy from the external environment for its operation, its parts remain constant and fixed, while in Professor von Bertalanffy's model, the parts are always undergoing change. So it isn't like a watch; it's a system in which not only energy is being utilized from the environment but also the parts are undergoing constant change themselves. Have I expressed correctly the essence of your model?

BERTALANFFY   Yes.

WECKOWICZ   My feeling is that Professor von Bertalanffy's model is not, as far as biology is concerned, a programmatic model, but it is a type of propositional theory. It's a propositional type of theory which can be empirically tested and possibly extended to psychology as, for instance, in the development of children.

Now, there remains only a very short remark, a minor point which is not relevant to the theory of open systems and to the subject of theoretical psychology. I disagree with one statement made by Professor von Bertalanffy. He said in his paper that the homeostatic model is applicable in psychopathology because it applies more to mental patients than to normals. I would like to take issue with this point. There is strong evidence that in schizophrenics there is an impairment of homeostatic mechanisms. Hoskins and his group at Western Mental Hospital found that in schizophrenics there is an impairment in function of many physiological homeostatic mechanisms and in the adaptation of the internal environment of the organism to changing conditions. Constancy of perception and conceptual thinking, a subject of my own study, may be viewed as a form of homeostatic mechanism which aids in maintaining stability (within specifiable limits) between the external environment and the organism. Constancy of perception and conceptual thinking are impaired in schizophrenic patients. The constancy of boundaries of concepts become very poorly delineated. These patients also show a greater intra-individual variance of performance on intelligence tests and other tasks than do normal controls. All these facts indicate that in schizophrenia we have an impairment of homeostatic and regular mechanisms.

Incidentally, although my remarks were focused on Professor von Bertalanffy, they also apply to Professor Frank, because although using a different language, he conveyed exactly the same message.

David Krech

I wish to record an objection. The two papers we are discussing have both been motivated by a search for novel and original concepts which might be of use to all psychologists. Obviously no sane man could publicly object to such an estimable goal – nor do I. What I do object to is the air of desperation which seems to permeate both papers. One gets the feeling from reading these two papers (and even more so from listening to the discussions provoked by their reading) that we psychologists are at some fateful "scientific crossroads," that we are ensloughed in some sort of "scientific mess," that we are facing a "scientific crisis" (I am here quoting phrases which have been bandied about in the last hour or so) – and because of all this it is time, nay time long past, that we make an agonizing reappraisal of our old conceptual mainstays, our methods, our work. My problem is that I simply don't share these feelings of crisis. I – and my colleagues, and my colleagues' colleagues – don't feel that we are in any sort of scientific mess! Most of my friends are Happy in Science! Permit me to justify what may seem to you like unbearable complacency with the *status quo*.

First of all, we agree, I take it, that the problems which psychologists tackle are very complex. This, of course, is an understatement. In my opinion, the psychological sciences are the most difficult of all the scientific enterprises. If this is so, we must take proper cognizance of the enormity of the task before us, and we must approach our work with great humility, great patience, and the willingness to be satisfied with little gains. Even little gains – in our business – are enormously more difficult to make, and have much more significance for mankind than the most dramatic kind of advances made by the relatively simple physical sciences. I am of the opinion that the degree of understanding we have achieved, into the mysteries of the brain's function, into the wondrous complexities of man's motives and personalities, in the beauties and order of his perceptual processes, are but little slivers of glimmerings of understanding – but they are wondrous glimmerings – glimmerings that shine in magnificence. And these little tiny advances are continuing at a happy rate and it is heartening to behold each year what advances we do make. And, therefore, I do not feel that we are in a "mess." This does not mean that I am not open to new ideas – I trust that I am – but simply that I feel no *desperate* need for a "conceptual revolution"!

Much has been said here about the need for a "scientific revolution." I am tempted to ask, "Hell, man – where have you been – we've been having an average of one revolution per year right along!" Compare the studies of brain and behaviour of today with that of the time of Lashley! Compare the work in perception today with that of fifteen to twenty years ago. Compare the early work of behaviour genetics with what is happening today. Compare the social psychology of today with that of pre-war (World War II, that is)! If you refuse to use the term "revolution" for anything less grand than a cosmic reorganization of *all* of psychology, very well then – will you settle for the term (ugh!) "revolution*ette*"? Please do settle for this because you will not get, I am afraid, any "Conceptual Revolution" which in one cosmic swoop will reorganize, integrate, unify and reorient all the psychological sciences. To seek that is to seek the will of the blind goose! One further remark. Too frequently, what the historians of science have called "conceptual revolutions" are merely cover stories invented decades or even centuries later by the philosophers and historians of science to give order and "meaning" to a whole series of somewhat independent "revolutionettes" brought about through the discovery of new data, the application of new techniques. The so-called "Conceptual Revolution", in other words, is often an epiphenomenal aftermath of scientific advance (not a directing influence) – and an effect which takes place only in the minds of the historian long after it can have any possible relevance to what is happening in science.

W. W. Rozeboom

During the discussion, two lists of abstract phrases were placed on the blackboard, one containing terms such as "robot model", "S-R", "linear causality", "homeostatic", "environmentalism", and "Cartesian dualism", which were held to characterize what has been wrong with past behaviouristic psychology, and the other describing such organized complexities as "imminent activity", "dynamic interaction", "creative processes", "growth development", and "symbolism" to which traditional theories have failed to do justice. I challenge the usefulness of this style of metaphorizing, suggesting (in parallel to Krech's previously stressed category of the "empty concept") that distinctions of this sort illustrate the "empty contrast" or "empty protest", wherein one applies some distasteful label to a metaphorical interpretation of an unesteemed theory, and then sets this in scornful opposition to some other phrase loaded with humanistic sentiment. This leaves unanswered whether the metaphor really catches what the criticized position has said technically, and whether the opposed humanistic phrase is really relevant to what is inadequate about the older view. In contrast Skinner is a theorist who really does personify all the metaphoric evils – reductionism, nothing-butery, and the like – which humanists abhor, yet to whose theoretical position none of the terms in the "robot model" list apply. For effective criticism of an outworn theory it doesn't help to say that it is inadequate because the metaphor doesn't feel right. We need to make clear what specifically is defective about it.

J. R. Royce

(Note: The following comment arose out of a challenge that it would not be possible to take general system theory beyond its present programmatic condition as it relates to behaviour.)

I would like to give an example of a multi-dimensional approach to a problem in organized complexity, involving invariant processes, which follows Bertalanffy's principle of equifinality, is consistent with the principle of open systems, and most importantly, could provide a bridge from a programmatic general systems theory to a propositional set of statements. My example is taken from factor theory, and I will use the domain of intelligence because it has been well explored and is generally known. However, further explication can best be achieved if I refer you to Fig. 5.1.

In this figure person A scores high on the Number, Space and Reasoning components and relatively low on all the others, whereas person B scored just the reverse. If we average each of these two profiles we get exactly the same values, a standard score of 50, equivalent to an IQ of 100. If the IQ were the only information available we would conclude that these two individuals are intellectually identical. They are in terms of overall intellectual performance (i.e. they have identical IQ's), and in their performance on the perception factor. Otherwise person A is essentially quantitative in his intellectual strength, whereas person B is essentially verbal. I trust it is obvious that this is merely an example of the

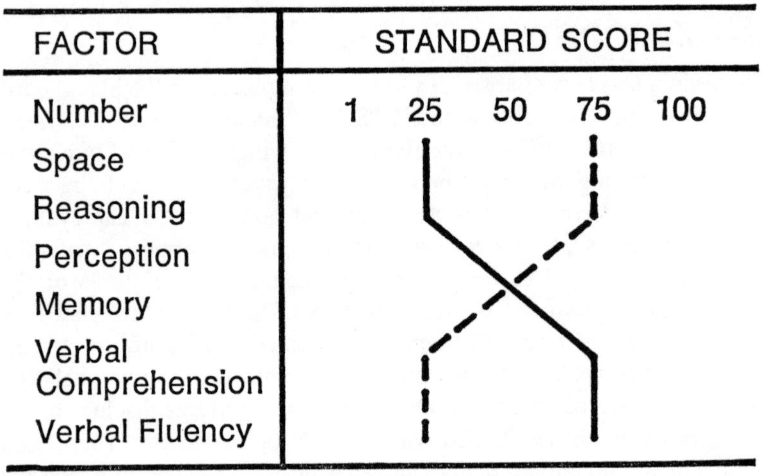

FACTOR	STANDARD SCORE
Number	1 25 50 75 100
Space	
Reasoning	
Perception	
Memory	
Verbal Comprehension	
Verbal Fluency	

FIGURE 5.1
Two persons, A (dotted line) and B (solid line) with same IQ, but with opposite mental ability profiles (Royce, 1957)

general case. That is, for any reliable and valid measure of general intelligence it is possible to generate all the permutations and combinations of the components (incidentally, the stance that factors or components are too atomistic and therefore, reductionistic, is irrelevant. The point is that *all* scientific efforts involve variables of some sort, varying from molecular to molar, etc. Factor theory is simply one strategy for identifying scientifically useful variables) of that measure which will result in a particular score on that measure.

I cite this as an example of how classic psychological findings can be seen as being consistent with Professor Bertalanffy's general systems theory – essentially on the grounds that persons A and B reach the same behavioural goal (equifinality) via different processes (i.e. factors). There can be little question that we are dealing with an open system, (the behaving human organism), organized complexity (intelligence), or a propositional set of statements (the theoretical-empirical findings of factor analysis). A possible debatable point is whether the factors in question constitute processes. My answer is that when the factors are organismic they clearly are processes, and further, they may also be processes when they are non-organismic (i.e. cultural processes). Whether or not all factors are processes, they are clearly the determinants or functional unities of the variability summarized in a given subset of covariation data (i.e. the correlation matrix).

Although I have elsewhere elaborated on factors as processes, the most general way to conceptualize factors is to view them simply as theoretical constructs or useful variables. In either case, whether theoretical construct or process, the similarity of intelligent behaviour attained by persons A and B in the example cited is reached via different psychological strengths and weaknesses. Unless I am misunderstanding the principle of equifinality, I see the factor analytic model as an extant approach which can provide a multitude of data which will allow us to take advantage of those aspects of general systems theory which have implications for advancing our understanding of behaviour.

Rebuttal: L. K. Frank

Referring to the comments by Weckowicz, the following remarks may be offered. It is especially difficult for us to formulate a precise and inclusive conception of organized complexities because our language is not capable of communicating the simultaneity and concomitance of a number of events which are closely coupled and entrained. We must rely upon a series of sequentially ordered statements, as in our conventional grammar and syntax, which compels us to describe one aspect or dimension of a multi-dimensional complex and ignore the other dimensions, until we can again formulate a statement about them in our language. Moreover, our language is oriented to the assertion of orderly relations of antecedent and consequent, of cause and effect, and largely biased in terms of linear relations. Consequently, we are unable to express in language the ongoingness of multi-dimensional, organized complexities such as organisms and personalities.

As Benjamin Whorf[5] has pointed out:

The categories and types that we isolate from the world of phenomena we do not find there because they stare every observer in the face; on the contrary, the world is presented to us in a kaleidascopic flux of impressions which has to be organized by our minds. ... We cut nature up, organize it into concepts, ascribe significance as we do, largely because we are parties to an agreement to do it in this way.

Science has difficulty in developing a symbol system for organized complexities because it has been primarily focused upon the discovery of isolated mechanisms by analytic methods which fractionate a whole and attempt to reduce it to a collection of variables to be isolated as far as possible from the context in which they occur. As described by Dkjksterhuis in his *The Mechanization of the World Picture* (Oxford University Press, 1961) the physical sciences have for the past three hundred and more years been intent upon the disclosure of mechanisms and have been aided and encouraged in this pursuit by the development of mathematics to further this aim. Consequently, the dominant scientific orientation has been analytic, and its symbol system has been formulated to express this conceptual orientation. Moreover, there is, I am told by mathematicians, only the beginnings of the non-linear mathematics which would be appropriate for processes as distinguished from mechanisms.

As Collingwood, in his *Philosophy of Nature*, and in his other writings, has emphasized, science has by this mechanistic orientation almost completely abandoned the earlier Greek concern for "wholeness" and has only recently begun to

5 Whorf, Benjamin, "Science and Linguistics," in *The Technological Review*, Vol. XLII, April 1940. MIT, Cambridge.

recognize some of the limitations of the prevailing assumptions and methods. This has been shown in *Models and Analogues*, edited by J. W. Beament (Academic Press, 1960) especially in the chapter by Niels Bohr.

The long accepted scientific requirement of predictability and the replication of any scientific findings seems to be appropriate only for homogeneous arrays and closed systems, since heterogeneous organizations, being open systems with continual inputs and outputs and ever-changing states, are difficult if not impossible to predict as to their future behaviour, and rarely can their performances and functioning be precisely replicated.

Organisms are not static, unchanging entities, but are engaged in growing, developing, ageing, and the continual replacement of cells, tissues and their chemical constituents. Thus, they persist by continually changing and maintaining their incessant intercourse with the environment. Furthermore, the human organism-personality develops a highly selective awareness and patterned perceptions as instrumental to the process of symbolic transformation whereby he transforms the actual world into a symbolic-cultural world, imputing or projecting the meanings and values by which his conduct is directed.

The many dualistic conceptions, such as vitalism and the difference between appearance and reality, are not necessary for a recognition that the individual is an organism-personality, who exists and functions in the world of nature but lives as a person in the symbolic world of his cultural traditions while responding both to the environmental impacts and stimulation and also to the symbolic meanings which he himself imposes on the world. To formulate the problems which a humanistic psychology might appropriately undertake to study it may be necessary for those psychologists who recognize the desirability, if not the urgency of this undertaking, to attempt to develop a scientific psychology with new assumptions and more appropriate concepts and with new criteria of credibility congruous with their revised frame of reference. But this would call for a self-conscious awareness of how much their professional orientation may need to be critically scrutinized and even radically revised, not to meet the criteria of the long-accepted scientific procedures, but primarily to enable them to formulate the problems and to develop the methodologies for advancing psychology and hopefully helping to unify it.

The task confronting these courageous individuals has been well described by Ortega y Gasset in *The Revolt of the Masses*, where he says:

Our scientific ideas are of value to the degree in which we have felt ourselves lost before a question, have seen its problematic nature, and have realized that we cannot find support in received notions, in prescriptions, proverbs, mere words. The man who discovers a new scientific truth has previously had to smash to atoms almost everything he had learnt, and arrives at the new truth with hands bloodstained from the slaughter of a thousand platitudes.

The statement by Krech that there is an "air of desperation" permeating the papers by Bertalanffy and myself seems to be an expression of irritation by one who does not wish to recognize the desirability, if not urgency, of some attempt to develop systematically, at least in one university, an institute dedicated to the advancement of humanistic psychology and hopefully to some unification of the many now conflicting subdivisions and schools of psychological studies. He is apparently convinced that the multiplication and intensification of the analytic study of isolated variables will eventually, by some mysterious process, become capable of providing an understanding of organisms-personalities. It is not difficult to understand why he says that he and his colleagues are "happy in science", since they can now find generous support and gain professional prestige by these investigations which are scientific contributions, but ignore the many crucial problems for an understanding of which we must look to psychology. It is noteworthy how many psychologists are concerned primarily with questions that are physiological and biological, and the use of methods derived from those disciplines which most appropriately involve animals. What is especially irritating and exasperating is the scepticism or even hostility exhibited by many psychologists toward anyone who ventures to deviate from the presently established research designs and analytic methodologies.

The advances which Krech justifiably celebrates can and will, we hope, continue, but as a number of biologists are now realizing, the further they go in their fractionation of the organism, the less they are capable of coping with the central and persistent problem of biology, the intact, functioning organism in its environmental context. Krech has reiterated the traditional empirical conviction that "the discovery of new data, the application of new techniques," can and does take place without an adequate conceptual framework. As Einstein remarked, "The great error of nineteenth century science was to believe that theory could be derived from facts". This error is still prevalent among those who naively refuse to examine their preconceptions, and who believe that facts automatically exhibit their scientific meaning without the symbolic interpretation (e.g. by language or mathematics) which makes those observations relevant and consistent with other scientific concepts.

Sooner or later psychology must strive to attain some conceptual clarification and unification, since at present it is divided and often conflicted by a number of irreconcilable assumptions and expectations which, like the various religious sects, vehemently attack each other as each asserts that it is the only true psychology. Obviously, we should encourage a diversity and often rival approaches, but a science requires some concensually validated concepts and assumptions and today should, as expressed in the purpose of this Conference, seek some beginnings toward unification and accept the obligation to develop a humanistic psychology. As the history of science clearly shows, every major advance has come with the formulation of new concepts and assumptions, as dramatically exhibited in the conceptual revolution in physics in the earlier years of this century. The amazing advances in physics and in chemistry were generated by new concepts and the replacement of the many old assumptions that had become anachronistic. The proposal that we recognize organized complexities and attempt to develop a series of models operating with processes rather than mechanisms seems to be congruent with this new climate of opinion.

The comments by Rozeboom seem to be more relevant to the other papers and their discussion than to my attempt to show the potential fruitfulness of the concept of organized complexities and the need for some conceptual models that recognize the operation of processes. My statement presented no polemics and did not express some of the metaphors which Rozeboom challenges, but was offered as a possible contribution to the development of the proposed Institute which, it is hoped, can and will explore new leads, and will recognize that the human organism-personality has a dual or co-existence, functioning as an organism in the natural environment but also living as a personality in a symbolic-cultural world which is generated by the process of symbolic transformation. Here humanistic psychology may find a promising opportunity to study how individuals and the cultural group imaginatively create the meanings and the evaluations which they impose or project upon the world and by which their conduct is so largely directed.

Royce's comment presents an ingenious but somewhat questionable attempt to reconcile the assumption of isolatable factors with the conception of a system operating through processes. As he says, we may view factors as "theoretical constructs or useful variables." But such constructs, implying isolatable variables and their correlation through statistical manipulation of measurements on a sample, seem to be an irreconcilable assumption. The concept of process implies a closely coupled and entrained sequence of functional operations occurring along with a number of other processes within an identifiable organism-personality as contrasted with anonymous measurements in a frequency distribution.

To apply the term equi-finality to the findings of factor analysis and/or correlational techniques seems to confuse what is essentially a scientific artifact, a statistical finding, with the psycho-biological operations of a process which, as previously emphasized, can and does produce different products according to when, where and how much it operates, while different processes can and do, produce similar or equivalent products, thereby exhibiting what Bertalanffy has called equi-finality. The factors which are assigned to assumed variables should not be confused with the products of operating processes which give rise to products that can be directly observed. As Paul Weiss, formerly at the Rockefeller Institute, remarked some years ago, we have been so intent upon observing and measuring the product that we have neglected to study the process which is all over by the time the product appears.

It is particularly important to recognize that factor analysis is based upon certain assumptions about what seems to be theoretically important, but it may perpetuate many of the older beliefs and assumptions of faculty psychology, and the imputation of specific capacities, drives and motives, all of which may be obstacles to the development of a humanistic psychology.

6
Psychological Phenomenology: A Propaedeutic to a Scientific Psychology

Robert B. MacLeod
CORNELL UNIVERSITY

6
Psychological Phenomenology: A Propaedeutic to a Scientific Psychology

Robert B. MacLeod
CORNELL UNIVERSITY

DR MACLEOD received his M.A. from McGill University in 1927, and his PH.D. from Columbia University in 1932. He began his teaching career at Cornell University where he remained until 1933. He taught at Swarthmore College from 1933–46 with a research break at the University of London in 1936. In 1939 he won a Fellowship of the Belgian-American Educational Foundation, and spent a year at the University of Louvain. Dr MacLeod moved to McGill University in 1946, and in 1948 returned to Cornell. He has had periods of research at the University of Pennsylvania (1957–8), and in East Africa (1951) and the Arab Middle East (1953–7) and has held visiting professorships at the University of California at Berkeley (1948), Stanford University (1961), and the University of Michigan (1953–4 and 1964–5). During the last war he served with the US Army Office of Strategic Services.

Dr MacLeod is past-president of the Psychology and the Arts, Teaching of Psychology, and History of Psychology Divisions of the APA. He has also been the Association's representative on the National Research Council, and the Social Science Research Council, and a member of the Education and Training Board, the Board on Scientific Affairs, and numerous committees. His interests are the experimental psychology of perception, language, and thinking, the history of psychology, psychological phenomenology, educational theory and practice, especially with respect to the "superior student," and cross-cultural studies. He has written extensively in all these fields, and his publications include: *The world of colour* (London: Kegan Paul, 1935), a translation of David Katz, *Der Aufbau der Farbheit* (Leipzig: Barth, 1930); *Psychology in Canadian Universities and Colleges* (Ottawa: Canadian Social Science Research Council, 1955); *Undergraduate education in the liberal arts and sciences*, 4 vols., mimeo. (The Educational Survey of the University of Pennsylvania, 1958); *William James: unfinished business* (as editor) (American Psychological Association, 1969), and chapters in numerous books, especially J. Rohrer and M. Sherif, *Social psychology at the crossroads* (NY: Harper, 1951) and T. W. Wann, *Behaviourism and phenomenology* (University of Chicago Press, 1964).

THESIS

The thesis presented here is that psychological phenomenology is a useful propaedeutic to a science of psychology, i.e. that it serves to define problems and to point
the way to possible answers. It does not, as such, provide answers, nor is it relevant
to all questions commonly termed psychological. It does, however, bring into focus
a good many problems which are frequently neglected in contemporary psychological research and theory.

Psychological phenomenology is not a theory, not a system or school, not a
philosophy; it is an approach, or a method. As such, however, it involves some explicit and implicit assertions about the subject-matter and method of psychology
which may be at variance with those contained in some of the popular psychologies
of today, and to this extent it may favour one kind of psychological theory rather
than another. It is consequently legitimate to speak of *a* phenomenological psychology, i.e. of a psychology which approaches its subject-matter phenomenologically, but never of *the* phenomenological psychology, unless this be qualified
by reference to a specific person or movement in psychology. Phenomenologists in
psychology have moved toward widely different modes of psychological conceptualization.

PSYCHOLOGICAL DISTINGUISHED FROM
PHILOSOPHICAL PHENOMENOLOGY

Psychology purports to be a science, i.e. a disciplined inquiry into a restricted range
of phenomena, conducted in accordance with methods which lead to generalized
and testable statements and ultimately to explanation in terms of acceptable constructs. The sciences may be distinguished one from another on the basis of: (i) the
problems they set out to investigate, (ii) the data they accept as relevant, (iii) the
methods they employ, and (iv) the constructs they consider to have explanatory
value. Historically science and philosophy were one, with philosophy the more
inclusive term. It is debatable whether philosophy today should attempt to retain
its historic role of synthesizer and interpreter of all knowledge, or be content with
a more modest critical role. In either case the task of the philosopher, whether as
interpreter or as critic, goes beyond that of the scientist. This has certainly been

true of the philosophic systems frequently classed as phenomenological or existentialist, e.g. those of Huserl, Scheler, Heidegger, Sartre, and Merleau-Ponty. Although these have begun with a descriptive analysis of experience which may appeal to the psychologist, they have without exception gone far beyond description and, especially in the case of the existentialists, have come to rely less and less on the description of phenomena as they deal with what for them are the more important problems of ontology. Thus, although philosophical and psychological phenomenology may have a common core of interest and method, the two must not be confused with one another. Psychological phenomenology presents itself as an approach to empirical science. As such, it may make its contribution to the philosophic enterprise, but it must not be identified, any more than is any other scientific discipline, with any particular system of philosophy. Psychological phenomenologists have on the whole been quite cautious in their excursions into philosophy, perhaps more so than have psychologists of other persuasions.

The confusion between the two types of phenomenology is further confounded by an increasingly loose use of the word both in philosophy and in psychology. Spiegelberg (1960) has pointed out that in philosophy we may speak only of a phenomenological movement, a movement which has now broadened to include the existentialist emphasis in literature and theology as well as in philosophy. In psychology the situation is even worse. Psychological phenomenologists are not only confused with their philosophical cousins; they are being increasingly identified with a movement in psychotherapy (*Daseinsanalyse – existential analysis*) which bears little relation to the phenomenology, either philosophical or psychological, of a half-century ago. One might with justice call for a revision of terminology. Since revisions of terminology have seldom proved successful, it is still advisable for any writer on phenomenology to identify which of the many meanings of the term he is accepting.

HISTORICAL NOTE

Although the modern history of phenomenology begins probably with the Cartesian *cogito*, the movement became explicit in recent philosophy in the early writings of Edmund Husserl, especially in the *Logische Untersuchungen* (1900–01). In his attempt to establish philosophy as a rigorous science (*strenge Wissenschaft*) Husserl emphasized the importance of the bracketing (*einklammern*) of presuppositions as prerequisite to the identification and description of the intuitively given essences of experience. For him a rigorous philosophy must begin with a rigorous descriptive psychology. It is unnecessary here to review the development of Husserl's philosophic thinking or the relation of his philosophy to that of his contemporaries and successors.[1] What is significant for an understanding of his relation to psychology is the fact that, although he was vigorously opposed to "psychologism" in any form and was impatient with much of the experimental psychology that was

---

1 Spiegelberg's (1960) survey and critique of the phenomenological movement is centred primarily about its place in recent philosophy. He includes, however, references to pertinent psychological contributions.

being developed in the laboratories of Leipzig, Berlin, and Göttingen, he recognized both the possibility and the value of a psychology based on the phenomenological method.[2]

Psychological phenomenology owes a great debt to Husserl. It would be incorrect, however, to regard it as merely an offshoot of Husserl's philosophy. Husserl gave expression to a mode of psychological thinking which was already taking shape in the 19th century. By giving it philosophic support he undoubtedly strengthened it; but he did not create it. The psychology of the late 19th century, typified by Wundt's group in Leipzig, was explicitly a psychology of consciousness, predominantly an analytic psychology patterned after Newtonian physics and employing the logical-genetic method of the post-Newtonian empiricist philosophy. For this kind of psychology the most satisfactory explanation rested on the discovery of the physical, physiological, and anatomical counterparts of the presumed elementary processes of consciousness. Given the elements, the more complex states and processes of consciousness could be explained by way of the laws of association. The popularization of Darwinian concepts did not, for the Germans at least, imperil this essentially Newtonian psychology. Biological genesis was merely added to logical genesis; and it might be argued that the notion of evolutionary origins involved nothing more than the injection of a dimension of time into what was essentially a logical rather than a psychological mode of explanation.

Resistance to this kind of psychology tends as a rule to be rationalistic or romantic rather than phenomenological; we find it in Thomas Reid's "common sense," in Rousseau's romanticism, in Hegel's objective idealism. The first recognizably phenomenological protest of the 19th century was probably Goethe's intemperate rejection of Newton's theory of colour (1810). Historians of science have too frequently been content to castigate Goethe for his bad physics, ignoring his brilliant descriptive analysis of the world of colour. The positive contribution of Goethe's argument is that, regardless of the physical composition of light, the colours as we see them must be accepted as legitimate phenomena. For the physicist, black is but the absence of light; for the phenomenologist, black is a true colour. During the nineteenth century, the psychology of perception was dominated by the attempt to specify stimuli, receptors, and neural conductors, with the categories of psychological description forced to conform to those of the physical and biological sciences. From time to time, however, there were suggestions that the description of psychological phenomena should be independent of hypothetical explanatory constructs. We find these, for example, in the work of Purkinje, and even more notably in Ewald Hering's approach to the study of vision. (*Zur Lehre vom Lichtsinn*, 1878.) We tend to think of Hering as the stout defender of nativism against the empiricism of Helmholtz. We need not share his nativistic theories, however, to recognize his importance as a pioneer in experimental phenomenology. Without using the word "phenomenology" he gave a new orientation to the experimental psychology of perception simply by insisting that the familiar phenomena of object constancy, explained away by Helmholtz and others as convenient illusions, should be taken at their face value and subjected to experimental

2 For a reconstruction of Husserl's own thinking about psychology see Drüe (1963).

investigation. How rewarding this approach has proved to be needs no elaboration. Suffice it to say that in his approach to the phenomena of vision Hering was deliberately suspending physical and physiological presuppositions and, by implication at least, defending the legitimacy of all psychological phenomena as facts. This did not prevent him, it must be noted, from seeking physical and physiological correlations for the complex phenomena which traditional psychology had "explained away" as secondary products of association or unconscious inference.

The subsequent history of psychological phenomenology can only be touched upon here. The most accessible field for phenomenological investigation is obviously that of perception, and the pioneer studies most frequently cited are possibly those of Stumpf on tone (1883, 1890), Katz on colour (1911, 1930) and touch (1925), Wertheimer on apparent movement (1912), and Rubin on figure-ground phenomena (1915). Broadly speaking, most of the European psychology of perception during the past half-century has been phenomenological in its orientation, and some of the most challenging of the new developments, e.g., Michotte's exploration of phenomenal causality (1946), have been explicitly phenomenological in their method. There can be little disagreement with the statement that phenomenology has helped to transform the psychology of perception and related cognitive processes from a somewhat dull into an exciting field of investigation.

Less dramatic and less successful, but equally important, have been the attempts to extend phenomenology to include the more intimate aspects of experience: the self and its properties, motivation, emotion, the relations between the self and "other selves," will, and the experience of freedom. Part of the instigation has undoubtedly come from such philosophers as Dilthey and Scheler, whose historical and ethical investigations led them to psychological phenomenology. Probably more important, however, was the challenge from the Freudian movement, with its disparagement of the phenomenal and its invocation of non-phenomenal constructs. Among the first of the psychologists to accept the challenge was Kurt Lewin, a member of the Berlin group, whose experimental studies of will and affect (1935) were grounded in phenomenology but attempted at the same time to deal with the problems of human dynamics which Freud had brought into focus. Lewin's influence has shown itself particularly in the growing interest in intra- and inter-group dynamics, and has been paralleled in developmental psychology by Piaget's attempt to reconstruct the world of the child. In both cases the initial approach is phenomenological, followed by a systematization which goes beyond phenomenology. In psychotherapy the phenomenological emphasis has been somewhat obscured by the normative concerns of the therapist, with the result that the question "What is?" may be replaced by "What ought to be?", and what begins as a phenomenology may end up as an ethics or an ontology. As of today the "existentialist" movement in psychotherapy looms as a possible major alternative to Freudian psychoanalysis. Whether or not this should be regarded as a part of the phenomenological movement is perhaps a debatable point. What is important to recognize, however, is that psychological phenomenology, which was born and reared in the laboratory, can no longer remain aloof from the rich and challenging evidence provided by the clinic.

THE PHENOMENOLOGICAL APPROACH

Psychological phenomenology calls for the bracketing of all presuppositions and the description of immediate experience in terms of its essential structures and attributes. This raises at once a number of questions, none of which can be answered simply and satisfactorily. (i) What do we mean by immediate experience? (ii) Is it literally possible to suspend one's presuppositions? (iii) Since description must be in terms of a language, what sort of language is required for a psychological phenomenology?

Immediate experience is what the phenomenologist observes and describes. The adjective "immediate" usually connotes either "instantaneous" or "unmediated." We are obviously not limiting ourselves to instantaneous experience, not merely because the word has little psychological meaning but also because experience as we have it continues and develops through time. The notion of mediation is equally unsatisfactory, since it implies a primary process which is somehow or other secondary to that which is mediated. The psychologist is interested in every experience, whether or not, or however, it may be mediated. We must consequently scrap the adjective "immediate."

What then do we mean by experience? The Germans make a useful distinction between *Erlebnis*, experience as we have it, and *Erfahrung*, past experience or experience as it has accumulated. The phenomenologist is concerned primarily with *Erlebnis*, for which there are such cognate terms as "consciousness" and "awareness." I suggest that for these terms there is no useful operational definition. Either we know what we mean when we say that we are conscious, or conscious of something, or we don't. We know the difference between red and blue, or we don't know it. The fact that we use verbal symbols to designate the difference is irrelevant. We could not use the symbols consistently if there were not differences in experience to which they refer. I shall not waste time on the supposed physical, anatomical, physiological, or chemical definitions of colour. These give us at best imperfect correlates of experienced colour which would have no meaning if we had not first experienced colour. This point becomes even clearer when we talk about experiences for which there are no known, or perhaps even postulated, physical, anatomical or physiological correlates. We are at present just guessing at the correlates of warm and cold, of sharp as compared with dull pain; and the attempts to find correlates for euphoria, anxiety, and guilt feelings have been almost ludicrous in their inadequacy – partly, I suggest, for want of an adequate phenomenology.

Phenomenology must begin, then, with the assumption that we know what we mean by experience. It is probably better simply to use the word "phenomenon," in its correct sense as "that which appears." We are observing and attempting to describe phenomena, the world of appearances, accepting this world as it is, passing no epistemological judgments. The phenomenologist is interested in all phenomena, whether they be the sturdy, resistant things which surround him and thrust themselves at him as real objects in a real world or the wispy, imaginary, intangible images of dreams and fantasies. All are phenomena, to be observed and to be described, eventually perhaps to be related meaningfully to the phenomena we call physical or physiological. The term "phenomenal world" as I am using it may at times be interchangeable with "phenomenal field," "psychological field," "behavioural world," or even "psychological life-space," as these have been used by other writers.

The bracketing of presuppositions required by Husserl's phenomenological reduction involved a very thorough housecleaning, in which metaphysical ghosts of all sorts were swept out of the attic and hung on the clothesline for airing. Husserl was prepared to expose to the light even the most sacred presuppositions of science, religion, and everyday living. It would do the psychologist no harm if he were to be equally ruthless in his housecleaning, although if he were to do this I am not sure that there would be any psychology left. If we were to put all presuppositions in temporary brackets our thinking might come to a stop, for we would be bracketing even the presupposition that thoughts are worth thinking. Husserl never went quite this far. He even wrote down his thoughts for the benefit of others and went through the agony of publishing them.

The bracketing procedure in psychological phenomenology is much more modest. In his role as scientist the psychologist is likely to leave unchallenged certain assumptions – about the possibility of observation, for instance, or about the rules of logical consistency – with which the philosopher must of necessity be concerned; but there is still ample room for the searching out and the identification of implicit assumptions which may be playing an unnoticed part in his observing and his theorizing. Titchener's caution against the stimulus error, while limited in its application, is still a healthy one; and so is the familiar caution against the confusion, so common in nineteenth-century associationism and in the early theories of instinct, between logical implication and psychological content. In an earlier publication (1947) I listed some of the "biases" commonly found in social psychological theory, among which were: the atomistic-reductive bias, the stimulus-receptor bias, the genetic bias, the logical bias, and the relativistic bias; and one could easily extend the list considerably. The word "bias" is probably an unfortunate one, because of its association with prejudice, and might well be withdrawn. The point is that with a little effort and discipline the psychologist can become aware of some of the presuppositions that are silently present in his observation and thinking. The fact that thinking totally free of presuppositions is an impossibility, and that at best presuppositions can be only partially and temporarily suspended, does not detract from the importance of the attempt to identify them.

Two further questions are frequently raised in connection with psychological phenomenology. (i) Does not the approach lead inevitably into a solipsism? (ii) Is not the bracketing of presuppositions precisely what every scientist does as part of his scientific procedure? The first of these can be brushed aside. Solipsism is no more, and no less, a threat to the phenomenologist than it is to any other inquirer. Devising an escape from solipsism is a healthful exercise for the beginner, one of the more interesting escape routes being, I think, by way of a careful phenomenology. The second question is to be answered with both a yes and a no: yes, in that in his attack on a specific problem the good scientist attempts to identify and challenge the implicit assumptions that are relevant to his problem; no, in that the scientist's interest is usually in the problem as set within the context of his science, not in the process of knowing as such. The phenomenological method might consequently be regarded, not as an alternative to the method of science, but rather as

its extension. Again it must be noted that, while in principle a complete phenomenology is conceivable, any phenomenological description is subject to the
limitations of the phenomenologist; which is ample ground for the conclusion that
phenomenology will always remain an approach and will never yield a fully satisfactory theory.

DESCRIPTIVE CATEGORIES FOR A
PSYCHOLOGICAL PHENOMENOLOGY

Since a complete phenomenological description of experience is impossible, any
proposed language of description must be quite tentative. The vocabulary and
syntax of such a language should ideally be dictated by the phenomena themselves
rather than impose their own structure on the phenomena. The only safeguard one
can suggest is that we be constantly aware of linguistic constraints and be prepared
to revise our descriptive categories in response to new observation. One useful
question to ask might be the following: Supposing we were to attempt the impossible and invent a language which could faithfully and efficiently communicate all
the essential data of experience, what would we have to build into that language to
render such communication possible? Our concern is not with the structural elements of the language, e.g., the vocabulary, or with such devices as word order
and intonation; we know from the comparative study of languages that similar
meanings can be communicated with approximately equal efficiency in a wide
variety of ways. We are asking, rather, for an identification of the forms and
properties of the meanings themselves, however these may be represented in any
given language; and this calls for a tearing aside of the screen of language and a
direct scrutiny of the phenomena. An impossible task, we agree, yet a task that is
worth attempting.

As a provisional framework for phenomenological description I suggest that we
begin with four crude categories, each of which will have to be subdivided further
and no one of which is to be considered as more than a convenient label. These
are: (i) structures; (ii) properties of structures; (iii) relations among structures;
and (iv) phenomenal dimensions. The chief advantage of such a categorization is
that it places in temporary brackets most of the traditional categories of psychological analysis, e.g., sensation, perception, memory, imagination, thinking, feeling, emotion, will, and encourages us to take a fresh look at the phenomena. Its
drawback, of course, is that any system of categories runs the risk of reifica-
tion. The proper way to avoid this is probably to keep revising one's categories.
It may be that in the long run the attempt to classify is more rewarding than is any
particular classification which may be achieved.

Phenomenal Structures
Traditional Aristotelian theory, with the support of most of the empirical psychologies since Aristotle, has imposed on psychological description a set of categories
based on the presumed sources of knowledge, or the channels through which
knowledge is presumed to come, namely the senses. While the qualitative differences which we label as sensory are readily recognized, and may eventually be
related to as yet unspecified sub-systems of the organism, there is no *a priori* justi-

fication for their unique status and there is no empirical basis for their acceptance as descriptive units. The redness I see is not an object in itself but one of many properties of the objects I see. This is the familiar argument against sensations as psychological units, and it need not be repeated here.

For want of a better term I suggest that we designate as *structures* the identifiable entities of the phenomenal world. The word *Gestalt* would be equally good, were it not so closely associated with a particular theory. Structures are not to be regarded as elements or units, in any metric sense, for they vary in their properties and can be ordered along many dimensions. To assert that the phenomenal world is structured is merely to recognize that, except in hypothetical extreme cases, it is always organized in some form or other, even if that organization involves nothing more than a dim distinction between "me" and "not-me." This point, too, is familiar from Gestalt psychology, and consequently needs no elaboration. What might be added, merely, is that the listing of phenomenal structures does not constitute an exhaustive description. Much of the phenomenal world is unstructured (William Stern, 1935, speaks of *Ungestalt*) and the unstructured aspects of the world are as truly "there" as are the structures.

Phenomenal structures may be loosely classified into: (*a*) things, (*b*) events, and (*c*) selves, no one of which is to be totally differentiated from the other two. A phenomenal thing, event, or self is, however, a bounded, segregated structure of the phenomenal world which to some extent at least maintains its identity. Such structures are usually labelled in our language with nouns, although not all nouns represent structures.

Things[3] are probably the stablest of phenomenal structures. For humans, at least, they are characteristically spatial in organization, fairly clearly localized, enduring in time but not dependent on time. We see and feel and lift things; we apprehend them as "really there." Unless we are sophisticated, we think of the physical world as a world of things.

Events, by contrast, are characteristically time-bound. An event has a beginning, a course, and an end. It may have spatial location, but this is less essential to its structure than are the spatial characteristics of a thing. An event may also be apprehended as "really there," but, for humans at any rate, events seldom carry as much "reality" as do things.

In the traditional sensory classification, "things" might be regarded as primarily products of vision, touch, and kinaesthesis, and "events" as products of "audition." While not to be disparaged, this distinction quickly loses its neatness when we observe the "event character" of visual movement and the "thing character" of certain noises. Furthermore, the distinction between thing and event begins to break down as we move into the modalities of smell, taste, temperature, and pain. In these categories, possibly, we have to do with *Ungestalt* rather than with *Gestalt*.

The self as a phenomenal structure has often been challenged but has never been completely banished. The stubbornness with which the first person (singular and plural) has maintained itself in every known human language would seem to support a firm place for it in a psychological phenomenology. I suspect that

---

3 This corresponds to the German *Ding*. The word "object" is avoided here because of the more restricted use of the word "objective" below.

our objection to the self as phenomenal datum is grounded in metaphysics rather than in phenomenology and reflects a bias which, in itself, should be of interest to the phenomenologist. Granted that the self is inescapably "there" in experience, the main question is whether or not it deserves to be classified as distinct from things and events. Certainly the self possesses much in common with things and events. It is segregated, bounded and localized in space, it has a recognizable if somewhat unclear temporal structure, and it maintains its identity in spite of change. Where it differs most from things and events is in the dynamic qualities which have invited such terms as intentionality and free will. This is not to suggest that phenomenal things and events are devoid of dynamic qualities, merely that in the self these are so much more prominent as to suggest a separate phenomeno-logical category.

Things, events, and the self are usually presented as here, now, and real; and as such we usually refer to them as percepts. For a phenomenology the traditional distinction between perception and memory, or between either of these and ima-gination, must be placed in brackets. A phenomenal structure is no less valid if it is then, there, and slightly irreal (a memory), or undated, unlocalized, and highly irreal (a fantasy). The tables and noises of memory and imagination are just as truly phenomenal structures as are the tables and noises of perception; and so may be the beliefs and concepts which at times, and with great reluctance, I have called "non-perceptual cognitive structures." As we move away from the here, now, and real of conventional perception, we are not forsaking one world and entering another; we are still in the phenomenal world, the structures, properties, and dimensions of which we continue to observe and describe.

Phenomenal Properties

Every phenomenal structure has a variety of properties, or attributes; and, for that matter, so do the unstructured components of the phenomenal world. These need not be listed in detail, since they can be found in any good textbook of experimental psychology. Things, for instance, usually have size and shape, and events have a temporal structure. Note, however, that the properties of phenomenal structures are not limited to the "sensory" attributes identified by the introspectionists, e.g., quality, intensity, extensity, duration, and clearness. Properties of things include modes of appearance, roughness, stability, and the like, and the structure of an event may include its velocity and its direction. The battle for the recognition of properties of organization as psychologically valid has seemingly been won.

To be emphasized is the fact that, while considerable progress has been made in the phenomenology of the more accessible forms of perceptual organization, particularly in vision, audition, and touch, litttle more than a beginning has been made in the phenomenology of tertiary or physiognomic properties or of the tradi-tional "higher thought processes," and of the affective and dynamic properties of the self; more about these presently.

Phenomenal Relations

Within, between, and among phenomenal structures are such familiar relations as before-after, right-left, inside-outside, louder than, sweeter than, and so forth. These have traditionally been accorded a secondary status as special products of

an act of judgment. So far as our psychophysics has been concerned, the consequences have not been catastrophic; the psychophysical curve is the same whether
we treat the relation as a phenomenon or as an inference. In psychological theory,
however, and in epistemology, this derogation of relations has been the source of
considerable confusion, although, again, the bias it reveals is in itself of phenomenological interest. We owe a debt to William James (1890) (in his famous
defense of the feelings of "if" and "and" and "but") for having restored relations
to their legitimate place as valid psychological phenomena.

This becomes particularly important as we proceed from the study of the simple
spatial, temporal, and intensive relations of classical psychophysics to relations
which are less readily quantifiable. Gestalt psychology has stressed such relations
as part to whole, thing to context, figure to ground, and some of the subtler relations of similarity; and such relations as those of phenomenal causality (Michotte,
1946) and phenomenal inherence (Benary, 1924), have been brought into the
laboratory. Where phenomenology has been most timid, however, has been in its
exploration of the dynamic relations of the self to other structures of the field,
phenomena which we have tended to reserve for a special psychology of motivation. When we speak of desire or fear or regret, we refer to phenomenal relations
between self and thing or event, and in love and hate we have a relation between
self and another structure which is present as a "self." These relations are characterized by activity, tension, the release of force. When Lewin introduced the terms
"valence" (*Aufforderungscharakter*) and "vector" he was distinguishing between
the properties of the thing or event which command or release action and the
resulting directedness of the self.

Lewin was evidently eager to restate as many as possible of the phenomena of
motivation in terms of properties of structures, particularly of those which could
be represented diagrammatically. This may have been an overreaction to Freud's
neglect of phenomenology. The fact remains, however, that his diagrams also
included needs, tensions, conflicts, and the like, which are not lodged in the self
or in the thing but are rather relations in the field. One might argue, of course, that
in the last analysis a relation is a property of a superordinate structure, the most
all-inclusive structure being the whole phenomenal world. This might have the
value of ridding us once and for all of such fictitious relations as "pure" space and
time, but I suspect that before long we would find ourselves reinstating the more
conventional use of the term.

The important point is that the phenomenologist must take another look at the
phenomena of motivation. A simple paradigm of motivated behaviour might involve a need, a goal, and certain conditions which sustain, regulate, or interfere
with progress toward the goal. Insofar as these are phenomenally present, the need
is there as a state of the self, but with a directedness beyond the self, and the goal is
there as something other than the self, but with a valence. The relation between the
two we call a desire, or a purpose, or a hope, or something similar. Whether we
call it a purpose or a hope will depend on the characteristics of the need, of the
goal, and of the other relevant conditions. Before we begin to theorize about basic
needs or ultimate goals it will obviously be profitable to find out what happens to
the self when it is in a state of need and what the phenomenal properties of a goal
are. What is called for is the same sort of scrutiny of dynamic phenomena as that

to which we have been subjecting the world of colours, sounds, and touches. Whether or not we can rest content with a mere phenomenology of motivation is another question. My own conviction is that, just as in the case of perception, we must transcend phenomenology if we are to develop a psychology, but that, as in the case of perception, it will be a better psychology if it is based on sound phenomenology.

The phenomenology of the self and its relations might lead us in various directions, into the psychology of communication, for instance, or into the problems of sympathy, empathy, and the perception of the "other self." Let me select one set of examples from a field in which the phenomenological approach seems to show some promise, namely psychological aesthetics. In the aesthetic judgment we have a relation between a perceiver (a self) and something that is not the self, e.g., a thing (a picture) or a complex event (a piece of music), and this relation is something other than that of simple size, distance, or loudness. It is frequently termed an emotional experience, but as such is differentiated from such emotional attitudes as those of reverence or of hatred. Two kinds of aesthetic theory are commonly advanced, one subjective and the other objective, with a number of compromises between the extremes. According to the subjectivist the aesthetic judgment is based on the affective response of the perceiver; the picture gives him pleasure, makes him feel good. According to the objectivist the judgment is a response to formal or other properties inherent in the structure of the picture.

I shall now use the terms "subjective" and "objective" in a strictly phenomenological way, disregarding the traditional distinction forced upon us by John Locke between "dependent on the perceiver" and "independent of perceiver." (In the last analysis, as Berkeley argued, every experience is dependent on the perceiver, and our inevitable fate is a meaningless solipsism.) An experience is phenomenologically subjective when it is a part of, a property of, or intimately related to the self. It is objective when it is independent of and unrelated to the phenomenal self. There can consequently be degrees of subjectivity and objectivity, and any given experience can usually be assigned a position on a continuum ranging from one extreme to the other. In the world of colour, for instance, organized visual objects are more objective than are the homogeneous colours of the *Ganzfeld*; a rough noise is more objective than a clear, pure tone; pains are predominantly subjective, but a dull, diffuse headache is likely to be more subjective than the sharply localized pain of a pin-prick in the finger; a touch may be either objective or subjective, depending on whether it is active or passive. As the phenomenal world becomes more elaborately structured it tends to become more objective; anything that destructures the world tends to make it more subjective.

The relevance of this to the aesthetic judgment is twofold. In the first place, it is precisely in the realm of the phenomenologically objective that our most delicate aesthetic judgments are made. (I am deliberately avoiding the problem of artistic creation, although the same phenomenological distinctions are relevant.) We have an aesthetics of colour, of sound and, to some extent, of active touch, all of which involve complex spatial, temporal, and intensive patternings; but we have no aesthetics of pain or temperature, and almost none of taste and smell. In our regrettably undeveloped aesthetics of food and drink, in fact, we find aesthetic judgments possible only when the flavour of the cheese or the wine is apprehended objectively as a property of something other than ourselves. This would seem to argue for an objectivist theory of the aesthetic judgment.

On the other hand, however, is the seemingly inescapable fact that the aesthetic judgment is usually tinged with emotion, and emotions are supposed to be subjective experiences. But are emotions really subjective, i.e., states or properties of the phenomenal self? The answer is not so clear. True, there are affective states which seem phenomenologically to be almost completely subjective. The simple pleasures and pains connected with physiological needs are very close to the phenomenal self; I feel good, or tired, or happy, or anxious. These might be considered as states of almost pure affectivity when simple needs are gratified or denied fulfillment. But this kind of affect is certainly not the foundation of the aesthetic judgment. In fact, although critics frequently use the language of affect (that picture is nauseating!), they are agreed that one's state of bodily well-being should be irrelevant to the judgment. The hedonic state of the judge may play a part in his judgment, but at most it is a generalized reinforcer and at worst a distractor.

Can we escape this easily, however, from the common association of aesthetics with emotion? The answer may lie in the fact that emotions as we know them are intentional, i.e., object oriented, and it is on the basis of their intentionality, not their affect, that we identify and classify them. Emotions are never affectively neutral, it is true, and they always involve the self; but they are not mere states of pleasantness or unpleasantness, or of arousal. A free-floating anxiety might conceivably be considered as a simple state of the self without specific objective reference, although I should question this; but what distinguishes fear from anxiety is the presence of something which is apprehended as a threat. What we call an emotion is thus a dynamic subject-object relation which can be fully characterized only if our description includes the properties of the objective structures as well as the properties of the self. A careful phenomenology of emotion would seem to complicate immeasurably the task of classifying "the emotions" and might even lead to an entirely new scheme, in which within a super-ordinate category of subject-object relations we find ourselves distributing the varied phenomena of emotion in a number of different sub-categories.

Whether or not such a new scheme is necessary, it would seem clear that the existence of a distinctive aesthetic emotion is open to question. What purport to be aesthetic judgments range from those based on diffuse and highly affective states of the self, as in the common response to a Tschaikowsky symphony, to those which rest on almost selfless absorption in objective structure. To lump all together as aesthetic is to ignore a great array of varied and interesting subject-object relations.

Dimensions

The familiar dimensions of psychophysics are space, time, intensity, and the like. Strictly speaking, these are not coordinate in a phenomenological description with structures, properties and relations. We do not perceive space as such; we perceive objects as having such and such a size, separated from ourselves and from one another by such and such distances. If we are to be precise in our description, however, we find it necessary to order the phenomena along some sort of hypothetical continuum, even if all points in the continuum are not phenomenally present. Thus, although we recognize certain judgments of hue or pitch as phenomenally "absolute," i.e., as seemingly independent of anchorage points on a scale, we find it easier to specify them by assuming the existence of a scale on which they can be assigned a position. Description in terms of dimensions has the further value that it keeps reminding us of the constantly changing character of the phenomenal world. Although many phenomenal structures are characteristically stable, as we know from the studies of perceptual constancy, this stability may be maintained only at the expense of radical changes in their properties and relations.

When Boring (1933) discussed the "physical dimensions" of consciousness he was obviously most interested in those psychological variables which can be coordinated more or less directly to the variables measured fairly simply by the physicist. Similarly, Gibson's (1959) attempt to coordinate more complex perceptual phenomena to "higher order" variables of stimulation also, although not as explicitly, turns to the physicist for psychological dimensions. The phenomenologist can have no quarrel with psychophysics, either in its classical or in its more recent form, provided that it does not claim to be giving an exhaustive account of all phenomenal dimensions. For the phenomenologist the dimensions of consciousness are to be discovered in the phenomena, not deduced from a prior analysis of the dimensions of the physical world. If physical (or anatomical or physiological) correlates can be established, so much the better; if not, the phenomenologist must continue his exploration of the phenomenal world without the aid of the physicist.

One might list, just as illustrations, a few significant dimensions which emerge in phenomenological analysis and which invite further study. These are best stated as pairs of opposites. Most of these are at least crudely scalable, but in some cases they may turn out to be multiple rather than single dimensions.

Similarity-Dissimilarity
This is obviously a multiple dimension, since "similar" is always "with respect to this or that feature." It is included merely because in most studies the relevant features are predetermined by the investigator. The most interesting judgments of similarity are those which are unanticipated.

Reality-Irreality
These words have no epistemological connotation. What is diagnosed as an hallucination may be phenomenally as real as something judged to be a percept.

Subjectivity-Objectivity
This is also without any epistemological connotation. A pain is likely to be more subjective than a visual object.

Positive and Negative Affectivity
This comprises pleasantness-unpleasantness or hedonic tone, more pronounced at the subjective end of the subject-object continuum.

Saliency-Embeddedness
Most frequently illustrated by means of figure-ground demonstrations, this is present in all phenomenal organization.

Stability-Instability
This too is a structural characteristic commonly reported in studies of constancy and of figure-ground fluctuations but which is even more important in the phenomenology of the self.

Inherent-Accidental
As used here this is characteristic of the phenomenal properties of a structure. The colour of an object may be phenomenally inherent, whereas the shadow in which it is seen may be phenomenally accidental. The distinction goes back to Aristotle, and although it led Aristotle into physical errors, e.g., in his assertion that weight is an inherent property, it is phenomenologically important.

Such a list could be extended almost indefinitely, but perhaps this is sufficient to indicate how even a somewhat casual phenomenology can suggest phenomenal dimensions that are worth exploring further. As we attempt to isolate dimensions, however, there are three points which might be kept in mind. (i) Dimensions emerge from free description, and the freer the better. Our language was not designed for phenomenological analysis, and it is often in the language of metaphor or poetry, or in the frustrated search for the appropriate expression, that we gain our best insights. To decide on our dimensions in advance is to violate the phenomenological method. (ii) As we move from the simpler phenomena of perception to the mercurial phenomena of motivation and thinking, we can no longer anchor our observations to controllable physical stimuli. Developments in scaling methodology, as in Osgood's semantic differential, offer encouragement; but it is clear that if phenomenology is to become precise we must have sharper tools. (iii) In the move from description to dimensional analysis there is always the danger that dimensions may become reified. The phenomenologist's only safeguard is to keep returning to observation and description. One of the more surprising remarks in Wittgenstein's *Philosophical Investigations* (1953, paragraph 66) is "*Denk nicht, sondern schau.*"

BEYOND PHENOMENOLOGY

The thesis I have been presenting is that phenomenology is a useful propaedeutic to a psychology, but is not in itself a psychology. A psychology must provide explanatory constructs, and for these we must go beyond phenomenological description and analysis. I concede that we could redefine psychology in such a way as to make phenomenology irrelevant. Watson tried to do this, with only partial success, and the current threat is from the computer enthusiasts who love to talk about inputs and outputs. I don't regard the computer as a threat, however. When the computer finally begins to ask searching questions, the phenomenologist will cheerfully resign. In the meantime, the phenomenologist will continue to ask the questions, and the computer will help to find the answers.

Any transcendence of the phenomenal world implies a metaphysics. I should like to dodge the metaphysical problem and suggest, as a basis for discussion, that there are at present five different languages in which psychologists are attempting to explain psychological phenomena:

Materialistic
This is the approach of modern science. Man is a part of Nature, governed by natural law. Psychological phenomena will ultimately be restatable in terms of neurophysiology, biochemistry, biophysics, and mathematics.

Teleological
This would include both the classical Aristotelian psychologies and the modern post-Darwinian psychologies which accord explanatory value to the concept of adjustment.

Quasi-Psychological
Lewin might be the best example, but some of the neo-Freudians might also be included. Explanatory constructs purport to be abstracted directly from the data of experience and behaviour.

Mathematical
These are the modern Platonists, for whom the ultimate explanation will be in the form of a mathematical model.

Existential
These are not strictly coordinate with the others, since they present no explanatory constructs. Experience cannot be explained in terms of the conventional constructs of the sciences; it can be "understood" only within the framework of an ontology.

All of these, and probably others as well, represent ways in which the phenomenal world can be transcended. The phenomenologist will not assert that one is correct and the others are false. He will merely ask the question: which kind of psychology does full justice to the phenomena?

SUMMARY AND CONCLUSIONS

As the term is used here, "propaedeutic" means "preliminary", and the argument that phenomenology is propaedeutic to a scientific psychology means simply and literally that a careful and rigorous descriptive analysis of experience should precede any attempt to develop a psychological system. A psychological system should endeavour to explain, whatever that means, in terms of independently definable constructs. Phenomenology makes no attempt to explain; it merely describes. To describe the world of experience, however, one must have descriptive categories, and this entails the use of language. No language has as yet been proposed which provides an adequate set of categories for phenomenological description, and one could easily defend the thesis that a completely adequate language does not exist and will never be invented. On the other hand, one might argue that every language, however imperfect, has evolved a set of categories which roughly represent the structures, properties, and dimensions of the phenomenal world. The thesis of the present paper is that within the context of the English language we can discover a set of descriptive categories which can, at least in preliminary fashion, serve as a basis for phenomenological description. There is no claim that these categories are in any sense final, and it is argued that the best way to avoid the pitfalls of language is to capitalize on its infirmities and, through the study of languages, to struggle toward the construction of a neutral language which will be adequate for phenomenological description. This may never be achieved, but the very search for such a language may improve our skill in describing and categorizing the world of experience.

References

BENARY, W., "Beobachtungen zu einem Experiment über Helligkeitskontrast." *Psychologische Forschung*, 5 (1924) 131–42

BORING, E. G., *"The physical dimensions of consciousness."* New York: Century, 1933

GIBSON, J. J., "Perception as a function of stimulation." *Psychology: a study of a science*, edited by S. Koch, vol. 1. New York: McGraw-Hill, 1959

VON GOETHE, J. W., *Zur Farbenehre*, 1810. Collected works, any edition

DRÜE, H., *Edmund Husserls System der phänemonelogischen Psychologie*. Berlin: de Gruyter, 1963

HERING, E., *Grundzüge der Lehre vom Lichtsinn*. Berlin: Springer, 1920. Revised edition of *Zur Lehre vom Lichtsinn*, 1878. English translation by L. M. Hurvich and Dorothy Jameson. Cambridge, Mass.: Harvard University Press, 1964

HUSSERL, E., *Logische Untersuchungen*, 1900–01, 2 vols. Revised in 3 vols. Halle: Niemeyer, 1913

JAMES, W., *Principles of psychology*, 2 vols. New York: Holt, 1890

KATZ, D., *Die Erscheinungsweisen der Farben*, 1911. Revised edition of *Der Aufbau der Farbwelt*. Leipzig: Barth, 1930. English translation by R. B. MacLeod and C. W. Fox. London: Kegan, Paul, 1935

KATZ, D., *Der Aufbau der Tastwelt*. Leipzig: Barth, 1925

LEWIN, K., *A dynamic theory of personality: selected papers*. Translated by D. K. Adams and K. Zener. New York: McGraw-Hill, 1935

MACLEOD, R. B., "The phenomenological approach to social psychology." *Psychological Review*, 54 (1947) 193–210

MICHOTTE, A., *La perception de la causalité*. Paris: Vrin, 1946. English translation by T. R. Miles. New York: Basic Books, 1963

RUBIN, E., *Visuell-wahrgenommene Figuren*. Danish edition, Copenhagen: 1915. German edition, 1921

SPIEGELBERG, H., *The phenomenological movement*, 2 vols. The Hague: Nijhoff, 1961. Revised edition, 1965

STERN, W., *Allgemeine Psychologie auf personalistischer Grundlage*. The Hague: Nijhoff, 1935. English translation by H. D. Spoerl. New York: Macmillan, 1938

STUMPF, K., *Tonpsychologie*, 2 vols. Leipzig: Hirzel, 1883, 1890

WERTHEIMER, M., "Experimentelle Studien über das Sehen von Bewegungen." *Zeitschrift für Psychologie*, **61** (1912) 161–265. Reproduced in *Drei Abhandlungen zur Gestaltpsychologie*. Erlangen: 1925

WITTGENSTEIN, L., *Philosophical investigations*. New York: Macmillan, 1953

Comments:
L. K. Frank

The strength of the phenomenological approach is in its insistence upon observing as closely and effectively as possible what occurs, and then calling upon whatever concepts and assumptions may be relevant and fruitful to put meaning into these observations. As MacLeod has emphasized, we must always be self-consciously aware of the language and the categories we impose upon our observations since we may obfuscate what is taking place, and thereby formulate problems that are no longer valid. For the proposed new Center this critical searching of what is not assumed may be highly productive of focusing study upon newly formulated problems, thereby freeing us from questions no longer relevant or fruitful.

W. W. Rozeboom

I wish we could get from MacLeod an explicit criterion for identifying reports which qualify as "phenomenological". From his exposition I take it that "I see a pitcher on the table" is a phenomenological report, whereas "there is a pitcher on the table" is not. By MacLeod's standards, therefore, it would seem that for a report to be classed as phenomenological, it has to be a description of an *experience*.

J. R. Royce

I think Rozeboom is right when he states that the phenomenologist, qua phenomenologist, is primarily concerned with *experience*. If this is so, then the phenomenological report will offer no distinction between the illusory and the veridical. Let us take autokinesis for example. It is my impression that the available empirical evidence indicates that the naive viewing of real movement compared with illusory movement cannot be differentiated. In fact, if anything, the illusory movement appears to have more reality character to it than actual movement. However, some research in which I have been involved suggests that a reliable tracking record of autokinetic movement is, in some sense, isomorphic with the phenomenological report of the extent and configuration of illusory movement. This presents an interesting and perhaps unsolvable problem on the similarities and differences between phenomenological experience, adaptive (i.e. veridical) behaviour, and epistemology.

David Krech

Professor MacLeod's paper deals with a psychological technique which is as important as it is neglected. It is my opinion that there hardly exists a single problem in human behaviour (including the problem of the physiological basis of behaviour) the solution to which cannot be aided by *starting* with a phenomenological description. Perhaps, in this company, it might be proper to point out to my reverend listeners that a common method of study may be one way of "unifying" diverse study areas. But, except for very few problems, psychologists have avoided the phenomenological approach. When Professor Crutchfield and I wrote our textbook, our plan was to precede the experimental analysis of each area of psychological inquiry (perception, motivation, emotion, social behaviour, learning, etc.) with a chapter in which we would give a phenomenological description of the events to be discussed in that section. We found this a relatively easy matter when dealing with perception, but, when it came to some of the other problem areas (learning, for instance), we had to scratch around to find useful phenomenological descriptions in the literature. In some instances we had to resort to home-made or do-it-yourself phenomenology.

We can all list many reasons for the neglect of this sovereign method by most contemporary psychologists – especially the American psychologists. Most of the reasons can be ascribed to the propaganda of the left-wing infantilism of the philosophically naive, so-called hard-nosed, Scientists produced by the Behaviourists and Neo-Behaviourists of recent memory. So be it! But some of the reasons for the neglect of phenomenology stem, I think, from the failure of people like Professor MacLeod. There is a belief – how well-founded no man knows – that phenomenological reports are not reliable, are not repeatable. But there exist precious little data to support or refute this belief. It seems to me that it is the responsibility of Professor MacLeod (America's "Mister Phenomenology") to do something about this. We need two kinds of studies. First, we need some carefully done studies which would set down the best procedures for obtaining useful phenomenological descriptions. Such studies might ask us to go back to "ancient" psychological procedures. Here is what I mean: I am sure that all of us, at one time or another, have told our students that the most important instrument for psychology is the psychologist himself. The psychologist must be a good observer, he must be well-trained, he must guard against bias, etc., etc., etc. Well, it may also be true that when the psychologist is working with human subjects that the instrument which may be more important than the psychologist, is the subject himself. Not only must the psychologist be trained to be a good observer, but, *so must the subject.* And so, as it must to all sciences, the pendulum of history may swing back again to the time when our human subjects are again first given careful training on how to *be* subjects before we record their responses, and human subjects will again be called os and not ss! (Shades of Titchener!)

In addition to this type of study (on how to obtain the best possible phenomenological reports), we need some carefully done experimental determinations of the degree of reliability and repeatability one can obtain with phenomenological procedures. No method in science has a reliability of unity. But, for every method in science, we must know *how* reliable it is. I am afraid that until both of these types of studies are done psychologists will shy away from using a method which, in my opinion, can be the beginning of wisdom *re* matters psychological.

Discussion: R. B. MacLeod

THE PHENOMENOLOGY OF THE COMMUNICATION PROCESS

AUDITOR   You make a fleeting reference to the phenomenology of communication. I'm interested in hearing a little more about what you had in mind.

MACLEOD   That's a dangerous question. I might let loose a long lecture, but ...
AUDITOR   Perhaps you could contrast it with other approaches, such as information theory.
MACLEOD   Some of us have expressed a certain amount of impatience with the information theory paradigm, which I find extremely useful for many purposes, particularly in computer programming and things like this. The information theory paradigm for communication grew out of the practical work of the Signal Corps during the Second World War when they had the problem of transmitting messages across simple media, the simplest being a single telegraph wire that can transmit only pulses that will vary primarily in their temporal characteristics. So the problem is, as in the Morse code, to translate the message that you want to send, which is inevitably fairly complex, into terms of the particular, limited variables that can be handled by the transmitting channel, and then, of course, they have to be decoded afterwards. So this is a simple paradigm, and it leads to theory of encoding and decoding, theory of transmission, with channel characteristics, noise, interference, and so on, and then as you complicate the paradigm to take care of channels of transmission that have greater possibilities of variation, obviously you can simplify the encoding and the decoding procedures and you can work out good quantitative analyses of these. Well, I would say this is all to the good. I have no objection to it at all when we are constructing computers or trying to simulate psychological processes, as we are doing with our perceptron at Cornell. And there are many concrete experimental problems which benefit from information theory. And if you are dealing with communication on a level which is pretty remote from human communication, the information theory paradigm seems to work well. Take, for example, the so-called language of the bees that Karl von Frisch studied. Now, I just don't see much point in trying to empathize with the bee. It's much easier to use the formal language of information theory and try to specify what the inputs are and what the outputs are, and so on. But, if we are interested in human communication, and we take two people talking to each other as our paradigm case, we are dealing with something very complex. Using a phenomenological framework, we have speaker and hearer, the s and the H, and we're focused at the speaker end with a person who lives in a phenomenal world – that is, a world as he apprehends it. We have the hearer in his own phenomenal world, too. Now, where person A, the speaker, communicates with person B, the speaker is speaking to the hearer. The point is that he is speaking, not to the real hearer, but to the phenomenal hearer, the hearer as he apprehends. Similarly, the hearer is listening to, not the real speaker, but the phenomenal speaker. Now, the medium ... let's limit ourselves to a linguistic system such as the English language. The English language considered independently as the linguist studies it is an enormously complex structure with tremendous vocabulary and very elaborate syntactical structures, parts of which are variations, and so on. It is so complex that it is no exaggeration to say that nobody has ever mastered the English language. This means each speaker and each hearer has his own degree of mastery of the English language, but even beyond this, in spite of serious efforts to communicate, the words that are used do not necessarily have identical meanings for speaker and hearer. This means the phenomenal speaker is speaking to the phenomenal hearer by way of a phenomenal

medium – that is, the language as he understands it – and we must replicate the whole thing for the world of the hearer. Now, the interesting problem in psycholinguistics that I am very much concerned with just now is the various ways in which a meaning can be conveyed through a linguistic system in such a way as to produce communication. We haven't any magical, external way of deciding whether communication has taken place, or how complete the communication is. Such matters are dependent on feedback. Sometimes feedback leads us to the conviction that communication has been complete, as in the case of a relatively simple language such as mathematics. Incidentally, the phenomenologist will duck the whole question of the ultimate verdicality of the communication. He is interested in the communication process itself. For me one of the most fascinating problems is the different ways a linguistic medium can be used to convey a meaning from speaker to hearer in such a way that communication is established. This is obviously tremendously complex compared to the simple things that happen in a telegraph wire, where we're just dealing with pulses patterned in simple time. In any standard language we have phonetic units, and we have morphological units – words; and we have syntactical structures, and characteristics of the whole communication process that we might call style. Now, all of these are psychologically interesting. The hearer hears not only certain elementary sounds, but he hears phonetic units and morphological units – words – as vocabulary. He hears these words arrayed in different ways and, in English particularly, the word order becomes significant. But then there are many other variables – for example, the physiognomic properties of words – that is, the expressive characteristics of words, which also contribute to the whole communication process. Well, I could go on at great length, but maybe this is enough to exemplify the relevance of phenomenological analysis.

7
The Serio-Comic Encounter of Clinical Psychology and Existential Philosophy

Herman Tennessen
UNIVERSITY OF ALBERTA

7
The Serio-Comic Encounter of Clinical Psychology and Existential Philosophy

Herman Tennessen
UNIVERSITY OF ALBERTA

PROFESSOR TENNESSEN received an advanced degree in Psychology and Philosophy from the University of Oslo, and has lectured there in logic, history of philosophy, and psychology since 1938. From 1947 to 1957 he was public examiner in these disciplines for all Norwegian universities. He was also a Fellow of the Norwegian Research Council from 1946 to 1948 and a member of UNESCO, Paris, 1948–9. From 1947 to 1957 he was Research Associate and Project Leader at the Institute for Social Research and from 1955–6 was acting Professor of Sociology of Law. He served as Assistant Professor at the University of California, Berkeley, California, from 1957 to 1961, Associate Professor at the University of Alberta from 1961 to 1966, and Professor of Philosophy since 1966. Professor Tennessen has published six monographs in the series *Filosofiske Problemer* (Oslo: Oslo University Press), and numerous articles in various scholarly journals. He has served on advisory boards of *The encyclopedia of philosophy*, The Macmillan Co., and in an advisory capacity to The Free Press and Appleton-Century. He is on the editorial boards of *Synthese, Inquiry*, and *Science and methodology*.

INTRODUCTION

In a Danish Encyclopedia, published around the turn of the century, a highly esteemed scientist wrote an article on "Flying Machines". "It is quite obvious," he concluded, "that none of these fantastic ideas shall ever materialize. Everybody knows that nothing heavier than water can ever float in water; by the same token, it is logically impossible that anything heavier than air can ever fly in the air." And while he jubilantly arrived at his unmistakable conclusion, outside his window birds sailed through the sky (Tennessen, 1964, p. 198). Analogous, and similarly ludicrous, so it has often been argued, was the situation of the dogmatic negativists who, until recently, denied the possibility of human space travel: the deniers were already on board a space-ship, soaring, whirling through an immense, absurdly indifferent, vast, vile void, totally vacuous, except for homeopathically sparse excipients of inconsequential motes of dust and specks of light: all blindly blank, deadly deaf, frigidly glaring with sublime apathy. ...

This image has now become commonplace (appearing even in the inaugural speech of a U.S. president). It is most frequently employed homiletically, to foster and promote human gregariousness: "We are all in the same boat," etc. More intriguing, however, seems to me a question, implicitly suggested in the metaphor: what wondrous mechanisms have permitted man to remain deluded about his own cosmic condition, and, in the face of all evidence to the contrary, caused him to maintain a basically Ptolemaic (if any) "Weltanschauung"? The shortest, if not simplest, explanation offers a reference to the (a) cognitive, and (b) empathetic "disintegrity" of human insights (or: "disintegratedness" of man): the ability (a) to hold cognitively incompatible views or positions, or (b) to prevent knowledge from penetrating "volitional" (etc.) personality layers and thus permitting it to remain purely "intellectual."[1] One of the, in this respect, most effective ontological and eschatological hebetants, is, according to Heidegger (1960, 1962, sections 27, 34–8, 71), man's knack for extracting intervals out of his total term of Being,

1 See, for a variety of approaches to this problem cluster: Ach, 1905; Cherry, 1957; Clive, 1964; Festinger, 1957; Heidegger, 1960, 1962; Jaensch, 1928, 1931, 1933, 1938; Kaila, 1935; Lynd, 1939; Riesman, 1950, 1960; Royce, 1959, 1962, 1964; Ruensch and Bateson, 1951; Shoemaker, 1963; Tennessen, 1964; and others.

and filling them with work and other pastimes, external sensations (*"Neugier"*), chatter and small-talk (*"das Gerede"*), etc. This, to return to the analogy, empowers the crew and passengers in the space-ship to go on, polishing brass and playing bridge, blissfully unaware of their "cosmic situation." They are all psychologically healthy, content, well-adjusted and accommodated: ontologically secure. They have a feeling of integral selfhood, of personal identity, and of the permanency of things. They believe in their own continuity, in being made of good, lasting stuff, and in meaning and order and justice in life and in the universe (see, e.g., Laing, 1960). In the most fortunate cases, there is a good, healthy, unconditional surrender and submission to the norms of nicety and normalcy of the average, square-headed, stuffed-shirted, sanctimonious, middle-class North-American churchgoer and bridge player, with his pseudo-intelligent, quasi-progressive, simili-cultured, platitudinal small-talk. Happy days, in this the best of all possible worlds! Time disappears as quickly and pleasantly as a lemon-chiffon pie, eaten while distracted by a picture of a luscious woman (or an exciting ball game). One doesn't notice, until too late. In short, *all is well* (since nobody notices the end of "all that is well"). Until one night: the day's work is well done; and all the ship's labour-crapulent fools frantically engulf themselves in a deadly serious game of bridge (till it is time for the night-cap and the tranquillizer). One of the "dummies," a champion brass polisher, suffering from an acute case of uncaused depression, goes to lie down for a while; he doesn't have a dime for the juke box; the room is painfully satiated with embarrassing silence. Instantly and unexpectedly he is struck by an execrative curse of inverted serendipity. He suddenly, in unbearable agony, sees himself as an upholstered pile of bones and knuckles, with the softer parts slung up in a bag on the front side, – and his whole life as a ludicrously brief interlude between embryo and corpse, two repulsive caricatures of himself (Zapffe, 1941, p. 112). As for this flying farce, this nauseatingly trivial burlesque in a whirling coffin, and its aimless, whimsical flight through the void – : "What is it all about?" The question permeates him with dread and anguish, with "ontological despair" and "existential frustration" (Ungersma, 1961, p. 18 ff.). "Angsten" (Kierkegaard) constrains out of him all his puny, piddling hatreds, and petty ambitions in brass and bridge, and fills him with care and compassion for his fellow travellers. In other words, he has become a philosopher, an alienated, nostalgic "cosmopath," and, *eo ipso*, a case for psychologists and psychotherapists, some of whom want to study him and label his "Daseinsweise," others to "unsick" him as well.

This is, in a metaphorical nutshell, the background for the tragicomic encounter of clinical psychology and existential philosophy.

WHY EXISTENTIAL PHILOSOPHY?

"What is it all about?" Mitja (in *The Brothers Karamasov*) felt that though his question may be absurd and senseless, he had to ask just that, and he had to ask it in just that way. Socrates claimed that an unexamined life is not worthy of man. And Aristotle saw man's "proper" goal and "proper" limit in the right exercise of those faculties which are uniquely human. It is commonplace that men, unlike other living organisms, are not equipped with built-in mechanisms for automatic maintenance of their existence; man would perish immediately if he were to respond to his environment exclusively in terms of unlearned, biologically-inherited forms of behaviour. In order to survive at all, the human being must discover how various things around him and in him operate. And the place he occupies in the present scheme of organic creation is the consequence of having learned how to exploit his intellectual capacities for such discoveries. Hence, more human than any other human endeavour is the attempt at a *total* view of man's function – or malfunction – in the Universe, his possible place and importance in the *widest conceivable cosmic scheme*, in other words: the attempt to answer, or at least articulate, whatever questions are entailed in the dying groan of ontological despair: *What is it all about*. ... This may well prove biologically harmful or even fatal to man. Intellectual honesty and man's high spiritual demands for order and meaning, may drive him to the deepest antipathy to life and necessitate, as one existentialist chooses to express it: "a *no* to this wild, banal, grotesque and loathsome carnival in the world's graveyard" (Zapffe, 1941, p. 503).

Philosophy and suicide have always been typical upper-class phenomena. Both presuppose some minimum amount of leisure time and a certain level of education. The recent desperate need among psychologists and psychotherapists for a "Philosophy of Man and his Fate" arises from the general improvement of living conditions and education. As David Riesman puts it (1960, p. 3 ff.): fifty years ago there was no problem as to what would constitute a *cure* or at least a step in a more "healthy" direction. Freud's patients were largely suffering from heavy hysteria, dramatic paralysations, inability to talk or move. The more advanced countries today have caught up with many Utopian ideals concerning economical poverty and unquestionably psychopath-creating, authoritarian family structures, while at the same time beliefs in gods and devils, heaven and hell, angels and immortality have almost vanished. In these countries people suffer less from nightmarish misery than from the more subtle disorders previously buried by the harsh and bitter struggle for existence. The clinical psychologists are unexpectedly confronted with patients who by all *social* criteria are tremendously successful and well adjusted. They have just – prematurely, as it were – anticipated the dying groan, Ivan Ilych's three-days-long shriek (Tolstoy, 1946): what is it all about? Thus what once was an obviously commendatory endeavour, to abolish poverty and ignorance, is slowly raising before us a problem – a problem, it seems, the severity of which will increase in correlation with increase in leisure time and socio-economic and educational "progress," *viz.*: the most humanly relevant question of all: *What does it mean to be man, what is the lot of mankind in cosmos?* What once was an object of idle contemplation, has recently become a concern for economists and theologians, for scientists and creative artists, psychologists, psychiatrists and educators.

VIA HISTORICA AD EXISTENTIALISMUM

The earliest idle contemplators, the so-called "Ionian philosophers of Nature," were rather naive and optimistic. "... they wondered originally at the obvious difficulties," says Aristotle[2] "then advanced and stated difficulties about the greater

2 *Metaphysica A2*, 982b, 13–7.

matters, *e.g.*, about the moon and the sun and the stars, and then about the genesis of the whole universe." The first severe criticism sets in with Heraclitus who, as everybody knows, became rather frightfully obsessed by the insight that everything changes; and some of his successors even more by the alleged consequences of this observation: "Nothing exists!" (in the Parmenides' sense of "exist"). Take for example the oil-capital of Canada, the city of Edmonton! I want to make a statement about Edmonton; but before I have managed to utter or even think: "Edmonton," that to which I intended to refer to by "Edmonton" has already changed. And since I don't want to use the same proper name to designate different objects, I might as well desist from making use of it altogether, throw up my hands and admit that there is no such thing as Edmonton. The ingenious counter-question is this: "But what *is* it then, this Edmonton of which you say: it does not exist? Clearly you must have had something in your mind." And the answer is: "Yes. That is precisely where I have it: *in my mind*. The 'Edmonton' in my mind, the concept, the form, the *idea of 'Edmonton'*, that is the Edmonton, the only Edmonton that exists with an endurance ("invariance") that permits a classification." It is quite easy to see how such an attitude, with the assistance of Pauline Christianity, might predispose the philosophers for that radical de-evaluation of all earthly sense-experiences which characterize so many of the most predominant trends of thought during the Medieval Ages and the first centuries thereafter. I shall refer to this type of philosophizing as "brain-philosophy." To a brain philosopher, sense experiences are either of negligible significance, totally irrelevant, or represent a more or less serious obstacle to knowledge perfection. Already Zeno (of Elea) may be used to illustrate a rather typical form of brain philosophy when he *proved* the fundamental impossibility of motion. "You claim that you can move?" asks Zeno: "tell me then: *where* does this alleged 'movement' take place?" It seemed to Zeno that there were only two possibilities: (i) Either you "move" *where you are*, in which case you are *not* moving, you are standing still; (ii) or you do this "moving" *where you are not*. But how can you do anything, let alone moving, where you are not? Diogenes from Sinope is said to have reacted to this lecture by silently leaving his seat, strolling around for a while, and then sitting down again. He undoubtedly meant by this to introduce a contra-argument to the Zenoist standpoint. But Zeno's response is obvious: "Thank you, my dear Diogenes," he would reply, "for this convincing illustration of my point of view. I take it that you all observed Diogenes perform what we have here called a notion, and which I have just shown to be in principle impossible. So let this be a lesson to you: don't ever believe your own eyes or any other sense-experience! They are bound to deceive you." The paradigm brain-philosopher is traditionally pictured: blindfolded in his ivory tower, meditating absolute and eternal forms in a world of abstract ideas.

Diogenes, on the other hand, may be seen as representing an alternative philosophical attitude, *viz.* what we shall call "the *eye-philosophy*".

As its first most typical exponent, Hippocrates, "the father of medicine," is usually mentioned. And this is no pure coincidence. It is commonly accepted as advisable for a physician to observe the patient before diagnosing. Few of us, I'm sure, would have much confidence in a brain surgeon who performed his operation blindfolded, concentrating on eternal forms. This truism drove Hippocrates to the other extreme. He warned against almost any form of theorizing, and advised his students to confine themselves to take down in their protocols all the observed symptoms of the patient *and nothing more*. These *protocol sentences* are the only things that can be known: 10.35 a.m.: Skin pallid, urine colourless, faeces grey.

What a distance to the noble meditator in his ivory tower! And yet, the two have *one* thing in common: their detachment from the external world, their attitude of "objective" non-commitment, their lack of emotional engagement. The doctor continues unruffled with his protocol: 10:45 a.m.: Pulse and respiration almost imperceptible; 10.48 a.m.: The death struggle has begun; 11.02 a.m.: No pulse, no respiration. The patient is dead. The undertaker can take over.

What thus seems to permit the eye-philosopher to take an equally detached attitude to what he perceives visually, as does the brain-philosopher to absolute forms, is the uniqueness of the vertebrate eye; it is not really a sense organ, as it were. It is part of the brain. Already Augustinus points to this exceptional position of our eyes in relation to our more peripheral sense organs. And he goes on to show how all the other senses imitate vision! "Ad oculos enim proprie videre pertinet. Ultimur autem hoc verbo etiam in ceteris sensibus cum eos ad cognoscendum intendium ... Dicimus autem non solum, vide quid luceat, quod soli oculi sentire possent, sed etiam vide quid sonet; vide quid oleat, vide quid sapiat, vide quam durum sit."[3] The whole brain-eye-distinction as an indication of two different epistemological attitudes and two different approaches to knowledge perfection – rationalism and empiricism – has thus been reduced to a mere matter of degrees. The brain-philosophy dominating up to the Renaissance and in Descartes, Leibniz, Spinoza, Hegel, and others, the eye-philosophy breaking through with the Renaissance (and its stress on bodily lust and sense-experiences) with Leonardo da Vinci, Galilei, etc., and later the British empiricists from Bacon to Locke, Hume, Mill ...

Existentialism as a "Heart Philosophy"
More conspicuous than the brain-eye-distinction is the ethical and epistemological distance from brain-eye philosophy on one hand, to, what one on the other hand might call "heart-philosophy." Generally speaking, heart-philosophy presents itself as a romantic reaction to the "existential lethargy" which allegedly characterizes the attitude of brain-eye-philosophers. It is a plea for a dynamic, Heraclitean world view in which human life is more than a mere puppet show, a plea for freedom, initiative, decision, responsibility, novelty, adventure, risk, chance, romance – a world which, with effort, we can fashion to our purposes and ideals, a world where *anything is possible*.[4] The existential "heart" philosopher refuses to submit to any external or internal forces demanding his obedience, such as: "logical laws," "laws of nature," "scientific laws," "ethical laws," "logical truths," "factual truths," "sense-data," "the structure of language," etc. They may all be worth considering,

3 *Confessiones*, Lib. X, Cap. 35.
4 See Thilly, Frank, "Romanticism and Rationalism". *Philosophical Review*, March 1913, and Tennessen, Herman, *Language Analysis and Empirical Semantics*. Edmonton: University of Alberta Bookstore, 1964, pp. 291–303.

but *the choice, the decision* is the individual's alone. And he must be thoroughly deprived of any pretext to avoid this responsibility.

I once gave a course in logic for high-ranking NATO officers. I suggested a possible procedure according to which one first has to make clear what the choice is all about, then evaluate (in some systematic manner) the consequences of various possible decisions, and then *make the choice.* I took a concrete example of a commander on board a Norwegian torpedo boat, who, under a war with Russia, discovers a huge Russian battleship helplessly cooped up behind a neutral tanker in the end of a narrow fjord on Greenland. I asked the officers first to map out the various possible choice-alternatives. But, to my surprise, they protested violently. I had, they claimed, attacked the problem from the wrong end. It turned out that what they resented was that *they* were going to make the choice. They did not like it a bit. And here is how they managed to avoid decision and responsibility. (i) There are, it seems, such things as "militarily relevant data." (ii) With each torpedo boat follows what one might call a "direction for usage."

What the commander is trained to do is just to compare direction and data; and the only correct course of action emerges more or less automatically out of this activity.

A somewhat similar experience came out of a course for lawyers who, at one time or another, had served as judges. They wanted to conceive of themselves as some sort of passive media, especially trained to compare a restricted set of juridically relevant data with a set of legal codes. This comfortable philosophy would permit the judge to send his fellow beings to long prison terms or economic ruin, with his face radiating good conscience, and without spoiling his appetite for a juicy steak at lunch.

The commander and the judge were both, the existentialists may contend, victims of brain-eye-philosophy. It is the task of the existential philosopher to break this spell, and awaken us all to come out and face our choice situations instead of cowardly hiding behind natural and logical "laws" and ratio-empirical "data."

An important obstacle here, however, is the ordinary language, the everyday prose. The heart-philosopher needs an extraordinary language, a poetic-dramatic transmitter in order to convey adequately to himself or his fellow beings what the choice is really about. Ordinary language, "die Umgangssprache," "das Gerede," represents "the public worldliness," "the intersubjective world," "das Man" (in Heidegger's terminology). It lulls us in to this platitudinal world of small-talk *where everything is taken for granted*: life, death, the world, and Man's fate in it, the society, the language. No reason to wonder or worry: everything is what it is and not another thing. The world is what it seems to be to a dry, unimaginative, down to earth, square-headed stuffed-shirt about mid-morning after a good night's rest. And as for such questions as what it *means* to live and die – there's nothing to it, it is commonplace, almost everybody does it. We need a poetic-dramatic, or, at least, a new and exotic transmitter to break through this barrier of ordinary language prose and realize through bones and marrow *what Man's Lot is like*. We are thrown into an absurdly indifferent world of stocks and stones and stars and emptiness. Our "situation" is that of a man who falls out of the Empire State Building. Any attempt at "justifying" our brief, accelerating fall, the inconceivably short interlude between our breath-taking realization of our "situation" and our inexorable total destruction, the "Big Hit on Broadway", is bound to be equally ludicrous, – *i.e.*, whether we choose to say: (*a*) "this is actually quite comfortable as long as it lasts, let us make the best of it", or: (*b*) "let us at least do something useful while we can," and we start counting the windows on the building. In any event: both attitudes presuppose an ability to *divert* ourselves from realizing our desperate "situation," abstract, as it were, every single moment of the "fall" out of its irreparable totality, cut our life up into small portions with petty, short time-span goals.

So much for the heart-philosophical concepts of "true" and "truth." As for "value," we are confronted with the chasm between (i) an authentic life worthy of Man, lived in clear and penetrating awareness of its utter absurdity, and (ii) a fraudulent, illusive life, lived in pleasant self-deception, essentially indistinguishable from the life of any other self-complacent, giddy-witted pig with some sense for cleanliness and indoor plumbing. The choice implies the unconditional acceptance of the value of *human dignity* at the cost of traditional, axiological objectives as, *e.g., adjustment, success, happiness, peace of mind*, etc. (Marcel, 1963 and 1964).

Existentialism and Knowledge Perfection
Another question, independent upon the acceptance of heart-philosophical truths and values, but of obvious didactic significance, is the question of whether such insights *can be taught*. In other words, we are approaching the concepts of "understanding" and "knowledge-perfection."

It has been usual to distinguish between a perfection of knowledge "in width" and "in depth," and so well known are these expressions that any further explication is hardly necessary. They reflect the elementary, psychological, relationship between attention span and attention concentration, between the man who knows almost nothing about almost everything and the man who knows almost everything about almost nothing. A two-dimensional space analogy will suffice to illustrate this relationship and the kind and degree of knowledge within such a *non*-engaged field of discourse. The so-called "engaged" discourse, introduced in heart philosophy, admits of a third component which we may tentatively designate "the degree of integration of knowledge." How integrated is our knowledge? An example will indicate what may be meant by the expressions "integrated" and "integration" in this connection.

During the Finnish-Russian War of 1939, the Finns caught a Russian spy behind their own lines. It was an obvious case. The spy confessed and was to be immediately executed. He knew that he would be shot at dawn, knew it, as well as anything can be known. Therefore, he appeared stoically in court. He knew the outcome. There was not the shadow of a doubt. The court scene was a theatre, a bureaucratic performance, demanded in every community founded on the rule of law, but ridiculously superfluous in his case. And still the stage does not leave him entirely untouched. Against his own will he gradually gets involved in the proceedings. When finally the death sentence is pronounced, he *collapses* completely. What on earth had happened? He knew the outcome with absolute certainty. He could not know it better. We should want to say: the spy *knows about* his imminent death now, in a *new* and *terrifying* way. He has suddenly obtained an insight, a knowledge which *penetrates* him, goes through bones and marrow and violently shakes up the total personality structure into its deepest and darkest labyrinths. This difference, this change in the attitude of the accused is what, according to a heart philosophical suggestion for language, may be described as "an increased integration of the spy's knowledge of his imminent death" (Kaila, 1935; Kern, 1962).

By the same token we should probably all answer the heart philosopher's demand for facing up to our fate by saying: "Sure I know I am going to die! All men are mortal you know," and all that. When confronted with a questionnaire asking: *Are you going to die?* we should, most likely without exceptions, all cross off in the right box, the box for "yes," and not for a moment consider "no," "I don't know" or "refuse to answer." But this question remains: do we know about our death the way the spy knew it (*a*) *before*, or (*b*) *after* the death sentence was pronounced? Unfortunately this "integration" (or "interiorizing," "internalization," "empathizing") of knowledge *cannot be taught* in any ordinary sense of teaching. The educator should have to resort to poetry and drama in order to break through the barrier of everyday prose, platitudinal small-talk, and superficial chatter. And only if this is didactically possible shall I ever see myself as I am:

> Me, like a perambulating
> Vegetable, patched with inconsequential
> Hair, looking out of two small jellies for the means
> Of life, balanced on collapsible legs, my sex
> No beauty but a blemish to be hidden
> Behind judicious rags, driven and scorched
> By boomerang rages and lunacies which never
> Touch the accommodating artichokes
> Or the seraphic strawberry, beaming in its bed:
> I defend myself against pain and death by pain
> And death, and make the world go round, they tell me,
> By one of my less lethal appetites:
> Half this grotesque life I spend in a state
> Of slow decomposition, using
> The name of unconsidered God as a pedestal
> On which I stand and bray that I'm best
> Of beasts, until under some patient
> Moon or other I fall to pieces, like
> A cake of dung.
>
> CHRISTOPHER FRY

A priceless example of Man's unwillingness to accept his fate in general, and his ephemerality in particular, is offered in Giradoux's *Amphitryon 38* (Acte Premier, Scène v, pp. 41, 42). Jupiter desires to seduce Alcmène, not as a god, but in flesh, as it were, as a man. Mercury examines him to ensure that the metamorphosis actually has taken place.

MERCURE   Avez-vous le désir de séparer vos cheveux par une raie et de les maintenir par une crême de Bryl?
JUPITER   En effet, je l'ai.
MERCURE   Avez-vous l'idée que vous pourrez mourir un jour?
JUPITER   Non. Que mes amis mourront, pauvres amis, hélas oui! Mais pas moi.
MERCURE   Alors vous voilà vraiment homme! ... Allez-y!⁵

Who Knows, What, How?

The heart *versus* brain-eye-philosophical controversy is in one respect a rather interesting one. The analytically oriented philosophers accuse the existentialists of not knowing what they are talking about because of their exotic, imprecise language (see Carnap's famous critique of Heidegger!). The existentialists return the compliment: analytic philosophers do not know what they are talking about, because of their lack of engagement, commitment. And this dimension of knowledge imperfection does not only prevent the analytic philosophers from realizing what Man's Lot is like, etc., but has a direct ethical relevance. A brain-eye philosopher, so say the existentialists, may have worked out the clearest, strictest set of moral rules and norms, and they may have no impact whatsoever on the philosopher's moral behaviour – as (over-)dramatized in the following little skit.

The professor sits immersed in his own work of constructing the ethically most valuable norm system of philosophical history, an ideal and effective combination of Spinoza and Gandhi.
A careful knock on the door. The professor does not react. Still a few knocks. Then the door is opened.
The stranger (with timid voice): Could the professor tell me when the post office closes today?
The professor (without looking up): Get out! I'm thinking.
The stranger: I should just have liked so much to know when the post office ...
The professor (as before, lifts one hand and points): Out!
The stranger: Oh dear Mr Professor, I'll go immediately, it was only the closing time ... You see ... it was only a package ... merchandise ... sample without value ... And then I knew that you had these letter scales ... And then I thought ... if they are open that late ... in the office, I mean ...
The professor, has, during the stranger's monologue, fiddled with his left hand in the desk drawer. Still without looking up from his work, his arm comes out of the drawer with a 38 caliber Smith and Wesson pistol. Finally, his gaze is torn away from the paper. He looks at the stranger and points in the same direction with the gun. A sharp report. The stranger collapses. The professor continues undisturbed with his work on the norm system.
    Some time passes. A door is opened in the background, and a cute young girl rushes into the room with a tennis racket in her hand.
The young girl: Time for tennis!

---

5 The paradoxical fact that man "knows" that he must die, but not *in bones and marrow*, has been repeatedly pointed out by both philosophers and psychiatrists.

Professor: Oh, is it that day today? I'll be there in a moment, dear.

The young girl discovers the stranger: Gosh, here's a body!

The professor: Oh, that. That was just a chap who was disturbing me. Impossible to get him to shut up while I was thinking.

The young girl: You don't mean to say that you have shot him ...

The professor nods absentmindedly.

The young girl: But isn't this an – er – action which – er – violated your norm system?

The professor (obviously animated and interested): No, you don't say! That I'll have to investigate.

(Pulls logarithm tables and slide rule out of the drawer. Gets up and chooses out of the shelves to the left a green bunch of IBM cards, places them in the IBM machine in the background, starts the distributor. One sees the professor excitedly noting the numbers which appear in their little windows. Suddenly the distributor stops. The professor runs across the floor with the notes, strikes a few numbers on the adding machine, compares results with a table on the wall to the right. And finally he turns excitedly towards the girl.)

The professor: Imagine, you guessed correctly! It did actually violate my norm system to kill the man. Did I not find that out quickly? There is no norm system like it, you see. The subsumption control took exactly thirty seconds. And absolutely reliable, that means ...

The young girl: It's the most ...

The professor: Well, well, we'd better get off. We're paying for the court.

Exeunt the girl and the professor.

Curtain.

This skit is meant to serve as an example of an extreme brain-eye-philosophical disintegration. The professor does not feel ethically obligated to follow his norm system. It does not engage him except in the most exterior cortical centres which in his case have little or no communication with the deeper, action-determining mechanisms. His ethical convictions are not interiorized, internalized, not sufficiently integrated. They have no *existential* validity.

The existentialists, however, may be said to be in another predicament. They over-emphasize existential validity, the exotic, poetic-dramatic, through-bones-and-marrow-conveyance of their messages, to such an extent that they lose sight of, or ignore the tenability, the "objective truth," if one wants, of the cognitive, epistemic (thought) content of these messages. Thus, during the reading of, say, Jean-Paul Sartre's celebrated novel The Wall (Le Mur), one can become deeply impressed by the wasteland and extreme distance between human minds, which has often occupied authors and dramatists through the years, not least in the 20th century. One is possessed by a terrible vision: "the loneliness of man," "lonely as a ship in a starless night" – and by a prophetic premonition: "and thus it will always be ..." Until one day one renews one's acquaintance with Leonid Andréjev's *The Seven Who Were Hanged*. And the mind is suddenly opened to a new insight, one diametrically opposite, it might seem. One feels forced by Andréjev to conclude that human beings are indeed able to understand each other, feel with each other, identify themselves with each other, and this to such an extent that these Andréjev's seven rebels cannot, as it were, be hanged apart and individually on the gallows. So it is also possible for human beings to be human towards each other.

If such types of literary descriptions, as for instance Sartre's and Andréjev's, are persistently emaciated by rational and ruthless analysis, the ready-peeled, objective skeleton will say something about the impossibility or possibility of human contact in stress-situations or during extreme circumstances of all kinds. It is clear that these dry, peeled-off formulations make it simpler for the cool and detached analyst to find effective methods for controlling the rules which apply to inter-human contact, the identification with other people, people-orientation, and even enable the analyst to draw practical inferences, of value for applied psychology, the "counselling" psychologist. However, the dilemma remains, not as a logico-philosophical paradox, but as a mere heuristic-didactic predicament. Is it practically possible to communicate in a useful way the course-of-life suggestions which such "precise" formulations may have been intended to transmit, without lowering the level of preciseness, and stressing empathy rather than clarity? Rather than "precising" language, we may have to "break through language in order to touch life," and turn the communicants involved into "victims, burnt at the stake, signalling through the flames" (Artaud, 1958). This may account for, say, Sartre's resort to drama for an empathetic transmission of his contentions. It is a question, however, if it vindicates (or can even be said to excuse) the general continental grandiloquence and the particularly pompous teutonic turgidity, in Heidegger's high-flown, glutinated conglomerate of bombastic neologisms. In a context of German philosophy, Heidegger's stylistic rhythm has the peculiarly mesmerizing effect of kettle-drums, finding a short-cut, as it were, from the receiver's tympanum directly to his volitional layers. Whereas the same style appears monstrously ludicrous in English, and within a clinical psychology frame of reference.

WHY CLINICAL PSYCHOLOGY?

"*Clinical* (Psychology)*"* is here used in a wide sense, including theory, observation and examination for diagnostic as well as for therapeutic purposes. In this sense of "clinical" there is hardly anything written that can plausibly be said to be: "existential" or: "phenomenological," and, at the same time: "non-clinical" psychology. True enough, after the two first expressions became such a fad, quite a few articles have appeared claiming to be both within non-clinical psychology and within existentialism or (now, more and more often) phenomenology. But in no case are "existentialist" and "phenomenological" used in a clearly philosophically relevant sense. On the other hand, there are works, like the early Sartrean essay: "La Transcendance de l'égo: Ésquisse d'une description phénoménologique."[6] This is not psychology, but basically "*eine Ausseinandersetzung*" with Edmund Husserl, whom Sartre accuses of self-contradiction. Or better, Sartre defends the

6 *Recherches Philosophique*, VI, 1936–7. The American translation (NY, 1957) has as subtitle: *An existentialist theory of consciousness.*

early Husserl (*Untersuchungen*) against the later Husserl (*Ideen*). The essay is only psychologically interesting in so far as it throws light on Sartre's concept: "consciousness", which is commonly considered incompatible with whatever Freud is referring to by the same expression. However (*a*) in the above indicated wide sense of "clinical," Sartre should be seen as concerned with clinical psychology, in so far as he is interpreted to attempt to settle an account with Freud. (*b*) What Sartre is doing to "conscious(ness)" is neither philosophically nor psychologically exciting: a banal rhetorical device, *viz*.: dilution of the concept, is employed to permit Sartre to speak a language where the possibility of "making sense," as it were, of "unconscious" or "subconscious" human actions is clearly ruled out. In two other publications (1948, 1964), supposedly dealing with "imagination," Sartre "proves" that eideticism in the Jaenschian (1931, 1933, 1938), not the Husserlian, sense, is logically impossible! It is a hair-raising example of extreme, dogmatic, brain-philosophy with a contempt for empirical evidence not surpassed even by Zeno in his (fictitious) disputation with Diogenes.

The Diagnostics

It has often been considered the major turning point in the history of psychoanalysis, when Elizabeth von R. reproached Freud for urging and pressing her to remember, instead of permitting a free flow of associations. This started the non-directive, client-centred analysis; never clearer, more succinctly expressed and accentuated, than in Freud's own works. He warns, in *Ratschläge für den Artzt bei der psychoanalytischen Behandlung* (1912), against the understandable ambition to make something particularly excellent out of the client, and prescribe for him the highest aims in life. In *Wege der psychoanalytischen Therapie* (1919) the purpose of psycho-analysis is described in terms of the clients (patients): self-completion, self-fulfillment, self-actualization. The analyst, says Freud, should chime in with the old French surgeon: "Je le pansai, Dieu le guérit."

The trends within clinical psychology, where this Freudian *epoché* (*i.e.*, suspension of all judgments) *vis-à-vis* the clients has been emphasized or furthered, shall here be referred to as: *diagnostic* (clinical psychology).

Sartre's analyses, from his early enquiry into Baudelaire, till his more recent *magnum opus* on Genet, are typically diagnostic (in this sense of "diagnostic"), *i.e.*, there is no criticism, no blame, or judgment, just a presentation à la Guy de Maupassant's: *Une Vie*.

The most extreme diagnostics among modern psychiatrists are Ludwig Binswanger and his followers, who are describing their activity as: "*Daseinsanalyse*" (an analysis of the patient's "mode of being" or "beingness"). They seem by and large uninfluenced by Sartre, and descend more directly from Husserl and Heidegger – in particular from the Heidegger of *Sein und Zeit*, *i.e.*, the existentialist position which, popularized, is conveyed in the introduction to the present paper. The most conspicuous Heideggerian influence on the diagnostics is, unfortunately, his thundering style. Heidegger's "hermeneutics of Man," his "Daseinsanalytik" or "existenziale Analytik" is defined by Binswanger as "die philosophisch-phänomenologische Erhellung der apriorischen oder transcendentalen

Struktur des Daseins als In-der-weltsein." And this is not even a representative example! In spite of the fact that the literature available on "Daseinsanalyse," or "onto-analysis," is usually fascinating, often also ghastly and grotesque, one cannot help wondering if the apparent indifference is as genuine as it seems on the surface. There is a nagging suspicion that the diagnostics are exploiting Heidegger's exotic language in order to "*keep talking*," and thus keep calm and unaffected by the horror of the bottomless *abyssus humanae conscientiae* with which they are incessantly confronted. The Freudian passivity, patience, and tolerance have in *Daseinsanalyse* been extrapolated into the phenomenological "reduction," "bracketing": the *epoché*, the complete abstinence from judgment, by means of which the absolute truth is revealed (*àlethéia*). Binswanger takes an attitude to the suicide, committed by his most famous patient, Ellen West, which was once described by Kierkegaard as characteristic of the aesthetic stage in life.[7] He seems like a Linnaeus, anxious only to find out what kind of plant he has at hand, so that he can give a thorough description and diagnosis. Sometimes the case is fairly obvious, the specimen is subsumed under a certain known class. But not too rarely does this Linnaeus find a plant so unique it deserves its own name.

One of the rather unconventional cases described by one diagnostic is Roland Kuhn's *Rudolf*. It turns out that what Rudolf really desires is a life of thrills ("ein Leben in der Spannung"). He has "eine vertikale Daseinsachse" which permits him to oscillate between the "die verwesende Welt des Kellers" and "die glänzende Welt der Strasse," or, it is also said: between *necrophobia* and *necrophilia*. When Rudolf is at his best he copulates with hogs in the moment when they are butchered. And it is quite clear that this is by no means a cause for raised eyebrows. On the contrary, what Kuhn's presentation seems to convey is rather a: "So what? Doesn't everybody?" This makes for a not too overly conventional, petit bourgeois psychotherapy. Recently a Swedish psychiatrist of this school, Lars Ullerstam[8], was touring Europe, in an attempt to reduce the shortage of corpses for necrophiles by persuading his audience to bequeath, not just eyes and kidneys, etc., but the whole body, to Necrophiles Anonymous. The underlying assumption is, of course, that we should not give in to the middle class, puritanistic, prejudice, according to which certain (conventional) forms of (say, sexual) life is in any way preferable, "healthier". ...[9]

Medard Boss[10] extends the total ethical indifference of existential analysis "both

7 *Cf.* Henrik Ibsen's poem: *Paa vidderne!*

8 *De erotiska minoriteterna.* Stockholm: Bonnier 1964.

9 For examples of predominantly "diagnostic" (or "diagnosticoforme") clinical psychology and its existentialist-phenomenological genealogy, see e.g., Astrada *et al.*, 1949; Binswanger, 1941, 1951, 1964, and "Der Fall Ellen West," *Schweizer Archiv für Neurologie u. Psychiatrie*, 1944, vol. 53, pp. 255–77; vol. 54, pp. 69–117, 330–60; 1945, vol. 55, pp. 16–40; Blauner, 1957; Boss, 1957; Clive, 1964; Elkin, 1961; Ellenberger, 1957; Kuhn, 1949; Laing, 1960; Maslow, 1962; May, 1958; Sartre, 1953; Sonnemann, 1954; Stern, 1953.

10 Boss, Medard, *The Analysis of Dreams.* New York: Philosophical Library, 1958, p. 119.

to psycho-therapeutic techniques and to practical consequences and aims." This may look most impressive as a phenomenological programme (with its "bracketing" and "epoché"), but is certainly not consistently carried out in practice.

The Prelatics

Even the most extremist diagnostics (Binswanger, Boss, Buytendijk, Kuhn) cannot be said to be completely freed from hortatory tendencies. The frequent references to "resoluteness," "authenticity," etc. (laudatory), and "Alltäglichkeit," "mauvaise foi," "despondency," etc. (derogatory) are unerring indications in this direction. However, the whole scene changes completely, when turning from any dubious diagnostic to typical exponents for what I shall here call "prelactics"[11].

During the first few years after the Second World War, a tendency to secede from the orthodox Freudian passivity and all-understanding tolerance, and return to a more expostulative old-fashioned Victorian attitude was vaguely detectable among psychotherapists. "Ah, don't give me that. Pull yourself together young man and save your silly excuses! You know you can if you want ... ." It wouldn't be too surprising if this psychotherapeutic metamorphosis were in fact rooted in some early (mis-)interpretations of post-war existentialists, whose main incentive, so it often seemed, was to fire a rocket in the rear of their fellow beings and shock them out of their "existential lethargy." Frankl (1963, p. 152) popularizes the difference between classic, Freudian, psychoanalysis and his own so-called "logotherapy" as follows: "In psychoanalysis the patient lies on a couch and must tell things that are disagreeable to tell." "In logotherapy the client sits erect and must hear things that are disagreeable to hear." This, of course, is not anything entirely unfamiliar to psychologists. The earliest Reicheans[12] were, perhaps, less verbose, but certainly more viciously aggressive in their attacks on patients' "character armour" and "neurotic equilibrium" than any of the rather nice and amiable prelatics – from Karen Horney, Carl Rogers, Maslow, Jourard[13] and Jahoda[14], to Ungersma and Viktor Frankl. In point of fact, they seem all rather anxious to please. They have – more so than any philosopher – really taken to heart McTaggart's famous line: "The utility of metaphysics is to be found in the comfort it can give us." When, for instance, a patient is found to be uncomfortably aware of his finitude, he suffers from "sickness unto death" or "Sein zum Tode," then, maintains Frankl, psychodynamic

---

11 Again, it is by no means easy to draw the line. The references section suggests some more or less typical examples of "Prelaticism": Allers, 1922, 1961 (?); Arnold, M. B. and Gasson, John A., *The human person*, New York: Ronald Press, 1954; Frankl, 1958, 1963, and 1967, and *The doctor and the soul, an introduction to logotherapy*, New York: Knopf, 1955; Fromm, 1942, 1947; Marcel, 1963, 1964; Maslow, 1962; May, 1961; Nikelly, 1964; Ungersma, 1961.

12 See, e.g., Reich, W., *Orgasmusreflex, Muskelhaltung und Körperausdruck*, Kbh. 1937, and *Character analysis* (English translation), 3rd edition. New York, 1949, Orgone Institute Press, p. 310.

13 Jourard, Sidney M., *The transparent self*. Princeton; Van Nostrand, 1964.

14 Jahoda, Marie, *Current concepts of positive mental health*. New York: Basic Books, 1959.

interpretations (!) simply will not do to "tranquilize away" his dread and anguish ("*Angsten*"). The only thing that can help here is: "philosophical understanding" (Frankl, 1958, p. 193). The task of the clinical psychologist is to determine the "beingness," the "mode of being," the "Daseinsweise" proper to the patient in question. It is then up to the therapist to prescribe the myths or metaphysics that will "unsick" (Maslow, 1962, p. 5) this particular "cosmopath," and to couch him into his metaphysic, his "philosophical" understanding, with such satanic cunning and deceiving finesse ("pull rather than push"!), that it gives the patient the pleasant illusion of having discovered "the meaning of (his) life" himself. In other words: this alleged "new approach in pastoral psychology" (Ungersma, 1961) is in theory and practice indistinguishable from the applied psychology of Dr Relling in Henrik Ibsen's *Wild Duck*, who furnished all his friends and acquaintances (of whom he suspected that they otherwise were liable to crack up, were they to face the horror of truth) with carefully selected, tailor-made "life-lies." The only difference is this: Dr Relling is pictured as a disillusioned, sophisticated high-brow, a warm-hearted, sentimental cynic, a "knight of infinite resignation" (Kierkegaard). The prelatics are completely devoid of this air of sophistication (which, incidentally, the Husserl-Heideggerian thunder-language to some extent seems to lend to the diagnostics). With open, unsuspecting enthusiasm, the prelatics devote themselves to their indisputably commendable mission: to save their fellow men from such pernicious views of life that it may cause "ontological uncertainty," "existential despair (frustration, vacuum)" by providing them with an impregnable metaphysical armour. The fact that a patient is classified as mentally or emotionally sick prevents the psychotherapist from enquiring into the possibility of whether (or to what extent) his patient may be cognitively right. During the last World War it became rather common to equip allied reconnaissance planes with some completely colour-blind observers, as it appeared that "patients" suffering from achromatopsia seemed on occasions to have a special knack for discovering concealed German V-2 positions. It is, by the same token, perfectly possible that a person with "thanatophobia," "existential frustration," "ontological despair" or, simply, "sub-clinical depression" may, because of his abnormal condition, be in a better position to look through the camouflage of life that still is deceiving the "healthy" psychotherapists.

On Suification in General

Among the most impressive existentialist writings are those of Peter Wessel Zapffe (1941, 1961, see the subsequent section). The lucidity of the presentation is only surpassed by the ruthless consistency in his existentialist position, his so-called "Biosophy." He sides with the other existentialists in considering self-awareness – awareness of one's own existence and its conditions – the differentiate earmark of Man, that which sets the human animal out from all other beings. Man's predicament is this: on the one hand we have Man's high spiritual demands for justice, order and meaning; on the other hand his, in principle, unlimited capacity for insight and knowledge-perfection, *plus* his intellectual honesty, constantly sharpened by increased sensibility of the most refined mechanisms of human self-deception, all combine to drive Man to face his own desperately incorrigible fate of futility, satiating him with the most sickening aversion from life in general,[15] human existence, and his own *"Dasein"* in particular. Man – if he desires *some* degree of psychological health – must either give up his high spiritual demands, *or* his unlimited capacities for knowledge-perfection. *Or*: he must overcome his inhibitions against deceiving himself. In short: he must resign *vis-à-vis* any attempt towards "self realization" (Jourard), "self-actualization" or "full-humanness" (Maslow), and seek himself a happier idol: the happy-go-lucky pig, grunting with whole-hearted contentment, and a complete peace of mind, with no demands beyond the garbage, a "vital" and "useful" life in unawareness of his existence and destiny. This is man's dilemma; this is the existential choice in biosophic perspective. The ordinary, "healthy" man tries to evade this choice. He may be paying lip service to the idea of humanization (towards "full-humanness" etc.), while at the same time surreptitiously practising *suification*[16] by exploiting the traditional ontological hebetants, i.e., work, religion, metaphysics, alcohol, drugs, lobotomy, everydayness, noseyness, external sensations, ordinary language prose, platitudinal small-talk or chatter, role-playing, role-expectancies, social norms, rigidity, insanity, or conformity.[17]

There cannot be much doubt that among the many means of suification, the safest long-time ontological hebetants are labour, ("useful") physical or mental exertion, and non-integrated religion (like, say, Søren Kierkegaard's contemporary Danish Lutheranism). Either one may be used as opium for the People. "Work," reads the Constitution of the USSR (1936), "is the duty of every citizen, according to the principle: ... He who does not work, neither shall he eat. ..." "Produce!" cried Carlyle: "Were it but the pitifulest, infinitesimal fraction of a product, produce it in God's name." The day is not far away[18] when two per cent of the USA population will be able to produce more than the other ninety-eight per cent can possibly consume. The Americans shall have to kill 600 billion more free hours. Leisure counsellors will have more than petty week-end-neuroses on their hands. Aristotle said that a society, unprepared for true leisure, will degenerate in good times. "Too much leisure with too much money has been the dread of societies across the ages. That is when nations cave in." (William Russell according to Bruce, 1965.) Robert Jungk (1952, 1956) has recently devoted a series of television programmes to a study of work addicts and their "leisure-osis" in more advanced societies (Scandinavia), where "die Zukunft hat schon begonnen." His solution is to form

15 "To this wild, banal, grotesque and loathsome carnival in the world's graveyard" (Zapffe, 1941, p. 503).

16 Of *sus*, swine.

17 See p. 1 of Stanley Palluch's enlightening comparison of existentialist (particularly Heidegger's) and modern socio-psychological theories in this area. Compare also Adorno, 1950; Asch, 1956; Frenkel-Brunswik, 1954; Garfinkel, 1959; Israel, 1956; Lynd, 1939; Rokeach, 1960, 1961; Shahn, 1957; Tolstoy, 1946; and Rommetveit, Ragnar, *Social Norms and Roles,* Oslo: Universitetsforlaget, 1953.

18 According to Richard Bellman of Rand Corp. quoted after Bruce, *Saturday Night,* **80** (1965) no. 3, p. 21.

quartets, repair (or build) one's own television sets, or better still, build *completely useless* machines! – something like Calder's "mobiles" with built-in motor. Whether this may be a "better answer" than anything that prelatic psychotherapists can offer, seems to me a toss-up. However: "It doesn't take a psychologist to predict that if we try to fill our leisure time by putting a small, white ball into a slightly larger hole, ..., we will as a people go quietly or noisily nuts" (Clifton Fadiman, see Bruce, 1965, p. 20). The time is close when professional baseball, football, hockey, wrestling and roller-skating just won't do to keep the labour force under a sufficiently permanent sedation. An increasing number is seeking higher thrills – or more thrilling "highs."

Someone said he had a friend who liked to shoot model airplane glue. No one else had heard of that. Sniffing glue, yes; but not shooting it. They had heard of people doing something to paregoric and shoe polish and then shooting it, but the high was reported to be no good. Heroin, of course, was the best. Heroin and a *bombita*. It gave the best high, completely relaxed, not a problem in the world."

"But that's not really the best high," one addict said. "Do you know what the best high *really* is?" The voice was serious. Everyone turned and stayed very quiet to hear, maybe, of a new kind of high that was better than heroin, better than anything else. "The best high" – the voice was low and sombre – "is death." Silence. "Man, that's outta sight, that's somethin' else. Yeah, no feelin' at all." Everyone agreed. The best high of all was death.[19]

The only flaw in this reasoning is simply that although true enough: the dead body has no feelings, there is no one in that body to enjoy this "best of all highs."

Even more unfortunate is the suificating impotence of religious myths. Atheism is extinct in the more advanced parts of the world – for lack of opposites. In Scandinavia a serious atheist is considered a slightly ludicrous bore. The myths are neither pompously condemned nor solemnly repudiated, but rather conceived as sweet and charming subjects for art and poetry – like old fashioned steam engines and antique hot-water bottles. Needless to say, the myths have in this form totally lost all consolation potentialities. They have ceased to serve as suificators.

On the other hand, an excessive stress on logico-rational knowledge perfection may in itself serve as an effective means to hebetate the death-awareness in man, and prevent the courage for dread and anguish to arise. A case *ad rem* is Tolstoy's *The Death of Ivan Ilych*[20]; a most impressive demonstration of the fact that the only decisive, crucial criterion for true insight in, and understanding of, one's own fate is the inwardness, the internalization of the awareness – and *not* tenable evidence or crystalline clarity. Ivan was thoroughly convinced of the logic of the syllogism: "Caius is a man, all men are mortal, therefore Caius is mortal."

That Caius – man in the abstract – was mortal, was perfectly correct, but he was not Caius, not an abstract man, but a creature quite, quite separate from all others. He had been little Ványa, with a mamma and a papa, with Mitya and Volódya, with the toys,

19 Mills, James, "The World of the Needle Park". *Life*, February 26, 1965.
20 *The Short Novels of Tolstoy*. New York: Dial Press, 1946, pp. 409–73.

a coachman and a nurse, afterwards with Kátenka and with all the joys, griefs, and delights of childhood, boyhood, and youth. What did Caius know of the smell of that striped leather ball Ványa had been so fond of? Had Caius kissed his mother's hand like that, and did the silk of her dress rustle so for Caius? Had he rioted like that at school when the pastry was bad? Had Caius been in love like that? Could Caius preside at a session as he did? Caius really was mortal, and it was right for him to die; but for me, little Ványa, Iván Ilych, with all my thoughts and emotions, it's altogether a different matter. It cannot be that I ought to die. That would be too terrible.

Such was his feeling.

If I had to die like Caius I should have known it was so. An inner voice would have told me so, but there was nothing of the sort in me and I and all my friends felt that our case was quite different from that of Caius. And now here it is!" he said to himself. "It can't be. It's impossible! But here it is.

Finally the truth filtered through to Ivan; and suddenly he realized in bones and marrow that his malady was not merely a matter of a diseased kidney, but of leaving behind him as pointless a life as any other life, and facing the ultimate and total annihilation. "For the last three days he screamed incessantly." (*The Death of Ivan Ilych*, p. 415.)

"Nothing," said Søren Kierkegaard, "is to me more ludicrous, than a man who rushes to his job and rushes to his food; when a fly rests on the busy executive's nose, or the draw-bridge (Knippelsbroe) goes up, or a tile falls down and kills him, my heart rejoices with laughter. He reminds me of the old hag, who, when her house was on fire, only saved the poker. What more does he save out of his life's conflagration."

Ivan Ilych was exactly such an assiduous executive. The major "welfare" problem facing modern man, and bewildering the clinical psychologists, is the fact that the enormous expansion of mass-education plus the explosion-like increases of leisure time will permit present and, not the least, future generations to anticipate Ivan Ilych's shriek with a margin of possibly thirty to sixty years, which will make for an awfully long shriek. Clinical psychologists in general, and prelatics in particular, are taking it for granted both that it is psychologically possible to forearm man against such pernicious insights, and that it is morally right (*e.g.*, in accordance with human dignity) to permit, or even tempt or lure man into some sort of more or less attractive, sophisticated, high-brow suifications, even at the expense of full "humanization," intellectual honesty, and although it may mean deliberate personality aberrations and distortions of intellectual processes and evaluations.[21]

---

21 An extensive outline of modern means of suification was presented before a joint meeting of The Canadian Humanities Association and Philosophical Society, October 1965 (and will appear in a forthcoming publication, *Happiness is for the Pigs*); it discussed suificants from body-freezing, the alleged "immortality" of germ-cells, to LSD and "cosmic consciousness," the revival of Illusionistic Vedanta, the Zen notion of *prajna*, etc.

Biosophy and Prelatic Psychotherapy

In a recent, popular, scientific non-fiction, an amateur anthropologist[22] observes that *homo sapiens* has matured as a species by accepting reality unconditionally, how awful or uncertain it may be, "by the capacity to absorb each disillusionment and still keep going." "Nonetheless," he concludes his chapter on The Romantic Fallacy, "should man ever attain a state of total maturity ... in sum, ever achieve the final, total, truthful disillusionment ..., then in all likelihood he would no longer keep going, but would simply lie down, wherever he happened to be, and with a long-drawn sigh return to the oblivion from which he came."

It is the view of Peter Wessel Zapffe, that this is the only decent, dignified thing for man to do, provided man neither intends to give up his intellectual honesty nor his demands for meaning, order and justice in the world.

One of the simplest forms of suification (offering happiness and peace of mind through the most comfortable evasions and illusions) consists in nothing more than just the lowering of the levels of such "meaning demands." A modern man may find satisfaction of his ontological needs in a combination of experience and imagination, in a *pia desideria* for "victory of the supreme good," "eternal peace," "a superior culture," "health and happiness for all men," "longevity," "liberation of unimaginable physical forces," "intergalactical space-flights," etc., one more unbearably exciting than the other. Or he may merely refuse to resent[23] "the haphazard contingency's inanely bizarre value destruction" (Zapffe, 1961, p. 86) and thus reduce the "power-draining," energy-exhausting, exasperating tension between nature and the human mind. It becomes increasingly apparent, as time goes by, that an ethically and ontologically obtuse or indifferent character shall tend to generate more viability, vivacity and zest for life, a richer, more spontaneous *joie de vivre*, than shall a sharper, keener, more sensitive and sagacious ethical consciousness and ontological awareness. Man's ability to "*stand out*" (ek-sistere) and, while still breathing, examine himself and his "total situation," is, from a biosophic view-point an insanely haphazard "short-circuit" in nature, a prerogative with which no other being hitherto has been blessed or cursed. The suification of Man may thus be regarded as a romantic: back to Nature, back to the unadulterated, ontological innocence and security *before* the great short-circuit! A popular suificating metaphysical hebetant is often found in Man's tendency to concentrate all energy and awareness on concrete objects, like the Company, the University, the Community, the Fatherland, Humanity, Culture, Civilization, etc. Other consolations may be sought in the existence of future generations: "My child is my immortality!" The latter position becomes particularly ludicrous, in the light of its inescapable implication: one is committed to see oneself and one's own life as "the answer" to hundreds of generations' dreams, struggles and painful renunciations! Such simple "life lies" (escapes from "life panic") are less and less likely to succeed. Modern men shall have to seek refuge in more solid metaphysical resorts. Typical cases here are the millionaires, who, after a lifelong

22 Robert Ardrey in *African Genesis*. New York: Dell, 1963, p. 145.
23 Let alone burst with boiling rage, or agonized in unbearable despair!

unceasing struggle to amass their millions, finally can settle down in California to enjoy their *otium cum dignitate*, and find neither enjoyment nor dignity, but realize in tormenting panic that: "this was your life ..." They have become a case for psychedelics, (Bishop, 1963) "pastoral" psychologists (Ungersma, 1961), and other prelatic psychotherapists. Their task will be to retard, or, if possible, reverse, their clients' development towards "full-humanness" (Maslow, 1962) and "self-realization," and rather save them from the vertiginously pernicious, insufferable insights into the monstrous absurdity of human life. In a near future I envisage whole generations who will have reached the millionaires' level of disillusionment at a much earlier age. They will shiver in their nakedness under the white, indifferent stars, and cry to psychotherapists for a solid and cosy metaphysical armour. But again there may be some, the true existentialist philosophers, who will rather risk to remain in the chilly out-doors, than to give up a jot of the noble privilege of human "ek-sistence." Here prelatic psychotherapy is ludicrously out of place. Were (say) Frankl to attempt to cure (say) Zapffe from his "existential frustration," "onto-logical despair," or "metaphysic-melancholic clairvoyance," the chances are that Zapffe (rather than "cured") would be baffled by Frankl's high-school-sophomoric philosophizing. "You may be psychologically healthier than I," Zapffe would gladly admit, "but I must insist that I am a better philosopher. A lifelong search for a meaning of Life in general, and of my life in particular, has led me – reluc-tantly, but with cataclysmic consistency and sleepwalker's certainty – to realize that it's all fantasy and delusions, divinely subsidized to put us at peace with our 'situation,' 'Man's Lot in Cosmos' ... You are certainly right, that psycho-patho-logical explanations of my biosophical pessimism, would be totally irrelevant; but I also fail to see what you can possibly accomplish with your naïve, maladroit metaphysics, behind which – if you will permit me to speak your language for once – I see but the profoundest, most fundamental trauma, and that great universal repression which prevents all fatal insights in man and his 'cosmic conditions,' the mysterious, grotesquely absurd origin and genesis of body and mind, their inalien-able interests, and their final and complete obliteration, the return of the synthesis to the absolute zero." The biosophist is fully aware of the many, marvellous meta-physics (theologies with or without a god, Vietta, 1946) offering "peace in heart," "reconciliation with the world," and "atonement with the almighty," or the like, to anyone who is willing to join this or that suificating sect, and replace intellec-tually honest experience with fictitious world views. The spiritual vacuum is often so painful, that if the fiction is sufficiently fix and form, and permanent, then it does not seem to matter much if it should turn out not to be so terribly pleasant (Eckblad, 1964), vol. 5, no. 1, pp. 47–8). In connexion with a year-long dis-cussion on the possible existence of a Hell, where human souls are being eternally tortured, one newspaper editorial expressed the view, that it would be to the advantage of everybody if the Church now would make up its (and our) mind *one way or the other*, "so people could compose themselves and calm down."

Prelatics are psychotherapists and not philosophers. Their "pastoral psycho-logy," "logo-therapy," etc., is based upon philosophical illiteracy in themselves and in their clientele. No one, of course, would ever object to "pastoral" and other counselling psychologists taking up amateur-philosophy as a hobby. The situation becomes farcical only when the hobby-man attempts to "unsick" the life-time, devoted philosopher; cure him, as it were, of being so insalubriously pessimistic! An encounter of Frankl with Zapffe would form a marvellous philosophical counterpart to the scene with Laërtes and Hamlet in Ophelia's grave[24]. Laërtes leaps into his sister's grave and demands: "Now pile your dust upon the quick and dead, ... till of this flat a mountain you have made ... to overtop old Pelion or the skyish head ... of blue Olympus" (see Vietta, 1946). Laërtes attempts to expostulate his emotion through pathetic sublimation; and Hamlet is immediately inspired. Not bad, Laërtes. Not bad at all! You're at the very threshold of life! But suddenly and painfully he sees the pulselessness of the other's attitude. And it infuriates him to witness this vulgar attempt to parry his own holy virtues by these shoddy means! In God's name, man, don't you see what you're doing? Lyrics and rhyme scheme! Has anyone heard such tomfoolery! If you can say, a mountain high as Pelion, then I can say a mountain reaching the sun! So what! Does it give any meaning to your grief for the dead? No, but you have disturbed life's order and now what will you do? What will you do with your sorrow, you who seem to guess what sorrow means. You who do not run, but cast yourself into the frightening question – you who dare to take it up. Good God, man, what will you do. ... Here I am, rotting away inwardly, being consumed alive because I can't begin to grasp what it's all about! But now you have grasped it and I want to see what you're going to do with it! Answer me, in the name of humanity, what are you going to do! Fight, weep, starve, tear yourself apart? Drink vinegar, eat a crocodile? For you certainly didn't leap into the flaming riddle's grave just to whine, did you – just to challenge me with boasting! A copy of your own birth certificate is all you need to keep you at peace with creation. Laërtes has no answer. His pretension in the direction of "great destiny" collapses and Hamlet adds a new "nothingness" to the notations of life.

SUMMARY AND CONCLUSION

I have in this paper concerned myself with theories of psychological treatment of "abnormal" behaviour in general, and mental "disorder" in particular, insofar as phenomenological and existentialist key-notions or general perspectives have been employed within the total explanatory system of these theories. Psychologists are themselves uncertain as to where the line should be drawn between "normality" and "abnormality" (Tennessen, 1964, p. 79, 80). Similarly controversial is (mental) "disorder." This does not imply that there are no obvious cases where "cure" or "treatment" is clearly suggested. If a student has difficulties in getting to the University because of fear of stepping on cracks in the pavement, this is not a problem to be taken seriously on the cognitive level; in other words, it doesn't raise the problem: "Is it really dangerous to step on cracks in the pavement?" It is quite a different story if the student has "working inhibitions," because he has struck up against the stark problem of death and annihilation. His stomach is clawed to shreds, his breathing throttled by the anguish of nothingness, the dread of being no more. His behaviour, his feelings and emotions, may deviate so far from what

24 See Zapffe, 1945, p. 504.

is presently considered customary that there is no question of their abnormality, in at least one possible sense of "abnormality." But the reasons for his "deviation" may *not* be troubles in adjusting to narrow "social" aspects of his environment, as in the case with our first student, but caused by an unusual awakening to a clear and penetrating awareness of a vast "cosmic" environment *to which there is no adjustment possible*. Max Scheler observes[25] that what insulates most modern men against the terrifying insight into their condition is their safe and busy way of life, which pushes back from their consciousness the intuitive certainty of death, until what is left is a mere rational knowledge of it. They constitute the "average," "normal," mentally "healthy" person, given the stage of human maturity presently prevalent in most civilized communities. This is the person who finds life enjoyable, at least within the limited environment of which he is aware, and to which he has so splendidly adjusted. The *clinical psychologists* want him to remain that way, and, in point of fact, make it one of their major endeavours to try to get back into the cosy fold the comparatively few who presently have transcended the narrow "*social*" environment, and therefore are incapable of enjoying and adjusting to it. The *existentialists*, on the other hand, find a life lived in utter unawareness of man's *cosmic* condition, to be a life void of human dignity, a life not worthy of being lived. Every human being should be forced to mature beyond what is biologically advantageous, or mentally "healthy," forced to face his fate, and open his eyes and mind to the unbearably agonizing insight into "the wild, banal, grotesque, loathesome, carnival in the world's graveyard" (Zapffe, 1941, 1961). What the man then wants to do about it, if anything, is irrelevant, as long as he has in all honesty, sincerity, authenticity, been confronted with the choice and made his decision. He may choose to suificate, and select any means of suification, from lobotomy to LSD, from conformity to insanity ("die Zuflucht zur Wahnsinn"), from hockey to religion, from brass to bridge. To Peter Wessel Zapffe, the fact that man is in this way overendowed with insights into his own preposterousness, is exactly what raises man's lot to qualify as a genuine tragedy (in the old Attic sense of "tragedy"); and the answer is clear: the only dignified exit for Man is to die out, not through a messy, unsavoury and unworthy suicide, but by deciding to abstain from propagating and to leave the Earth deserted behind him. Not in despair, but in triumph over finally having realized "what it is all about," and saying his final "no more."

This eschatological position, however, is unfortunately epistemologically unwarranted. It is rather optimistic and naïve in its presupposition that knowledge can so readily and finally be reached. Men are not angels, living in an eternally stable paradise where their eyes are opened to all possible mysteries of the world. Human beings, on the contrary, are only on the threshold of the most preliminary steps to the mysteries of man and cosmos. There is not a single sentence among what we today should look upon as adequate transmitters of our most important, surest, and most indisputably significant assertions, which may not at another stage of our insight become an object for ridicule and painful shame. Thrown into an eternally changing universe, human beings cannot be tied by a set of rigid rules for

---

25 In *Schriften aus dem Nachlass*. Berne: Franke, 1933, vol. 1, "Tod und Fortleben," p. 6. (See, more generally, pp. 1–51 and 397–413.)

language, thought, or action. Assuming that we, and most of our fellow beings, choose to exist, and to increase our insight, perfect our knowledge about ourselves, our fate and our cosmic situation, we should never express any judgment of value or truth without carefully considering the status of present relevant research. It seems that the only incorrigible knowledge we have ascertained so far is the fact that there is no incorrigible knowledge. Let's grant the existentialists that, given all available insights anno 1966, it is hard to see that man's lot in the universe is not totally absurd. It is clearly important that we realize this, and do not intend to small-talk us out of our insight. However, we may most certainly still improve our language, our conceptual tools, our methodological approach, and add to the quantity and quality of our present information about the mechanisms within and around us. It is hard to predict today what we may *not* be able to predict within the coming millennia. This seems in itself fascinating: Without man in the universe, any later state of the universe might at any given time be predictable with a maximum of certainty to a Laplacian superscientist – at least on the macroscopic level. With man in the world: anything is possible. Just add the homoeopathic ingredient, man, to the universe and it makes all the difference in the world! There is no conceivable cosmic catastrophe which could not either be produced or prevented if man put his mind to it for a million millenia or so. Hence the battle cry sounds: Man, let's go on! – not because we have a mission in the world, not because it makes us happy or proud, but merely because we are different. Man is the only remarkable thing in the world. But it shall not make him conceited. He is accidentally thrown into this world as its sole principle of uncertainty. That's all (Tennessen, 1964, pp. 304 and 305).

References

ACH, NARCISS, *Uber den Willenstätigkeit und das Denken*. Bamberg: C. C. Buchners Verlag, 1910

ADORNO, T. W., et al., *The authoritarian personality*. New York: Harper, 1950

ALLERS, RUDOLF, *Über Psychoanalyse*. Heft 16. Berlin: S. Karger, 1922

ALLERS, RUDOLF, *Existentialism and psychiatry*. Springfield, Ill.: Thomas, 1961

ALLPORT, G. W., et al., *A study of values: a scale for measuring the dominant interest in personality*. Boston: Houghton Mifflin, 1951

ARTAUD, ANTONIN, *The theatre and its double*. New York: Grove, 1958

ASCH, S. E., "Studies of independence and submission to group pressure: I A minority of one against a unanimous majority." *Psychological Monographs*, (1956), 70 (9), (no. 416)

ASTRADA, C., BAUCH, K., BINSWANGER, L., HEISS, R., KUNZ, H., RUPRECHT, E., SCHADEWALD, W., SCHREY, H. H., STAIGER, E., SZILASI, W., and VON WEIZÄCKER, X. F., *Martin Heideggers Einfluss auf die Wissenschaftern*. Bern: A. Francke, 1949

BINSWANGER, LUDWIG, "On the relationship between Husserl's phenomenology and psychological insight." *Philosophical and Phenomenological Research*, 2 (1941–2) 199–210

BINSWANGER, LUDWIG, *Grundformen und Erkenntnis menschlichen Daseins*. München: Reinhardt, 1964

BINSWANGER, LUDWIG, "Daseinsanalytik und Psychiatrie," *Nervenarzt*, Jan. 1951, pp. 1–11

BISHOP, M. G., *The discovery of love, a psychedelic experience with LSD-25*. New York: Dodd, Mead, 1963

BLAUNER, J., "Existential Analysis: L. Binswanger's *Daseinsanalyse*". *Psychoanalytic Review*, 44 (1957) pp. 51–64

BOLLNOW, OTTO FRIEDRICH, "Deutsche Existenzphilosophie." *Bibliographische Einführung in das Studium der Philosophie,* Herausgegeben von I. M. Bochenski. Bern: A. Francke, 1953

BOLLNOW, OTTO FRIEDRICH, *Existenzphilosophie.* Stuttgart: W. Kohlhammer, 1955

BOLLNOW, OTTO FRIEDRICH, *Neue Geborgenheit, Das Problem einer Überwindung des Existentialismus.* Stuttgart: W. Kohlhammer, 1960

BOSS, MEDARD, *Psychoanalyse und Daseinsanalytik.* Bern: Huber, 1957

BOSS, MEDARD, *Analysis of dreams.* London: Rider, 1957

BRUCE, HARRY, "Can we stand life without work?" *Saturday Night,* **80** (1965) no. 4, 22–4

BRUCE, HARRY, "Will more free time kill freedom?" *Saturday Night,* **80** (1965) no. 3, pp. 19–21

CHERRY, COLIN, *On human communication.* Cambridge: Technology Press of MIT, 1957

CHORON, JACQUES, *Death and western thought.* New York and London: Collier, 1963

CLIVE, G., "The inauthentic self." *Journal of Existentialism,* **5** (1954) no. 17, 51–66

CRUTCHFIELD, RICHARD S., "Conformity and character." *American Psychologist,* **10** (1955) 191–8

DELFGAAUW, B., "Heidegger en Sartre." *Tijdschrift voor Philosophie,* **10** (1948) 289–336, 403–46

ECKBLAD, GUDRUN, "The attractiveness of uncertainty." *Scandinavian Journal of Psychology,* **4** (1963) no. 1, 1–13; **5** (1964) no. 1, pp. 33–49

ELKIN, HENRY, "Comment on Medard Boss' approach to psychotherapy." *Journal of Existentialism,* **2** (1951) 203 ff.

ELLENBERGER, H. F., "Phenomenology and existential analysis." *Canadian Psychiatric Association Journal,* **2** (1957) 137–46

FEIFEL, HERMAN (editor), *The meaning of death.* New York, Toronto; London: McGraw-Hill, 1959

FENICHEL, OTTO, "On the psychology of boredom." From *Organization and pathology of thought,* translation and commentary by David Rapaport. New York: Columbia University Press, 1951

FESTINGER, LEON, *A theory of cognitive dissonance.* Evanston, Ill.: Row, Peterson 1957. (See also BREHM, J., and COHEN, A., *Explorations in cognitive dissonance.* New York and London: Wiley, 1962)

FRANKL, VICTOR, "On logotherapy and existential analysis." *American Journal of Psychoanalysis,* **18** (1958) 28–37

FRANKL, VICTOR, *Man's search for meaning. An introduction to logotherapy.* New York: Washington Square Press, 1963

FRANKL, VICTOR, *Psychotherapy and existentialism.* New York: Washington Square Press, 1959

HANDY, ROLLO and KURTZ, PAUL (editors), *A current appraisal of the behavioural sciences. Section 5: Psychology.* Great Barrington, Mass.: Behavioural Research Council for Scientific Inquiry into the Problems of Men in Society, 1964

JAENSCH, WALTER, *Grundzüge einer Physiologie und Klinik der psychophysischen Personlichkeit.* Berlin: J. Springer, 1926

JASPERS, KARL, *Allgemeine Psychopathologie,* dritte Ausgabe. Berlin: Springer-Verlag, 1948

JASPERS, KARL, *Psychologie der Weltanschaunger,* zweite Ausgabe. Berlin: Springer, 1960

JASPERS, KARL, *Existenzphilosophie.* Berlin: W. de Gruyter, 1938

JASPERS, KARL, *Vernunft und Wiedervernunft.* München: R. Piper, 1950

JASPERS, KARL, *The philosophy of Karl Jaspers,* edited by Paul Arthur Schilpp. New York: Tudor, 1957

JUNG, C. G., *Seelenprobleme der Gegenwart.* Zürich: Racher, 1930

JUNG, C. G., "Life after death." *Atlantic Monthly,* Dec. 1962, 39–44

JUNGK, ROBERT, *Die Zukunft hat schon begonnen.* Stuttgart: Scherz & Goverts, 1952

JUNGK, ROBERT, *Heller als tausend Sonnen.* Stuttgart: Scherz & Goverts, 1956

KAILA, EINO, *Personlighetens Psykologi.* Tammersfors: Natur och Kultur, 1935

KAILA, EINO, *Den mänskliga kunskapen.* Helsinki: Natur och Kultur, 1939

KAILA, EINO, *Tankens oro.* Helsinki: Natur och Kultur, 1951

KERN, EDITH (editor), *Sartre.* Englewood Cliffs, NJ: Prentice-Hall, 1962

KIERKEGAARD, SØREN, *Samlede Vaerker,* Bd 1–14, Kbh. 1901–6

KLUBERTANZ, G. P., *Introduction to the Philosophy of being*. New York: Appleton-Century, 1963

KUHN, ROLAND, "Daseinsanalyse im psychotherapeutischen Gespräch," *Schweizer Archiv für Neurologie und Psychiatrie*, **67** (1951), 52–60

LAING, R. D., *The divided self*. London: Tavistock, 1960

LOPEZ, IBOR and JUAN, J., "Existential psychology and psychosomatic pathology." *Review of Existential Psychology and Psychiatry*, **1** (1961) 140 ff.

LYND, ROBERT S., *Knowledge for what*. Princeton: Princeton University Press, 1939

MARCEL, GABRIEL, *The existential background of human dignity*. Cambridge, Mass.: Harvard University Press, 1963

MARCEL, GABRIEL, *Creative fidelity*. New York: Farrar, Straus, 1964

MASLOW, A. H., *Towards a psychology of being*. Princeton, NJ: Van Nostrand, 1962

MAY, ROLLO, *The meaning of anxiety*. New York: Ronald Press, 1950

MAY, ROLLO, *Man's search for himself*. New York: Norton, 1953

MAY, ROLLO (editor), *Existence – a new dimension in psychiatry and psychology*. New York: Basic Books, 1958

MAY, ROLLO (editor), *Existential psychology*. New York: Random House, 1961

MOLINA, FERNANDO, *Existentialism as philosophy*. Englewood Cliffs, NJ: Prentice-Hall, 1962

NATANSON, M., *A critique of Jean-Paul Sartre's ontology*. University of Nebraska Studies, new series, no. 6. Lincoln, Nebraska: 1951

NIKELLY, ART, "Existentialism and education for mental health." *Journal of Existentialism* **5** (1964), no. 18, 205–12

O'FLAHERTY, JAMES, *Unity and language: a study in the philosophy of Johann Georgg Hamann*. Chapel Hill, NC, University of North Carolina, 1952

PALUCH, STANL, "Sociological aspects of Heidegger's *Being and Time*. *Inquiry*, **6** (1963) 300–7

POLAK, P., "Existenz und Liebe." *Jahrbuch für Psychologie und Psychotherapie*, **1** (1953) 355–64

POSATIN, PH. and PHILTINE, ELLEN G., *How psychiatry helps*. Toronto, New York: Collier, 1965

RAPAPORT, DAVID (translation and commentary), *Organization and pathology of thought*. New York: Columbia University Press, 1951

RIESMAN, DAVID, *The lonely crowd*. New Haven: Yale University Press, 1950

RIESMAN, DAVID, *Faces in the crowd*. New Haven: Yale University Press, 1952

RIESMAN, DAVID, *Individualism reconsidered*. Glencoe: Free Press, 1954

RIESMAN, DAVID, *The search for challenge*, in *New university thought*, Spring 1960

ROKEACH, MILTON, *The open and closed mind*. New York: Basic Books, 1960

ROKEACH, MILTON, "Authority, authoritarianism and conformity," in *Conformity and deviation*, edited by Irwin A. Berg and Bernhard M. Bass. New York: Harper, 1961

ROSNER, JOSEPH, *All about psychoanalysis*. New York, London: Collier, 1964

ROYCE, JOSEPH R., "The search for meaning." *American Scientist*, **47** (1959) no. 4, 515–35

ROYCE, JOSEPH R., "Psychology, existentialism and religion." *Journal of General Psychology*, **66** (1962) 3–16

ROYCE, JOSEPH R., *The encapsulated man*. Princeton, NJ: Van Nostrand, 1964

RUESCH, JURGEN and BATESON, GREGORY, *Communication, the social matrix of psychiatry*. New York: Norton, 1951

RUGGIERO, GUIDE DE, "Lesistenzialismo," from *Filosofi del novecento (agiunta)*. Bari: Laterza, 1942

RUITENBEEK, HENDRIK M. (editor), *Psychoanalysis and existential philosophy*. New York: Dutton, 1962

SARTRE, JEAN-PAUL, *La nausée*. Paris: Gallimard, 1938. (American translation: *Nausea*. Norfolk, Conn.: New Directions, 1949)

SARTRE, JEAN-PAUL, *Being and nothingness*, special abridged translation. New York: Citadel, 1964

SARTRE, JEAN-PAUL, *The psychology of imagination*. New York: Philosophical Library, 1948

294 Toward Unification in Psychology

SARTRE, JEAN-PAUL, *The emotions: outline of a theory*. New York: Philosophical Library, 1948

SARTRE, JEAN-PAUL, *Existential psychoanalysis*. New York: Philosophical Library, 1953

SARTRE, JEAN-PAUL, *Imagination*. Ann Arbor: University of Michigan Press, 1962

SCHRAG, CALVIN O., *Existence and freedom. Towards an ontology of human finitude*. Evanston, Ill.: Northwestern University Press, 1961

SCHÖFER, ERASMUS, *Die Sprache Heideggers*. Stuttgart: Neske, 1962

SHAHN, BEN, "Nonconformity." *Atlantic Monthly*, Sept. 1957, 36–41

SHOEMAKER, SYDNEY, *Self-knowledge and self-identity*. Ithaca: Cornell University Press, 1963

SONNENMANN, ULRICH, *Existence and therapy. An introduction to phenomenological psychology and existential analysis*. New York: Grune & Stratton, 1954

STERN, ALFRED, *Sartre, his philosophy and psychoanalysis*. New York: Liberal Arts Press, 1953

TENNESSEN, HERMAN, *Language analysis and empirical semantics*. University of Alberta Bookstore, 1964. (In particular, chap. 18: "Anything is possible," pp. 281–327)

TOLSTOY, LEO, "The Death of Ivan Ilych." In *The short novels of Tolstoy*. New York: Dial Press, 1946, pp. 409–73

UNGERSMA, A. J., *The search for meaning. A new approach in psychotherapy and Pastoral psychology*. Philadelphia: Westminster Press, 1961

USHER, ARLAND, *Journey through dread*. New York: Devin-Adair, 1955

VIETTA, EGON, *Theologie ohne Gott*. Zürich: Artemis, 1946

WAELHENS, ALPHONSE DE, *Une philosophie de l'ambiguité: l'existentialisme de Maurice Merleau-Ponty*. Louvain: Publications universitaires de Louvain, 1951

WEBER, MAX, *The protestant ethic and the spirit of capitalism*. London: Allen & Unwin, 1930

ZAPFFE, PETER WESSEL, *Om det tragiske*. Oslo: Gyldenal Norsk Forlag, 1941

ZAPFFE, PETER WESSEL, *Indføring i litteraer dramaturgi*. Oslo, Bergen: Universitetsforlaget, 1961

Comments:
W. W. Rozeboom

Is existential awareness, as construed by Tennessen, a cognitive condition or an emotional state? That is, if a person realizes the absurdity of life but doesn't let it bother him, has he got Tennessen's message or must he also feel *despair* before his appreciation is complete? Tennessen indicates that, in principle, it would suffice merely to have awareness of life's meaninglessness, but that without the feeling it wouldn't be real knowledge. I concede a point on emotional involvement, but question whether the emotion has to be *angst* – e.g., couldn't one just as well feel an existential exhilaration over the meaninglessness of it all? It should also be pointed out, contrary to the prevailing opinion which has somehow crept into the discussion, that the goal of Tennessen's paper is not to relieve angst in those who already suffer it, but to *arouse* it in those who have not yet become burdened by the existentialist predicament.

J. R. Royce

As a partial answer to Rozeboom I should like to offer an elaboration on one aspect of why this business of existential crisis is important. As I see it, existentialism has extremely potent implications for clinical psychology, particularly for our conception of what we mean by mental health, and what we see as the major goal of psychotherapy. More specifically, existential insights clearly throw the disease concept of "mental illness" into question, and suggest that greater awareness would be a more adequate goal of therapy. (In my judgment, this is what Tennessen is driving at.)

Szasz has suggested that the term mental illness is a term we use for difficulties we have in the task of coping with life. I propose that we interpret these aberrant efforts to cope with life, these efforts which have misfired in one way or another, and hence have been dubbed mental illness, as man's strivings to make sense out of a meaningless universe. I propose that man cannot help but try to make sense out of the totality of things, and that he finds the futility of the twentieth century particularly devastating. I propose that the need for meaning on the one hand, combined with the relativity of values on the other hand, leads to a state of existential ambiguity which overwhelms individual men under specifiable conditions. In short, I propose that the search for meaning and values is at the centre of our conceptual confusion regarding what we call mental illness. This means substituting a psycho-philosophical framework for the traditional medical model because a purely medical approach is not adequate to the task. At this juncture I refer you to the schematic diagram I offered in my paper (see chapter 1, figures 1.4 and 1.5), where I replaced the organism-in-environment scheme with man-in-the-universe. The purpose here was to focus on the cosmic issues of "being" on this earth. Such a schematic diagram allows us to cast the more philosophic aspects of man's behaviour within the traditional definition of psychology as involving organism-environment interactions. The only difference is that we are now operating at the more cosmic level.

The dilemma of man-in-the-universe is man's essential alienation with respect to his environment; not only the social environment, but the total environment. That is, man's need to understand the universe on the one hand, and his inability to do so completely on the other hand. In short, the dilemma is the fact of uncertainty and ambiguity in the face of a need to evolve a meaningful and stable philosophy of life. The relevance of this point to mental health is pointed up in the line in Samuel Becket's play, *Endgame* which reads: "You're on earth. There's no cure for that." Similarly, in MacLeish's play *J.B.*, a modern version of the *Book of Job*, the author trots out three varieties of cure in the form of organized religion, political ideology, and psychoanalysis. They are dismissed with the excruciatingly satirical line, uttered by God, "They don't sound much like comforters to me." Both the "theatre of the absurd" and the existentialists have been pointing to the reality of what might be termed an existential ache. We yearn for meaning spelled with capital letters, but the universe merely echoes the void. Surely the dramatists and philosophers are right in suggesting that life is not so simple as merely to require a pill (medical model) or the right culture (social adjustment model) in order to straighten out the ills of the world.

Within the context of what I will now refer to as an existential-symbolic-philosophic orientation it should be possible to recast the issue of mental health as the many-faceted problem that it obviously is. Just as psychology is appropriately seen as a multiple causation or a multi-variable discipline, so mental health is best seen as a multi-model set of phenomena. No one model, such as the medical model of sickness, is adequate as a basis for understanding the multiple complexities of disturbed behaviour. This means that several models are likely to be required in dealing with the conception of mental health. I should think, for example, that we might wish to retain the concept of mental illness (i.e., sickness) where it is relevant, possibly whenever direct medical intervention will relieve symptomatology (e.g., in performing a vagotomy for psychogenic ulcers). We would also test out the adequacy of the game theory model in accounting for the social aspects of behaviour, a self-actualizing or individuation model for the inner aspects of the psyche, a homeostatic-adaptation model for the biological aspects of behaviour, and learning theory as a basis for the re-educational type of psychotherapy. Each of these components would be seen as aspects of the more general philosophic-value perspective, namely, as manifestations of man's search for a meaningful existence.

III
Epilogue

David Krech
UNIVERSITY OF CALIFORNIA

III
Epilogue

David Krech

UNIVERSITY OF CALIFORNIA

DR KRECH received his undergraduate degree in psychology from New York University in 1930 and completed his M.A. (1931) and his PH.D. (1933) in psychology at the University of California. He has been a faculty member of the University of California, Berkeley since 1947 and was appointed Professor in 1951.

He is one of the few true generalists in the discipline of psychology. With Tolman (under whom he took his doctorate), he hypothesized hypotheses in rats; with Lashley (as a post-doctoral fellow and research assistant), he did brain lesion research; with Kohler (at Swarthmore), he investigated perception in rats; inspired by Bertalanffy, he dabbled in open-system theory; with George Klein, he contributed to personality theory; with Crutchfield, he published textbooks in introductory and social psychology; with kindred zealots, he founded the Society for the Psychological Study of Social Issues; with Berkeley colleagues in psychology, biochemistry, and anatomy, he initiated a research program in brain chemistry and behaviour; and with Senator Fulbright's aid, he has taught in foreign climes – social psychology in Oslo (1949–50), learning theory in Nijmegen, Holland (1963–4), and Berkeley psychology in Cambridge (Massachusetts).

He feels the scientist should be involved in social issues not only *qua* citizen but also *qua* scientist. He has edited a radical newspaper in the Midwest, has been dismissed from the faculty of a midwestern university for "subversive activity," and, in his later years, has conducted (jointly with Nevitt Sanford) *The Activists' Corner* in the *Journal of Social Issues*. He believes the future of society is with the free souls of the richly educated generalists, and the future of psychology with the disciplined and carefully trained specialists – and of these specialists, he cherishes the psychobiologists above all others.

Professor Krech is the co-author of *Theory and problems of social psychology* (New York: McGraw-Hill, 1948) (with R. S. Crutchfield); *Elements of psychology* (New York: Knopf, 1958) (with Crutchfield and E. L. Ballachey); *The individual in society* (New York: McGraw-Hill, 1962) (with Crutchfield); and *Elements of psychology* (New York: Knopf, 1969) (with Crutchfield and Livson).

We are often admonished to start with first things first. Good advice – but what are "first things"? In thinking about the nature of problem-solving, for example, the Gestalt psychologists were wont to distinguish between two approaches – problem-solving from "below," and problem-solving from "above." In the first instance the problem-solver starts from the "givens" and seeks to make progress toward the solution; in the second approach the problem-solver starts from the end – the solution – and works back toward the start. The native Vermonter who said, in response to the tourist's request for information on how to get to St Johnsbury, "If I were you, I wouldn't start from here (!)" may have been giving voice to more generally sound advice than would at first appear. Unlike the bewildered tourist, for much of our business we do not always have to start from "here"; "first" things do not always come first.

These ruminations were prompted by reading Professor Royce's Prologue before attempting to write what was to have been the Epilogue to this volume. It seems clear, to me, that Professor Royce wrote his Prologue long after the Banff Conference had ended, after the papers and discussion notes had been revised and edited, and long enough afterwards to have second – and third – thoughts about the whole affair. But if Professor Royce prepared the major part of his Prologue after the event, I found, when it came my turn to write, that I had already written my Epilogue beforehand.

When I was first invited by Professor Royce to participate in a conference which would explore the possibilities of achieving order and unity in psychological theory, I felt that he was espousing a lost cause. However, I agreed to accept the task of Devil's Advocate at the conference and to prepare an Epilogue for the volume to be published afterwards. I am glad that I did accept, but I find myself shamefully without any new post-conference thoughts; so my pre-conference pre-judgment will have to serve as an epilogue-surrogate.

I have said that I was glad I went to the party, and indeed I am. Much was accomplished at Banff. The contents of a respectable proportion of the papers prepared for the Conference merited the calling together of the distinguished scholars and scientists who attended; the distinction and wisdom of those who came is reflected in the ensuing comments and discussion recorded in this volume; and Professor Royce's reference to "the excitement of the conference" is not merely the wishful over-reaction of a man closely identified with the Conference, it is a quite justified characterization of what took place during both the formal and the informal (and thus unrecorded) discussions. This is no mean achievement. The sustained intellectual excitement of the Conference – among conferees, staff, students, and visitors – generated great expectations in many of us who had come to wish the University of Alberta well in its new enterprise. The obvious success of this Conference argued well for the usefulness of a Center for Advanced Study in Theoretical Psychology, and augured well for its future. But, I suspect that the great and lasting achievement of this First Banff Conference on Theoretical Psychology lies in this: it lowered the sights of its sponsors.

As I read again Professor Royce's opening paper, *The Present Situation in Theoretical Psychology*, it seems to me that his call to come and gather in Banff was indeed prescient. He attempted to convene diverse men who "should bring out the full range of our discipline" (p. 3) to the end that the dimensions of a Mansion which would accommodate us all might be delineated. And thus we found at the Conference physiological and clinical psychologists, psychophysicists and humanists, philosophers of science and animal men, existentialists and perceptionists.

Unification was, I think, the initial hope and the sustained aim. But it soon became apparent – indeed on the first evening when MacLeod and others commented on Royce's paper – that this aim might remain unfulfilled. As MacLeod said, "If the unity we seek is something that is common to all people who call themselves psychologists, then it is a silly quest" (p. 38). Having delivered this observation, which I think is sound, MacLeod went on to suggest his own guide-line for unification of psychology. Even von Bertalanffy, who subscribed to the thesis behind the Conference, was moved to issue a personal disclaimer, "Of course, there is not and probably never will be a 'unified' psychology, but only a number of different fields subsumed under this name" (p. 40). Not all is lost, however, for von Bertalanffy proceeds to assure us, in the very next paragraph, that "*there are unifying concepts and principles in science ...*" and while these may not lead to a total unification, "they do help to bring different phenomena and more special theories into a general framework" (p. 41). My own position – which I have already indicated – was more unyielding than that of either MacLeod or von Bertalanffy: "there is not, and perhaps cannot be, a 'science of psychology.' What we have is a mélange of sciences, technologies, professions, arts, epistemologies, and philosophies – many of them but distantly related to each other – all called 'Psychology.' ... What, then, does it mean when we say that we seek to 'unify' *psychology*? Why seek to unify the potpourri now called 'psychology'?" (p. 43). My answer to MacLeod who would seek for "the essential unity of any science ... in the questions it asks" would be this: the various enterprises dubbed psychological share only the most trivial of questions. I am tempted to make a similar answer to von Bertalanffy's suggestion that, abandoning hopes of total unification, we may still find some general concepts and principles which would unify psychology. This is possible but these unifying concepts and principles – when stretched to envelop the entire range of the "psychologist's" activities – would prove to be a flimsy cover, knit together with trivia.

The reader can imagine how lively and interesting the proceedings became after such a beginning. Unification reared its noble head again and again – now this man, now that, rose to affirm his faith and hope in psychology unified, meaningful, and integrated. But as each private plan for Psychology Fulfilled was unrolled, it became increasingly clear that these were men who would build not a mansion of many chambers, but a street of semi-detached, and in many instances of completely detached, houses in which physiological psychologists, humanists, and perceptionists, clinicians, existentialists, and animal psychologists would live – in comity, *perhaps* – but in separate though equal houses.

And now for my Charge Direct! It was after the Conference, after analysing what happened there, that Professor Royce rethought its original objectives and lowered its sights. Read again his Prologue. Not only (he tells us) was this Conference designed to make but the merest hint of a beginning *toward* a possible unification, but "The point is that theoretical unification is where you find it, and if it results in fragmentation, then so be it, for our primary concern is to understand behaviour rather than perpetuate a historical chapter heading for political or historical reasons" (p. 4). And Royce then continues to outline what manner of things conferences such as this one, and the Center for Advanced Study in Theoretical Psychology might accomplish. And these are good and necessary things for all psychologists, whatever their persuasion. He makes clear to all of us how difficult can be the problem of thinking and writing theory. Only to have "scratched the surface of each of the papers prepared for the conference," he points out, yielded many pages of discussion. His suggestion of the necessity of a Center which would examine *critically* the theories of psychology is a well-taken suggestion indeed. *Where* in all of the psychologies is there another place where men can gather to think about matters which need thought? And even if the Centre in Alberta does no more than make short shrift of ill-begotten theories, it will make a great contribution to the disciplines called psychological. For to prevent pseudo-solutions, and to search out pseudo-achievements is just as much the proper business of science as to forge ahead with partial solutions and partial achievements. If Professor Royce and his colleagues continue to work to the pattern which Royce delineates in his Prologue, then the Centre will surely flourish.

Index